Dance and the Corporeal Uncanny

Dance and the Corporeal Uncanny takes the philosophy of the body into the field of dance, through the lens of subjectivity and via its critique.

It draws on dance and performance as its dedicated field of practice to articulate a philosophy of agency and movement. It is organized around two conceptual paradigms – one phenomenological (via Merleau-Ponty), the other an interpretation of Nietzschean philosophy, mediated through the work of Deleuze.

The book draws on dance studies, cultural critique, ethnography and post-colonial theory, seeking an interdisciplinary audience in philosophy, dance and cultural studies.

Philipa Rothfield is an academic, a dancer and a dance reviewer. She is an honorary staff member in Philosophy and Politics at La Trobe University, Australia, and an honorary professor in Dance and Philosophy of the Body at the University of Southern Denmark. She is Creative Advisor at Dancehouse, Melbourne. She is co-author of *Practising with Deleuze: Design, Dance, Art, Writing, Philosophy* (2017).

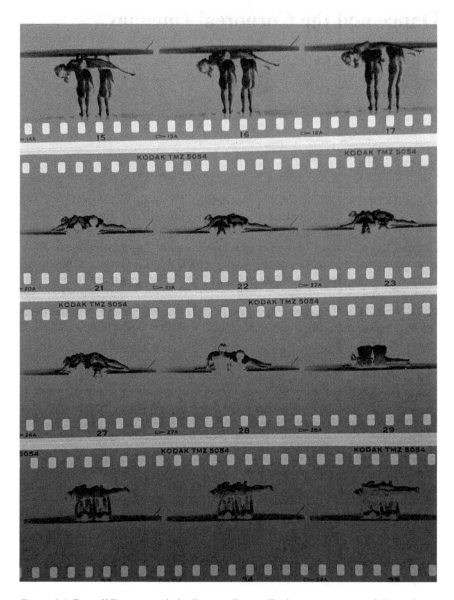

Figure 0.1 Russell Dumas, artistic director, Dance Exchange, courtesy of the artist.

Dance and the Corporeal Uncanny
Philosophy in Motion

Philipa Rothfield

Routledge
Taylor & Francis Group

LONDON AND NEW YORK

First published 2021
by Routledge
2 Park Square, Milton Park, Abingdon, Oxon OX14 4RN

and by Routledge
52 Vanderbilt Avenue, New York, NY 10017

Routledge is an imprint of the Taylor & Francis Group, an informa business

British Library Cataloguing-in-Publication Data
A catalogue record for this book is available from the British Library

Library of Congress Cataloging-in-Publication Data
A catalog record has been requested for this book

ISBN: 9780367508425 (hbk)
ISBN: 9781003051510 (ebk)

Typeset in Times New Roman
by Newgen Publishing UK

This book is dedicated to my parents, Rose Rothfield and Jessel Rothfield.

Contents

Figures

Acknowledgements

They say it takes a village to bring up a child. The same could be said of this book. A book about dance, it could not have been written without the corporeal generosity of numerous master dancers and practitioners. How I learnt, who I learnt from and how I dance matters to this book.

Perhaps not from my time as a youngster at Corona Acting Academy, London, but certainly 13 years dancing with Margaret Lasica, in class and in the *Modern Dance Ensemble*. Margaret was a great teacher who, informed by Feldenkrais technique, would take the time in class to investigate the nuances of movement. She was also a beautiful and lyrical dance-maker. It was a joy to dance her movement materials. Margaret's investigative attitude also made it possible for me to work intermittently but intensely with Russell Dumas over several years.

Russell's rigorous choreographic practice and the emergent mutability of his movement vocabularies challenge the dancer's knowing subjectivity. And yet, there is great pleasure to be found through his work too, in its sensations, feelings, shifts of weight and perceptions of gravity; in its references and innovations; and in its demands.

As well as Russell and Margaret, there are many others whose insight and generosity informs my writing: in the studio with Linda Sastradipradja, improvising with Alice Cummins, workshops and performances with Deborah Hay, and class with Eva Karczag, Joan Skinner and Lisa Nelson amongst others. I am also indebted to Feldenkrais technique, mediated through Leonie Hearn and Julia Scoglio, and the Alexander Technique with Shelley Senter, Shona Innes and Gary Levy. Thanks to you all. Finally, on the movement front, I thank Master Liu DeMing, Abby Lee and Ralph Spethmann for their Qigong teachings.

Key to my engagement with dance studies as a field was joining and then co-convening the Choreography and Corporeality Working Group (International Federation of Theatre Research), organized by Susan Foster and Lena Hammergren, who passed on their roles to Thomas DeFrantz and myself. Meeting with scholars and choreographers around the world has been invaluable as has reading each other's work in progress. Inspiration is also due to Erin Manning and Brian Massumi (the Sense Lab) for their stimulating and wonderful events of research-creation and positive intellectual engagement.

On an academic front, my thanks go to those who took the time to read my work. I am especially grateful to Elizabeth Grosz and Thomas DeFrantz for reading the entire manuscript. Thank you Liz, for suggesting I read Nietzsche. Big thanks also to Susanne Ravn, Jack Reynolds and Jon Sherman for your feedback on my Merleau-Ponty section, and to Liz Conor, Toula Nicolacopoulos, George Vasillacopoulos and Priya Srinivasan for reading draft chapters. While I'm at it, I would also like to thank my colleagues from the Philosophy Department at La Trobe University, Melbourne, Australia, who, over many years, showed themselves to be people of great warmth, integrity and rigour.

I would also like to thank Keith Gallasch and Virginia Baxter, editors of *RealTime Magazine*, for engaging me to review dance over so many years. This was a great learning experience for me and a welcome change from academic writing protocols.

In regard to my work on Korean dance, I would like to acknowledge the tremendous hospitality of SIDance (Seoul International Dance Festival, Director Lee Jong-ho), who exposed me to so much Korean culture, tradition, dance, food and many people, and also to Lee Dong-min, Yoon Yeo-ick, Lee Ji-hyeon and Kim Seo-ryoung.

Finally, to those whom I love a great deal: Thanks to my brother Steven, who would enquire after my progress every few days, listening sympathetically to my writing dramas; to my loving daughter Tilly, who understands all too well the intensity of academic study (and for her Photoshop brilliance); and to my partner, Tony, who thinks I've been working on this book ever since I met him 30 years ago – *I haven't* – but Tony has done everything in his power to support this project. To my friends, family and colleagues, thank you for being who you are.

Introduction

Hanging out in the body

Dance and the Corporeal Uncanny aims to contribute to the field of dance and performance studies by targeting the parameters through which it can think the body. Although articulated along philosophical lines, this book is the beneficiary of the depth and breadth of dance scholarship, which has long sought to accommodate the body within its remit. It has done so by drawing attention to the plurality of bodies embedded in dance practices, their modes of visibility, differentiation, valorization and marginalization, opening itself to the problematic of their enunciation. As a field, dance studies has endeavoured to accommodate the author's corporeality, bodily experiences and provenance as a way of situating research in the body of the researcher. Drawing on feminism, Marxism, cultural studies, psychoanalysis, performance theory, ethnography and political philosophy, also queer theory, postcolonial and critical race theory, the field has availed itself of an interdisciplinary breadth of resources. In that sense, it is part of a larger conversation occurring in the humanities and social sciences gathered around the politics of difference.

This book parallels the focus of dance scholarship on the body. It is not a repudiation of that work, rather an attempt to think through the question of difference by other means. In particular it is focused on the philosophical question of subjectivity in its relation to the body. This is expressed through the figure of the dancer. The figure of the dancer allows us to ask to what extent different dance traditions, cultures and milieus impact the subjectivity of the dancer so as to explore how this is expressed in movement terms, at the level of the body. This is a question of difference in the dancer's body, conceived in relation to agency and action. On the other hand, it is the argument of this book that we need not assume that the activity of dancing is the work of the dancer. Was Yeats right to suggest that we cannot separate the dancer from the dance? Or, to put it differently, can we subtract the dancer from the dance? Organized around two conceptual paradigms, one phenomenological, the other an interpretation of Nietzschean philosophy, *Dance and the Corporeal Uncanny* offers two ways of thinking the status of the dancer within the dance. Their differences concern the place of the subject within a philosophy of action. Taken together, they allow us to ask: Are we the authors of our actions? For phenomenology, the subject is the key. Without the dancer, there would be no dance. Nietzschean philosophy takes a different view. It suggests we can think the dance without the dancer. Through pursuing these two kinds of approach, *Dance and the Corporeal Uncanny* takes philosophy of the body into the field of dance, through the lens of subjectivity and via its critique. Its aim is to open up a discussion of the body in dance without settling on a singular solution, not only to fully explore the subject-position of the dancer but also to open up a corporeal conversation beyond the plane of the subject.

This book is both practice-based and philosophical in orientation. Its emphasis on practice – on what a body does – is an expression of an ontological approach towards the moving body. Ontology in this context represents a focus on the existential character of dance practice and its implications for conceiving the body. It looks to the nuances of movement expressed within the dance. As a work of philosophy, this text must negotiate the tensions that exist between conceptual abstraction and the concrete. I am very fond of quoting Michel Foucault and Gilles Deleuze on this point, through the figure of a relay between theory and practice. Their claim is that theory will at some point hit the brick wall of practice, but equally, that "practice is a set of relays from one theoretical point to another".[1] *Dance and the Corporeal Uncanny* acknowledges that its philosophical concepts are tethered to practice, that they are in some sense its offspring. Time and again, I have had minor epiphanies while dancing in the studio, for it is while dancing that I am able to think about the body in philosophy. But, by the same token, it's only through writing that such thoughts acquire any conceptual traction. There is a tension then in the attempt to produce a conceptual understanding of the body in dance, which has an ear for practice. For *which* practice is to count? And when it does, *how* does it count? Although it acknowledges the heterogeneity of dance testified by dance discourse, *Dance and the Corporeal Uncanny* cannot purport to incorporate that diversity. Its inability to do so is a corollary of the failure of totalizing philosophies to achieve what Donna Haraway calls "the god trick", an all-encompassing vision.[2] It is not possible to achieve 360-degree vision because knowledge is the product of multiple positions and practices, which are themselves open to critical evaluation from other points of view. For Haraway, knowledge needs to recognize its situated character, thereby to accept the link between conceptual thinking and practice.

The situation of this book is articulated and informed by the location and specificity of its author. The need to elucidate that specificity is context-driven. For example, I have elsewhere elaborated my own positionality as a white feminist, working in an Australian, colonizing context.[3] That aspect of my subjectivity re-emerges towards the end of this book, in the form of a collective, colonizing subjectivity, belonging to white Australia, theorized by Toula Nicolacopoulos and George Vassilacopoulos as a mode of "occupier being".[4] The partial, perspectival nature of this book will come as no surprise to those committed to a corporeal point of view. For if we are to say that thought is refracted through the body, then we are entitled to ask after that particular body. The references to practice in this book are for the most part the result of my corporeal encounters, founded on body to body relationships – in the studio, watching work, drawing on the corporeal insights of others. *Dance and the Corporeal Uncanny* thereby owes a debt of gratitude to the corporeal generosity of a great many master practitioners across a variety of situations. To that extent, this book has an underlying corporeal history. I hesitate to write about dancing that I haven't encountered one way or another. This is not to say that the encounter entails objectivity. The encounter is formative. It shapes that which a body can do, its perspectives and preferences, skills and tendencies. Nietzsche makes clear that the body interprets in light of its own history and that history for its part produces its own interpretation of the body. This book seeks to flesh out these claims.

It is the argument of this book that dance is perceived, experienced and evaluated through the body, that its perspective is mediated by practice which is in turn the ground of corporeal formation. Since there is no disinterested perspective, the event of its encounter with the body must be deciphered in terms that allow for questions of difference, privilege, power and politics. Practices of subjectivity, politics, culture and society are embedded within these dynamic encounters. They are at work in the philosophical gesture, in its selection, interpretation and deployment. Their force is felt at every level of dancing, in the studio, training institution, performance space, compound or dirt floor as well as in its manner of reception, criticism, evaluation and transmission. The encounter lays bare all these modes of difference. It offers a field and problematic of interpretation that is witness to its own partiality.

This has implications regarding the status of the example and its discussion. The totalizing perspective sees the example as a mere instantiation of the general concept. According to this way of thinking, particulars exemplify the universal. Although subject to individual variation, insofar as they are particulars, they function in the same way, by way of instantiation. Scientific theory is often thought to operate in this fashion – making out law-like claims and then seeking proof or disproof in the particular instance through observation and experiment. Joseph Rouse contests the hierarchical distinction between the universal and the particular in science, arguing that scientific practice functions via adaptation from local context to local context.[5] Rouse's model is similar to the figure of the relay insofar as theory experiences a series of encounters with practice. According to the relay, theory is itself a mode of practice, movement and adaptation from site to site. This is not a form of localism. The site is not immune to wider social and political influence. Rather, the adoption of theoretical insight is a situated affair requiring adaptation on the part of the theoretical perspective towards the exigencies of the situation. Rouse and Haraway, Foucault and Deleuze lend weight to the specificity of the situation which plays a greater part in the development of theory than mere instantiation. Theory encounters its outside in and through the example of practice, which provokes change on the part of theory. The same could be said of philosophy, in its encounter with that which differs. The example then – important in its own way – can no longer be thought of as exemplary. Perhaps it is better understood as an exemplar. The exemplar does not seek to represent. Rather, it functions as a way of reviewing and situating the concept, through practice. The exemplar speaks to the sense in which the conceptual is already oriented, inviting movement from one milieu towards another while recognizing that adaptation is itself a mode of transformation. The exemplar offers a line of thought, which traverses the contingency of practice. Its role is to further conceptual discussion through a process of contextualization. To that extent, the exemplar may invite adaptation towards *another* concept, fit for purpose rather than faithful to its origins. That said, it is unclear at what point a concept becomes other than itself, particularly when part of a wider conceptual field. Deleuze and Guattari speak of "the inseparability of variations in the concept".[6] Quite apart from its relation to practice (via the exemplar), the mutability of the concept puts philosophy in "a perpetual state of digression" or motion.[7] If so, then the exemplar, as metonym for the encounter with practice, nudges the concept towards even greater variation, felt in relation to citations of movement practice.

Dance and the Corporeal Uncanny traverses two conceptual landscapes, both corporeal in focus, but divided on the question of subjectivity and its relation to the body. Part I is centred upon the figure of experience, in particular, the experience of the dancer. It looks at the activity of dancing from the dancer's point of view, drawing on Maurice Merleau-Ponty's phenomenological philosophy in order to account for the dancer's experience of movement. Its adaptation of Merleau-Ponty's philosophy of perception emphasizes the subjectivity of the dancer, her feelings of agency, thoughts and perceptions, habits and dispositions. Following Merleau-Ponty, the discussion cleaves to that which the dancer experiences in motion. It seeks to explain the dancer's kinaesthetic point of view through theorizing the impact of practice upon the body. In so doing, it distinguishes between different modes of subjectivity as they are found within and formed through practice. Chapter 1 begins with an overview of Merleau-Ponty's phenomenological philosophy, which draws upon the everyday in order to acknowledge the nexus between perception and the body.[8] As several commentators have noted, for Merleau-Ponty, it is the body that perceives, acts and experiences.[9] This is not a mechanistic body, evacuated of all thought and experience. This body is lived. A blend of perceptual experience, thought and action, the body in Merleau-Ponty is the source and site of subjectivity, the means by which we perceive the world and act within it. It is material and, importantly, experiential. Merleau-Ponty does his best to capture – via philosophical reflection – these many facets of corporeal life. He does so by offering a general characterization of the way we live as corporeal beings. It is Merleau-Ponty's observation that, in general, we are immersed in whatever it is that we do. Our thinking is embedded in pragmatic concerns and projects. These inform the kinds of perceptions we seek and the sorts of actions we perform. The body is for the most part in the background in everyday life. It is an enabler, an 'I can', the seamless embodiment of skills and habits which enable us to follow through on our intentions without a second thought. But the body need not function in this way. Merleau-Ponty's *Phenomenology of Perception* supplements its general depiction of corporeal life with a number of existential variations. In large part, they take the form of pathological cases drawn from the medical literature. By acknowledging these lived variations, Merleau-Ponty makes room for the non-conforming instance, thereby to allow for difference in the lived body.

That difference is leveraged in Chapter 2, to develop a phenomenological approach to dance which recognizes the diversity of kinaesthetic practices and their allied modes of subjectivity. It begins with Maxine Sheets-Johnstone's *Phenomenology of Dance*, a work that seeks to extract the essence of dance from its experience. This chapter will argue that the essential project is doomed to failure, due to its inability to incorporate the heterogeneity of the field. The discussion thereby renounces the orthodoxy of phenomenological philosophy, eschewing the pursuit of essential insight for a more contingent appreciation of corporeal diversity. Retaining phenomenology's commitment to the plane of the subject, it aims towards a conception of the dancer felt through the historical specificity of dance practice. The concept, movement subjectivity, is introduced as a means of tracing the contingent agency of the dancer. Movement subjectivity is individual. It refers to the specific dispositions and embodied tendencies of the dancer. It is perspectival, pertaining to what the dancer feels and thinks as she dances. It is also enactive, an action-based conception that incorporates the skills and habits that coalesce in the body. Movement subjectivity is a practice-based account of subject-formation. It draws on what a body does, as a means of understanding what it is. It is also situated. It speaks to the sense in which a dancer acquires facility within a distinctive cultural and kinaesthetic milieu. Movement subjectivity represents the impact of that milieu on the dancer's agency and inclinations. Although powerful, the dancer's situation is not fully determining. Chapter 2 makes two claims in this regard, that movement subjectivity is produced through practice, but also, that the body is an active participant in that practice, bringing to the encounter the dancer's history, orientation, preferences and projects. Movement subjectivity is thereby the offspring of practice but also a mode of singular variation.

There are two components of movement subjectivity, the perceptual attitudes and attentions of the dancer towards her moving body, and the embedded skills manifest in her corporeal demeanour. Chapter 2 takes up Shaun Gallagher's distinction between body image and body schema in order to account for these two moments, one perceptual, the other organizational.[10] As conceived by Gallagher, body image and body schema dynamically interact. They emerge through practice and are embedded in the body's individual inclinations. It will be argued that body image and body schema can be adapted to acknowledge the dancer's distinctive demeanour, while linking that demeanour to her kinaesthetic, cultural context. The notion of context is widely construed here, to include the many factors that enter into the dancer's situation. It represents the dancer's kinaesthetic and cultural everyday, including its shaping by wider social and political forces. These are multi-faceted, as complex as the social itself. It is not possible to extract the dancer from her social environment, nor movement subjectivity from the dancer's provenance, background and history.

Movement subjectivity varies from body to body, situation to situation. It is a dynamic formation, linked to but not reducible to practice. Its existential diversity is reflected in the many perceptual orientations belonging to each field. Chapter 3 addresses an implication of that diversity, that dance may be perceived in terms other than its own and is therefore liable to be judged according to entirely different criteria. Its overarching problematic is the encounter with difference. While that encounter may be entirely positive, this chapter will canvas the political and ethical problems which can arise in the encounter with difference. It will argue that movement subjectivity is implicated within a wider politics of perception. The ensuing discussion draws on the field of ethnography for its capture of the encounter with difference. Chapter 3 cites the corporeal ethnography of Thomas Csordas, who builds on Merleau-Ponty's perceptual philosophy to characterize the ethnographic encounter. Csordas draws attention to the bodily perceptions of the ethnographer, which he frames as a culturally situated state of affairs. Csordas introduces the notion of somatic attention as a way of acknowledging the bodily impact of culture on perception. Chapter 3 extends this thinking into the kinaesthetic domain, through the concept of kinaesthetic sensibility. The concept of kinaesthetic sensibility addresses the concerns of recent dance scholarship on corporeal difference by thinking the social and political in a perceptual register. Kinaesthetic sensibility is embedded within a politics of perception, which exerts itself through the non-reciprocal deployment and imposition of kinaesthetic value. This emerges in relation to the perception and evaluation of dance through norms of spectatorship and hegemonic conceptions of kinaesthetic value. Kinaesthetic sensibility is a way of highlighting the kinaesthetic, cultural specificity of the one who apprehends difference. It conceptualizes the insights of so many dance ethnographers that the perceptual subject is, as Theresa Buckland puts it, no *tabula rasa*.[11] It also draws attention to the ways in which particular kinds of sensibility come to govern the perception of dance. Chapter 4 poses the question of kinaesthetic sensibility, perception and spectatorship in relation to a non-western cultural context, specifically, that of Korean dance. It looks at the ways in which Korean dance has been represented in relation to questions of modernity, modernism and tradition. These issues are in part subject to a politics of classification, theorized by Lena Hammergren and Ananya Chatterjea. Chapter 4 draws on Dipesh Chakrabarty's project of postcolonial history, to suggest a pluralized approach towards the categorization of Korean dance. It also draws on the work of Luce Irigaray to characterize the strategic interventions of dance critic, Daisuke Muto, to stage work in Asia for an Asian spectatorship.

The first half of *Dance and the Corporeal Uncanny* seeks an account of the body in subjective terms. It draws on the figure of experience as it emerges in practice, in the body of the dancer. Its acknowledgement of difference is felt in perceptual and organizational terms, made manifest through the formation of movement subjectivity and its allied modes of kinaesthetic sensibility. Practice is refracted through the body, embedded in the dancer's demeanour and expressed in action. Although qualified by wider social and political forces, and situated in relation to multiple domains of practice, its field of discussion remains on the plane of the subject.

Part Two draws on a quite different conceptual landscape, predicated upon a critique of the subject. It begins with Friedrich Nietzsche's famous declaration that there is no doer behind the deed. Subjectivity is, for Nietzsche, symptomatic, a pathological formation imbued with morality if not agency. Nietzsche claims that experience is not indicative of the way things are, that "Actions are *never* what they appear to be".[12] Beneath the veneer of subjective experience lie a multiplicity of other factors, drives and forces, impulses and affects which are responsible for all that occurs. Nietzsche offers the following illustration:

> Suppose we were in the market place one day and we noticed someone laughing at us as we went by: this event will signify this or that to us according to whether this or that drive happens at that moment to be at its height in us – and it will be a quite different event according to the kind of person we are. One person will absorb it like a drop of rain, another will shake it from him like an insect, another will try to pick a quarrel ... in each case a drive has gratified itself, whether it be the drive to annoyance or to combativeness or to reflection or benevolence. This drive seized the event as its prey: why precisely this one? Because thirsty and hungry, it was lying in wait.[13]

The market analogy suggests that the phenomena of subjectivity – our conscious thoughts, perceptions, intentions and rationalizations – are symptomatic of underling forces that function on an entirely different plane. It posits subjectivity as a post-hoc formation, a hermeneutic overlay on the opacity of the drives. Although all our actions and experiences are the work of these underlying drives, we are bound to interpret our thoughts and feelings as if we were their author. Such is the imperative of subjectivity.

The Nietzschean critique of subjectivity paves the way for a reformulation of the body in terms of force. Chapter 5 asks after the Nietzschean body in light of its displacement of (phenomenological) subjectivity. It engages a line of philosophers who oriented Nietzsche towards a corporeal line of interpretation.[14] A precursor to Deleuze and Foucault, Pierre Klossowski offers a way of thinking the body through the lens of Nietzschean philosophy. He makes sense of the Nietzschean claim that there is no doer behind the deed by distinguishing between the body and its experience. For Klossowski, the body is a wholly transitory phenomenon, a succession of corporeal states which come into being, then pass. The body in Klossowski passes through a serial trajectory of becoming states. Klossowski illuminates Nietzsche's critique of the self by posing our experience of the body as a hermeneutic problem. The problem is articulated thus: In order to experience ourselves as subjects, we need to understand ourselves as a coherent identity, a subject amongst others. The kind of thinking that makes this possible is primarily oriented towards the group. Such thinking is ill-suited to discern the serial singularity of corporeal becoming that precedes and underlies identity. To that end, Klossowski outlines two very different registers, one governed by the intersubjective needs of the group, the other linked to the transitory character of corporeal becoming.

Deleuze similarly poses the body in dynamic terms thought apart from subjectivity. He uses Nietzsche's distinction between active and reactive forces in order to show how forces combine to produce the body. For Deleuze, the body arises from the difference between forces. Forces enter into relation and a body forms when one force (active force) selects and works another, which forms a reaction. Together, active and reactive forces enter into relation to produce the body. Deleuze writes:

> What is the body? We do not define it by saying that it is a field of forces, a nutrient medium fought over by a plurality of forces. For in fact there is no "medium", no field of forces or battle ... Every force is related to others and it either obeys or commands. What defines a body is this relationship between dominant and dominated forces. Every relationship of forces constitutes a body – whether it is chemical, biological, social or political.[15]

Corporeal formation ensues from relations of force, whose constituent differences find provisional and dynamic resolution. Thought in this way, the body is itself a form of movement, the dynamic resolution of relations of force. Chapter 5 draws on these alternative figurations of corporeality in order to rethink the activity of dancing in relation to the workings of force. It asks: What are the forces that constitute the activity of dance? How do forces combine to produce what Erin Manning calls "the becoming-body"?[16] An ontology of force facilitates a reading of dance as the expression of mastery over a field of circumstance. Forces master other forces in the production of movement. These coalesce into corporeal formation, a transitory state of affairs that takes shape then gives way to further articulation. The body of the dancer stands for an underlying multiplicity of activities and formations, found in transit from formation to formation. Chapter 5 endeavours to make sense of these terms in relation to the activity of dance, the force of history, habit formation and kinaesthetic provenance. The dancer's agency, central to phenomenological thought, is reformulated here amongst relations of force.

Chapter 6 returns to the question of subjectivity, asking after the fate of the dancer according to this distinctive philosophical landscape. It begins with Deleuze's take on typology, as the attempt to analyse modes or patterns of existence in terms of their constituent forces. Typology allows Deleuze to show that the body and subjective experience represent entirely different types. The body represents one kind of formation, subjectivity another. These are different in kind and have implications for how we might approach the question of agency within dance. The typological distinction between subjectivity and the body paves the way for a reformulation of dance beyond the plane of the subject. Chapter 6 takes up the typological framework in order to rethink the dancing body, away from the agency of the dancer and towards the agency embedded in relations of force. It seeks to explain the dancer as a formation of force, as well as account for the kinaesthetic incorporation of sensation, thought and experience in action. In so doing, it offers an alternative conception of the ways in which experience can be deployed in movement. Chapter 6 also theorizes cultural production as a mode of subject-formation, felt through the workings of force. Combining the work of Foucault and Deleuze, it poses the trained individual as the vehicle of cultural reproduction but also as a means of cultural change. This is addressed in relation to the potential for virtuosic dancing to move beyond the givens of culture. The concept of virtuosity is offered here as a means of kinaesthetic destabilization and cultural reconfiguration. It draws on the Nietzschean figure of the Sovereign Individual, the one who actively engages rather than merely reproduces cultural norms. The virtuosic represents the possibility of cultural change, from within, but also beyond the terms of culture. Finally, the question of agency is reconvened, through the lens of Nietzschean overcoming. Although Deleuze's Nietzsche excludes agency as phenomenology would have it, there is room for a strategic move of sorts on the part of the subject. What follows is a discussion of the ways in which certain kinaesthetic practices can be seen to embrace the Nietzschean notion of overcoming. This is made possible through the figure of active destruction, a precursor to Deleuzian affirmation. Chapter 6 explores the sense in which we might reconceive subjectivity as a mode of desubjectification. It suggests that postmodern and somatic practices can be seen to involve the strategic deployment of subjectivity. The exemplar of postmodern and somatic practice represents a practice-based interpretation of the Nietzschean conceptual apparatus. Its speculative gesture towards desubjectification paves the way for a range of potential adaptations of the Nietzschean landscape towards a variety of corporeal and kinaesthetic becomings. These are a mode of corporeal reinterpretation, the reconfiguration of force towards other ways of thinking the subjectivity of the dancer.

Dance and the Corporeal Uncanny is informed by practice. Its concepts aim to show the impact of practice on the body, however elaborated. It pursues two ways of thinking the body, with and without the benefit of subjective agency. Its final chapter draws on these two paradigms in order to acknowledge its place, the situation of this book. Chapter 7 is a work of context, of a situated, colonial history and the survival, agency and creative expression of its First Nations peoples. It acknowledges that to enter a dance studio, walk, run or jump in Australia is to set foot on Aboriginal land. Australia has never properly recognized the sovereignty of its Indigenous owners, as that which was never ceded to British colonizers. Chapter 7 draws on the work of Toula Nicolacopoulos and George Vassilacopoulos who invert the colonizing gaze of contemporary Australian culture to focus on the being of the colonizer. Nicolacopoulos and Vassilacopoulos argue that Indigenous sovereignty poses a threat to what they call the occupier being of white Australia. Chapter 7 supplements the work of Nicolacopoulos and Vassilacopoulos, with the writings of Indigenous scholars, Gary Foley, Larissa Behrendt and Aileen Moreton-Robinson, to explore the perceptual terrain of white spectatorship in relation to two powerful expressions of Indigenous sovereignty, the performance work of SJ Norman, and the on-field dancing of footballer, Adam Goodes. It juxtaposes the relational subjectivity of occupier versus sovereign being with the potential of Indigenous performance to destabilize these very categories. To that end, it will be argued that Goodes and Norman were able to destabilize the colonial force of the white Australian imaginary, yielding an untimely provocation towards another kind of Australia.

There is more than one way to think difference in relation to the body and within dance. For phenomenology, difference enters into the embodied subjectivity of the dancer, whose agency is an expression of a range of kinaesthetic, social, cultural and political factors. According to this line of thought, difference informs but stops short of determining the subjectivity of the dancer and her actions. The Nietzschean paradigm is somewhat different but equally capable of attending to the social and political circumstances of dance. It does so through decentring a metaphysics of subjectivity for a dynamic understanding of kinaesthetic provenance, subject-production and corporeal formation. The social and political is at work here, to be discerned within and according to relations of force, which in turn inform the serial adventures of corporeal formation.

It is my hope that the thinking of this book will make itself available to other areas of thought that aim to think the body in cultural, performative terms. It presents its reader with a series of choices, felt between two conceptual terrains, one formulated around the subject, the other predicated on an ontology of force. The focus of the book is kinaesthetic, but its implication concerns the ways in which we might think of action and cognition, agency and experience. To that end, it speaks to the philosophy of action through the lens of a dedicated field of practice. It also offers a corporeal rendition of decentred, anti-humanist approaches, whose (post)structuralist origins were struck in the days of the linguistic paradigm. Rather than the notion of subject address and interpellation, it offers an account of corporeal and subject-formation through the becomings of force.

There is a tendency to gloss over the practice-based nature of philosophy, to give it transcendental powers which set it apart from history. Deleuze and Guattari's account of philosophy as the creation of concepts draws attention to the practice of its creation.[17] As a field of practice, the concept has its historical roots. This book is made possible by the work of dance scholars, philosophers, cultural theorists and political analysts. It has its roots in the studio, in the filaments of transmission between bodies and the corporeal generosity of master practitioners. But the concept is not merely historical. It has an untimely and indeterminate future. One of those futures lies in its encounter with difference. Difference informs the relay between theory and practice – it is the dynamic of its motion. Difference also portends another means of evaluation (beyond the domain of concepts), through its appeal to other conditions and circumstances. Foucault and Deleuze claim that

> theory is exactly like a box of tools. It has nothing to do with the signifiers. It must be useful. It must function. *And not for itself*. (emphasis mine)[18]

Their point is that theory acquires value by connecting to an outside, signified here through the concept of practice. Practice is no longer in the shadow of theory, it is an interlocutor. Insofar as this book gives voice to certain kinds of practice, it aims to open itself to other voices, situations and perspectives, which embody the potential to destabilize its thinking, towards an entirely different conceptual orbit.

Notes

1 Michel Foucault and Gilles Deleuze, "Intellectuals and Power: A Conversation between Michel Foucault and Gilles Deleuze", in *Language, Counter-Memory, Practice: Selected Essays and Interviews by Michel Foucault*, trans. Donald F. Bouchard and Sherry Simon, ed. Donald F. Bouchard (New York: Cornell University Press, 1977), 206.
2 Donna Haraway, "Situated Knowledges: The Science Question in Feminism and the Privilege of Partial Perspective", *Feminist Studies* 14, no.3 (1988): 581.
3 Philipa Rothfield, "A Narrative on the Limits of Theory", in *Australian Women: Contemporary Feminist Thought*, ed. Norma Grieve and Ailsa Burns (Melbourne: Oxford University Press, 1994), 108–119.
4 Toula Nicolacopoulos and George Vassilacopoulos, *Indigenous Sovereignty and the Being of the Occupier* (Melbourne: re-press, 2014), 35.
5 Rouse accounts for the appearance of universality within the scientific paradigm through norms of standardization which ensure that scientific research follows the same protocols of investigation and documentation. Standardization enables research to appear independent of its origins and masks the adaptation of research from site to site, Joseph Rouse, *Knowledge and Power: Towards a Political Philosophy of Science* (Ithaca: Cornell University Press, 1987), esp. Chapter 4, "Local knowledge", 69–126.

6 Gilles Deleuze and Félix Guattari, *What Is Philosophy?*, trans. Hugh Tomlinson and Graham Burchell (New York: Columbia University Press, 1994), 23.
7 Ibid., 23.
8 Maurice Merleau-Ponty, *Phenomenology of Perception*, trans. Donald A. Landes (London and New York: Routledge, 2014).
9 For example, David Morris, "Body", in *Merleau-Ponty: Key Concepts*, ed. Rosalyn Diprose and Jack Reynolds (Stocksfield, UK: Acumen, 2008), 111–120; Shaun Gallagher, "Body Schema and Intentionality", in *The Body and the Self*, ed. José Luis Bermudez, Anthony Marcel and Naomi Eilan (Cambridge, MA: MIT Press, 1995) 225–244; and Harry Adams, "Expression", in *Merleau-Ponty: Key Concepts*, ed. Rosalyn Diprose and Jack Reynolds (Stocksfield, UK: Acumen, 2008), 152–162.
10 Gallagher, "Body Schema and Intentionality". Although body image has a wider deployment in the field of psychology, especially around body dysmorphia, it is adapted here to signify the subject's conscious thoughts and perceptions in regard to her own body in movement.
11 Teresa Buckland, "Shifting Perspectives on Dance Ethnography", in *The Routledge Dance Studies Reader: Second Edition*, ed. Alexandra Carter and Janet O'Shea (London and New York: Routledge, 2010), 339.
12 Friedrich Nietzsche, *Daybreak: Thoughts on the Prejudices of Morality*, trans. R.J. Hollingdale (Cambridge, Cambridge University Press, 1997), 72.
13 Ibid., 120.
14 These include Georges Bataille, Pierre Klossowski, Michel Foucault, Gilles Deleuze, Luce Irigaray, Sara Kofman and Eric Blondel. For further discussion, see Alan Schrift, *Nietzsche's French Legacy*, (London and New York: Routledge, 1995), esp. Chapters Two and Three, also, David Allison, ed., *The New Nietzsche* (Cambridge, MA: MIT Press, 1985).
15 Gilles Deleuze, *Nietzsche and Philosophy*, trans. Hugh Tomlinson (New York: Columbia University Press, 1983), 39–40.
16 Erin Manning, *Relationscapes: Movement, Art, Philosophy* (Cambridge, MA: MIT Press, 2012), 6.
17 Gilles Deleuze and Félix Guattari, *What Is Philosophy?*, trans. Hugh Tomlinson and Graham Burchell (New York: Columbia University Press, 1994).
18 Foucault and Deleuze, "Intellectuals and Power", 208.

Bibliography

Adams, Harry. "Expression". In *Merleau-Ponty: Key Concepts*, edited by Rosalyn Diprose and Jack Reynolds, 152–162. Stocksfield, UK: Acumen, 2008.
Allison, David B, ed. *The New Nietzsche*, Cambridge, MA: MIT Press, 1985.
Buckland, Theresa. "Shifting Perspectives on Dance Ethnography". In *The Routledge Dance Studies Reader: Second Edition*, edited by Alexandra Carter and Janet O'Shea, 335–343. London and New York: Routledge, 2010.
Foucault, Michel and Gilles Deleuze. "Intellectuals and Power: A Conversation between Michel Foucault and Gilles Deleuze". In *Language, Counter-Memory, Practice: Selected Essays and Interviews by Michel Foucault*. Translated by Donald F. Bouchard and Sherry Simon, edited by Donald F. Bouchard, 205–217. New York: Cornell University Press, 1977.

Gallagher, Shaun. "Body Schema and Intentionality". In *The Body and the Self*, edited by José Luis Bermudez, Anthony Marcel and Naomi Eilan, 225–244. Cambridge, MA: MIT Press, 1995.

Haraway, Donna. "Situated Knowledges: The Science Question in Feminism and the Privilege of Partial Perspective". *Feminist Studies* 14, no. 3 (1988): 575–599.

Manning, Erin. *Relationscapes: Movement, Art, Philosophy*. Cambridge, MA: MIT Press, 2012.

Merleau-Ponty, Maurice. *Phenomenology of Perception*. Translated by Donald A. Landes. London and New York: Routledge, 2014.

Morris, David. "Body". In *Merleau-Ponty: Key Concepts*, edited by Rosalyn Diprose and Jack Reynolds, 111–120. Stocksfield, UK: Acumen, 2008.

Nicolacopoulos, Toula and George Vassilacopoulos. *Indigenous Sovereignty and the Being of the Occupier: Manifesto for a White Australian Philosophy of Origins*. Melbourne: re-press, 2014.

Nietzsche, Friedrich. *Daybreak: Thoughts on the Prejudices of Morality*. Translated by R.J. Hollingdale. Cambridge, Cambridge University Press, 1997.

Rothfield, Philipa. "A Narrative on the Limits of Theory". In *Australian Women: Contemporary Feminist Thought*, edited by Norma Grieve and Ailsa Burns, 108–119. Melbourne: Oxford University Press, 1994.

Rouse, Joseph. *Knowledge and Power: Towards a Political Philosophy of Science*. Ithaca: Cornell University Press, 1987.

Schrift, Alan. *Nietzsche's French Legacy*. London and New York: Routledge, 1995.

Part I

1 Merleau-Ponty and the lived body

Introduction

The aim of this chapter is to set the scene for thinking dance from the point of view of the dancer. It looks to the work of Maurice Merleau-Ponty in order to offer an account of the body that makes room for the dancer's perspective. The body is central to Merleau-Ponty's thought, which is organized around the figure of experience. The alignment of philosophy with experience appeals to subjectivity – how we feel and think – as the basis of philosophical insight. The emphasis on experience leads Merleau-Ponty to take stock of the ways in which mind and body intertwine. Merleau-Ponty's term for this is the lived body. The lived body offers a way to understand the agency and experience of the dancer. Its existential emphasis allows for a formulation of the dancer's subjectivity in terms that acknowledge the role of practice in the formation of the dancer's means and manner of movement.

The lived body begins with the subject. Merleau-Ponty writes:

> Everything that I know about the world, even through science, I know from a perspective that is my own.[1]

The reference to a first-person perspective is a statement about its priority with respect to objective thought. Merleau-Ponty asserts that subjective experience is primary and objective thought secondary. It's not that the objective perspective is wrong. It is, rather, derivative. Even science must rely upon first-person observation in order to develop its theoretical insights.[2] For Merleau-Ponty then, "the fundamental philosophical act would thus be to return to the lived world beneath the objective world".[3] This is the task of philosophy, to situate itself in life so as to tease out its features. Philosophical reflection does not withdraw from the world, rather it aims "to match reflection to the unreflective life of consciousness".[4]

Merleau-Ponty's philosophy is thus answerable to the character and content of actual experience. It is distinguished from empiricism, which emphasizes objectivity, and from what he calls intellectualist (Kantian) philosophy, which posits the deployment of the intellect upon sensuous input.[5] By situating itself within the domain of existence, philosophical reflection privileges the realm of the pre-reflective (as that which occurs prior to philosophical reflection). The appeal to the pre-reflective is an attempt to cleave to the world of actual experience, to faithfully render its character. David Morris writes:

> Merleau-Ponty thus radicalizes philosophical method, since his philosophy begins by installing itself and being responsible to a pre-philosophical setting that exceeds it.[6]

Embedded in existence, reflection is not purified of life, it never loses contact with its object. The grounding of reflection in life gives it a rather contingent, provisional character, ever in debt to the nuances of existence. In this sense, reflection is by nature incomplete.[7] This is not a sign of inadequacy, though, rather a mark of the field within which the philosopher must think. Philosophical reflection is an ongoing task then, oriented towards pre-reflective life, yet critical of itself, acknowledging its own insights as provisional rather than known in advance. It is in short a "style" or "manner" of thinking, a philosophical journey situated in the world, in the life and context of its practitioners.[8]

Phenomenology of Perception identifies perceptual life as that through which we experience and live in the world.[9] Its understanding of perception as the background for all thought brings the body to light as our pivotal means of connection with the world. It is because we are bodily beings that we are able to live, think, even have a world. Merleau-Ponty distinguished his approach towards the body from those that reduce it to an object. He rejected the Cartesian separation between mind and body by holding to a notion of the body that is both subjectively felt and objectively discernible. It's not that the body is not objective but that it's not *merely* objective. The body is never just an object for Merleau-Ponty because the body is my means of living in the world. The body is the perspectival means by which we encounter the world. Although often implicit within experience, the body is nonetheless the seat of all activity.

Phenomenological philosophy was first established by Edmund Husserl. Husserl's starting point was Franz Brentano's notion of the intentionality of consciousness, the insight that consciousness is always a consciousness of something (the object of consciousness). The goal of Husserlian phenomenology is to determine the essence of consciousness in relation to its object, the object of thought. One of its innovations is to 'bracket' ontological concerns regarding the status of the object of consciousness, as a means to analyse its key structures. Husserl proposed that we can learn a great deal about the ways in which consciousness relates to the world once ontology is put aside. Bracketing what Husserl called the natural attitude is the first step in the phenomenological method.[10] Husserl called this operation the phenomenological reduction or *epoché*.[11] Once the phenomenological reduction is activated, we must remain neutral regarding the existential status of the object. It matters not, according to Husserl, whether or not the object of thought exists. What matters is the relationship between consciousness and its object, manifest through the intentionality of consciousness, its (*noetic*) actions and meanings (*noemata*). A further phase involves what Husserl called eidetic variation, the attempt to consider one's object of analysis from a multiplicity of perspectives in order to determine that which remains constant. Eidetic variation aims to reveal the invariant structures of consciousness, thereby to produce essential modes of insight. Although Merleau-Ponty did not break with the Husserlian project, and indeed retained the word phenomenology in his title (*Phenomenology of Perception*), he tended to emphasize the lived rather than manipulate the given towards a conception of the invariant. He also deepened Husserl's understanding of the corporeal, giving it a particularly perceptual inflection. Rather than consciousness towards its intentional object, Merleau-Ponty depicted a body towards the world (of objects and others). In so doing, he shifted intentionality onto the plane of movement, towards a conception of "motor intentionality" as the corporeal means by which we relate to the world.[12] Motor intentionality acknowledges that intentionality is not merely an interior set of experiences but is expressed in action.

Merleau-Ponty's work on the body, perception and movement offers a subject-centred account of action and its experience. His attempt to depict the lived character of experience – its existential thrust – leads to a number of general characterizations, aimed to capture how it is that we live as bodily beings. This chapter looks to the ways in which Merleau-Ponty portrays the everyday in relation to the body and its perceptual experience. Shaun Gallagher's distinction between body image and body schema will be utilized to clarify Merleau-Ponty's understanding of movement and its perception. The following discussion will canvass a number of themes as they are found in *Phenomenology of Perception,* which emphasizes the everyday character of intentional life. *Phenomenology of Perception* features a subject at grips with the world. The body is typically in the background here, 'on call' but not in focus. Merleau-Ponty acknowledges that not everyone is able to rely on their bodies in this way. His discussion of the medical literature makes the case for acknowledging existential differences between lived bodies. This recognition and Gallagher's working definition of body image and body schema set the scene for a kinaesthetic treatment of Merleau-Ponty's perceptual philosophy.

The body towards the world

Merleau-Ponty was a mid-twentieth century philosopher, a contemporary of the existentialists, Jean-Paul Sartre, Simone de Beauvoir and Albert Camus. He was at times closely aligned with them, co-editing the political journal, *Les Temps Modernes*, alongside Jean-Paul Sartre. Although he predicated his work on Husserlian phenomenology, there is a strong sense of the existential in his work, manifest in the use of concepts such as milieu, setting and situation.[13] There is also in his work a commitment to the sensory, encapsulated in his sustained elaboration of perceptual life. While Sartre concerned himself with the exigencies of consciousness, Merleau-Ponty preferred to delve into sensory life as the crucible of thought. His commitment to materiality and its experience elevated perception over and above pure thought, while acknowledging their interdependence.[14] Why perception? Perception for Merleau-Ponty is allied to life. Perception underlies all our thinking, experience, our every move. For Merleau-Ponty, the role of philosophy is not to explain perception but to "coincide" with it, remaining as close as possible to how it is for us.[15] The philosophy of perception seeks to understand the experiential relationship between the subject and his or her milieu. Merleau-Ponty approaches perception through the lens of phenomenological philosophy. He extends the intentionality of consciousness to depict a subject oriented towards the world:

> My "psyche" is not a series of "states of consciousness" that are rigorously closed in on themselves and inaccessible to anyone but me. My consciousness is turned primarily toward the world, turned toward things; it is above all a relation to the world.[16]

Pre-reflective life reveals a subject towards the world, embedded in life's undertakings, recalling Sartre's characterization of human being as a mode of transcendence.[17] The identification of transcendence as the mark of the human is related to a number of Husserlian terms which Merleau-Ponty employs in the context of his discussion. These are, firstly, the intentionality of consciousness, which says that all consciousness is a consciousness of something, suggesting that consciousness is a form of movement beyond itself (whether towards an immanent or transcendent object of thought). This is enhanced by Husserl's concept of the lifeworld (*lebenswelt*), which signals the socio-historical dimension of human intersubjectivity. Merleau-Ponty also refers to Husserl's notion of operative intentionality, an extended understanding of intentional life.[18] Operative intentionality is distinguished from act intentionality, "the intentionality of our judgements and voluntary decisions", in that it incorporates the wider context within which we act.[19] Operative intentionality establishes "the unity of the world and our life".[20] It is the lived texture of our being in the world within which our actions have meaning. Taken together, these concepts support the view that perception is a movement beyond the self into the world, understood in terms "inseparable from subjectivity and intersubjectivity".[21] It's in this context that Merleau-Ponty cites Heidegger's notion of the *ek-stase* of experience, to indicate the transcendent thrust of perceptual activity.[22] These concepts characterize perceptual experience as a complex of "intentional threads" running from the subject to the world.[23] Perception does not begin with the subject, however, and then extend towards the world. It is already in the world.

Most importantly, for Merleau-Ponty, the relation between the subject and the world is a bodily relation. My access to the world is mediated by my body. My actions are bodily actions. This is not a Cartesian body, servant of an animating consciousness, rather a fully cognizant, living body. To say that the body, my body, is oriented towards the world is to reframe intentionality in corporeal terms. Once intentionality becomes corporealized and existentially situated, however, the body towards the world is equally a body at large, in and of the world. Merleau-Ponty's term for this is the lived body. The lived body expands the intentionality of consciousness towards a bodily conception of subjective life. It is action-based but also open to the width and breadth of lived corporeality. To say the body is lived is not to suggest it is always experientially present. Merleau-Ponty is quite clear that, for the most part, we are more oriented towards the world than to our own bodies. The following discussion traces Merleau-Ponty's efforts to depict the ways in which the lived body typically finds itself in the midst of things.

The lure of the object

Ludwig Wittgenstein writes:

> My life shews that I know or am certain that there is a chair over there, and so on – I tell a friend e.g. "Take that chair over there, shut the door", etc. etc.[24]

For Merleau-Ponty also, objects feature in the context of life. The object is nested within our "motor projects" (actions) – there for the taking, to be opened or shut.[25] The object is a practical concern, a focus puller:

> Our perception ends in objects, and the object, once constituted, appears as the reason for all the experiences of it which we have had or that we could have.[26]

The focus on the object is the flip side of the body towards the world. It is the manner in which perception is felt, the subject-matter of our perceptual content. We are occupied with the object because we are busy doing things. Inasmuch as objects feature in my actions, I become "anchored" in them, and come to "inhabit" them.[27] I hold this pen, pat my dog, drink my tea, roll on the floor.

This posture of practical absorption means that I may not fully acknowledge the role played by my body in all this. I hold the pen in order to write. I bring the cup to my lips because I want to sip my drink. My body's contribution to these habitual achievements is rarely appreciated as such:

> Obsessed with being, and forgetting the perspectivism of my experience, I henceforth treat my experience as an object and deduce it from a relationship among objects. I consider my body, which is my point of view upon the world, as one of the objects of that world.[28]

Pre-reflective life fosters a sort of corporeal amnesia – forgetting the body's role as perceptual facilitator – in favour of simply getting on with it, so that "in the end, experience believes it draws from the object everything that experience itself teaches us".[29] Were I to examine my actions, however, I would see that my perceptual encounters are always framed in relation to my body. I see the table, in fact, weight pours through my forearms onto it as I grasp the pencil and guide its shapely formations. Wittgenstein's chair over there is 'there' to my body's 'here', that door's proximity to me puts it within shutting distance, the pen lies within reach of my arm:

> When the word "here" is applied to my body, it does not designate a deter-minate position in relation to other positions or in relation to external co-ordinates. It designates the installation of the first co-ordinates, the anchoring of the active body in an object, and the situation of the body confronted with its tasks.[30]

Bodily perspective

My body's relation to the object informs these perceptual interactions. I always look from a certain point of view. My touch is guided by the zone of contact between my flesh and the thing, by the placement of my weight, its direction and force. In fact, all perception has this corporeal, perspectival character. I sit on this chair angled forwards in virtue of my body's orientation towards the table, according to the way my spine looms over the paper, my head resting on my hand. This is the way the world enters my life, the manner in which I act in the world.

I see that house always from a certain point of view, a point of view which is informed by my corporeal relation to the house. I can, of course, extend that experience to include another point of view – by moving away perhaps or looking at a photo or entering the house and walking through its rooms. Each of these alternatives offers me another perspective on the house. While the human gaze never takes in more than one version of the object at a time, we are over time able to have multiple experiences of one and the same object. Merleau-Ponty draws upon the Husserlian notion of the horizon in order to account for this. The horizon conjoins Gestalt theory as a means to describe the organization and character of lived perceptual experience. According to Gestalt theory, all percep-tion involves the perception of a figure against a background.[31] In each case, my perception will involve a figure in the foreground, posed against the rest of the field as background.[32] The concept of the horizon comes into play when we shift attention from one perceptual focus to another.

The horizon is that which ensures the identity of the object in all my various experiences of it. I hear my dog bark. I call her, she comes, rolls over for a pat and I lean down to rub her stomach. These are not fully distinct experiences but a series of encounters with my dog. The horizon stands for my practical understanding of the object (my dog) as a sensible unity experienced over time. I do not have one experience and then another completely isolated one. Rather, the horizon is my way of relating to what I understand to be the same object in the variety of perspectives I have of it. It guides my movements, my sensory attentions and underlies what I understand by this or that particular object. These experiences need not be temporally contiguous. I can just as easily return to the object later. The horizon enables this return to be a return.

Objects come to prominence through our focusing on them against a background, in relation to other perspectives of one and the same object. This is in part a question of the Gestalt and its requisite focus. But it is also a question of perspective, or rather, the movement from one perspective to another. The notion of perspective is built into the functioning of the horizon:

> The object-horizon structure, that is, perspective, thus does not hamper my desire to see the object. Although it may be the means that objects have of concealing themselves, it is also the means that they have of unveiling themselves.[33]

In other words, the object is revealed to me in the course of multiple experiences. Never fully given in any one experience, I become familiar with objects through exposure to them but also through their suggestiveness, the suggestion of more to come.[34] The horizon stands for that suggestion. It enables its pursuit.

Merleau-Ponty presents us with an account of perceptual experience which is corporeally situated and refracted through the subject's own body – perspectival in nature, yet organized according to the subject's active understanding of the object as an inexhaustible, yet ordered, source of experience. Merleau-Ponty rejects impartial, effectively disembodied, accounts of the object seen from all sides. The horizon is an aspect of perceptual life that follows the "consistency and coherence" of the thing.[35] The horizon incorporates both experience and its object because it concerns the way in which experience has embedded within it the possibility of more encounters with the object. The horizon works because we are corporeal. It functions via the body's activity. While I enter the house from the front, I could walk around it to come in the back door. I pat my dog, lean down and rub her fur. For David Morris, the objects of perceptual experience are not given all at once but rather portend hidden aspects through the horizon's structure of "premeditated potentialities" according to which the "thing unfolds".[36] This conception of unfolding is elaborated as a lived relation within the flow of perception. Future encounters are prefigured or adumbrated within perception. They arise from the world and are felt as sensory premonitions, in the folds of perspective by which an object is apprehended.

Body schema and body image

The horizon represents an ability on the part of the subject to appreciate the coherence and consistency of the external world in the context of one's own bodily integrity. The horizon works in virtue of the subject's bodily perspective, felt in action. Merleau-Ponty adopts the term, body schema, in order to explain the ways in which the subject is able to navigate and participate in the world.[37] It is important to clarify the difference between body schema and body image, especially since there exists a certain degree of confusion and overlap between these two concepts.[38] The following discussion adheres to Shaun Gallagher's clarification of body image and body schema as it relates to Merleau-Ponty's phenomenological philosophy.[39] For Gallagher, body image and body schema are entirely different in character and function. The body image is a conscious perception of one's own body. It is an intentional object (or series of intentional experiences), "a conscious representation of the body or a set of beliefs about the body".[40] A body image may express a person's perceptions, attitudes, thoughts and feelings towards their own body.[41]

The body schema is less an image than a particular way of moving in the world. The body schema is an acquired facility or capacity to move, developed over time. It belongs to, or rather, characterizes the subject's own distinctive movement palette. Gallagher describes the body schema as "the body's nonconscious appropriation of habitual postures and movements, its incorporation of various significant parts of the environment into its own experiential organization".[42] Gallagher credits the body schema with the ability to walk or run, to pick up a pen, to catch a ball, determine depth of field or read a book.[43] Knowing where one is and how to measure and perceive items relative to one's body forms the background for the pursuit of intentional actions. It complements the formation and pursuit of intentional projects.[44] The body schema is habitual, 'automatically' available in a way which fosters and makes possible intentional action.[45] It is the subject's movement-based *modus operandi.*

Merleau-Ponty writes of an integrated whole between movement and its background.[46] The body schema is an "overall body plan" that facilitates lived experience.[47] It functions as a "sensorimotor unity of the body".[48] Its organizational unity differs from the episodic nature of body images, which are momentary and individuated. In that sense, the body schema is systemic. It functions as an action-based, corporeal Gestalt.[49] The body schema underlies those activities that comprise everyday life. It is the basis of our motor projects (actions). The body schema anchors me in my own body in a situational, spatial sense. It enables me to know where I am in relation to the world without having to think.

The body schema can also be seen in ecological terms. This is because it emerges through the nexus between the body and its world.[50] Being an ecological, relational system of skills and abilities, the body schema is a creature of habit, inculcated through practice. The idea that the body schema is formed and functions in relation to the world informs Merleau-Ponty's understanding of posture as a dynamic, movement-based facility. Merleau-Ponty writes:

> Psychologists often say that the body schema is *dynamic*. Reduced to a precise sense, this term means that my body appears to me as a posture towards a certain task, actual or possible.[51]

The body schema captures the dispositional nature of posture, its way of understanding itself in the world as a means of navigating within it. It offers a sense of posture as that which is oriented and situated.

Although formed in relation to its milieu, the body schema is not a mere product of its environment. Gallagher makes this clear by claiming:

> How the body reacts to a particular environment, even if automatic, is not a matter of simple mechanics or reflex … the body *meets* stimulation and organizes it within the framework of its own pragmatic schemata.[52]

In other words, the organization implicit in the body schema develops within the context of the person's interests, actions and background skills, which inform the ways in which a body will acquire its own manner of moving. Gallagher writes of a certain kind of "selectivity" nested in the process of body schematic development.[53] Selectivity, while related to the subject's "intentional interests", is not a matter of conscious decision-making.[54] One does not acquire skill by fiat but through practice. Skill emerges in the body through a process of inculcation. Nineteenth-century philosopher, Félix Ravaisson, wrote a short book on habit in which he set out the process by which a body acquires habit or, in this case, develops a specific bodily schema.[55] Ravaisson detailed habit's pathway from initial, mindful effort towards non-conscious ease of execution.[56] The selectivity of body schematic development is expressed in the transition between conscious awareness and non-conscious, embodied flow. It informs the shape of habit.

While the subject's interests, history and background may well inform the nuances of the process, the formation and exercise of the body schema work on another level, beneath conscious intentionality. Gallagher is in that respect right to say that the "body operates according to a 'latent knowledge' it has of the world, a knowledge anterior to cognitive experience".[57] Ravaisson's work shows why it is that the body schema is anterior to conscious experience in that he traces the shift from deliberate action to embedded habit. Once embedded, habits find expression outside conscious awareness.[58] This is what is meant by organization in the body. I cannot be said to have the skill of writing unless my body schema is able to pragmatically merge with my pencil so that I can concentrate on articulating my thoughts. The body schema is the background means whereby we are able to conceive and act in the same motion.

The body schema broadens our understanding of embodied subjectivity beyond the frame of consciousness by allowing for a level of non-conscious activity.[59] To that extent, it marks a break with Husserlian phenomenology.[60] Gallagher argues that Merleau-Ponty developed an expanded notion of intentionality beyond a merely noetic understanding of the body's intentional remit. While noetic intentionality remains wholly available to conscious reflection, the body schema can be said to function in pre-noetic terms, as the skilful givenness which enables the articulation of thought in action. How we walk, reach, touch and act involves a set of skills that function seamlessly within the realm of habit rather than conscious deliberation.

The distinction between body image and body schema shifts the plane of phenomenology beyond the frame of conscious awareness. It allows for a fuller understanding of the impact of the way we move on the way we perceive. The demarcation between (conscious) body image and (non-conscious) body schema is most easily maintained when the subject functions in an everyday, habitual context. In such cases, the body schema is the non-conscious corporeal means by which the subject acts in the world. A person's body schema can of course become the subject of explicit (re)negotiation. In rehabilitation for example the body schema may become the subject of explicit awareness.[61] Any attempt to expose and engage habitual movement tendencies would need to bring to the fore that which normally functions outside awareness. It is for that reason that Gallagher claims that the body schema (and its difference from the body image) is most easily understood on an everyday level, when the focus is not upon one's own body as such.[62]

The body at grips with the world

Merleau-Ponty's appreciation of the body shifts phenomenological thinking into a fuller acknowledgement of the body's importance for thought and action. The perspectival character of perception, for example, is due to our bodily relation to the perceptual object. My ability to engage in motor projects (movement-based actions) is conditioned by my body's ability to organize itself in the world. The horizon works through the body, through its motility amongst a world of objects, creatures and people. I touch because my body seeks contact, I look through inhabiting my gaze. The senses work together because my body works as a whole in the world. The lived body is an active body, able to think in action, as an integrated whole, which combines conscious perception (body image) with corporeal facility (body schema). Merleau-Ponty refers to the body as an "I can", as a capable body-subject who acts without reflecting, within the habitual every day.[63] These are the features of a body "at grips with the world".[64]

The notion of grip is a pragmatic term. The grip of a handshake is infused with practical, corporeal intelligence. Part initiation, part response, my grip enters a duet with the hand of another. I mould my hand to its shape while exerting my own hold. To grip is to act in relation to the world, to the grip of the object, the world's riposte to our situation. Alphonso Lingis portrays the world as issuing demands such that the body responds to the "commands" of the thing, to its character as revealed through my grip.[65] He uses the term "imperative" to suggest that the world calls forth perceptual activity.[66] My gaze, for example, is drawn to these books, this pad of paper. The toothbrush and toothpaste call forth my tooth-cleaning. The car in my driveway invites my driving. These invitations are not reducible to their embedded objects, in that their significance is found within the context of my life. The order of the world – its "ordinance" – is none other than its sensible configuration, the meaningful contours of my environment.[67] The will of the world is its character, its commands, an invitation to connect. Grip is an activity framed in accordance with the world. It signifies the relation between an active subject and the world framed in terms of its practical significance. Komarine Romdenh-Romluc describes the subject's environment as embracing a variety of "suggestions": "entities that are edible, throwable, kickable and so on".[68] Lingis takes suggestion one step further, towards a form of address, whereby "kickable" becomes 'kick me', "throwable" becomes 'throw me' and so on.[69] In order to pursue tasks, one attends to the world's initiatives: "suddenly the sensible takes possession of my ear and my gaze".[70] Yet, perception is neither centred on the subject (as grip) nor the object (as command) but lies between the two. Nor can we say which it is that takes the lead. In his later work, Merleau-Ponty writes:

> What is this talisman of color, this singular virtue of the visible that makes it, held at the end of the gaze, nonetheless much more than a correlative of my vision, such that it imposes my vision upon me as a continuation of its own sovereign existence? How does it happen that my look, enveloping them, does not hide them, and, finally, that, veiling them, it unveils them?[71]

The same could be said of the body's grip: how is it both activity and response? Tango might seem the ultimate in dominant machismo, but unless the 'leader' cleaves to the actions of their partner, there is no dance. Alexander Technique proceeds through touch – between teacher and pupil – but the Alexander teacher cannot simply 'will' a certain result. Touch must submit as well as exert.[72]

Merleau-Ponty's quest for a true and accurate picture of pre-reflective life, of lived perceptual experience, follows the contours of a certain kind of philosophical anthropology, that is, a manner of posing human being. His analyses of the pre-reflective domain yield a tapestry of embedded competencies that express the perceptual relation between subject and object. The focus is on everyday activities which manage the world through a series of corporeal praxes or "conducts at work in the world".[73] Lingis calls this a "phenomenology of perceptual competence".[74] It is discerned in pre-reflective life, emerges from our situation, through our (motor) projects without necessarily calling attention to itself. In that sense, our competence is habitual, reliable and familiar. Subjectivity is practically and existentially dispersed. The world itself is an extension of our being, its setting incorporated into what we do, determining (imperative) but also responsive (the field of our activity).

Merleau-Ponty's typification of perceptual activity has been taken up by scholars who want to emphasize the corporeal agency inherent in thought and action.[75] The body-subject's characteristic immersion in the object is posed as a relational praxis, holding between the body and its environment. The environment solicits our everyday actions which are expressed through the pursuit of motor projects. It is our existential setting made familiar over time and through myriad projects and patterns. It is our social and cultural milieu.

Dreyfus and others have developed the theme of everyday coping inherent in Merleau-Ponty's work.[76] Dependent on norms of absorption and flow, everyday coping is an extension of the bodily 'I can' posed within a conception of the human situation as environment. The body is seen to embody skills and knowledges which are brought into play as the situation demands. The notion of absorbed coping posits skills acquisition as the prelude to coping. It follows the movement from learning to facility. Absorbed coping posits a subject who inhabits a familiar world, one which elicits 'unthinking' though skilled responses to its solicitations. There are those who disagree with Dreyfus' characterization, who question the character and degree of absorption inherent in a variety of practices.[77] These debates turn on the kind of account one gives of particular actions, their degree of absorption and skill, awareness, deliberation, focus and immersion. They also extend to nuanced discussion of other sensory matters, such as spatial management and awareness.[78] What follows addresses another kind of focus felt in action, less a question of absorption than the attempt to manage one's existential situation.

The lessons of Schneider

Phenomenology of Perception features an ongoing dialogue with the scientific research of its time. It also engages the medical literature on perceptual and cognitive pathology. Johann Schneider was a First World War soldier who suffered acquired brain injury from an exploding mine. He came to the attention of the German physicians, Goldstein and Gelb, who drew on his case in order to develop their version of Gestalt theory.[79] Although Schneider suffered a wide range of symptoms, Merleau-Ponty's discussion is concentrated on his distinctive movement qualities as relayed by Gelb and Goldstein. Schneider is able to perform a number of tasks in the context of his daily life. He can strike a match, blow his nose, even hold down a job, stitching leather wallets.[80] But he cannot repeat the very same movements outside of their usual setting. For example, he can stitch shoes at work but he cannot mime these actions. When bitten by a mosquito, Schneider scratches the felt itch. If, however, he is asked to repeat the scratching movement without feeling the itch, he experiences difficulty. He cannot move his arm, leg or even bend a finger to order even though he might flex a finger in the course of his work.[81] He can grasp and touch but cannot point to his nose. When attempting to do so he tracks his arm by watching it swing to and fro, and then visually follows its passage through space towards his nose.[82]

Merleau-Ponty surmises that Schneider lacks the ability to move his body as such, to shape it according to an external perspective. Schneider cannot imagine a possible situation in which he might perform certain bodily movements, even though those very same movements occur in the context of his everyday life. Schneider's condition limits him to the sphere of what Goldstein and Gelb call concrete action.[83] Schneider functions in the field of absorbed activity. He has difficulty composing his body outside the domain of the actual. Merleau-Ponty points out that this distinction in ability cannot be explained in purely behavioural terms because the behavioural perspective fails to distinguish between concrete and imaginary settings. A body scratching a real itch or miming a scratch is, from a behavioural point of view, performing the same actions. Yet the two actions are not the same for Schneider who can perform one action with ease but not the other. The discussion of Schneider's case prompts Merleau-Ponty to posit a third term – the body – to supplement Gestalt's distinction between focus and ground. Merleau-Ponty argues that "one's own body is the always implied third term of the figure-background structure".[84]

The tri-partite Gestalt (body-figure-ground) allows Merleau-Ponty to distinguish between very different movement qualities, while maintaining the body's intrinsic habitual character. For the most part, the body functions as an implicit agency, the *éminence grise* that provides "the darkness of the theatre required for the clarity of the performance".[85] In habitual, everyday activities, the body is tacit. It is the enabler, an 'I can', competently performing habitual tasks. This represents our usual manner of moving according to the dictates of the object, without any explicit experience of the body's activity. Schneider inhabits this manner of moving and therefore living. But there are other existential possibilities.

Although the body is not typically at the forefront of experience, it can become so. Some tasks require an explicit appreciation of the body's spatial occupation. Pointing for example requires an awareness of the arm's directionality in relation to its object. Mime also calls for an understanding of the body's external appearance. Marcel Marceau's encounter with an imaginary wall is so well executed that we can almost sense its solidity. Merleau-Ponty claims that in these cases the body is no longer experientially implicit. Its difference concerns the need to occupy objective space in a particular manner. In such instances, the subject is no longer merely immersed in the object but has to configure his/her body in specific terms. In the case of pointing, the necessity to position the body in objective space involves the intention to achieve an actual bodily configuration (rather than some other practical efficacy). Its focus on what the body is doing as such elevates the experience from mere

absorption in the task at hand. These factors lead Merleau-Ponty to distinguish between what he calls the phenomenal and objective body:

> It is never our objective body that we move, but our phenomenal body,
> and there is no mystery in that since our body, as the potentiality of
> this or that part of the world, surges towards objects to be grasped and
> perceives them.[86]

The phenomenal body is the body as it is lived and felt, whether dancing or
doing the most ordinary of things. Most of the time the phenomenal, lived
body gets on with it, inhabiting the material world, which for its part speaks
to the subject in practical terms. My body anticipates, responds and creates,
depending upon its situation, task or goal. The pen forms the words on this
page as my hand shapes these letters. These movements are unthinking, mar-
ginal to my conscious thoughts. But I could watch these words form in virtue
of my hand's pathway, feel the tension in my fingers and shoulder, the contact
with the pen, attend to the weight falling through my thighs onto the chair.
And I could, in principle, reproduce these movements, according to and from
the point of view of an outside eye. The phenomenal and objective bodies
represent two perspectives on one and the same entity. The phenomenal body
is that aspect of ourselves that we move, sense and feel. The objective body
is the phenomenal body from an external point of view. The question for
Merleau-Ponty is to account for these two perspectives and to show how the
one also speaks to the other.[87]

Merleau-Ponty discusses the sense in which we are able to shift focus from
the lived, phenomenal body to an appreciation of its objective character.
This occurs for example when performing actions with an imaginary component beyond the concrete every day. Following Merleau-Ponty, Komarine
Romdenh-Romluc calls this "the power to reckon with the possible".[88]
Romdenh-Romluc illustrates action beyond the concrete everyday through
the example of a martial arts expert miming a fight against an imaginary
foe as part of a film sequence. Although digital technology will ultimately
insert an opponent, the martial artist must project around herself a substitute,
imaginary setting in which to battle. Such activities depend upon a sense of
the greater intentional setting within which we live. Merleau-Ponty describes
this in the following way:

> So let us say instead, by borrowing a term from another work, that the
> life of consciousness – epistemic life, the life of desire or perceptual life –
> is underpinned by an "intentional arc" that projects around us our past,
> our future, our human milieu, our physical situation, our ideological situ-
> ation and our moral situation, or rather, that ensures that we are situated
> within all of these relationships. This intentional arc creates the unity of
> the senses, the unity of the senses with intelligence, and the unity of sensi-
> tivity and motricity. And this is what "goes limp" in the disorder.[89]

Schneider is unable to imagine or re-imagine any setting beyond the concrete activities of his life. If he walks past his doctor's house without specifically attending an appointment, he will not recognize the house. Schneider's relation to his own body is largely limited to its habitual domain. He cannot shape his body to order nor facilitate its movement in relation to any imaginary situation. His intentional arc is thereby compromised by his own specific cognitive and motoric pathology.

And yet, Schneider can attempt non-habitual actions. In order to do so, however, he needs to resort to non-conventional means. For example, to locate the spot where another touches his body, he moves his entire body. When attempting to point, he will swing a limb to determine the position of his forearm.[90] Although Schneider does not easily perform non-habitual actions, he is able to call upon and execute certain strategies (with varying degrees of success). Merleau-Ponty contrasts Schneider's limited abilities with the breadth of possibilities available to "the normal subject".[91] And yet, there is another aspect to the discussion. Although Schneider is unable to recreate imaginary situations, he does try, calling upon quite ingenious strategies in order to do so. This is not a picture of absorbed coping, rather of conscious endeavour in a situation of fallible grip.

Gayle Salamon draws on the autobiographical writings of two women, one with rheumatoid arthritis, the other with a congenital and progressive physical disability, to challenge the surety of grip typified in conceptions of absorbed coping and perceptual competence.[92] Salamon questions Dreyfus' notion of 'maximal grip' as typifying the subject's relation to the world by introducing the experience of those who cannot consistently exert grip in their everyday lives. She cites Mary Felstiner's daily experience of joint pain and muscle stiffness, which undermines her ability to perform everyday tasks such as writing, unscrewing a jar or peeling an orange:

> Felstiner's description of her daily life stands, or painfully sits, in stark contrast to the Dreyfusian philosophy of life as maximal grip. On her very best days, Felstiner can achieve only *minimal* grip.[93]

Salamon depicts Felstiner's grip as a variable and complex project, a "compensation for lost bodily intentionality".[94] Her discussion of grip also draws on Harriet John's management of her electric wheelchair. Salamon cites John's highly skilful negotiation between her body and her chair, working a dynamic and delicate balance between gravity, grip and weight. For Salamon, the nuanced skill needed to negotiate John's chair in a physically weakened state is a mark of less not more grip, calling into question the normativity embedded in Dreyfus' concept of maximal grip. She sees the grip exerted by John and Felstiner as compromised by their physical condition, leading to an interrupted bodily intentionality and minimal sense of grip.[95]

I would argue that there is another way of viewing their efforts, as the incredibly skilful endeavours of people who experience movement difficulties.

Like Harriet John's wheelchair manoeuvres, Australian dancer Melinda Smith exerts great skill in managing her environmental milieu. As a dancer with cerebral palsy, Smith can be seen in performance actively negotiating a physical terrain of unwilled bodily movements.[96]

In her solo work, *Spasmotive*, Smith sets up physical challenges for herself, allowing her audience to apprehend her endeavours, drawing attention to the challenges of spasmodic movement.[97] Smith's dancing could be construed as the consummate expression of grip upon her physical condition. There is a sense then in which Felstiner, John and Smith can be seen to exert great skill in relation to their motor projects, which call for a dedicated and situational virtuosity. Whether they succeed in the particular instance, the complexity of their engagement signals a high degree of complexity that isn't faced by those whose movement is habitually seamless. If not the expression of 'maximal grip', the endeavours of those whose bodily intentionality is challenging are a powerful example of non-absorbed coping.[98] From the point of view of grip, facing such challenges may not be that different from rock climbing, competition golf or potting a billiard ball. The difference is that for Felstiner, John and Smith, everyday actions cannot simply be achieved under the guise of absorbed coping because their motor intentionality is no easy matter. Their coping is explicit, to be found in their active engagement with the complex task of moving in everyday life. And yet, the distinctive virtuosity of so-called disabled movement can be appreciated in terms that acknowledge its dedicated

Figure 1.1 Melinda Smith, *Spasmotive*, Melbourne, 2018. Photographer: Dianne Reid.

complexity and creative engagement.[99] Schneider's example, and the complex physical situations of others, makes it clear that there is more than one kind of lived body, that there are bodies with a range of facilities, facing a range of challenges, and that the world cannot guarantee our coping.

Schneider's case does two things for Merleau-Ponty. It allows him to posit the lived, phenomenal body as the source and site of human agency but it also opens the door to differentiating its manner of execution. Schneider is living proof that there is more than one kind of lived body, that there are those with a range of facilities, who move in a plethora of ways. While Merleau-Ponty depicts life in habituated terms which suggest absorption and immersion, *Phenomenology of Perception* is also full of unusual cases, 'pathological' instances that call for philosophical engagement. Schneider's case allows Merleau-Ponty to acknowledge other ways of moving as legitimate unto themselves.[100] If there is a normative current in Merleau-Ponty's work, *qua* the presumption of everyday facility, there is also room for discussing ways of doing and living that depart from the general picture.

Towards a conception of movement subjectivity

Merleau-Ponty's discussion of bodily movement in *Phenomenology of Perception* lays the groundwork for a phenomenological approach to the dancing body. It posits the agency of the lived body, while offering a number of conceptual tools to analyse the breadth of human movement. Taken together, they point towards a conception of dancing which is articulated through relations between the body and its habitual environment or setting. Chapter 2 introduces the concept of movement subjectivity in order to shift the generality of motor intentionality in Merleau-Ponty towards the specificity of (dance) practice. Movement subjectivity is my term for the dancer's inculcated, habitual manner of moving. It is formulated to acknowledge difference in terms that seek an account of subject-formation in the midst of practice. Movement subjectivity represents the view that motor intentionality can be found across a range of kinaesthetic practices, and that movement and its experience are shaped by its existential milieu. The suggestion is that motor intentionality can be differentiated, depending upon its context and lived character. It will be argued that there is in Merleau-Ponty a precedent for this gesture, established through his discussion of illness. Merleau-Ponty devoted a great deal of thought to unpacking the distinctive ways in which illness is lived, so as to detail its singular modes of expression. Although his motivation may have been to reveal something about so-called normal function (as that which the ill person lacks), his nuanced attention to lived difference paves the way for an attention towards other kinds of difference, thought of as the embodiment of specificity rather than lack. The dancer's movement subjectivity is one such specificity. Rather than taking subjectivity as the universal ground of all perceptual experience, movement subjectivity proposes a practice-based notion of subject-formation. Felt at the level of perception, and expressed as a mode of agency, movement subjectivity emerges through practice. Its values and means of attending to the body in action speak to those practices from which it arises.

Notes

1 Maurice Merleau-Ponty, *Phenomenology of Perception*, trans. Donald A. Landes (London and New York: Routledge, 2014), 9.
2 "We will no longer say that perception is a nascent science, but rather that classical science is a perception that has forgotten its origins and believes itself complete", ibid., 75.
3 Ibid., 57.
4 Ibid., lxxx.
5 *Phenomenology of Perception* is marked by an ongoing engagement with other philosophical positions and scientific analyses. Merleau-Ponty used these interactions to differentiate his own thinking, which he hoped would capture the qualities of everyday life. While empiricism and intellectualism are traditionally thought in oppositional terms, Merleau-Ponty identified a common problem between them: that each in its own way proceeds from a split between mind and body, privileging one or the other side of this Cartesian separation rather than acknowledging the interconnectedness of mind and body. Empiricism's emphasis on the objective basis of thought looks to the causal origins of perception, thereby seeking in sensation the crux of perception, while intellectualism prioritizes the *a priori* structures of thought and understanding, thereby downplaying the actual field of perception. Their joint problem, according to Merleau-Ponty, is that they focus on the objective world without adequately appreciating the production of the object within and according to perceptual experience, *Phenomenology of Perception*, 28. See, Taylor Carman, "Between Empiricism and Intellectualism", in *Merleau-Ponty: Key Concepts*, ed. Rosalyn Diprose and Jack Reynolds (Stocksfield, UK: Acumen, 2008), 44–56.
6 David Morris, "Body", in *Merleau-Ponty, Key Concepts*, ed. Rosalyn Diprose and Jack Reynolds (Stocksfield, UK: Acumen, 2008), 111.
7 Ted Toadvine, "Phenomenology and 'Hyper-Reflection'", in *Merleau-Ponty: Key Concepts*, ed. Rosalyn Diprose and Jack Reynolds (Stocksfield, UK: Acumen, 2008), 26.
8 Merleau-Ponty, *Phenomenology of Perception*, lxxi.
9 "The task of knowing perception will always belong to perception. Reflection never transports itself outside of all situations, nor does the analysis of perception remove the fact of perception … Reflection is not absolutely transparent for itself, it is always given to itself in an experience", Merleau-Ponty, *Phenomenology of Perception*, 45.
10 Edmund Husserl, *Ideas: General Introduction to Pure Phenomenology*, trans. W.R. Boyce Gibson (London: Allen and Unwin, 1976).
11 "We put out of action the general thesis which belongs to the essence of the natural standpoint, we place in brackets whatever it includes respecting the nature of Being …", Husserl, *Ideas*, 110.
12 Merleau-Ponty, *Phenomenology of Perception*, 113.

13 For example, see Merleau-Ponty, *Phenomenology of Perception*, lxxvi, 26, 81, and 109.

14 See M.C. Dillon, *Merleau-Ponty's Ontology* (Bloomington: Indiana University Press, 1988), 52–3.

15 Merleau-Ponty, *Phenomenology of Perception*, 47.

16 Maurice Merleau-Ponty, "The Child's Relations with Others", *Primacy of Perception*, trans. William Cobb (Evanston, Ill: Northwestern University Press, 1964), 116–7.

17 Jean-Paul Sartre, "Existentialism is a Humanism", in *Existentialism from Dostoevsky to Sartre*, ed. Walter Kaufmann (New York: Meridian, Penguin Books, 1975), 345–369.

18 Merleau-Ponty, *Phenomenology of Perception*, lxxxii.

19 Ibid., lxxxii. Shaun Gallagher writes that:

> the concept of operative intentionality attempts to capture the idea that the experiencing agent is intentionally engaged with the world through actions and projects that are not reducible to simple mental states, but involve an intentionality that is motoric and bodily.
> (Shaun Gallagher, *Phenomenology* [London: Palgrave Macmillan, 2012], 76)

20 Merleau-Ponty, *Phenomenology of Perception*, lxxxii.

21 Ibid., lxxxiv.

22 Ibid., 73.

23 Ibid., 108.

24 Ludwig Wittgenstein, *On Certainty*, trans. Denis Paul and G.E.M. Anscombe, ed. Elizabeth Anscombe and G.H. von Wright (Oxford: Blackwell, 1969), 2e.

25 Merleau-Ponty, *Phenomenology of Perception*, 112–114. The term, project, is part of the existential lexicon, which sees human existence as a mode of individual endeavour. In the context of a perceptual phenomenology, the notion of project becomes a form of movement, where action is conceived in relation to its object(ive).

26 Merleau-Ponty, *Phenomenology of Perception*, 69.

27 Ibid., 70, 71.

28 Ibid., 73.

29 Ibid., 73. In *The Absent Body*, Drew Leder develops this observation – that we tend to forget the body's active role in perception because we are so focused on the world – in part to explain the Cartesian tendency to render the body as (inert) materiality, but also to describe the embedded character of the body in everyday life, Drew Leder, *The Absent Body* (Chicago and London: University of Chicago Press, 1990). Others argue for a sense of transparency rather than absence, Dorothée Legrand, "Myself with no Body? The Body and Pre-reflective Self-consciousness", in *Handbook of Phenomenology and Cognitive Science*, ed. Shaun Gallagher and Daniel Shmicking (Dordrecht: Springer 2010), 181–200, Dorothée Legrand, "Pre-reflective Self-consciousness: On Being Bodily in the World", *Janus Head* 9, no. 2 (2007): 493–519. See also Dorothée Legrand and Susanne Ravn, "Perceiving Subjectivity in Bodily Movement: The Case of Dancers", *Phenomenology and the Cognitive Sciences* 8 (2009): 389–408.

30 Merleau-Ponty, *Phenomenology of Perception*, 103.

31 Ibid., 4.

32 Gestalt theory famously engages the Müller-Lyer illusion, according to which two lines of equal length 'seem' unequal, because each is framed by arrows, one heading inwards, the other, heading outwards. Ambiguous figures such as drawings of a cube are also discussed, where the cube will be perceived differently depending upon how the lines are seen. These figures are used to draw out the more general character of perception, that it is organizational and holistic rather than atomic.

33 Merleau-Ponty, *Phenomenology of Perception*, 70.

34 Alphonso Lingis develops this theme, that the object is known through multiple encounters, to suggest that the thing is known in "continuous transition", between and through experiences rather than via the singular event, Alphonso Lingis, "Imperatives", in *Merleau-Ponty Vivant*, ed. M.C. Dillon (Albany, NY: State University of New York Press, 1991), 93.

35 Lingis, "Imperatives", 92. For Lingis:

> Merleau-Ponty's phenomenology showed, beneath or prior to nature as objectively represented by theoretical or scientific nature, not a pure sensuous medley, but sensible things. The relationship between the sensible aspects of a thing is not that of external relations or additive juxtaposition ... A sensible thing has the consistency and coherence of a *Gestalt*, where the parts both implicate and express eachother.
> (Alphonso Lingis, "The Elemental Imperative", in *Re-reading Merleau-Ponty: Essays Beyond the Continental-Analytic Divide*, ed. Lawrence Hass and Dorothea Olkowski [New York: Humanity Books, 2000], 219)

36 Morris, "Body", 212.

37 The notion of the body schema originated in the work of Henry Head and Gordon Holmes, who see it as a postural mode of organization, Henry Head and Gordon Holmes, "Sensory Disturbances from Cerebral Lesions", *Brain* 34, nos. 2–3 (1911): 102–254, and Henry Head, *Aphasia and Kindred Disorders of Speech* (Cambridge: Cambridge University Press, 1926).

38 The English translations of *Phenomenology of Perception* reflect this confusion: where Colin Smith's English translation of *Phenomenology of Perception* translates *le schema corporeal* as body image, Donald Landes' subsequent translation uses body schema. See also Landes, "Translator's Introduction", in Maurice Merleau-Ponty, *Phenomenology of Perception*, trans. Donald A. Landes (London and New York: Routledge, 2014) xlix; Shaun Gallagher, *How the Body Shapes the Mind* (Oxford: Oxford University Press, 2005), 19–23; and Shaun Gallagher, "Body Schema and Intentionality", in *The Body and the Self*, ed. José Luis Bermudez, Anthony Marcel and Naomi Eilan (Cambridge, MA: MIT Press, 1995), 232.

39 Gallagher, "Body Schema and Intentionality"; Gallagher, *How the Body Shapes the Mind*, esp. Chapter 1.

40 Gallagher, "Body Schema and Intentionality", 228.

41 Ibid., 226.

42 Ibid., 226.

43 Ibid., 235.

44 Gallagher writes: "The body operates according to a 'latent knowledge' it has of the world, a knowledge anterior to cognitive experience", ibid., 233.

45 Gallagher puts this in the following way, by asking: "Are there not factors that have an effect on us, that operate in a way that is 'behind our back' and yet efficaciously anterior with respect to our experience?", ibid., 232.

46 Merleau-Ponty, *Phenomenology of Perception*, 113.
47 Ibid., 101.
48 Ibid., 102.
49 Merleau-Ponty writes of the body schema as a "global awareness of my posture in the inter-sensory world, a 'form' in Gestalt psychology's sense of the word", ibid., 102.
50 Gallagher, "Body Schema and Intentionality", 234.
51 Merleau-Ponty, *Phenomenology of Perception*, 102.
52 Gallagher, "Body Schema and Intentionality", 235.
53 Ibid., 235.
54 Ibid., 236.
55 Félix Ravaisson, *Of Habit*, trans. Clare Carlisle and Mark Sinclair (London and New York: Continuum, 2008).
56 Ravaisson traces the shift from effort to ease in the acquisition of habit. An action that may have required conscious effort becomes easier through the formation of habit, *Of Habit*, 51.
57 Gallagher, "Body Schema and Intentionality", 233.
58 Ravaisson claims that habit is established beneath consciousness in such a way that there is a "fusion" between thought and action, *Of Habit*, 55. I clean my teeth in habitual fashion, free to think about other things as I work the toothbrush.
59 Gallagher puts this in the following way, by asking: "Are there not factors that have an effect on us, that operate in a way that is 'behind our back' and yet efficaciously anterior with respect to our experience?", "Body Schema and Intentionality", 232.
60 Gallagher teases out the sense in which the body schema marks a point of departure from Husserlian phenomenology, whose methodology of bracketing existence can only accommodate the body as body image (insofar as it appears in consciousness), ibid., 231. The phenomenological reduction thereby excludes the body's pre-noetic functions, that is, the sense in which the body facilitates (movement) in the background. Gallagher writes that for Husserl, "Everything of importance happens in full phenomenological view, 'out in front' of the noetic act", ibid., 232. For Gallagher, the Husserlian emphasis on consciousness tends to underplay "the role of the body as it functions on the other side of the intentional relation, that is, as it functions to make perception possible and to constrain intentional consciousness in various ways", ibid., 226.
61 See, for example, Øyvind F. Standal, "Re-embodiment: Incorporation through Embodied Learning of Wheelchair Skills", *Medical Health Care and Philosophy* 14 (2011): 177–184.
62 Gallagher, *How the Body Shapes the Mind*, 24.
63 Merleau-Ponty, *Phenomenology of Perception*, 139.
64 Maurice Merleau-Ponty, *Phenomenology of Perception*, trans. Colin Smith (London: Routledge and Kegan Paul, 1962), 303.
65 Lingis, "Imperatives", 97.
66 Ibid.
67 Ibid., 98.
68 "The direct objects of perception, on Merleau-Ponty's account, are things that have a value or meaning for the perceiver in terms of her capacities to interact with them. One's surrounding environment is immediately presented in perception

as 'requiring' or 'suggesting' a certain sort of behaviour such that the perceiver is not confronted with things that have merely objective qualities such as size, shape, etc., but with entities that are edible, throwable, kickable, and so on." Komarine Romdenh-Romluc, "The Power to Reckon with the Possible", in *Reading Merleau-Ponty: On Phenomenology of Perception*, ed. Thomas Baldwin [London and New York: Routledge, 2007], 45.

69 Kickable and throwable are terms found in Romdenh-Romluc (*supra*).
70 Merleau-Ponty, *Phenomenology of Perception*, 219.
71 Maurice Merleau-Ponty, *The Visible and the Invisible*, trans. Alphonso Lingis, ed. Claude Lefort (Evanston: Northwestern University Press, 1968), 131.
72 See also Lingis, on the "perceptual adjustment" according to which touch opens itself to the textures of the touched, Alphonso Lingis, "Translator's Preface", Maurice Merleau-Ponty, *The Visible and the Invisible*, trans. Alphonso Lingis, ed. Claude Lefort (Evanston: Northwestern University Press, 1968), xl–xlvi.
73 Merleau-Ponty, "The Child's Relations with Others", 117.
74 Lingis, "Bodies that Touch us", *Thesis Eleven* 36 (1993): 165.
75 David Morris links Merleau-Ponty's work on practical, perceptual conduct with debates in cognitive science. Morris refers to scientific research on AI and robotics to establish the view that bodily, skilful coping is a mode of cognition, David Morris, "Empirical and Phenomenological Studies of Embodied Cognition", in *Handbook of Phenomenology and Cognitive Science*, ed. Daniel Schmicking and Shaun Gallagher (Dordrecht: Springer 2010), 235–252; also, Sean D. Kelly, "What Do We See (When We Do)?", in *Reading Merleau-Ponty: On Phenomenology of Perception*, ed. Thomas Baldwin (London and New York: Routledge, 2007), 23–43.
76 Hubert L. Dreyfus and Stuart E. Dreyfus write of a body whose competence is beyond the ability of consciousness to keep up, citing the example of the trainer pilot whose expert eye movements were well beyond his/her ability to consciously track them, "The Challenge of Merleau-Ponty's Phenomenology of Embodiment for Cognitive Science", in *Perspectives on Embodiment: The Intersections of Nature and Culture*, ed. Gail Weiss and Honi Fern Haber (New York and London: Routledge, 1999), 114; see also Dreyfus, "Reply to Romdenh-Romluc", in *Reading Merleau-Ponty: On Phenomenology of Perception*, ed. Thomas Baldwin (London and New York: Routledge, 2007), 59–69.
77 For example, Daniel Barbiero, "On 'Absorbed Coping': G-intentionality, R-intentionality, and the Agent's Access", *Philosophy Today* 43, no. 4 (Winter 1999): 386–397; Dow, "Just Doing What I Do: On the Awareness of Fluent Agency", *Phenomenology and the Cognitive Sciences* 16 (2017): 155–177; Romdenh-Romluc, "The Power to Reckon with the Possible"; and Barbara Montero, "A Dancer Reflects", in *Mind, Reason and Being-in-the-World: The McDowell-Dreyfus Debate*, ed. Joseph Shear (New York: Routledge, 2013), 303–319.
78 Susanne Ravn, "Dancing Practices".
79 Kurt Goldstein, K and Adhémar Gelb, "Psychologische Analysen hirnpathologischer Falle auf Grund von Untersuchungen Hirnverletzer", in *Zeitschrift fur die gesamte Neurologie under Psychiatrie* 41 (1918): 1–142.
80 Merleau-Ponty, *Phenomenology of Perception*, 105.
81 Ibid., 106.
82 Shaun Gallagher discusses the movement qualities of a patient, Ian Waterson, who experiences similar problems:

If I ask Ian to sit, close his eyes, and point to his knee, he has some difficulty. If, in this situation, I move either his knee or his arm, he is unable to point to his knee since, without vision or proprioception, he does not know where either his knee or his hand are located.

(*How the Body Shapes the Mind*, 43)

83 Concrete action is habitual, absorbed action, oriented towards the world in the context of one's everyday motor projects. Abstract action, by contrast, lies outside the subject's usual domain of action, requiring a different kind of focus.
84 Merleau-Ponty, *Phenomenology of Perception*, 103.
85 Ibid., 103.
86 Ibid., 106.
87 See also Ibid., 517, note 20.
88 Romdenh-Romluc, "The Power to Reckon with the Possible".
89 Merleau-Ponty, *Phenomenology of Perception*, 137.
90 Ibid., 109.
91 Ibid., 107.
92 Gayle Salamon, "The Phenomenology of Rheumatology: Disability, Merleau-Ponty, and the Fallacy of Maximal Grip", *Hypatia* 27, no. 2 (Spring 2012): 243–260.
93 Ibid., 246.
94 Ibid., 248.
95 Vivian Sobchak also analyses her moving with and without prosthesis as a kind of interrupted intentionality, which she describes in terms of a "rupture of bodily transparence and fluidity", "Choreography for One, Two, and Three Legs: A Phenomenological Meditation in Movements", *Topoi* 24, no.1 (2005): 63.
96 Melinda Smith is a dancer and mentor/educator in the field of disability and education. In 2010, Melinda Smith helped to establish a small dance troupe of wheelchair users, known as Wheel Women. She has collaborated with dancer and filmmaker, Dianne Reid, over several years, improvising together, performing with Reid in *Dance Interrogations*, choreographed by Dianne Reid, 2017, and more recently, created the solo work, *Spasmotive*, choreographed and performed by Melinda Smith in collaboration with Franca Stadler, Dianne Reid, Stefanie Robinson and Mark Lang, 2018.
97 Smith's work, *Spasmotive*, draws attention to the "spasmic" character of Smith's corporeal existence, "*Spasmotive*: *Showings by Melinda Smith*", The Drill Hall, Women's Circus, Melbourne, Australia, February 17–25, 2018. Smith fully acknowledges the spasms that constitute and disrupt her movement. *Spasmotive* works with rather than in spite of Smith's unpredictable spasms. It highlights them in movement and textual terms.
98 Given Montero's argument against the assumption of absorption in respect of elite sports actions, one might call into question the normative status of absorbed coping and replace it with a more existential attention to that which happens in practice, Barbara Montero, "Thinking in the Zone: The Expert Mind in Action", *The Southern Journal of Philosophy* 53 (2015): 126–138.
99 See Erin Manning, *Always More than One* (Durham and London: 2013) and Hickey-Moody, *Unimaginable Bodies: Intellectual Disability, Performance and Becomings* (Rotterdam, NL: Sense Publishers, 2009) for a discussion of neurodiversity and corporeal diversity drawn from a different conceptual milieu, one which does not frame difference in terms of lack.

100 "Illness, like childhood or like the 'primitive' state, is a complete form of existence
     ... The normal cannot be deduced from the pathological ...", Merleau-Ponty,
     Phenomenology of Perception, 110.

Bibliography

Barbiero, Daniel. "On 'Absorbed Coping': G-intentionality, R-intentionality, and the
Agent's Access". *Philosophy Today* 43, no. 4 (Winter 1999): 386–397.

Carman, Taylor. "Between Empiricism and Intellectualism". In *Merleau-Ponty: Key
Concepts*, edited by Rosalyn Diprose and Jack Reynolds, 44–56. Stocksfield,
UK: Acumen, 2008.

Dance Interrogations. Choreographed by Dianne Reid, 2017.

Dillon, M.C. *Merleau-Ponty's Ontology*. Bloomington: Indiana University Press,
1988.

Dow, James, M. "Just Doing What I Do: On the Awareness of Fluent Agency".
Phenomenology and the Cognitive Sciences 16 (2017): 155–177.

Dreyfus, Hubert, L. "Reply to Romdenh-Romluc". In *Reading Merleau-Ponty: On
Phenomenology of Perception*, edited by Thomas Baldwin, 59–69. London and
New York: Routledge, 2007.Dreyfus, Hubert, L. and Stuart E. Dreyfus. "The
Challenge of Merleau-Ponty's Phenomenology of Embodiment for Cognitive
Science". In *Perspectives on Embodiment: The Intersections of Nature and Culture*,
edited by Gail Weiss and Honi Fern Haber, 103–120. New York and London:
Routledge, 1999.

Gallagher, Shaun. "Body Schema and Intentionality". In *The Body and the Self*, edited
by José Luis Bermudez, Anthony Marcel and Naomi Eilan, 225–244. Cambridge,
MA: MIT Press, 1995.

———. *How the Body Shapes the Mind*. Oxford: Oxford University Press, 2005.

———. *Phenomenology*. London: Palgrave Macmillan, 2012.

Goldstein, Kurt and Adhémar Gelb. "Psychologische Analysen hirnpathologischer
Falle auf Grund von Untersuchungen Hirnverletzer". *Zeitschrift fur die gesamte
Neurologie under Psychiatrie* 41 (1918): 1–142.

Head, Henry. *Aphasia and Kindred Disorders of Speech*. Cambridge: Cambridge
University Press, 1926.

Head, Henry and Gordon Holmes. "Sensory Disturbances from Cerebral Lesions".
Brain 34, nos. 2–3 (1911): 102–254.

Hickey-Moody, Anna. *Unimaginable Bodies: Intellectual Disability, Performance and
Becomings*. Rotterdam, NL: Sense Publishers, 2009.

Husserl, Edmund. *Ideas: General Introduction to Pure Phenomenology*. Translated by
W.R. Boyce Gibson. London: Allen and Unwin, 1976.

Kelly, Sean, D. "What Do We See (When We Do)?". In *Reading Merleau-Ponty: On
Phenomenology of Perception*. Edited by Thomas Baldwin, 23–43. London and
New York: Routledge, 2007.

Leder, Drew. *The Absent Body*. Chicago and London: University of Chicago
Press, 1990.

Legrand, Dorothée. "Pre-Reflective Self-consciousness: On Being Bodily in the
World". *Janus Head* 9, no. 2 (2007): 493–519.

———. "Myself with no Body?: The Body and Pre-reflective Self-consciousness". In
Handbook of Phenomenology and Cognitive Science, edited by Shaun Gallagher
and Daniel Shmicking, 181–200. Dordrecht: Springer 2010.

Legrand, Dorothée and Susanne Ravn. "Perceiving Subjectivity in Bodily Movement: The Case of Dancers". *Phenomenology and the Cognitive Sciences* 8 (2009): 389–408.

Lingis, Alphonso. "Translator's Preface". In Maurice Merleau-Ponty, *The Visible and the Invisible*. Translated by Alphonso Lingis, edited by Claude Lefort, xl–lvi. Evanston: Northwestern University Press, 1968.

———. "Imperatives". In *Merleau-Ponty Vivant*, edited by M.C. Dillon, 91–115. Albany, NY: State University of New York Press, 1991.

———. "Bodies That Touch Us". *Thesis Eleven* 36 (1993): 159–167.

———. "The Elemental Imperative". In *Re-reading Merleau-Ponty: Essays Beyond the Continental-Analytic Divide*, edited by Lawrence Hass and Dorothea Olkowski, 209–234. New York: Humanity Books, 2000.

Manning, Erin. *Always More than One*. Durham and London: 2013.

Merleau-Ponty, Maurice. *Phenomenology of Perception*. Translated by Colin Smith. London: Routledge and Kegan Paul, 1962.

———. "The Child's Relations with Others", *Primacy of Perception*. Translated by William Cobb, 96–155. Evanston, Ill: Northwestern University Press, 1964.

———. *The Visible and the Invisible*. Translated by Alphonso Lingis, edited by Claude Lefort. Evanston: Northwestern University Press, 1968.

———. *Phenomenology of Perception*. Translated by Donald A. Landes. London and New York: Routledge, 2014.Montero, Barbara Gail. "A Dancer Reflects". In *Mind, Reason and Being-in-the-World: The McDowell-Dreyfus Debate*, edited by Joseph Shear, 303–319. New York: Routledge, 2013.

———. "Thinking In the Zone: The Expert Mind in Action". *The Southern Journal of Philosophy* 53 (2015): 126–138.

Morris, David. "Body". In *Merleau-Ponty: Key Concepts,* edited by Rosalyn Diprose and Jack Reynolds, 111–120. Stocksfield, UK: Acumen, 2008.

———. "Empirical and Phenomenological Studies of Embodied Cognition". In *Handbook of Phenomenology and Cognitive Science*, edited by Daniel Schmicking and Shaun Gallagher, 235–252. Dordrecht: Springer 2010.

Ravaisson, Félix. *Of Habit*. Translated by Clare Carlisle and Mark Sinclair. London and New York: Continuum, 2008.

Ravn, Susanne. "Dancing Practices: Seeing and Sensing the Moving Body". *Body and Society* 23, no. 2 (2016): 57–82.

Romdenh-Romluc, Komarine. "The Power to Reckon with the Possible". In *Reading Merleau-Ponty: On Phenomenology of Perception*, edited by Thomas Baldwin, 44–58. London and New York: Routledge, 2007.

Salamon, Gayle. "The Phenomenology of Rheumatology: Disability, Merleau-Ponty, and the Fallacy of Maximal Grip". *Hypatia* 27, no. 2 (Spring 2012): 243–260.

Sartre, Jean-Paul. "Existentialism is a Humanism". In *Existentialism from Dostoevsky to Sartre*, edited by Walter Kaufmann, 345–369. New York: Meridian, Penguin Books, 1975.

Sobchack, Vivian. "Choreography for One, Two and Three Legs: A Phenomenological Meditation in Movements". *Topoi* 24, no. 1 (2005): 55–66.

Spasmotive. A dance showing, choreographed and performed by Melinda Smith in collaboration with Franca Stadler, Dianne Reid, Stefanie Robinson and Mark Lang, February 17–25, 2018.

Standal, Øyvind F. "Re-embodiment: Incorporation through Embodied Learning of Wheelchair Skills". *Medical Health Care and Philosophy* 14 (2011): 177–184.

Toadvine, Ted. "Phenomenology and 'Hyper-Reflection'". In *Merleau-Ponty: Key Concepts*, edited by Rosalyn Diprose and Jack Reynolds, 17–29. Stocksfield, UK: Acumen, 2008.

Wittgenstein, Ludwig. *On Certainty*. Translated by Denis Paul and G.E.M. Anscombe, edited by Elizabeth Anscombe and G.H. von Wright. Oxford: Blackwell, 1969.

2 Movement subjectivity and the phenomenology of dance

Introduction

Merleau-Ponty's phenomenological philosophy discerns human subjectivity at the heart of the perceptual relation. Perception reveals itself in the field of everyday life, as the sensory medium within which human affairs are conducted. It pervades the subject's lived situation, projects and goals. Since all experience is ultimately perceptual in origin, life itself is perceptual to the core, perception the living conduit between the body and its world. Perception is nested in everyday life. It is typically action-based, the modality and setting for our intentional projects. Merleau-Ponty develops a number of movement-based concepts, such as motor intentionality, motor signification and motor project to depict the corporeal nature of lived experience. The notion of motor intentionality offers an embodied, situated philosophy of action that aims to reflect the ways in which everyday life is enmeshed with what a body does.

The body is the key perceptual player in Merleau-Ponty's work. Merleau-Ponty does his best to characterize the ways in which we experience life through our bodies. He gives voice to the fact that, more often than not, the body is not the explicit focus of action. It is rather the means whereby we do what we do. The body schema is a way of conceptualizing the body's capacity to inhabit the everyday in movement terms. The body schema is a creature of habit, as are we. It is also that which enables a body to be a body and not a series of disconnected experiences. Its implicit manner of function frees up the subject to conceive and act without an explicit bodily focus. On the other hand, in certain contexts, the body may well become a focus of attention. In such a case, the body becomes an intentional object, the perceptual subject and object of attention, a momentary body image. Merleau-Ponty uses the example of Schneider to portray the mutability of the lived body, implicit one minute, explicit the next. This is not to treat the inflexible Schneider as incomplete. Merleau-Ponty is very clear that illness is fully lived on the part of the subject.[1] The recognition that the body can be lived in many ways enables Gayle Salamon to critically review the normativity embedded in certain extensions of Merleau-Ponty's thought, especially around notions of coping, competence and grip. Salamon's work, and indeed, Merleau-Ponty's own discussion of the singularities of illness, poses a limit to generalization through highlighting the nonconforming instance. There are therefore two trajectories in Merleau-Ponty's thought, one towards the typical, the other towards the atypical. The typical is the phenomenological goal of existential phenomenology, which aims to depict the subject's general perceptual demeanour. The lure of the object, bodily perspective and the body towards the world are all examples of its general character. The atypical comes about when considering the variety of ways in which a person might inhabit their situation. Disruptive variations between thought and action, intentionality and body schema, habit and motor intentionality, impact upon what a body can do and how it does it.

Merleau-Ponty's work seeks to honour the typical but also to acknowledge the atypical. Insofar as these tendencies co-exist, a phenomenology of dance must find a way of functioning in both these respects. The existential thrust of Merleau-Ponty's work translates into dance as an open-ended focus upon practice. The challenge then is to open phenomenology to the exigencies of the form, its situation and those who practise it. The following discussion begins with Maxine Sheets-Johnstone's landmark text, *The Phenomenology of Dance*.[2] Written at a time when there were few scholarly publications on dance, *The Phenomenology of Dance* is a sustained and systematic attempt to capture "the lived experience" of dance.[3] Sheets-Johnstone offers a framework for thinking dance from the point of view of the dancer, including a bold formulation of its essential character. It will be argued that the attempt to discern the phenomenological essence of dance is fraught with difficulty. The problem lies with the embedded nature of the theorist's own perspective, itself situated in practice, which is in turn an unfolding historical enterprise. These issues, of fact and essence, method and temporality, put dance phenomenology in touch with the question of difference, between subjectivities, practices, corporealities and their situation. Dance studies has long grappled with these matters, treading a careful path towards the recognition and iteration of difference. This chapter and the next will endeavour to think difference in relation to the lived body. It will do so through introducing two concepts: movement subjectivity and kinaesthetic sensibility, with a view to opening Merleau-Ponty's conceptual framework to the multiplicity of situations and subjectivities in relation to which dancing is practised.

The phenomenology of dance

The Phenomenology of Dance, by Maxine Sheets-Johnstone, was first published in 1966. It begins by focusing on the lived experience of dance, whether from a performer or audience point of view. Sheets-Johnstone writes:

> It is the lived experience which is of paramount significance. Through the lived experience we arrive at not only the sense of any particular dance, but also at the essence of dance.[4]

The goal of Sheets-Johnstone's phenomenological project is to extract the essence of dance from its lived experience. For Sheets-Johnstone, the lived experience of dance is pre-reflective, the subject of an immediate encounter, felt by way of direct apprehension.[5] The encounter between the subject and the dance is, by implication, without presupposition, untainted by the kinaesthetic provenance of the observer, in time but independent of history. Since the phenomenon of dance is given immediately and fully, without the mediation of reflection or knowledge, the phenomenologist is in a position to develop a complete account based upon that which appears in the lived encounter. The phenomenological enterprise thereby requires the analyst to repeatedly return to the immediate encounter, whether in the studio or in performance, to analyse it in its "totality" as exemplar of the form.[6] Sheets-Johnstone is very definite that the embodied history of the observer has no impact on its lived experience:

> Whatever knowledge we may have of dance, in general or in particular, is extraneous to the lived experience of any dance. Such knowledge may only affect our aesthetic expectations and judgments of that experience. Hence, the kinds of dances we have seen before, the extent of our own participation in dance – all prior experiences with dance influence the manner in which, and the level at which we approach and evaluate it. But to be pre-reflectively involved in what is now appearing before us on the stage is to be fully and exclusively responsive to it, such that the sense of that appearance is *immediately and directly apprehended.*[7] (emphasis mine)

For Sheets-Johnstone, there is therefore a mode of pre-reflective experience which is able to furnish direct insight into the essential character of dance. Historical contingency thus sits outside the immediacy of dance and its perception.

Although the embodied accumulation of kinaesthetic experience is extraneous to its lived encounter, it is still possible to look at its formation, to analyse what it takes for a dance work to assume 'the form' of a dance. Sheets-Johnstone is in this respect guided by Susanne Langer's aesthetic theory of symbolic function within art. Following Langer, Sheets-Johnstone focuses on the illusory aspects of art in assuming symbolic form. Taking dance to be a symbolic form, Sheets-Johnstone surmises that it must transcend the actual so as to achieve some kind of virtual presence. The virtual in this context denotes the illusory power of dance to create meaning beyond actual, physical movement. Sheets-Johnstone approaches the matter in terms of abstraction:

> It is clear that the form of dance is therefore an abstracted form in two senses: it is abstracted from the continuum of form in everyday life ... and secondly, it is abstracted from actual content so that it is divorced from any actual and specific feeling.[8]

Abstraction gives dance a non-physical, non-affective character, allowing it to achieve symbolic status. As a consequence, its lived experience has no kinaesthetic elements.[9] It is "ineffable" rather than actual – a formal achievement in the virtual, symbolic realm.[10] This leads to the following discovery:

> If we look at the phenomenon of movement, at its pure appearance untied to any actual affective or practical condition, movement appears as a *revelation of force*; it appears in and of itself as power or energy. All qualities of movement are therefore describable in relation to the global phenomenon of force: each quality describes a particular and apparent structure of movement as a revelation of force.[11]

Sheets-Johnstone systematizes the movement qualities of dance according to four essential qualities: tensional, linear, areal and projectional.[12] Each of these qualities is expressed and intuited on the part of the observer as an aspect of the revelation of force. Tension, for example, does not refer to the actual effort or muscular tension needed to produce movement but that aspect of tension which appears to be conveyed through movement and is (immediately) apprehended. The linear arises through the lines created by the body in motion, for example, whether in diagonal or zigzag lines.[13] The areal concerns the shape of the body and that which is created spatially through moving,[14] and the projectional refers to the manner in which force is said to be projected, for example, whether in an "abrupt, sustained … [or] ballistic" fashion.[15] According to Sheets-Johnstone, these four qualities together qualify each and every dance work. They collectively characterize the appearance of dance in its lived immediacy. Whence do they arise? Sheets-Johnstone writes:

> These terms describe the qualitative structures of the total illusion of force. As far as is known, they have never before been used. They emanate from the author's own experience of movement as a revelation of force.[16]

Thus we have the gist of Sheets-Johnstone's phenomenology of dance. Predicated upon the artwork's inherent symbolic iteration, dance is produced in the immediacy of its lived experience, and appears as the revelation of force via the specific configuration of its four essential qualities. This represents the totality of dance, its structure as a global phenomenon, alongside its essential phenomenological analysis.

The general thrust of *The Phenomenology of Dance* is to account for dance as a whole, as a global phenomenon, fully present to the person experiencing it. To that end, Sheets-Johnstone explicates lived experience as a medium of immediacy and direct apprehension. It matters not who experiences the dance or from what perspective, since its appearance is unaffected by history or circumstance. Sheets-Johnstone proceeds to tease out the key qualities of this expressive, symbolic art, from its inherent break with everyday life to its shift towards virtual power. Dance emerges from this encounter as the revelation of force, a unified phenomenon available to all who encounter it. The phenomenon is further qualified according to four essential characteristics. By Sheets-Johnstone's own account, these qualities, never articulated before, were revealed through "the author's own experience of movement".[17] What is the status of the author's movement experience here? Is it representative of others' experience of movement or is it a key eidetic insight which others may or may not apprehend? What would be the status of four *different* essential qualities, as apprehended by another mover? The aim of these questions is to open up the question of eidetic insight – knowledge of essences. In Husserlian phenomenology, the eidetic reduction involves a series of intentional operations. Insofar as essence is revealed through the experience of movement, it is apprehended through the lens of motor intentionality, and is found in the way a person moves, their dancing and its experience. I argue that this is a situated affair, marked by history and felt within and according to its kinaesthetic milieu.

Sheets-Johnstone's kinaesthetic context – American modern dance – informs her characterization of what dance is, an issue for anyone endeavouring to describe the entirety of dance. In the Preface to the Second Edition of her book, written 13 years after its initial publication, Sheets-Johnstone noted the emergence of a new form of (post)modern dance, one which consists of movement *qua* movement.[18] The existence of an emergent form of dance, which is neither symbolic nor expressive, contravenes certain assumptions made about dance in the book. For example, dance was no longer confined to the domain of symbolic expression.[19] Dance had become a form which could incorporate the pedestrian,[20] felt sensation,[21] or examine its separation from the everyday.[22] In other words, the 'totality' of dance had changed (as thought within the confines of American modern and postmodern dance). The physical body had become a perfectly legitimate focus. Steve Paxton's *Small Dance*, for example, calls for the dancer's sensory attentions to the micro-movements implicit in very minor movements.[23] This marks a shift from the dancer's immersion in the dance to the exclusion of physical sensation, effecting a break with immediacy as characterized by Sheets-Johnstone. *Small Dance* elicits the dancer's momentary perceptions of movement. A dancer steeped in these concerns no longer excludes the kinaesthetic from their lived experience. Sheets-Johnstone's response to these localized, historical changes is to signal the need for certain revisions in her work, some of which she alludes to in her own subsequent writing.[24] Phenomenology is after all a provisional endeavour, open to changes in its very formulation. What is less clear, however, is how (and whether) the phenomenological enterprise can ever deliver the essence of 'the' dance experience. The four defining qualities of movement were revealed to Sheets-Johnstone in the context of her own movement experience. Their manner of revelation was situational and embedded.

Although Sheets-Johnstone endeavoured to achieve total generality in her depiction of the lived experience of dance, her account is indelibly marked by the corporeal specificity of the encounter and its milieu. Sheets-Johnstone could not have possibly known the turn that (post)modern dance was to take towards the kinaesthetic investigation of movement. What does this say about the 'totality' of dance (as posed within a thoroughly western paradigm)? Is it 'essentially' unaffected by historical development? If so, then in principle Sheets-Johnstone could have provided for the subsequent turn towards kinaesthetic investigation; the job was flawed but feasible. On the other hand, if history impacts upon essence, then experience can only appear within the confines of historical practice. Foucault puts it this way: while experience may "harbour universal structures", these are never felt apart from their social and historical context, which in turn sets out the conditions within which experience can be thought.[25] If Foucault is correct, then each and every experience will be particular, contingent and inextricably caught up in the conditions of its articulation. According to this view, there is no moment where structure reveals itself to a subject outside history. Rather, its 'appearance' is always affected by its conditions of articulation and the corporeal specificity embedded in the event of its encounter.

Sheets-Johnstone's historical 'omission' was not a lack of eidetic vision on her part but an indication of the corporeal register according to which movement is experienced. Phenomenological grip is an exercise of corporeal agency. It is kinaesthetically, culturally and historically specific. The experiential aspect of dance, which we might call its perception, is an embodied corporeal act, one which is embedded in the conditions of its articulation. When phenomenology concerns itself with an elaborated domain such as dance, the project is exposed to the vicissitudes of practice.[26] The issue is not merely one of content, of practice as the object of analysis. It also concerns the means by which it is perceived. Postmodern, poststructural and postcolonial forms of discourse dispute the notion that the immediate is prior to and analytically separable from the influence of social life, suggesting instead that the sphere of subjectivity is constituted through discursive and representational means. They take the view that experience is 'always already' mediated, that there is no zone of pre-reflective immediacy available to the subject.[27] Merleau-Ponty's work makes clear that experience is 'always already' corporeal. The mediation of the social is therefore also a corporeal matter, registered in the lived body. Elizabeth Grosz writes of the sense in which power relations and systems of representation do not merely traverse the body but "actively constitute the body's very sensations, pleasures – the phenomenology of bodily experience".[28] In other words, discursive and representational practices function through creating an interior, a phenomenology of bodily experience, which for its part informs the perceptual appreciation of dance. This represents a genealogical understanding of the lived body, one which contends that the lived body has a history.[29]

Movement subjectivity

What follows is an attempt to think through the impact of history on the lived body in terms which allow for the dancer's provenance, situation, and greater social and historical milieu. Rather than seeing the phenomenological project as a means to draw out the essence of dance, the suggestion is that the dancer's subjectivity can be posed as a variable and contingent formation. The notion of movement subjectivity is introduced so as to highlight lived differences amongst dance practices and their embedded forms of subjectivity. In post-structural parlance, this is the dancer's subject-position, corporeally understood and found within practice. According to movement subjectivity, movement and its perception are conceived along multiple pathways, each with its own preoccupations, preferences and priorities. Movement subjectivity is a practice-based approach towards subject-formation.[30] It is an adaptation of Merleau-Ponty's perceptual competence – the body-subject as an 'I can' – to the terrain of dance. Its elaboration of practice represents a qualification of motor intentionality, posed in relation to the dancer's kinaesthetic milieu. Movement subjectivity is a plural phenomenon which speaks to the sense in which a dancer acquires facility within a distinctive cultural and kinaesthetic milieu. Informed by Merleau-Ponty's conceptual universe, it depends upon the range of factors that coalesce around the lived body. Its explication is open-ended, dependent upon its origins, context and milieu. It follows no single trajectory, corporeal or historical. The concept, movement subjectivity, makes itself available to the vicissitudes of practice and includes the ways in which a particular dance form is culturally elaborated, its techniques, modes of transmission, performance and pedagogy.

Movement subjectivity may be described in terms internal to its situation, according to its kinaesthetic origins and values, or in relation to wider factors, contexts and conditions. From a subject-oriented perspective, movement subjectivity speaks to the dancer's concerns, kinaesthetic agency, motor intentionality and body schema. It underlies the dancer's perceptual demeanour, her conscious perceptions, thoughts and feelings. It also reflects the dancer's kinaesthetic and cultural everyday. Movement subjectivity is embedded in the domain within which it is articulated. It has a provenance but also its own unfolding history. Movement subjectivity offers a genealogy of the subject's perceptual demeanour, distinctive agency and kinaesthetic origins. It can only be approached on the plane of practice, through its situation and provenance. It is in that sense contingent.

Movement subjectivity is emblematic of its kinaesthetic situation and representative of the dancer's individual style and embodied history. Insofar as movement subjectivity is linked to its situation, it will take on the characteristics of its milieu but it will do so in its own way. Movement subjectivity is allied to the two moments of corporeal thinking in Merleau-Ponty's work, conceptualized in the body schema and body image. Body schema and body image are at play in the dancer's demeanour and facility, which incorporates a certain perceptual style (mode of perceptual attention) and an acquired, ready-to-hand facility. The body schema, as articulated in Chapter 1, is an established mode of movement organization that enables a person to reach out and grab a pencil, lift a box or enter a room without thinking about how they are doing so. To that end, the body schema functions beyond intentional awareness.[31] It represents the body's capacity to act without requiring a conscious focus on what the body is doing. Gallagher argues that the body schema extends the sphere of embodied intentionality towards a wider understanding of bodily function beyond the Husserlian model of noetic intentionality.[32] The body schema complements the pursuit of our intentional projects. It "precedes" experience, but also contributes to its character.[33] It frees up the subject to focus on other aspects of their actions or to complement their habitual activities with a conscious focus on other matters. Unlike the body image, which is partial and momentary, the body schema is an entire mode of organization, drawing together how a body does what it does. Merleau-Ponty's concept of motor intentionality embraces this wider sense of intentional life, as that which is nested in our actions.[34]

According to Gallagher, the body schema functions almost automatically. There is no doubt movement subjectivity incorporates a great deal of automatic, habitual action. There is also a strong sense of organization in the trained dancer. But movement subjectivity also incorporates the subject's perceptions, attitudes and conscious engagement in motion. This is where the body image (the body as intentional object) comes to the fore. The body image represents all the conscious images, thoughts, perceptions, feelings and representations a person may entertain with respect to their own body. It poses the body as an intentional object. The everyday subject who is oriented towards the world may have no need of explicit bodily perceptions, but the dancer will likely entertain a great deal of conscious perceptions (sensations, attentions, feelings). To that extent, movement subjectivity incorporates habitual ways of moving, *plus* a range of intentional engagements (body images). While some actions may be automatic and unthinking (body schematic), others will involve a dynamic interplay between conscious intentionality (body image) and embedded facility (body schema). Particular modes of practice may well prefigure a certain manner of interaction, for example, a focus on sensation, imagery, muscular quality or regional organization (breath, feet, the pelvis, length in the back and so on). Others may require a particular focus or mode of attention, perhaps spiritual or nature-based. Practices are distinguished from other modes of practice in part because of these characteristic relationships between perceptual and organizational elements. These are elaborated in practice, through the ways in which dancing combines a body's dispositional tendencies and the intentional experience of dancing. The interplay between conscious and organizational factors pertains to the dancer's awareness and attention towards her body in movement. Linda Sastradipradja's conception of the dancer's *auteurship* highlights this interplay.[35] For Sastradipradja, *auteurship* concerns the relation between the dancer and her dancing. It is exhibited in the intentional choices she makes within the context of enacting movement material. For Sastradijpradja, *auteurship* complements the dancer's body schema through the pursuit of explicit intentional strategies, whether a question of focus, qualitative detail, sensory attention, exploration or experimentation. To put the matter in terms of movement subjectivity, Sastradipradja outlines an element of movement subjectivity explicitly devoted to the dancer's enacted, intentional relation to her dancing.[36] Put in phenomenological terms, the dancer's relation to her dancing is iterated in the relation between her noetic, intentional acts (of consciousness) and the operative intentionality embedded in her movement choices.[37] *Auteurship* is a mode of kinaesthetic agency. It makes sense in the context of a postmodern kinaesthetic milieu, which is able to embrace an interrogatory, interactive movement approach.[38] It also embodies a certain kind of (movement) individualism, which speaks to the kind of subjectivity a dancer feels herself to exert.

Russell Dumas is also concerned with the nuances of the dancer's relation to her dancing. In his view, the work is done in the body of the dancers. Russell Dumas is a choreographer with a great breadth of experience and knowledge. Before returning to Australia over 30 years ago to make work, Dumas performed with a number of classical ballet companies, including the Royal Ballet, Ballet Rambert and Nederlans Dance Theatre. He has also worked and performed with Twyla Tharp Dance and Trisha Brown Dance Company. He draws on contact and ideokinesis, and conducts dance residencies in Larret, France and Bali, Indonesia. His dance style has been described as "sensuous, non-decorative, pedestrian classicism".[39] I have known Russell Dumas for many years. Over a period of five years (2005–2010), I worked relatively intensively with him, travelling, occasionally performing in showings, but mainly hanging out and dancing in the studio, where I was exposed to a great many of his insights, which hail from a multiplicity of traditions and practices. For Dumas, the work is done in the body of the dancers. Working with Russell changed the way I perceive movement – my own and others'. As a dance reviewer since 1997, I wondered what and how I saw dance before working with Russell. That shift in perception and understanding is testimony to the formative impact of practice on perception and the body.

Like Sastradipradja, Dumas highlights the dancer's relation to movement material, citing Roland Barthes' taking a walk through the same park every day. Although the pathway remains the same, it is repeated anew with each iteration. The walking thereby opens itself to difference.

In "Signature, Event, Context", Derrida draws out a tension in relation to a person's writing their signature. Although "a signature must have a repeatable, iterable, imitable form", it is not clear that there is a pure signatory event which is utterly reproducible.[40] And yet, the repetition of the signature is an everyday occurrence. Choreographic material is repeated, iterated and reiterated, but can we say that there is a single form which is repeated? Or is there rather an ongoing reiteration which does not devolve upon a singular

Figure 2.1 Russell Dumas, artistic director, Dance Exchange, courtesy of the artist.

moment, 'the' choreography?[41] And if this is the case, the daily walk or the dancer's relation to her dancing material is an ongoing problematic to be resolved each time in the dancing. Hence the suggestion from Sastradipradja that dancers are able to confront this tension in their dancing, thereby to express an individual mode of *auteurship*. Sastradipradja and Dumas are each in their own way indicating an element of the dancer's movement subjectivity as it pertains to a certain kind of intentional-body schematic nexus (one which privileges the relation between act and operative intentionality). Their work is informed by a postmodern kinaesthetic milieu which makes space for such a nexus. Such an approach, although specific and contingent, need not be confined to a western movement paradigm. Classically trained Thai dancer, Pichet Klunchun, describes his own work as bridging "traditional Thai classical dance language with contemporary sensibility".[42] Klunchun's solo work, *I am Demon,* addresses Klunchun's apprenticeship learning the Khon Demon character from master dancer, Chaiyot Khummanee.[43] *I am Demon* offers a range of perspectives (visual, audio, movement) on the development of Klunchun's movement subjectivity but also speaks to his intentional approach towards his own embodied history and the subsequent elaboration of his classical heritage. Klunchin speaks of deconstructing the practice of Khon, of telling its story from his own viewpoint.[44] He has written about the 'basic movement' of Khon dance, in which he offers a range of possible thoughts in the body as it develops mastery of Kohn's basic step (for the Demon and Monkey characters). Klunchun writes:

> If one does "Ten Sao" and thinks about the dancing step, managing body movement, weight distribution, and the relationship between the left and right feet, it means that this person is going to be good at dancing soon.[45]

Klunchun offers a way of thinking dancing in the process of skills acquisition. His suggestions propose a series of intentional queries, to be directed towards the practising body as it acquires the bodily schemata associated with Khon classical dance. These three formulations, from Sastradipradja, Dumas and Klunchun, express a way of thinking the individual's approach to her dancing, an approach which may itself be embedded in a particular mode of movement subjectivity.

The enunciation of movement subjectivity – its expression in movement – thereby involves a dynamic interplay between conscious perceptions of the body (intentional body images) and embedded competencies (body schemata). The manner of that interplay may be a feature of the field itself, insofar as the field cultivates specific modes of intentional relationship towards the act of dancing. Other practices may instead de-emphasize subjectivity altogether in favour of other kinds of relationship, spiritual, social, cultural, cognitive, collective, ontological or metaphysical. The subtleties of these relationships are embedded in the field, taken up and expressed in action.

Movement subjectivity represents the refraction of these kinaesthetic qualities in the dispositional demeanour and agency of the dancer. There is an element of the habitual in movement subjectivity insofar as it represents an identifiable assemblage of qualities and dispositions. These emerge in the body by way of habit formation. In other words, movement subjectivity is a form of sedimentation. The emphasis on (movement) habits signals a corporeal emphasis upon subject-formation.[46] Habit is a way of thinking the consolidation of movement subjectivity in corporeal terms. It speaks to the body's acquired movement tendencies and intentional dispositions. There are two aspects of habit formation with regard to movement subjectivity, one centred upon the schematic incorporation of its environment, the other to do with the dancer's characteristic modes of intentional attention (body images). The body schema represents the incorporation of the subject's environmental milieu through a mode of organization felt in the body. Movement subjectivity speaks to the specificity of the body schema, to its origins within a distinctive kinaesthetic milieu and its adaptive, embedded facility. The influence of the kinaesthetic environment on the subject's body schema comprises the non-conscious, habitual component of the dancer's movement subjectivity.

Selectivity and signature

One of the features of the body schema is the selective manner in which it forges a movement-based relation with its environment. Gallagher puts this as a case of the body's 'meeting' rather than merely reflecting its environment. For Gallagher, the body actively participates in the formation of its body schema, organizing its sensory experiences according to "the framework of its own pragmatic schemata".[47] The inculcation of bodily schemata is therefore informed by the person's corporeal history and intentional concerns, movement tendencies, background and interests.

The notion of selectivity explains how movement subjectivity can be both idiosyncratic and typical. It does so through linking the body schema with its environment without claiming that the body schema is fully determined by it. Gallagher writes that the body schema cannot be reduced to physiological stimuli (the environmental encounter) but is informed by the person's practical concerns and intentional interests. The point is that while the body schema is a response to its environment, it is not reducible to it. That the body schema reflects its environment speaks to the characteristic component of movement subjectivity's body schema. This is felt through the adoption of a certain style or set of techniques. That the body schema is not reducible to its environment explains the idiosyncratic aspect of an individual's habitual movement organization, which could be called the dancer's *movement signature*.[48] Numerous dancers can be trained in a given technique, say ballet, Graham or release, and not turn out the same. And yet, the subject's kinaesthetic environment is the medium within which habitual modes of organization emerge. The selectivity of the body schema (its singular and embedded character) is built up by the way in which practice cultivates and embeds movement habits *and* the sense in which a body extracts and builds habit from its circumstance. Style is transmitted through the body schema but not as some faithful reproduction of an ideal form. Its expression is itself a mode of practice, open to historical variation and innovation.

Selectivity explains why movement subjectivity is conditioned but not determined. The two aspects, determination and relative autonomy, are reflected in cultural theories of subject-production.[49] David Morley contests the notion of a "single, original (and mythic) interpellation", according to which subjectivity can be read off the page.[50] Morley reminds us that "subjects have histories" within which actual encounters are framed.[51] These histories underlie the subject's pragmatic concerns. Morley argues that actual relations between subjects and discourses are an "unstable, provisional and dynamic" affair.[52] As Judith Butler writes:

> To claim that discourse is formative is not to claim that it originates, causes or exhaustively composes that which it concedes; rather, it is to claim that there is no reference to a pure body which is not at the same time a further formation of that body.[53]

The point is not to reject the concept of subject-production altogether but to make space for a degree of indeterminacy in its formation, signalled in Gallagher by the claim that the body actively organizes, rather than merely reflects, incoming stimuli. Dancers enter into kinaesthetic environments with a range of interests, backgrounds and concerns. These inform the kinds of impact an encounter is able to make. For example, a dancer engaging in the Alexander Technique may have her own movement issues, injuries, problems or habits which she wants to address. These might be deeply embedded in the way she moves and therefore not easily shifted by fiat. Her encounter and response to the technique will be refracted through these concerns as they manifest in her movement. There is thus a meeting between where a body is at and a body of practice such as Alexander Technique. Changes at the level of movement organization occur with respect to the body schema. Intentional strategies (noetic acts) to be carried out as part of the technique's distinctive practice call for the activation of body images. Over time, these intentional strategies may become incorporated into a modified body schema. In the case of the Alexander Technique, the body's tendency towards contraction may become less habituated, open to the sensory enjoyment of expansion. Similarly, the head might enjoy a greater dynamic range in relation to the spine. For Alexander, habit can never be entirely overcome but it might loosen its grip, as reflected in a body schema (mode of organization) that responds to Alexander's intentional agenda.

The relation between body schema and body image can take many forms. Movement practices offer their own interpretation and pragmatic concerns regarding the dynamic relation between the two, whether intimately engaged, relatively autonomous or otherwise. Engaging in somatic practice can generate all sorts of movement questions which may reflect on established movement patterns (resident body schemata) while establishing some habits of their own, for example, an habituated commitment to regular practice. Alexander Technique for instance articulates its own distinctive combination of conscious and non-conscious elements. This is embodied in the Alexander concept of non-doing. Non-doing aims to occupy a middle ground between deliberate and habitual, non-conscious action. It is activated through a specific set of intentional gestures (inhibition, and the Alexander directions), yet is itself not a deliberate action. For the Alexander Technique, habit (the body's resident movement tendencies) is in constant need of intentional disruption. The use of intentional strategies – inhibition (non-doing) and the Alexander directions – is aimed at undermining habitual contraction (as embodied in the body schema). The Alexander Technique therefore puts forward a set of body images at odds with the body schema. The technique's characteristic body image strategies do not supplement so much as defuse the subject's functioning body schema. To that extent, the Alexander Technique purports its own mixture of conscious intentionality, non-conscious operative intentionality and non-habitual action.

Other somatic practices espouse their own distinctive strategies in order to destabilize the subject's body schema. For example, ideokinesis draws on the activation of imagery in order to promote the incorporation of new movement qualities.[54] Ideokinetic practice is most commonly conducted in the constructive rest position, a horizontal formation that transports the subject away from the vertical everyday. It involves the entertainment of movement images such as imagining the body as a collapsing suit of clothes,[55] or that the pelvis is a bridge that walks,[56] or that the clavicle is the clasp of a cape flowing down the back,[57] or that the diaphragm is an umbrella that opens and shuts.[58] The idea is for the imagery to become incorporated but not through conscious directives.[59] Like the Alexander Technique, ideokinesis subscribes to a notion of non-doing, of allowing the image to occur in action, rather than through 'doing' or performing the image. Explicit intentionality is initially involved in this process, through entertaining the image, but gradually, the image takes on a life of its own, in motion.[60] There is thus an anticipated shift from explicit (noetic) thinking to movement thinking. Non-doing can also be quite pared back. Working in the studio recently, it was suggested to me that allowing my body to fall backwards into a walk could involve the thought of weight into the back of the head as distinct from 'putting' the weight into the back of my head.[61] As it turned out, thinking without doing allowed for a different kind of doing than doing per se.

Gallagher's notion of selectivity offers a corporeal perspective on the ways in which the dancer's kinaesthetic situation plays a part in the formation of the dancer's movement subjectivity. It also acknowledges the distinctive, idiosyncratic component of the body's response, which consists of an actual encounter (or series of encounters) informed by the subject's history (Morley) and pragmatic concerns (Gallagher). The result is a form of provenance which is typical yet also individual. People have distinctive movement signatures. These cannot be totally attributed to the dancer's environment or 'determining' situation. Rather, the situation offers the conditions for agency within which the dancer develops and enacts their own facility and movement style.[62] Some dance forms may favour more individualistic variations than others but, ironically, it is in improvisation that a signature style can become evident. Perhaps this is because the dancing is not masked by choreographic phrase material. I watched a structured improvisational piece recently (as a dance critic) in which I observed four dancers improvising alongside each other.[63] I was familiar with the work of one particular dancer, who I noticed tended to keep to a certain style of movement; letting his body drop according to gravity, catch the drop, hold his head and neck, eyes focused inward and tip the body towards the hip joints; the spine is held upright unless tipped, the legs mostly move through hip flexion such that there is a pronounced break at the hip joint. There is a sense in which this dancer was performing his distinctive movement style, his own habitual movement signature. Another occasion featured accomplished improviser, Ros Crisp, creating movement through bending her joints.[64] While Crisp pursued a great many jointed variations – in location, cumulative effect, rhythm and repetition – there was a sense in which the registration of joint activity counted as dancing for Crisp. This observer was drawn to felt sensation in the joints – joint-thinking – noticing their articulation as constituting, producing the movement. It's not that movement signatures are hermetically sealed nor improvisation predictable.[65] Improvisation is full of happenstance and in-the-moment serendipity, inspiration and stimulus. It is just that improvisation can also reveal what dancing means to that particular body. This was made quite apparent to me when observing a dance season of improvised works entitled "*The Dance Card*".[66] Dancers would begin 'outside' the dance event, then settle into a version of what counted for them as dancing: a palpable relation between thought and action, of movement phrasing, muscular exertion, timing, rhythm and occupation of space. One dancer even slipped into the diagonal exhibition of phrase material, legacy of the class format. In each case, there was a marked difference between an initial demeanour and its subsequent transformation into dancing.[67] There is no need, however, to assume that movement subjectivity is fixed once and for all, nor that a dancer cannot change.[68]

Habit formation

The process by which corporeal schemata and movement signatures are laid down is informed by the many different ways in which dance is transmitted. Habits are cultivated in a great variety of contexts, whether in a university, training institution, class, artisinal, familial, tribal, club, festival or intergenerational setting. They arise through ritual social practices, classroom pedagogy, group activity, bespoke modes of apprenticeship as well as the cultural everyday. What these differing contexts share is the incorporation of distinctive movement practices into the subject's corporeal schema. This is the non-conscious, habitual component of movement subjectivity. The non-conscious, habitual character of the body schema is complemented by its intentional other, the subject's body image. By this is meant the ways in which the body features within the dancer's intentional experience, her corporeal perceptions, feelings and thoughts as they occur in action. The subject's body schema and explicit intentionality (body image) complement each other, working the division between awareness and absorption.[69] For example, the ballet dancer's daily barre offers the opportunity not only to work habitually but also to interact with habit's enunciation, to focus on particular elements of a given repertoire, to pay attention to problematic or difficult actions or to take in the sensory experiences associated with its reiteration. Performance likewise sets the scene for an intentional interaction in movement. The dancer's daily practice may be more or less attentive, more or less intentional. Similarly, different approaches may require distinct combinations of intentional activity and habitual enunciation, including a sense of the kinds of intentional relation a dancer might assume towards her dancing.

The acquisition of movement subjectivity equally involves a dynamic relation between conscious and non-conscious facility. In the case of dance training or its social equivalent, the emergence of movement subjectivity will likely forge a complex and changing relationship between body schema and body image. Félix Ravaisson offers a way of thinking the emergence of habit within movement subjectivity, as a progression from conscious effort to non-conscious ease.[70] Ravaisson details the means whereby a body acquires habit, beginning with conscious effort (bodily perceptions) and ending with non-conscious facility (body schematic adoption). He notes that the conscious effort needed to perform a new action will decline with repetition. The diminution of effort and the concomitant emergence of ease (of movement) signal the birth of habit:

> as effort fades away in movement and as action becomes freer and swifter, the action itself becomes more of a tendency, an inclination that no longer awaits the commandments of the will but rather anticipates them, and which even escapes entirely and irremediably both will and consciousness.[71]

Habit thereby establishes itself beneath consciousness, "further down into the organism" so to speak.[72] This is an effect of habit, that habitual disposition no longer requires conscious effort in order to initiate activity. Ravaisson writes that the actions established by habit are the result of a "fusion" between the idea and its performance, so that ultimately "nothing separates the subject and object of thought".[73] Ravaisson traces the passage from body image to body schema in the formation of habit. His work draws attention to the role played by the body image in the formation of the body schema. It also explains why, once formed, the body schema (habit) no longer relies upon the intercession of an intentional body image. Once acquired though, the dancer's intentional focus is freed up to complement the bodily schema, in action, whether through the individual exercise of agency (à la movement signature) or according to the physiognomy of practice.

Conclusion

The concept of movement subjectivity was introduced to think through the impact of history on the lived body. Movement subjectivity is a practice-based account of subject-formation. It is itself a form of practice. Insofar as it is organized around habitual facility, it will coalesce around the subject's body schema. The body schema represents the ways in which a body implicitly organizes itself in action. Gallagher's clarification of the body schema shows how movement subjectivity incorporates both conscious body images and non-conscious body schemata. The body schema explains the link between movement subjectivity and its kinaesthetic milieu. The selectivity of the body schema allows for the development of individual movement signatures – idio-syncratic movement habits – while nevertheless positing the influence of the kinaesthetic environment on the dancer's formation. This is because the body schema develops in light of the individual's pragmatic interests, intentional projects and dance background. Although the dancer's kinaesthetic milieu has a formative effect upon the dancer's movement subjectivity, there is a degree of individual variation. Individual movement signatures (the selective uptake of body schematic elements) intersect with the characteristic facility belonging to the field (the habitus of the practice). Style and signature are enmeshed in the body. Gallagher describes the body schema as pre-personal in the sense that it functions outside of conscious awareness.[74] To my mind, there is nothing more personal than the way a body organizes itself in movement. Yes, the dancer's kinaesthetic environment is a form of social practice that extends beyond the individual, embedding itself deep in the habit, sensibility and musculature of the dancer. But, as a characteristic mode of organization, found in movement, the body schema is large component of who the dancer is.

This is not to dismiss the conscious, intentional component of dancing, the many ways in which noetic thinking meshes with the body schema in action. Body image and body schema are complementary aspects of movement that come to be articulated in motion. Different traditions will have their own take on the dancer's relation to her dancing, thereby to articulate their own interpretation of the intentional-organizational nexus. The shifting current between *thought within action* and *thought felt in relation to action* is an indication of the variety of ways in which a dancer may engage her dancing. Particular traditions and modes of somatic practice may well have something to say about this relation. Taken together, these differing approaches inform the formation and enunciation of the dancer's movement subjectivity. Although the concept of body schema has been forwarded in unified terms, as a corporeal Gestalt, which enables a body to function as a whole, there is a sense in which dancers may well acquire more than one mode of organization in the body. Heterogeneous components, which hail from more than one technique, style or milieu, may combine to form a complex range of (even incompatible) competencies.[75] To that end, it may become important to identify the plurality of bodily schemata as they nonetheless coalesce to form a single functional whole.

Such thinking is not limited to invocations of the body image, but also extends to perceptions of others' bodies and of the environment within which the dancing occurs. This is an important feature of dancing, however realized, one which is not captured by the concept of the body image, which is formulated to address perceptual experiences of one's own body. There is of course a sense in which one's own bodily sensations differ in kind from those of others. My pain cannot be felt by another. And yet, many dance practices develop a finely honed appreciation of sensory relationships beyond one's own corporeal envelope. And they do so in signature ways. Social dancing is but one example of an ensemble practice which may incorporate particular, intersubjective modes of perception not reducible to the self-regarding attentions of the body image. A colleague recently described to me his experience as a child in Greece, joining a circle of dancing villagers. Korean master dancer, Ha Yong-Bu, leads his village into dance each year. These events, and their allied modes of movement subjectivity, are founded in the group. Insofar as they inculcate a kind of movement subjectivity, they suggest a mode of perceptual attention which cannot be confined to the concept of the body image.

Social dance is a movement practice, with its own features, embedded sociality and sense of what dancing is. Ritual, tribal, shamanistic and trance-based dance may also be aligned with a mode of movement subjectivity. They signal the intersubjective, social register of movement subjectivity. An amplification of these wider possibilities extends beyond the scope of this text, towards the multiplicity of practices that create their own communal body.[76] The same might be said of 'the difference' between the body and its environment, a given for western sensibilities but not necessarily other traditions. Skewed towards a very specific range of perspectives, it is no coincidence that the illustrations offered here cluster around the author's own movement experiences. It is in virtue of these situations and their experience that I can talk about movement subjectivity at all.

Sastradipradja's notion of *auteurship* and Dumas' account of the (re)iterative nature of choreographic enactment are movement approaches that make sense in the studio, in the context of dancing which is in turn connected to a particular kinaesthetic paradigm. These experiences are constitutive of my own movement subjectivity and influence my very understanding of what that might be. Such is the tension between the phenomenological perspective and its conditions of articulation.

The situated nature of movement subjectivity has perceptual implications, not merely for dancers and their audiences but also for the phenomenological project itself. Merleau-Ponty's own body permeates *Phenomenology of Perception*. He leans on the table, picks up his pipe, stares out the window, attending to these actions so as to flesh out their analysis. If these descriptions verge upon universality, they are nevertheless corporeal in an existential, lived sense. The lived body is indelibly historical, cultural and social. To what extent

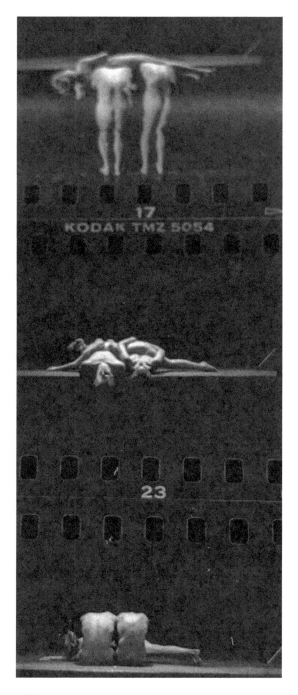

Figure 2.2 Russell Dumas, artistic director, Dance Exchange, courtesy of the artist.

does this impact on the phenomenological project? One way of framing the issue is to question the place of universality within the corporeal sphere and to ask whether a body thoroughly marked by history can rise above its own historicity. In perceptual, phenomenological terms, the question concerns the degree to which the phenomenologist's own perceptions are historically constituted and perceptually particular. To what extent is the phenomenological project marked by the provenance and milieu of the phenomenologist? Does phenomenology embed its own subject-position? My own interest concerns the way in which the conceptual vocabulary associated with and emergent from Merleau-Ponty's *Phenomenology of Perception* can be brought to bear upon the diversity of dance practice and its associated subject-positions. This makes dance phenomenology a more contingent and interest-driven enterprise, one whose concepts are answerable to the vicissitudes of practice and whose elaboration is by its very nature situated. There need to be no limit to its armoury of concepts which may well be context- and interest-driven.

The following chapter seeks to develop a companion concept to the notion of movement subjectivity. Informed by Thomas Csordas' work on somatic attention, the notion of kinaesthetic sensibility denotes the perceptual tendencies embedded in particular kinds of kinaesthetic experience. A concept born from the recognition of cultural difference, kinaesthetic sensibility represents a way of perceiving dance, of attending to the body in particular ways. It is also a filter, a way of seeing. To that extent, the deployment of kinaesthetic sensibility has political implications, insofar as a particular way of seeing dance holds sway.

Notes

1 A number of writers have developed this insight, drawing attention to the specific ways in which illness or disability is lived, in particular, Kay Toombs, "The Body in Multiple Sclerosis: A Patient's Perspective", in *The Body in Medical Thought and Practice*, ed. Drew Leder (Dordrecht: Kluwer Academic Publishers, 1992), 127–137, and Vivian Sobchack, "Choreography for One, Two and Three Legs: A Phenomenological Meditation in Movements", *Topoi* 24, no.1 (2005): 55–66. See also Drew Leder, "A Tale of Two Bodies: The Cartesian Corpse and the Lived Body", in *The Body in Medical Thought and Practice*, ed. Drew Leder (Dordrecht: Kluwer Academic Publishers, 1992), 17–35, Philipa Rothfield, "Attending to Difference: Phenomenology and Bioethics", in *Ethics of the Body: Postconventional Challenges*, ed. Margrit Shildrick and Roxanne Mykitiuk (Cambridge, MA: MIT Press, 2005), 29–48, and Philipa Rothfield, "Living Well and Health Studies", in *Merleau-Ponty: Key Concepts,* ed. Rosalyn Diprose and Jack Reynolds (Stocksfield, UK: Acumen, 2008), 218–227.
2 Maxine Sheets-Johnstone, *The Phenomenology of Dance*, second edition (London: Dance Books, 1979).
3 Ibid., 4.
4 Ibid.

5 Ibid.
6 Ibid., 7.
7 Ibid., 4.
8 Ibid., 61.
9 "It is clear then that the immediate lived experience of dance is an intuition of whatever feeling the form is symbolic of. It is not an experience of actual sorrow, rage, love, jealousy, or whatever. Neither is it a matter of empathy, of "going through" the movements kinaesthetically", ibid., 65.
10 Ibid., 65.
11 Ibid., 50.
12 Ibid.
13 Ibid., 53.
14 Ibid., 54.
15 Ibid., 56.
16 Ibid., 50.
17 Ibid.
18 Ibid., xiii.
19 Yvonne Rainer's manifesto, "'No' to Spectacle", is often cited in relation to these changing concerns, Yvonne Rainer, "'No' to Spectacle", in *The Routledge Dance Studies Reader,* ed. Alexandra Carter (London and New York: Routledge, 2010), 35.
20 For example, *Satisfyin' Lover*, choreographed by Steve Paxton (1967).
21 *Small Dance* choreographed by Steve Paxton (1977). See also Steve Paxton, "Small Dance", *Contact Quarterly* 11, no. 1 (1986): 48–50.
22 For example, Deborah Hay claims that "Every day the whole day from the minute you get up is potentially a dance", in Susan Foster, *Reading Dancing: Bodies and Subjects in Contemporary American Dance* (Berkeley and Los Angeles: University of California Press, 1986), 6.
23 Paxton, *Small Dance*.
24 Sheets-Johnstone, *The Phenomenology of Dance*, xii–xiv.
25 Foucault writes:

> Singular forms of experience may perfectly well harbour universal structures; they may well not be independent from the concrete determinations of social existence. However, neither those determinations nor those structures can allow for experiences (that is, for understandings of a certain type, for rules of a certain form, for certain modes of consciousness of oneself and of others) except through thought … this thought has a historicity which is proper to it. That it should have this historicity does not mean that it is deprived of all universal form, but instead that the putting into play of these universal forms is itself historical.
>
> (Michel Foucault, *The Foucault Reader*, ed. Paul Rabinow [Harmondsworth: Penguin Books, 1986], 335)

26 There are a number of phenomenological approaches which aim to do just that, for example, Susanne Ravn, "Dancing Practices: Seeing and Sensing the Moving Body", *Body and Society* 23, no. 2 (2016): 57–82; Susanne Ravn, "Embodying Interaction in Argentinean Tango and Sports Dance", in *Choreography and Corporeality: Relay in Motion*, ed. Thomas F. DeFrantz and Philipa Rothfield (London: Palgrave Macmillan, 2016), 119–134; Philipa Rothfield, "Playing the

Subject Card: Strategies of the Subjective", in *Performance and Phenomenology Traditions and Transformations*, ed. Maaike Bleeker, Jon Foley Sherman, and Erini Nedelkopoulou (London and New York: Routledge Books, 2015), 97–110; Anne Cooper Albright, "Situated Dancing: Notes from Three Decades in Contact with Phenomenology", *Dance Research Journal* 43, no. 2 (Winter 2011): 7–18; Susan Kozel, *Closer: Performance, Technologies, Phenomenology* (Cambridge, MA: MIT Press, 2007); Phillip Zarilli, "The Actor's Work on Attention, Awareness, and Active Imagination: Between Phenomenology, Cognitive Science, and Practices of Acting", in *Performance and Phenomenology: Traditions and Transformations*, ed. Maaike Bleeker, Jon Foley Sherman, and Erini Nedelkopoulou (London and New York: Routledge Books, 2015), 75–96; Carolina Bergonzoni, "When I Dance my Walk: A Phenomenological Analysis of Habitual Movement in Dance Practices", *Phenomenology and Practice* 11, no. 1 (2017): 32–42; Sigrid Merx, "Doing Phenomenology: The Empathetic Implications of CREW's Head-Swap Technology in 'W' (*Double U)*", in *Performance and Phenomenology: Traditions and Transformations*, ed. Maaike Bleeker, Jon Foley Sherman, and Erini Nedelkopoulou (London and New York: Routledge Books, 2015), 204–222; Sondra Fraleigh, *Dancing into Darkness: Butoh, Zen and Japan* (Pittsburgh: University of Pittsburgh Press, 1999), Anna Pakes, "Phenomenology and Dance: Husserlian Mediations", *Dance Research Journal* 43, no. 2 (2011): 33–49; Chantel Ehrenberg, "A Kinesthetic Mode of Attention in Contemorary Dance Practice", *Dance Research Journal* 47, no. 2 (August 2015): 43–62; Peta Tait, "Fleshing Dead Animals: Sensory Body Phenomenology in Performance", in *Performance and Phenomenology: Traditions and Transformations*, ed. Maaike Bleeker, Jon Foley Sherman, and Erini Nedelkopoulou (London and New York: Routledge Books, 2015), 111–120; and Janna Parvainen, *Bodies Moving and Moved: A Phenomenological Analysis of the Dancing Subject and the Cognitive and Ethical Values of Dance Art* (Vammala: Tampere University Press, 1998).

27 The always already hails from the work of Jacques Lacan on subjectivity and was taken up by Louis Althusser into the realm of social (re)production, by claiming that "*individuals are always-already* [social] *subjects*", "Ideology and the State: Ideology and Ideological State Apparatuses (Notes Towards an Investigation)", *Essays on Ideology* (London: Verso Editions, 1984), 50. In cultural critique, the always already counters humanistic claims that subjectivity exists prior to the social.

28 Elizabeth Grosz, *Sexual Subversions: Three French Feminists* (Sydney: Allen and Unwin, 1989), 111.

29 Margaret Whitford writes, "The phenomenological account of the lived body and the lived world needs to be complemented by the awareness that there is an interaction between the live experience, the imaginary, and the discursive and social construction of both", *Luce Irigaray: Philosophy in the Feminine* (London and New York: 1991), 152.

30 Although working with different concepts, Susan Foster's attention to the differences between dancing bodies resonates with the notion of movement subjectivity, "Dancing Bodies", in *Incorporations*, ed. Jonathon Crary and Sanford Kwinter (New York: Zone Books, 1992), 480–495. Rather than movement subjectivity, Foster forwards the notion of a "dancing bodily consciousness", addressing the question of corporeal specificity by distinguishing between the various bodies

implicit in particular dance techniques, ibid., 485. For Foster, each technique constructs a distinctive body, with its own characteristic relations between body and self. Foster describes the dance class as the vehicle for the production of a dancerly sensibility, repetition and drill as the means by which a body is produced, through the daily production and reiteration of habit. The similarity between the two approaches is to be found in their appeal to modes of practice as the basis for generating modes of corporeal subjectivity.

31 Shaun Gallagher, "Body Schema and Intentionality", in *The Body and the Self,* ed. José Luis Bermudez, Anthony Marcel and Naomi Eilan (Cambridge, MA: MIT Press, 1995), 228.

32 For Gallagher, the body schema opens our understanding of the lived body beyond the Husserlian paradigm which would reduce the body to an intentional object: "In Husserl's transcendental analysis, the body is reduced to a perceived object and appears to have no role in the production of perceptual experience", ibid., 233. "For Merleau-Ponty, the body cannot be reduced to consciousness of the body ... To capture this truth, he develops an expanded model of intentionality that includes a role for the prenoetic functions of the body schema", ibid., 232. According to Gallagher, the body schema is prenoetic. It functions at the edge of consciousness, "behind the scene", ibid., 235. This is a point of departure from a strictly Husserlian point of view. Sheets-Johnstone's account of the immediate experience of the dancing body conforms to the Husserlian view that the body is an intentional object. Sheets-Johnstone parts ways with Gallagher on the question of (phenomenological) availability. For Gallagher, the "prenoetic role of the body schema is impenetrable to phenomenological reflection and must be worked out conceptually with the help of the empirical sciences", "Body Schema and Intentionality", 233.

33 Merleau-Ponty writes:

> If the need was felt to introduce this new word, it was in order to express that the spatial and temporal unity, the inter-sensorial unity, or the sensorimotor unity of the body is so to speak, an in principle unity, to express that this unity is not limited to *contents* actually and fortuitously associated in the course of our experience, that it somehow *precedes them* and in fact makes their association possible (emphases mine).
>
> (Maurice Merleau-Ponty, *Phenomenology of Perception*, trans.
> Donald A. Landes [London and New York: Routledge, 2014], 102)

Gallagher draws upon this enlarged sense of embodied intentionality in order to "develop an account of how the body, prior to our outside of cognitive experience, helps to constitute the meaning that comes to consciousness", "Body Schema and Intentionality", 233. See also Merleau-Ponty, *Phenomenology of Perception*, 441. The body schema thus plays an important complementary role in the development of perceptual and kinaesthetic consciousness.

34 The shift towards action-based conceptions of the lived body has been developed towards an enactivist paradigm, one which sees intentionality as built into bodily action, for example, Varela Evan Thompson and Eleanor Roche, *The Embodied Mind: Cognitive Science and Human Experience* (Cambridge, MA: MIT Press, 1991), Shaun Gallagher, *Enactivist Interventions: Rethinking the Mind* (Oxford: Oxford University Press, 2017).

35　Linda Sastradipradja, *Agency, Authorship and Embodied Aesthetics: The Dancer as Auteur*, PhD diss., Victoria University, Melbourne, Australia, 2019.

36　Ibid.

37　Merleau-Ponty, *Phenomenology of Perception*, lxxxii, 441.

38　Linda Sastradipradja is a dancer, dance-maker and teacher. She was a member of Mikhail Baryshnikov's White Oak Dance Project and spent many years working and performing with Sara Rudner in New York. Although I have danced in only one of Linda's showings – *Inside/Out*, choreographic collaboration with Sara Rudner, Linden Centre for Contemporary Art, Melbourne, 2012 – I have been the beneficiary of learning from and dancing with Linda in the studio over a number of years.

39　"Russell Dumas Dance: About", www.russelldumasdance.com/about/index.html, accessed November 5, 2019.

40　Jacques Derrida, "Signature, Event, Context", *Margins of Philosophy*, trans. Alan Bass (Chicago: University of Chicago Press, 1982), 328.

41　Dumas often speaks of the instability of choreographic material, a lack of fixity felt in relation to its reiterative character, personal communication, 2006.

42　Pichet Klunchun, "Life", www.pklifework.com/life.html, accessed March 21, 2011. Pichet Klunchun is a classically trained Thai Dancer, who trained in Khon dance under Master Chaiyot Khummanee. Klunchun has created and performed a number of solo works, including, *Nijinsky Siam* (2010) and *I am Demon* (2005). Klunchun also choreographs for his company, Pichet Klunchun Dance Company, most recently, *Dancing with Death* (2017).

43　*I am Demon*, choreographed by Pichet Klunchun, 2005.

44　Preeti Gaonkar, "Merging the Classical with the Contemporary: An Interview with Picket Klunchun", *Magazine, Asia-Europe Foundation*, https://culture360. asef.org/magazine/merging-classical-contemporary-interview-pichet-klunchun/, accessed November 4, 2019.

45　Pichet Klunchun, "Ten Sao", www.pklifework.com/Articles%20Pages/03%20 TenSao.html, accessed March 21, 2011.

46　Cultural theory's adoption of interpellation (subject-address) as the means of subject-formation has historically focused on the discursive production of identity in terms of, for example, gender, race, ethnicity and sexuality. Movement subjectivity, like interpellation, is grounded in social practice but it is also importantly an account of the uptake of movement practice at the level of disposition, demeanour and agency. Its emphasis is upon the performative means by which a body articulates its kinaesthetic situation. To that end, habit formation and its enunciation play a key role in the distinctive movement subjectivity of the dancer.

47　Gallagher, "Body Schema and Intentionality", 235.

48　Jenny Roche addresses the dancer's signature movement style through the notion of the historical trace. Roche writes of the dancer's acquiring "a 'corporeal portfolio' of movement traces", which leads to a "moving identity or signature way of moving", "Dancing Strategies and Moving Identities: The Contributions Independent Contemporary Dancers Make to the Choreographic Process", in *Contemporary Choreography: A Critical Reader,* ed. Jo Butterworth and Liesbeth Wildschut (London and New York: Routledge, 2017), 155. Gallagher's account of the selective nexus between the body and its environment in the course of laying down the body schema represents one way of explaining how the trace becomes a mode of agency. Movement subjectivity enables the distinctive specificity of intentional body images to be added to the picture so as to depict the combination of experience, agency and organization belonging to the dancer.

49 Relative autonomy is a term used by Louis Althusser to explain the independence of cultural formations (ideological state apparatuses) from the determining impact of the economic. Althusser's way of putting this was to claim the relative autonomy of the ideological state apparatus from the influence of the economic which is nevertheless seen as determinant in "the last instance", Louis Althusser, "Contradiction and Overdetermination", *For Marx*, trans. Ben Brewster (London: Verso Editions, 1977), 112.

50 David Morley, "Texts, Readers, Subjects", in *Culture, Media, Language*, ed. Stuart Hall et al. (London: Hutchinson, 1980), 163–173.

51 Morley refers to the tension in Althusser's work on ideological subject-production between the 'always already' and the actual. Althusser's essay on ideology distinguishes between ideology in general ("the category of the subject and its functioning", the mythic aspect of the always already) and the historical specificity of Ideological State Apparatuses, which grounds the actual encounter between subjects and the social, "Texts, Readers, Subjects", 166.

52 Morley, "Texts, Readers, Subjects", 166.

53 Judith Butler, *Bodies That Matter: On the Discursive Limits of 'Sex'* (London and New York: Routledge, 1993), 10.

54 Ideokinesis hails from the work of Mabel Todd and was further developed by a number of cardinal practitioners, such as Barbara Clark, Lulu Sweigard and Andre Bernard. See Mabel Todd, *The Thinking Body* (Brooklyn: Dance Horizons, 1968).

55 The image of a collapsing suit of clothes originated in the work of Lulu Sweigard, *Human Movement Potential* (Lanham, MD: Harper & Row, 1974), 333–335.

56 The notion of the pelvis as a bridge was taught by Shona Innes, using the work of John Rolland, in Melbourne, August 2014.

57 Pam Matt, a student of Barbara Clark, offered this image during a series of classes held in Ubud, Bali, July 2004.

58 The image of an umbrella opening and closing was put forward by Jane Refshauge, during, *Winter Intensive*, Dancehouse, Melbourne, June 2012.

59 Jane Refshauge sees the image moving from conscious thought to a mode of incorporation, such that the image is "present without effort", *Winter Intensive*, Dancehouse, June 2012.

60 Refshauge recounts a child telling Mabel Todd, "First you see it, then you think it, then you forget it, then it happens", ibid.

61 In the studio with Linda Sastradipradja, November 2018.

62 Butler writes of a materializing process of reiteration (practice), as a "reiterated acting that is power in its persistence and instability", *Bodies That Matter*, 9. The notion of persistence and instability is a way of thinking the sedimentary aspect of the body schema alongside the recognition that it is open to performative variation.

63 See Philipa Rothfield, "Responsive Objects", *RealTime Magazine* 89 (June–July 2009): 38, www.realtimearts.net/article.php?id=9477, accessed December 4, 2019.

64 Ros Crisp has been dancing for over 30 years, in Australia and Europe. She founded Omeo dance studio in Sydney, a home for experimental dance, and became the first choreographic associate of the Atelier de Paris, Carolyn Carlson. She has collaborated with dancers Céline Debyser, Max Fossati, Lizzie Thomson, Andrew Morrish, Helen Herbertson, musicians Bo Wiget & Hansueli Tischhauer,

multi-media artist Vic McEwan, dance scholars Isabelle Ginot & Susan Leigh Foster. *No One will tell us...*, choreographed by Ros Crisp, 2011. See also Keith Gallasch, "Dance Like Never Before", www.realtime.org.au/dance-like-never-before/, accessed February 14, 2019.

65 Indeed, Crisp's dancing took on new characteristics once the musician, Tischhauser, participated, giving way to a more intense, sensual, exuberant movement quality. Similarly, Andrew Morrish's humorous interludes provoked a hermeneutic difference in Crisp's work, offering the possibility of humour through ignoring Morrish as much as in staging a response.

66 *The Dance Card,* curated by Helen Herbertson, Dancehouse, 2003. See also John Bailey, "Bodies as Signals, Nodes, Networks", www.realtime.org.au/bodies-as-signals-nodes-networks/, accessed February 14, 2019.

67 Not all dance forms embrace a marked difference between the everyday and dancing. Russell Dumas would sometimes speak of walking into dancing, to suggest a continuity between everyday actions, such as walking, which are already in motion, and that which counts as dancing.

68 Lisa Nelson writes of her experience of not dancing for two years: "During those two years I knew I was loosening the bonds of certain movement habits that were there. Through resting, not doing, I knew I was letting them drop away. That was one very good way to do it. Just to stop reminding my body of these movement habits, which I had no use for in my daily life. Pointed toes, for example, weren't reinforced by any movement in my daily life. Those stylised movements atrophied and disappeared in those two years. That was very nice ... After two years, I started dancing again and I felt I would start from the beginning ... So this was my chance to be a beginner", "The Sensation is the Image: It's What Dancing is to Me", *Writings on Dance* 14, (Summer 1995/1996): 10.

69 Gallagher writes: "The body image is not always intentionally present, that is, one is not always conscious of one's own body as an intentional object. This effacement of the body is possible because in normal circumstances a particular body schema functions in a way that makes movement and posture close to automatic and in no need of conscious control ... Whatever the degree of body consciousness, however, the body schema continues to function in a nonconscious way, maintaining balance and enabling movement. Yet by defining the body schema in terms of its prenoetic function, I do not mean to rule out the possibility that the body image and body schema can work (or fail to work) together in a complementary fashion", "Body Schema and Intentionality", 229–230.

70 Félix Ravaisson, *Of Habit*, trans. Clare Carlisle and Mark Sinclair (London and New York: Continuum, 2008). See also Rothfield, "Beyond Habit: The Cultivation of Corporeal Difference", *Parrhesia* 19 (2013): 100–112, www.parrhesiajournal. org/parrhesia18/parrhesia18_rothfield.pdf, accessed December 4, 2019.

71 Ibid., 51.

72 Ibid., 53.

73 Ibid., 55.

74 Gail Weiss also writes of a "prepersonal generality" that "persists in and through the idiosyncratic, subjective, singular perspective of each individual", "Ambiguity", in *Merleau-Ponty: Key Concepts*, ed. Rosalyn Diprose and Jack Reynolds, (Stocksfield, UK: Acumen, 2008), 139.

75 Heterogeneity may be the mark of economic circumstance on the production of movement subjectivity. Writing in 2002, Veronica Dittman draws out the influence

of economic factors on the formation of New York dancers like herself, "A New York Dancer", in *The Body Eclectic: Evolving Practices in Dance Training*, ed. Melanie Bales and Rebecca Nettl-Fiol (Urbana and Chicago: University of Illinois Press, 2008), 23–27. Dittman outlines the context in which New York dancers at this time were able to train and work. Like many others, Dittman moved between individual projects: "I venture that the biggest factor contributing to the rise of dancers like us is the collapse of the modern dance economy in the early 1990s", ibid., 23. For Dittman, the dearth of available funds had consequences for the individual who was unable to access to the kind of "bone-deep unison" (between bodies) that comes from working long-term in the one company, ibid., 26. Nor will such a dancer be able to enjoy an enduring professional relationship with the one choreographer. As a result, the majority of dancers at that time exercised individual agency in regards to their own training, moving between more collaborative, choreographic projects.

76 This is not to confine the communal to the field of social dance. Faye Driscoll's *Thank You for Coming: Attendance* becomes a communal dancing body, for example, formed out of a merger between dancers and their audience, *Thank You for Coming: Attendance*, choreographed by Faye Driscoll, 2014. On the other hand, Eirini Nedelkopoulou's discussion of the in-common draws out the communal aspects of participatory, interactive art and performance, without necessarily creating a form of community, "The In-Common of Phenomenology", in *Performance and Phenomenology: Traditions and Transformations*, ed. Maaike Bleeker, Jon Foley Sherman, and Eirini Nedelkopoulou (London and New York: Routledge Books, 2015), 152–172.

Bibliography

Althusser, Louis. "Contradiction and Overdetermination", Louis Althusser, *For Marx*. Translated by Ben Brewster, 87–128. London: Verso Editions, 1977.
———. "Ideology and Ideological State Apparatuses (Notes Towards an Investigation)", 1–60. *Essays on Ideology*. London: Verso Editions, 1984.
Bailey, John. "Bodies as Signals, Nodes, Networks". www.realtime.org.au/bodies-as-signals-nodes-networks/, accessed February 14, 2019.
Bergonzoni, Carolina. "When I Dance My Walk: A Phenomenological Analysis of Habitual Movement in Dance Practices". *Phenomenology and Practice* 11, no. 1 (2017): 32–42.
Butler, Judith. *Bodies that Matter: On the Discursive Limits of 'Sex'*. London and New York: Routledge, 1993.
Cooper Albright, Ann. "Situated Dancing: Notes from Three Decades in Contact with Phenomenology". *Dance Research Journal* 43, no. 2 (Winter 2011): 7–18.
The Dance Card. Curated by Helen Herbertson, 2003.
Dancing with Death. Choreographed by Pichet Klunchun, 2017.
Derrida, Jacques. "Signature, Event, Context". *Margins of Philosophy*. Translated by Alan Bass, 307–330. Chicago: University of Chicago Press, 1982.
Dittman, Veronica. "A New York Dancer". In *The Body Eclectic: Evolving Practices in Dance Training*, edited by Melanie Bales and Rebecca Nettl-Fiol, 23–27. Urbana and Chicago: University of Illinois Press, 2008.

Ehrenberg, Chantel. "A Kinesthetic Mode of Attention in Contemporary Dance Practice". *Dance Research Journal* 47, no. 2 (August 2015): 43–62.

Foster, Susan Leigh. *Reading Dancing: Bodies and Subjects in Contemporary American Dance*. Berkeley and Los Angeles: University of California Press, 1986.

———. "Dancing Bodies". In *Incorporations*, edited by Jonathon Crary and Sanford Kwinter, 480–495. New York: Zone Books, 1992.

Foucault, Michel. *The Foucault Reader*, edited by Paul Rabinow. Harmondsworth: Penguin Books, 1984.

Fraleigh, Sondra. *Dancing into Darkness: Butoh, Zen and Japan*. Pittsburgh: University of Pittsburgh Press, 1999.

Gallagher, Shaun. "Body Schema and Intentionality". In *The Body and the Self*, edited by José Luis Bermudez, Anthony Marcel and Naomi Eilan, 225–244. Cambridge, MA: MIT Press, 1995.

———. *Enactivist Interventions: Rethinking the Mind*. Oxford: Oxford University Press, 2017.

Gallasch, Keith. "Dance Like Never Before". www.realtime.org.au/dance-like-never-before/, accessed February 14, 2019.

Gaonkar, Preeti. "Merging the Classical with the Contemporary: An Interview with Picket Klunchun". *Magazine, Asia-Europe Foundation*. https://culture360.asef.org/magazine/merging-classical-contemporary-interview-pichet-klunchun/, accessed November 4, 2019.

Grosz, Elizabeth. *Sexual Subversions: Three French Feminists*. Sydney: Allen and Unwin, 1989.

I am Demon. Choreographed by Pichet Klunchun, 2005.

Inside/Out, Choreographed by Linda Sastradipradja in collaboration with Sara Rudner, Linden Centre for Contemporary Art, Melbourne, 2012.

Klunchun, Pichet. "Life". www.pklifework.com/life.html, accessed March 21, 2011.

———. "Ten Sao". www.pklifework.com/Articles%20Pages/03%20TenSao.html, accessed March 21, 2011.

Kozel, Susan. *Closer: Performance, Technologies, Phenomenology*. Cambridge, MA: MIT Press, 2007.

Leder, Drew. "A Tale of Two Bodies: The Cartesian Corpse and the Lived Body". In *The Body in Medical Thought and Practice*, edited by Drew Leder, 17–35. Dordrecht: Kluwer Academic Publishers, 1992.

Merleau-Ponty, Maurice. *Phenomenology of Perception*. Translated by Donald A. Landes. London and New York: Routledge, 2014.

Merx, Sigrid. "Doing Phenomenology: The Empathetic Implications of CREW's Head-Swap Technology in 'W' (*Double U*)". In *Performance and Phenomenology: Traditions and Transformations*, edited by Maaike Bleeker, Jon Foley Sherman, and Eirini Nedelkopoulou, 204–222. London and New York: Routledge Books, 2015.

Morley, David. "Texts, Readers, Subjects". In *Culture, Media, Language*, edited by Stuart Hall et al., 163–173. London: Hutchinson, 1980.

Nedelkopoulou, Eirini. "The In-Common of Phenomenology". In *Performance and Phenomenology: Traditions and Transformations*, edited by Maaike Bleeker, Jon Foley Sherman, and Eirini Nedelkopoulou, 152–172. London and New York: Routledge Books, 2015.

Nelson, Lisa. "The Sensation Is the Image: It's What Dancing Is to Me". *Writings on Dance* 14 (Summer 1995/1996): 4–16.

Nijinsky Siam. Choreographed by Pichet Klunchun, 2010.

No One will tell us.... Choreographed by Ros Crisp, with Andrew Morrish and Hansueli Tischhauser, Dance Massive Festival, Dancehouse, Melbourne, March 17, 2011.

Pakes, Anna. "Phenomenology and Dance: Husserlian Mediations". *Dance Research Journal* 43, no. 2 (2011): 33–49.

Parviainen, Janna. *Bodies Moving and Moved: A Phenomenological Analysis of the Dancing Subject and the Cognitive and Ethical Values of Dance Art*. Vammala: Tampere University Press, 1998.

Paxton, Steve. "Small Dance". *Contact Quarterly* 11, no. 1 (1986): 48–50.

Rainer, Yvonne. " 'No' to Spectacle". In *The Routledge Dance Studies Reader*, edited by Alexandra Carter, 35. London and New York: Routledge, 2010.

Ravaisson, Félix. *Of Habit*. Translated by Clare Carlisle and Mark Sinclair. London and New York: Continuum, 2008.

Ravn, Susanne. "Dancing Practices: Seeing and Sensing the Moving Body". *Body and Society* 23, no. 2 (2016): 57–82.

———. "Embodying Interaction in Argentinean Tango and Sports Dance". In *Choreography and Corporeality: Relay in Motion*, edited by Thomas F. DeFrantz and Philipa Rothfield, 119–134. London: Palgrave Macmillan, 2016.

Roche, Jenny. "Dancing Strategies and Moving Identities: The Contributions Independent Contemporary Dancers Make to the Choreographic Process". In *Contemporary Choreography: A Critical Reader*, edited by Jo Butterworth and Liesbeth Wildschut, 150–164. London and New York: Routledge, 2017.

Rothfield, Philipa. "Attending to Difference: Phenomenology and Bioethics". In *Ethics of the Body: Postconventional Challenges*, edited by Margrit Shildrick and Roxanne Mykitiuk, 29–48. Cambridge, MA: MIT Press, 2005.

———. "Living Well and Health Studies". In *Merleau-Ponty: Key Concepts*, edited by Rosalyn Diprose and Jack Reynolds, 218–227. Stocksfield, UK: Acumen, 2008.

———. "Responsive Objects". *RealTime Magazine* 89 (June–July 2009): 38. www.realtimearts.net/article.php?id=9477, accessed December 4, 2019.

———. "Beyond Habit: The Cultivation of Corporeal Difference". *Parrhesia* 19 (2013): 100–112. www.parrhesiajournal.org/parrhesia18/parrhesia18_rothfield.pdf, accessed December 4, 2019.

———. "Playing the Subject Card: Strategies of the Subjective". In *Performance and Phenomenology, Traditions and Transformations*, edited by Maaike Bleeker, Jon Foley Sherman, and Eirini Nedelkopoulou, 97–110. London and New York: Routledge Books, 2015.

Sastradipradja, Linda. *Agency, Authorship and Embodied Aesthetics: The Dancer as Auteur*. PhD diss., Victoria University, Melbourne, Australia, 2019.

Satisfyin' Lover. Choreographed by Steve Paxton, 1967.

Sheets-Johnstone, Maxine. *The Phenomenology of Dance*, Second Edition. London: Dance Books, 1979.

Small Dance. Choreographed by Steve Paxton, 1977.

Sobchack, Vivian. "Choreography for One, Two and Three Legs: A Phenomenological Meditation in Movements". *Topoi* 24, no. 1 (2005): 55–66.

Sweigard, Lulu. *Human Movement Potential*. Lanham, MD: Harper & Row, 1974.

Tait, Peta. "Fleshing Dead Animals: Sensory Body Phenomenology in Performance". In *Performance and Phenomenology: Traditions and Transformations*, edited by Maaike Bleeker, Jon Foley Sherman, and Eirini Nedelkopoulou, 111–120. London and New York: Routledge Books, 2015.

Thank You for Coming: Attendance. Choreographed by Faye Driscoll, 2014.

Todd, Mabel. *The Thinking Body*. Brooklyn: Dance Horizons, 1968.

Toombs, Kay. "The Body in Multiple Sclerosis: A Patient's Perspective". In *The Body in Medical Thought and Practice*, edited by Drew Leder, 127–137. Dordrecht: Kluwer Academic Publishers, 1992.

Varela, Francesco, J., Evan Thompson and Eleanor Roche. *The Embodied Mind: Cognitive Science and Human Experience*. Cambridge, MA: MIT Press, 1991.

Weiss, Gail. "Ambiguity". In *Merleau-Ponty: Key Concepts*, edited by Rosalyn Diprose and Jack Reynolds, 132–141. Stocksfield, UK: Acumen, 2008.

Whitford, Margaret. *Luce Irigaray: Philosophy in the Feminine*. London and New York: 1991.

Zarilli, Phillip. "The Actor's Work on Attention, Awareness and Active Imagination: Between Phenomenology, Cognitive Science, and Practices of Acting". In *Performance and Phenomenology: Traditions and Transformations*, edited by Maaike Bleeker, Jon Foley Sherman, and Eirini Nedelkopoulou, 75–96. London and New York: Routledge Books, 2015.

3 Kinaesthetic sensibility and the politics of difference

Introduction

This chapter is concerned with the perceptual implications of thinking the subjectivity of the dancer in relation to her kinaesthetic situation. Its focus is on the ways in which perception is shaped and deployed in the wider field of dance. Although open to a degree of contingent variation, the dancer's subjectivity is deeply informed by the kinaesthetic milieu within which she dances. Movement subjectivity aims to capture the impact of that milieu on the dancer's agency, perceptual demeanour and organizational facility. Its acknowledgement of the dancer's situation takes a genealogical approach towards the provenance of the dancer. Genealogy functions through practice to create patterns of perception, rhythms and habits, ways of moving and ways of approaching that moving.

Foucault writes that the "body manifests the stigmata of past experience".[1] This chapter is concerned with the ways in which such 'stigmata' function at the level of perception. It takes as its point of departure Shaun Gallagher's recognition that, for Merleau-Ponty, "the body is doing the perceiving".[2] It also begins with Judith Butler's view that "there is no reference to a pure body which is not at the same time a further formation of that body".[3] The development of Merleau-Ponty's thought towards a conception of perceptual specificity opens the lived body to a politics of difference. Difference comes into play when thinking the deployment of corporeal perception towards the heterogeneity of practice: How does the body perceive difference? How are dance practices themselves the bearers of particular ways of attending to the body? And in what ways is this made performatively and discursively manifest? The argument of this chapter is that the differentiation of the lived body opens itself to a politics of perception, one which acknowledges relations of power in the wider experience of dance. It commences with the ethnographic encounter. Insofar as it conceives itself as an encounter with difference, ethnography has the potential to flesh out what is at stake in the deployment of perceptual sensibility. Thomas Csordas' work on somatic attention theorizes the impact of culture on perception. Valuable for identifying the cultural nature of perception, somatic attention is shifted onto the plane of movement through the concept of kinaesthetic sensibility. A companion concept to movement subjectivity, kinaesthetic sensibility differs through its being a social practice, somewhat akin to Bourdieu's *habitus*. Kinaesthetic sensibility represents the ways in which a form of practice coalesces around the body. It also speaks to the sense in which one form of sensibility is able to impose itself upon others. This occurs when one mode of perception assumes a mode of authority over another field of practice. Authorization is an expression of power, the power to discern, to represent, articulate and evaluate that which is foreign to itself. Globalization, market forces, performative conventions, colonial and postcolonial factors impact upon the devolution of perceptual authority. This chapter will conclude with the view that these dynamics call for an ethics and politics of perception, so as to account for the deployment of thought in the field of dance.

Somatic attention

The discussion begins with Thomas Csordas' work on the body and culture. Csordas is a cultural phenomenologist who has oriented Merleau-Ponty's work towards the field of ethnography. Csordas' *The Sacred Self* is notable for its focus on the body within the experience of charismatic healing.[4] Csordas is also noteworthy for emphasizing the body of the ethnographer.[5] This is made possible through his concept of somatic attention. Somatic attention signifies those "culturally elaborated ways of attending to and with one's body in surroundings that include the embodied presence of others".[6] There are two salient features of somatic attention: first, we attend with or through the body, and second, such a body's mode of attention is culturally and socially informed. In other words:

> neither attending to nor attending with the body can be taken for granted but must be formulated as culturally constituted somatic modes of attention.[7]

Cultural phenomenologists claim that cultural beliefs and values shape somatic, perceptual experience. There is no neutral body. Rather, the immediacy of experience is always already synthesized with the "multiplicity of cultural meanings in which we are always and inevitably immersed".[8] The inter-subjective ground of somatic attention conveys its inherent sociality. This is manifest even in the individual instance, where "Attention *to* a bodily sensation can thus become a mode of attending to the inter-subjective milieu that gives rise to that sensation".[9] The individual body thereby bears the traces of culture, through its manner of attention either towards itself or to others.

The synthesis of body and culture within somatic attention extends to the sensorium, incorporating the ways in which the senses are both organized and deployed. The cultural specificity of somatic modes of attention and their situated differences is explicated by Csordas via his ethnographic study of religious healing rituals.[10] Csordas contrasts the somatic attentions exercised by ritual healers from two different cultural milieus. The first group, the American Catholic Charismatic Renewal Community, stages ceremonies for the conduct of ritual forms of healing. Faith healing occurs in these events, through the actions of the Christian faith healer who is a channel for God's work. The work of the faith healer involves the exercise of somatic attention. Faith healers are guided by their own bodies, which lead them towards the problems of others. In the process, Christian Charismatic faith healers experience a range of spontaneous bodily events – including images, words and sensations – most of which concern the client's body. They also lay on hands as part of the healing ritual.[11] These bodily events are regarded as the word of God, an expression of the divine found through healing. The process is dynamic and transformative. Healers might experience changes in these sensations, such as a tumour palpably shrinking or evil spirits leaving the body.[12] For their part, clients may undergo a shift in their own somatic attentions, developing a greater sensitivity towards the emergence of problematic symptoms.

Although they also attend to their own bodies, Csordas argues that Puerto Rican faith healers have an entirely different set of corporeal experiences. The Puerto Rican *Espiritismo* tradition deals primarily with spirits which take possession of people's bodies, causing harm and distress. By attending to their own bodies, Puerto Rican *Espiritistas* encounter the evil eye (*ojo oculto, ojo malo*), experience physical events (in the *boca del estomago*) and the passage of fluids in the body (*fluidos*). While there are common elements between these two groups of healers – attention to the healer's body, embodied imagery, sensations and spiritual encounters – Csordas makes the point that the *deployment* of the senses is culturally specific.[13] Not only do the American healers report a greater proportion of visual experiences (as a matter of sensory emphasis), there are embodied differences between experiencing the word of God and following spirits and fluids coursing through the body.

The tendency to deploy a certain kind of sensibility is in part a disposition of the body. The view that sensibility is culturally differentiated is indebted to Bourdieu's account of the social production of taste.[14] Bourdieu developed the concept of the *habitus* as a practice-based system of dispositions which are grounded in the body.[15] The socially informed body has a number of distinctive tastes, habits and sensory preferences which depend upon the subject's class affiliation or, in ethnographic terms, depend upon cultural modes of belonging. These refer to the body's situatedness or *habitus*, which is in turn a matter of social practice. The body's sensible orientations are found in and emerge through social practice.

The cultural link between sensibility and social practice is evident in Robert Desjarlais' work amongst the Nepalese Yolmo wa.[16] Desjarlais locates Yolmo sentience in the realm of the everyday, claiming that:

everyday actions are rooted in local sensibilities; this rootedness forces us
to rethink how we talk of moralities, bodies, pain, healing and politics.
For Yolmo wa, the aesthetic values that govern how a person dresses in
the morning or talks with a neighbour constitute a tacit moral code, such
that ethics and aesthetics are one.[17]

According to Desjarlais, not only is sensibility embedded within social practice, the conduct of everyday life informs and reveals Yolmo cultural values
concerning the body, health and illness.

Ceres Victora also invokes social practice as the basis for understanding
local sensibilities.[18] Victora studied working class women's experiences of
pregnancy in Puerto Alegre, Brazil. Her interviews with women reveal bodily
experiences of an organ (*mãe do corpo*, the body's mother) which has no
equal in western biomedicine.[19] According to Victora, an explanation for this
difference is to be found in the practices of the community within which it
is found. Victora refers to the local organization of space and time as the
corporeal staging ground for the phenomenon and experience of 'the body's
mother', arguing that the lived everyday of working class Puerto Alegrans
underpins the ways in which pregnancy is experienced. This includes "the
ways their families are organised, the way they relate to other people, the way
they raise their children, the way they cook, the way they love, the way they
look after the ill".[20] According to Victora, the fluidity of domestic modes of
organization in Puerto Alegre, manifest in the mobility of bodies between
households, facilitates "a more fluid notion of body organs and systems".[21]
Such fluidity differs from the rigidity of medical models, leading to her claim
that "people know their bodily facts in different ways".[22] This is another way
of framing somatic attention, by bringing the perceptual object into focus
and through showing how the cultural deployment of the senses can give a
cultural inflexion to the body's morphology.[23]

Although somatic attention was introduced via the conceptual distinction
between self and other, the very distinction between self and other may take
on decidedly local characteristics. Anne Becker's account of Fiji islanders
reveals a great degree of permeability between bodies, signifying a somatic
mode of attention that also functions in fluid, relational terms.[24] Becker's
work overall lends support to Leenhardt's observation that Melanesian
cultures have an undifferentiated sense of body and world.[25] Although Fijian
islanders are quite capable of distinguishing between self and other, Becker
describes a body that is a matter of collective, rather than individual, significance. Accordingly, individual bodies enjoy extensive attentions from the
community. Changes in bodily appearance, for example, are the subject of
ceaseless jokes and banter on the part of the group. The humour does not
target individual body shape and size in terms of individual merit or lack
thereof but rather addresses the group.

The body's well-being is a matter for the collective. According to Becker,
this is felt especially in the realm of food, where the communal distribution of

food resources in Fiji underlies the collective interest in the individual body. This trickles down to the family who is in charge of feeding individuals. The body thus comes to be monitored by others as the bearer of good care and proper feeding. The social character of food and feeding is reflected in the public display of meals, which are served with windows and doors flung wide open. Hospitality remains the order of the day. In fact, passers-by are routinely entreated to join the group, an invitation unlikely to be accepted only because people tend to dine with their own family unit. The carbohydrate basis of the Fijian diet means that meals can be easily expanded to accommodate extra guests. A well-fed body reflects favourably upon the family unit, and visitors need to return home looking healthy.[26]

The social orientation of the body towards others must be sustained. Any attempt to sequester the individual body is doomed to failure, even disaster:

> a Fijian has no choice but to reveal her pregnancy simply because her body is unable to contain the experience as a personal event. Her body divulges the pregnancy in token catastrophes: cakes not rising, chairs falling flat, and boats encountering rough seas in her presence. More threatening are the effects of her undisclosed pregnancy which manifest in other bodies. The hair she cuts may fall out, her glance may dry up the milk of a lactating mother, or her very touch may contaminate food.[27]

Not only is undisclosed pregnancy problematic, the permeability of bodily boundaries means that any attempt to stop the flow of information will ultimately find expression in the bodies of others as the subject of others' somatic attentions.

Although affiliated with anthropology of the body rather than Csordas' cultural phenomenology, Andrée Grau also addresses the question of bodily boundaries in a cross-cultural study of western classical ballet and Tiwi islander dance.[28] Grau writes:

> For many Tiwi there is no real separation between the body and the self, between persons and their environment, between the past and the present. Indeed bodily, social, ecological, historical and spiritual worlds are seen as being interconnected and part of a fluid universe: the Dreaming, a space-time more real than reality itself.[29]

These understandings underlie the difference between the ballet dancer's body as an ontologically discrete entity and an unbounded sense of the Tiwi body, at "one with the land", and part of a greater inter-corporeal continuum with Country.[30]

The ethnographic literature cited here does two things. Firstly, it gestures towards the plasticity of perception, the senses, objects, even concepts. And secondly, it situates the ethnographer's own perceptions, rendering the encounter with difference in a relationship between multiple modes of embodiment. Somatic attention is not merely about the cultural other's perceptual apparatus then. It concerns the corporeal means by which the ethnographer perceives and understands social practice.

Kinaesthetic sensibility

The concept of somatic attention emphasizes the cultural component of perception, including its sensory configuration and deployment. Although grounded in social practice, it is often offered as a perceptual registration and interpretation of a bodily state. The following is an attempt to mobilize somatic attention towards an action-based conception of perceptual difference through the concept of kinaesthetic sensibility. Kinaesthetic sensibility represents the sorts of attention exercized in dance towards dance. It reflects the ways in which dancing organizes the senses, whether visual in emphasis, internally oriented, touch-based and so on. It characterizes the dancer's perceptual dispositions towards movement which in the previous chapter was organized around the notion of body image but is here extended to the perception of others' bodies. Kinaesthetic sensibility is formulated to draw attention to the corporeal, cognitive and kinaesthetic values embedded within a particular field of practice. The existential plasticity of its expression aims to deflect universalist presuppositions regarding 'the' dance experience, also to register the many different concerns found within dance. Although enacted by the individual, kinaesthetic sensibility refers to the ways in which a mode of practice organizes perception in the body. It refers to the kinds of things attended to, the way attention is deployed, its sensory emphases and priorities. Here, however, kinaesthetic sensibility also refers to the ways in which the subject attends to *other* bodies. A companion concept to movement subjectivity, kinaesthetic sensibility is less about the individual than a manner of perception wielded by the dancer 'on behalf' of and in relation to a field of practice. To a degree, then, kinaesthetic sensibility typifies the field. It is a social concept, dependent for its character on the social and kinaesthetic practices within which it is framed.

Kinaesthetic sensibility is a marker of deep kinaesthetic difference: in understanding, sensation, attention, perception and ontology. Each mode of sensibility will have a view on what a body is and what a body does. That view may be hybrid in origin or adhere to a well-defined mode of practice. Kinaesthetic sensibility addresses the great range of mental states, thoughts, images and suppositions found in dance practice, such that the cognitive and imaginary merge with perception. It cannot be confined to one way of thinking dance. It is found in the extraordinary imagination of Butoh and Body Weather, the embodied physiology of Body Mind Centering and the image-actions of ideokinesis. It pertains to the heterogeneity of non-western dance practices, as well as the novel sensibilities embedded in new choreographic work. It may be shaped to incorporate collective modes of perceptual consciousness (dancing together), dancing with nature or as nature. Its existential range is to be found in the diversity of practices created through dance. It is idiomorphic, a contingent arrangement articulated in and over time. Like movement subjectivity, kinaesthetic sensibility depends upon a series of encounters, themselves a gathering of origins and practices.

Kinaesthetic sensibility need not suppose that a field of practice is wholly individuated. Some fields may be but others will consist of diverse (even incommensurable) movement tendencies and traditions. Susan Foster has questioned the assumption that (dance) "culture is relatively stable, cohesive and distinct".[31] If a mode of practice is emergent and unstable, then its affiliation with kinaesthetic sensibility will be correspondingly complex. The existential plurality of the concept allows for an assemblage of sensibilities in the particular instance, distributed amongst bodies and practices. Kinaesthetic sensibility makes sense in the context of the field's distinctive bodily schemata, through its relation towards what a body does by way of its belonging to a particular milieu. The identification of its constituent elements is itself an exercise of kinaesthetic sensibility and therefore opens to critical evaluation. The impossibility of a 'God's eye view' rules out the possibility of a context-free perceptual neutrality.[32] It contests Sheets-Johnstone's position that dance can be apprehended independently of the observer's background and experience. Although subject to a great many influences, the enunciation of kinaesthetic sensibility is dancerly. It is about the ways in which dancing is perceived.

Dancing provides the setting within which kinaesthetic sensibility is formed and maintained. Its exercise is not confined to the dancer but is also found in the relation between the spectator and the work. Spectatorship is in part context-driven.[33] For example, certain theatre spaces have a tendency towards a particular perceptual style, whether coded for visual display (associated with proscenium arch and black box theatre spaces) or more haptic forms of connectivity (to be found in more intimate spaces). Classical ballet (and opera) has had an historical part to play in the performative *habitus* of large-scale theatre spaces.[34] This in turn impacts upon the sorts of corporeal attentions brought to bear upon its staging. Immersive, installation dance works, on the other hand, call for a different kind of participatory engagement on the part of the spectator. Maaike Bleeker discusses the impact of Rainer's work on canons of spectatorship, beyond the frontal availability of proscenium arch performance.[35] For Bleeker, Rainer's *Trio A* altered the ways in which a spectator might engage with the dance.[36] Bleeker writes:

> Rainer's modes of sculpting spectatorship point to the role of affordances in perception: how the way in which movement is structured affords modes of perceiving it.[37]

Affordances are embedded, environmental cues for action, somewhat like Alphonso Lingis' notion of the imperative.[38] The suggestion is that the work itself is a kind of environmental cue, which makes possible certain modes of spectatorship. Lisa Nelson similarly offers an inter-sensory account of the audience relation to the work, which also depends upon the cues found in performance. Nelson writes of "constantly shifting from one sense to another in constant dialogue with my sensations to construct my experience of the performance".[39] She looks for cues in the work to provoke her own sensory dialogue. There are many factors that condition the kinds of attention exercised by audience members. Audiences have their own expectations, seasons are curated, framed and promoted, while the work itself may espouse a certain kind of perceptual agenda. Different kinds of social dancing will also embed their own manner of spectatorship, whether familiar, shared amongst practitioners or calling for certain kinds of audience response.

And yet, spectators are able to exert their own agency in relation to the dance. For example, Priya Srinivasan offers an account of her own position as an "unruly spectator" of Bharata Natyam dance.[40] Deeply literate in the field, Srinivasan asserts her own right to move "between different positions, discourses and gazes to revel in, critique, historicize, deconstruct and participate" in the performative elements of the form.[41] Srinivasan traces the sweat (a corporeal metonym of the body's labour) exhibited on and offstage as a way of opening an individual performance to the complex history of Bharata Natyam.[42] She also offers a phenomenology of dance spectatorship which wanders between her own sweating body, political analyses, historical understanding and serial encounters with those whose labour supports the artform. Srinivasan moves between a close perceptual reading of individual performances, detailing her own perception and cognition within a cultural narrative that incorporates the history of *devadesi* dancers, their post-independence fate and the recent emergence of diasporic Bharata Natyam dance. Although an activist form of intervention, Srinivasan's spectatorship is marked by her provenance in Bharata Natyam.[43] She draws upon her kinaesthetic literacy to interrogate her bodily interactions with the dance in the midst of an informed understanding of the form's historical past. Her attention towards the sweating body highlights the corporeal nature of the encounter, beyond an idealized conception of the form and its 'proper' spectator. Although an expression of critical agency then, Srinivasan's spectatorship is informed by the kinaesthetic sensibilities embedded in the field.

Csordas' work on somatic attention was introduced for its theorization of the corporeal encounter in perceptual terms. Cultural phenomenology reflects this emphasis on the corporeal nature of perception. Dance ethnography, a long-standing and important component of dance studies, is equally corporeal in emphasis, offering many examples of the incorporation of authorial corporeality within its research. Dierdre Sklar explicitly draws on Csordas' notion of somatic attention to support a corporeal epistemology within dance ethnography, one which recognizes the centrality of the researcher's movement experience.[44] For Sklar:

> While it has been traditional practice to erase the researcher's body from the ethnographic text, "subjective" bodily engagement is tacit in the

process of trying to make sense of another's somatic knowledge. There is no other way to approach the felt dimensions of movement experience than through the researcher's own body.[45]

This is reflected in the work of Sally Ann Ness, who argues for a participatory model of dance ethnography. Ness articulates the features of an embodied mode of participation in dance research, which highlight the role of the researcher's own body for understanding a field of practice, drawing attention to the work of Cynthia Novak and Barbara Browning as key examples of such an approach.[46] Adrienne Kaeppler similarly writes of a participant observation, which takes part in a field of practice through learning its movements.[47]

The point of the detour through ethnography is to extract something from the ethnographic paradigm, namely its encounter with otherness. Its point of departure is the recognition that there are a great many forms of social practice and that their perception is distilled through the embodied sensibilities of the observer. Csordas argues that the very concept of somatic attention decentres the privilege of ethnographic subjectivity and that, as a consequence, participant observers are ever vulnerable to the "challenge of reflexivity".[48] The challenge is in part a response to the following: if cultural difference is refracted through the sensibilities of the ethnographer, which is in turn culturally produced, how can the ethnographer guarantee the veracity of their perceptions? Does the ethnographer really see what there is to see or do they merely filter their object of perception through their own social values? The situation is further qualified by the historically elevated status of the ethnographer, often situated within a network of asymmetric power, colonial and postcolonial relationships.[49] To what extent are these issues felt in the field of dance? Is the expression of kinaesthetic sensibility similarly troubled by questions of reflexivity? In the case of dance, the exercise of kinaesthetic sensibility may not see itself as the expression of particularity. Specificity can be submerged, concealed and erased where the façade of universality and universalism prevails as a matter of course. This occurs when certain values become institutionalized and therefore invisible in their expression, that is, neutral, unmarked and anaesthetized to their own modes of privilege and epistemic authority.

Once values take root (and this is how they emerge), they become normalized, bearers of value through notions of, for example, virtuosity, authorship, training, composition and the allocation of space and time within funding models. The provocation of reflexivity in relation to ethnographic research is more likely to surface as a question of value in dance. The need for reflexivity arises when dance is being judged according to some notion of merit which is itself indebted to certain perceptual assumptions. For example, state funding is purportedly allocated according to merit. In situations where balletic notions of technical facility prevail, choreography is liable to be conceived of as a process that is conducted 'on' bodies, who are always already able to dance. Inasmuch as movement vocabularies are grounded in recognizable patterns and familiar sensory states, such a process may not require extensive periods of research and development. This is reflected in funding models which suppose, for example, that six weeks is a reasonable period within which to stage a creative development.[50] Practices that do not (indeed, cannot) conform to this notion may be regarded as too costly, lacking value for money and unable to furnish sufficient budgetary justification on obscure aesthetic grounds. The issue revolves around whether the body is regarded as a site of investigation, both as a performing body but also within and according to the terms of choreographic practice itself. A body that is already trained and ready to perform may well be worked 'on' within a matter of weeks. A choreographic practice that investigates the body or the form as a matter of its process may not be able to produce work within such short time frames. A related issue concerns the sustainability of dance culture. How are dance cultures identified, and how are they deemed worthy of state support?[51]

The issue of state support is in part a question of rationality within a funding system that is predicated on certain normative practices. Jon Willis' work on the provision of palliative care for remote Australian Indigenous communities illustrates the sense in which funding models may reflect the norms of one culture, and thereby resist accommodating another. Willis notes that the Australian health system's budgetary rationale presumes the normative force of certain ways of living and therefore dying.[52] These are amenable to metropolitan, hospice-based forms of palliation. Pitjantjatjara ways of dying in Country through a return to land require different modes of palliative care delivery, calling for resources that cannot be 'justified' according to models that "are bound up in the 'way of dying' of the [non-Aboriginal] culture in which they originated".[53]

Audience behaviours can also embody cultural norms. As Jasmin Gunaratnam has shown, institutional norms extend to conceptions of order and proper behaviour. Gunaratnam's study of multicultural palliative care in the UK illustrates the ways in which standards of order and control reflect and perpetuate institutionalized racism.[54] Gunaratnam argues that the UK hospital system implicitly embodies Anglo-centric norms of death and dying and that this is expressed in the notion of order in the hospital context. These norms are transgressed by vocal and communal expressions of grief endemic to many non-Anglo cultures. The problem is that certain cultural behaviours come to represent a disturbance to the peace, order and good governance of the institution.

Audience behaviours are likewise implicitly normative. Thomas DeFrantz cites a dance critic's response to a warm and vocal audience reception towards work made by African American dance artists. DeFrantz is alert to the suggestion that African American audiences "cheered hysterically" while "we [white critics] saw amateurish performances or half finished ideas".[55] Was this 'hysterical' response a transgression of behavioural norms that belong to the perceiver's cultural milieu? The difference in audience response could be attributed to the difference between dominant norms of aesthetic appreciation including their distinctive behaviours, and those embedded in African American circulations of community, aesthetics, spirituality, call and response.[56] And yet that difference was not acknowledged in the critical moment. What authorizes the critic to judge work and how are these judgements made?[57] This particular example illustrates the sense in which a set of norms can combine with perception in unacknowledged ways. It suggests a form of hegemonic dominance where certain norms are so embedded within a particular scene or cohort that their perceptual deployment is indiscernible. How likely is it for a critic to question their own authority, in relation to their own kinaesthetic literacy? Insofar as the reflexive gesture signifies an acknowledgement of partiality, will it undermine the critic's standing? Or conversely, give it substance? Srinivasan deploys a self-conscious criticality to construct a resistant spectatorship at odds with the good spectator who conforms to Bharata Natyam's political aspirations. Such an approach is no less attentive to the nuances of the practice. Srinivasan's deployment of Bharata Natyam's kinaesthetic modes of attention is not diminished by her refusal to conform. Her deep literacy of the form is evident throughout. And yet, she allows her mind to wander, to abandon her thinking to other related considerations. Srinivasan's unruly spectator is constructed through a montage of cognitive musings, as they appear in the midst of her corporeal encounters – in the performance space, in the taxi, temple and sari shop – also in relation to her own perceptual observations of her own body and those of others. Her writing opens up a mode of difference, less between two modes of sensibility, than a complication of what kinaesthetic sensibility can mean for someone whose social, political and historical concerns are inseparable from her perceptual connection with the dancing. Srinivasan's approach recalls David Morley's view that spectatorship cannot be read off the page but is complicated by the historical background each subject brings to bear upon the discursive encounter.[58] Srinivasan accordingly brings her own historical difference into her deployment of Bharata Natyam's kinaesthetic sensibility, thereby to combine a close reading of its performance with a materialist reading of the labouring body.

Normativity is not confined to questions of criticality and reflexivity. It also underlies a politics of classification, whereby a work is allocated a certain range of potential values. For example, Susan Foster highlights the differential framing of dance works in a curated program staged in the US, where the work of an American company was deemed "an instant classic", while the other, the work of a Russian company, was represented as providing "exuberant evocations of traditional dance".[59] Foster questions the allocation of one dance work to an aesthetic register, and the other to an 'ethnic' dance platform, the point being that classification is itself an expression of presumed value. Csordas writes that "the attempt to define a somatic mode of attention decenters analysis such that no category is privileged and all categories are in flux between subjectivity and objectivity".[60] The problem here is that these categories of kinaesthetic classification and perception are not at all in flux but are rather geared around the ethnocentric and aesthetic assumptions embedded in its curation.

One of the features of hegemonic dominance in the perception of dance is the ability to determine the conditions of visibility under the guise of neutrality. Russell Dumas writes:

> Most dance that's been committed to film is done with dancers and choreographers who have been trained in ballet, this technique that is designed to be perceived at a distance. It's akin to semaphore signals. Ballet is about certain extremes and the subtlety of something like Trisha Brown's involvement with transition is likely to be lost and in an extreme case not even recognised as movement. Techniques like ballet put railways tracks through the sensibility. A ballet dancer reads movement and looks at it ... oh what did you do? Well you went to first position and then you went to second position and that squitchey thing ... that's not dance, that's not movement, that's nothing ... so that you end up with this very peculiar distortion in perception. It becomes your frame of reference; basically how you see movement is by how you learned it.[61]

The problem is not that ballet "puts railways tracks in the sensibility" – *for what practice does not*? The problem is rather political, that one kind of kinaesthetic sensibility is able to purport neutrality, exert its specificity and consequently negate or nullify difference. Neutrality is the face of normalization, where hegemonic values come to stand in for value per se. There are many divergent instances and fields of power within which this occurs. The articulation within dance of hegemonic forms of value is shaped by a range of socio-political factors including colonization, globalization, commodification, western ethnocentrism, modernity and modernization.

It should be noted that Dumas' remarks were made in an Australian context, where the colonial origins and legacy of classical ballet persist as the marker of skill and virtuosity. According to Sally Gardner, "the hegemony of ballet – as an aesthetic and system of training – has never been effectively countered" in Australia.[62] Elizabeth Dempster likewise claims that Australia has not developed an alternative source of kinaesthetic value sufficient to call into question ballet's primacy. It's not merely that ballet is dominant, it is, for Dempster, univocal:

> In the absence of a significant counter tradition, ballet sets the terms of reference – it knows what is dance and what is not.[63]

According to Dempster, hegemony prevails in the absence of any counter-tradition, here, the unrealized potential of a modern and postmodern aesthetic practice, whose origins, teachers and mentors lie elsewhere. And yet, Australia is host to some of the longest standing Indigenous traditions on the planet. To what extent can Australian Indigenous dance threaten the colonial ascendancy of ballet within Australia?[64] Can Indigenous dance represent a counter-tradition, thereby to disrupt ballet's hegemonic hold? If Indigenous dance were to be regarded as a counter-tradition, would it need to occupy the same kinaesthetic terrain as ballet's kinaesthetic sensibility or could it exercise its own kinaesthetic autonomy? And if dealing with two modes of sensibility, how are these to be commensurated in the absence of an Archimedean perspective?

In the case of Australia's leading Indigenous dance company, Bangarra Dance Company, it is not possible to pit one sensibility against another for they are not wholly distinct. Bangarra's Artistic Director, Stephen Page, incorporates classical ballet into company class, as well as contemporary, Yoga and Pilates.[65] Page combines his training in Graham technique with "traditional dancing which allows you to draw your weight into the ground".[66] Such hybridity, in conjunction with the ambivalent positioning of white spectatorship, makes for a complex assessment of tradition, hegemony and counter-tradition.[67] There is a further complication, a question of classification and colonial critique somewhat akin to Foster's example of dance classification. It concerns the reception of Bangarra's work abroad, specifically in the United Kingdom. Page took Bangarra's London critics to task for expressing an expectation that Bangarra would perform what Page calls, "traditional anthropological dance", dismissed as a desire for "ooga booga dancing".[68] According to Page, Bangarra's British critics could not accept that his work was a contemporary engagement with Indigenous culture.[69]

The demand for anthropological authenticity limits Bangarra's work to offering what Fiona Nicoll calls a "window on aboriginal culture approach", according to which the role of art is to present culture for a non-Indigenous spectatorship.[70] As a mirror for culture, art can do no more than re-present that which exists. The window on culture approach judges work in terms of accuracy or authenticity with respect to a stable, cultural referent. Traditional practices are thereby condemned to repeat themselves to the crack of doom, while art plays its part in the commodification of the nation's culture. Bangarra are often required to represent Australia in international cultural events, an irony not lost on the company.[71] It is perhaps unsurprising that an anthropological expectation was discerned in England, the colonial source of Indigenous dispossession and anthropological discourse. It is a further irony that a land which was deemed by the British, *terra nullius* (uninhabited), is now exhorted to demonstrate the cultural being of its Traditional Owners so as to legitimate the validity of colonial tenure. Despite the incongruity of presenting "traditional anthropological work" on a contemporary London stage, the discussion raises questions about the ways in which Bangarra's work is able to be framed, and according to what kind of perceptual sensibility.

Ranajit Guha's analysis of vernacularity draws attention to the struggle between a practice's own embedded values and the dominant perspective of a colonizing consciousness.[72] According to Guha, the vernacular embodies two historical moments, the relative autonomy of vernacular practice, alongside its simultaneous insertion into colonial modes of subjection. Insofar as Bangarra Dance Theatre enunciates its own relation to indigeneity (seen in so many of its works and community projects), yet finds itself inserted into Australia's colonial system, the company is subject to the hegemonic factors that condition vernacular forms of practice. Guha characterizes the vernacular in relation to Indian Indigenous social and cultural practices. Bangarra not only draws on Indigenous vernacularity but it also reterritorializes Indigenous tradition. To what extent then can Indigenous dance draw upon but also exceed its vernacular origins so as to contest ballet's colonial hold (as posited by Dumas, Dempster and Gardner)? This is not a question of mere classification, whether traditional or contemporary, but an issue of a practice and its perception. What does it take to counter an established tradition and how can the specificity of that challenge command a perception which does justice to its own modes of sensibility? The hybridity of Bangarra's vernacular terrain, which incorporates modern and classical sensibilities, cannot simply be opposed to colonial tradition. If Bangarra is to be regarded as a mode of counter-tradition, its challenge is to be found in the ways in which Bangarra reterritorializes tradition beyond the confines of colonial sensibility, and through its displacement of the single temporal axis of traditional, modern and contemporary art.[73]

Conclusion

This chapter began with the view that perception is cultivated, through practice. It appealed to the ethnographic literature on somatic attention to claim the cultural plurality of perception. Kinaesthetic sensibility looks to the origins of kinaesthetic perception in dance. The diversity of kinaesthetic sensibility is testament to the plurality of dance practices, the plasticity of perception and the variety of ways in which dance can be experienced and bodies sensed. It is also a register of perceptual difference, of embedded norms and values, complex histories, situations and subjectivities. The pluralization of kinaesthetic sensibility locates perception in the heterogeneity of practices that make up the dance. As a concept, kinaesthetic sensibility is local in origin. In practice, it is informed by wider social forces. Arjun Appadurai's approach towards locality embraces these two moments. It does so through focusing on "the production of locality".[74] Appadurai argues that locality cannot merely function as a background to ethnographic research, claiming that we need to pay attention to the social means by which localities emerge. There is nothing more local than the body and its perceptions. And yet, the production of corporeal locality is a social, political and kinaesthetic affair.

Dance scholarship takes stock of the wider social and political landscape. Kinaesthetic sensibility supplements that approach by thinking the social and political in a perceptual register.[75] This is felt not merely in the production of kinaesthetic sensibility but also in relation to its exercise. A window on embodied difference, kinaesthetic sensibility reveals the asymmetric deployment and imposition of ways of seeing and experiencing dance. As itself a form of practice, kinaesthetic sensibility is part of a wider network of social and political relations. It is no surprise then that particular kinds of kinaesthetic sensibility are authorized while others are subjugated. Kinaesthetic sensibility is found in the widespread deployment of unacknowledged norms of classification, skill, behaviour and value. Underpinned by wider relations of power, kinaesthetic sensibility is deployed to evaluate, elevate and diminish, also to sense, feel and attend.

The production of kinaesthetic sensibility is a complex affair. In the particular instance, kinaesthetic sensibility may well be hybrid, informed by historical matters, power relations and discursive factors. That said, it would be a mistake to think that any given form of sensibility, however complex, determines its manner of deployment. The deployment of kinaesthetic sensibility is a singular event, kinaesthetically informed to be sure, but not a matter of mechanistic application. In Chapter 2, I argued that the formation of movement subjectivity is a selective matter: environmentally conditioned yet idiosyncratic in its take up and rendering of the individual's movement signature. I want to argue here that the deployment of kinaesthetic sensibility is likewise conditioned by circumstance and curated by the perceptual subject. David Morley's notion of the *active audience* offers a way of thinking these two tendencies.[76] Morley sees the audience experience as both shaped by "cultural formations and practices pre-existent to the individual" but also open to individual variation.[77] For Morley, particular people in particular contexts form their own relation to cultural formations. This is not to deny the power of the cultural but an attempt to "better understand *how* that power operates, in conjunction with the fact that people *do* make choices and do make their own interpretations".[78] Morley speaks of the resistant audience as "the ability of a person to re-interpret or re-use" cultural technologies.[79] The audience experience is thus a variable concept, articulated in the singular instance, yet always felt through the lens of power relations. The deployment of kinaesthetic sensibility is likewise poised between the individual and a collective set of social practices. A combination of circumstance, individual history, social formation and cultural practice, its deployment is open to individual variation, whether strategic, resistant or symptomatic. For example, Anita Ratnam describes her work as Neo Bharatnam.[80] Ratnam draws on her classical training to make new work she describes as "contemporary classicist".[81] Watching Ratnam perform *MA3KA, The Triad Supreme*, it was evident to my semi-literate understanding that there was a great deal of play between the givenness of the form and what Ratnam describes as improvisation.[82] A post-performance artist talk with an expert panel drew attention to the work's feminism, cultural critique, kinaesthetic play and Hindu redeployment. Following Morley, it might be said that the largely Indian audience brought their cultural and religious literacy to the encounter, fully alert to Ratnam's citation and deviation with respect to the three Hindu goddesses, as well as the founding elements of Bharatnam dance. And yet, Ratnam also spoke of her Tai Chi and Qigong, of her feminism and cultural critique. Some spectators may have picked up her reconfiguration of the Hindu goddesses; others, her feminist reorientation of the gaze. I, on the other hand, was drawn to Ratnam's play between the classical from and its improvisational variation, aware of my inability as a spectator to determine exactly when the form moved into a mode of variation, yet drawn to pose the question. Each set of imagined perceptions speaks of a range of kinaesthetic concerns and sensibilities, a contingent partiality negotiated somewhere between the dancing and its experience.

Kinaesthetic sensibility recalls the relation between the dancer and her dancing, between her body imagery and bodily schemata. It speaks to the ways in which a body's actions are perceived. While perception may well have all the general qualities observed by Merleau-Ponty, perception in dance belongs to a greater kinaesthetic milieu, one which shapes and guides perception according to its own set of priorities, thoughts and conceptions. Perception can become detached from its origins and superimposed on other practices and contexts. In so doing, it enters a wider field of market, cultural, social and political forces. To that end, kinaesthetic sensibility invites an ethical and political reading of its employment. Whereas the ethical cleaves to the corporeal encounter, leaning towards a fine calibration of its intensive impact, the political draws attention to the porosity between social and corporeal matters. Taken together, the ethical and the political offer a complementary set of perspectives to be directed towards the bodily encounter. That these encounters can be surprising, as well as dispiriting, is testament to the potential for bodies to move in ways we do not and cannot yet know.

Notes

1 Michel Foucault, "Nietzsche, Genealogy, History", in *Language, Counter-Memory, Practice: Selected Essays and Interviews by Michel Foucault*, trans. Donald F. Bouchard and Sherry Simon, ed. Donald F. Bouchard (New York: Cornell University Press, 1977), 138.

2 Shaun Gallagher, "Body Schema and Intentionality", in *The Body and the Self*, ed. José Luis Bermudez, Anthony Marcel and Naomi Eilan (Cambridge, MA: MIT Press, 1995), 233.

3 Judith Butler, *Bodies that Matter: On the Discursive Limits of 'Sex'* (London and New York: Routledge, 1993), 10.

4 Thomas Csordas, *The Sacred Self: A Cultural Phenomenology of Charismatic Healing* (California: University of California Press, 1997).

5 See, for example, *Embodiment and Experience: The Existential Ground of Culture and Self*, ed. Thomas Csordas (Cambridge: Cambridge University Press, 1994).

6 Thomas Csordas, "Somatic Modes of Attention", *Cultural Anthropology* 8 (1993): 138.

7 Ibid., 140.

8 Thomas Csordas, "Embodiment and Cultural Phenomenology", in *Perspectives on Embodiment: The Intersections of Nature and Culture,* ed. Gail Weiss and Honi Fern Haber (New York and London: Routledge, 1999), 143.

9 Csordas, "Somatic Modes of Attention", 138.

10 Csordas, *The Sacred Self.*

11 Ibid., 53–55.

12 Csordas, "Embodiment and Cultural Phenomenology", 153, 173.

13 Ibid., 153.

14 Bourdieu, *Distinction: A Social Critique of the Judgement of Taste Distinction: A Social Critique of the Judgement of Taste,* trans. Richard Nice (Cambridge: Harvard University Press, 1984).

15 Bourdieu writes:

> The *habitus* – embodied history, internalized as second nature and so forgotten as history – is that active presence of the whole past of which it is the product. As such, it is what gives practices their relative autonomy with respect to external determinations of the immediate present. This autonomy is that of the past, enacted and acting, which, functioning as accumulated capital, produces history on the basis of history and so ensures the permanence in change that makes the individual agent a world within the world.
>
> ("Structures, *Habitus*, Practices", 280)

16 Robert Desjarlais, *Body and Emotion: The Aesthetics of Illness and Healing in the Nepal Himalayas* (Philadelphia: University of Pennsylvania Press, 1992).

17 Ibid., 248–249.

18 Ceres Victora, "Inside the Mother's Body: Pregnancy and the 'Emic' Organ 'the Body's Mother'", *Curare* 12 (1997): 169–175.

19 Ibid., 171.

20 Ibid., 171.

21 Ibid., 171.

22 Ibid., 170.

23 This sense of morphology follows Grosz' reading of the body in Luce Irigaray as that which differs from essentialist conceptions of the body's anatomy insofar as it is caught up in economies of language and representation, Elizabeth Grosz, *Sexual Subversions: Three French Feminists* (Sydney: Allen and Unwin, 1989), 111–113. The morphological body suggests that the lived body – the experience of the pregnant body in Victora's work for example – cannot be reduced to a common anatomical body, but is traversed by the social and psychical meanings which are part of a wider network of "socio-linguistic" forces, ibid., 111.

24 Anne E. Becker, "Nurturing and Negligence: Working on Others' Bodies in Fiji", in *Embodiment and Experience: The Existential Ground of Culture and Self,* ed. Thomas Csordas (Cambridge: Cambridge University Press, 1994), 100–115.

25 Ibid., 110.

26 Not having enough food for a visitor brings shame upon the household. Becker writes:

> Whether a potential guest is a friend or relative stranger is immaterial. In fact, if a guest is known to be staying in the village, households will carry a food offering (*kabekabe*) to the household in which he or she is staying in order to pay their respects to the stranger.
>
> (Ibid., 106)

27 Ibid., 110.

28 Andrée Grau, "When the Landscape Becomes Flesh: An Investigation into Body Boundaries with Special Reference to Tiwi Dance and Western Classical Ballet", *Body and Society* 11, no. 4 (2005): 141–163.

29 Ibid., 153.

30 Ibid., 157.

31 Susan Foster, "Worlding Dance: An Introduction", in *Worlding Dance*, ed. Susan Foster, (Basingstoke and New York: Palgrave Macmillan, 2009), 7.

32 Donna Haraway, "Situated Knowledges: The Science Question in Feminism and the Privilege of Partial Perspective", *Feminist Studies* 14, no. 3 (1998): 575–599. See also Introduction.

33 On this point, see Matthew Reason and Dee Reynolds, "Kinesthesia, Empathy and Related Pleasures: An Inquiry into Audience Experiences of Watching Dance", *Dance Research Journal* 42, no. 2 (Winter 2010): 49–75.

34 Lincoln Kirstein writes: "Only after the French Revolution were court theatres replaced by city opera-houses with subsidized academies of music and the dance serving them. In the big municipal theatres arose the need to amplify movements whose delicacy and finesse had long been attached to their birth in ballrooms. Increased legibility was demanded, and it broadened the language ... With an increase of virtuosity, legibility remained the first concern. What was danced had to be not only well danced but also cleanly seen. It was increasingly diffi-cult to read tiny movements without blurring from the upper reaches of the bal-conies", Kirstein, "The Classic Ballet: Historical Development", in *The Classic Ballet: Basic Technique and Terminology*, ed. Lincoln Kirstein, Muriel Stuart and Carlus Dyer (London: Adam and Charles Black, 1977), 6–7. The demand for legi-bility is the direct result of what Kirstein calls "the opera-house partnership", ibid., 6. Russell Dumas calls ballet's adherence to spectacular notions of display, a technique of exaggeration inasmuch as it can be read from the balcony, the stalls or the God's, personal communication, February 10, 2010.

35 Maaike Bleeker, "Movement as Lived Abstraction: The Logic of the Cut", in *Performance and Phenomenology: Traditions and Transformations*, ed. Maaike Bleeker, Jon Foley Sherman, and Erini Nedelkopoulou (London and New York: Routledge Books, 2015), 35–53. Bleeker refers to Lambert-Beatty's discussion of Rainer's work as drawing attention to "what happens in seeing movement", ibid., 39.

36 Ibid., 45. See also John T. Sanders, "Affordances", in *Perspectives on Embodiment: The Intersections of Nature and Culture,* ed. Gail Weiss and Honi Fern Haber (New York and London: Routledge, 1999), 121–141.

37 Bleeker "Movement as Lived Abstraction", 45.

38 Alphonso Lingis, "Imperatives", in *Merleau-Ponty Vivant*, ed. M.C. Dillon (Albany, NY: State University of New York Press, 1991), 91–115. See also Chapter 1.

39 Lisa Nelson, "The Sensation is the Image: It's What Dancing is to Me", in *Writings on Dance* 14 (Summer 1995/1996): 13.

40 Priya Srinivasan, "A 'Material'-ist Reading of the Bharata Natyam Dancing Body", in *Worlding Dance*, ed. Susan Foster (London: Palgrave Macmillan, 2009), 53–75.

41 Ibid., 56.

42 See also Janet O'Shea, *At Home in the World: Bharata Natyam on the Global Stage* (Middletown, CT: Wesleyan University Press, 2007), for an account of Bharata Natyam's transnational mobility.

43 See Baya Ou Yang, "Interview #36: Dr Priya Srinivasan", www.liminalmag.com/
    interviews/priya-srinivasan, last accessed November 3, 2019.
44 Dierdre Sklar, "On Dance Ethnography", *Dance Research Journal* 32, no. 1
    (Summer, 2000): 70. Elsewhere she writes of relying on her "body as a research
    tool", Dierdre Sklar, "CORD Awards Panel 2014: Celebrating the Scholarship of
    Dierdre Sklar: Rigor: A Personal Essay", *CORD Proceedings 2015* (Fall 2015): 19.
    See also Dierdre Sklar, *Dancing with the Virgin: Body and Faith in the Fiesta of
    Tortugas: New Mexico* (Los Angeles: University of California Press, 2001).
45 Sklar, "On Dance Ethnography", 71.
46 Ness cites the work of two scholars, Cynthia Novak and Barbara Browning,
    both of whom highlight their own embodied understanding as a means to
    account for a particular field of practice, Sally Ann Ness, "Being a Body in a
    Cultural Way: Understanding the Cultural in the Embodiment of Dance", in
    Cultural Bodies: Ethnography and Theory, ed. Helen Thomas and Jamilah Ahmed
    (Oxford: Blackwell, 2004), 140; also Cynthia Novak, *Sharing the Dance: Contact
    Improvisation and American Culture* (Madison: University of Wisconsin Press,
    1990); and Barbara Browning, *Samba: Resistance in Motion* (Bloomington: Indiana
    University Press, 1995).
47 Adrienne L. Kaeppler, "The Mystique of Fieldwork", in *Dance in the Field: Theory,
    Methods and Issues in Dance Ethnography*, ed. Theresa Buckland (Basingstoke:
    Palgrave Macmillan, 1999), 20.
48 Csordas, "Somatic Modes of Attention", 145.
49 Not all ethnographers enjoy western forms of privilege. Priya Srinivasan refers to
    a growing body of research in South Asian ethnography, in which "the 'natives'
    have written back", "A 'Material'-ist Reading", 72. Coorlawala writes of the
    hybrid territory of split subjectivity from a position of overdetermined otherness,
    "Speaking Back", *Dance Research Journal* 33, no. 1 (Summer 2001): 93. Srinivasan
    cites the work of Lila Abu-Lughod, *Remaking Women: Feminism and Modernity in
    the Middle East* (Princeton: Princeton University Press, 1998), Arjun Appadurai,
    Modernity at Large: Cultural Dimensions of Globalization (Minneapolis: University
    of Minnesota Press, 1996) and Kamela Visweswaran, *Fictions of Feminist
    Ethnography* (Minneapolis: University of Minnesota Press, 1994), to which we
    might add Sara Ahmed, *Strange Encounters: Embodied Others in Post-Coloniality*
    (Hoboken: Taylor and Francis, 2013). These examples of situated ethnography
    build upon feminist and postcolonial discourse to subvert the historical legacy of
    colonial and western anthropology. Paula Saukko also indicates the existence of
    a new ethnography, one which aims to balance a greater attention to difference
    with an acknowledgement of the partial nature of the ethnographic perspective,
    Paula Saukko, *Doing Research in Cultural Studies: An Introduction to Classical and
    New Methodological Approaches* (London: Sage, 2003), 55. The existence of mul-
    tiple, potentially contradictory perspectives casts doubt on the adequacy of critical
    self-reflexion. Its situated character will inevitably offer partial results. However,
    ignoring the ethnographer's subject-position altogether is no solution.
50 Australian funding for dance projects will often be split into short periods of paid
    work, where professional dancers work on other projects in between. A chore-
    ographer recently complained that she has to "detrain" her dancers each time
    they come to her as they will have picked up the tendencies and mannerisms
    embedded in other projects. Other than the Australian Ballet, no other dance com-
    panies in Melbourne offer dancers continuing employment. As a result, dancers

are constantly on the move between projects, a form of employment discussed by Randy Martin, "Dance as a Social Movement", *Writings on Dance* 8 (Winter 1992): 9–21; and Susan Foster, "Dancing Bodies", in *Incorporations*, ed. Jonathon Crary and Sanford Kwinter (New York: Zone Books, 1992), 480–495.

51 In Australia, for example, contemporary dance is founded on a western paradigm. Non-western dance forms are funded under the rubric of multicultural or Indigenous arts. While Federal funding acknowledges the importance of diversity, there are numerous non-western dance subcultures whose excellence and virtuosity fall outside the canons of (western) contemporary dance and its principles of selection. The recognition of kinaesthetic difference calls for an expanded literacy which may be lacking on the part of decision-makers. On the other hand, there is a growing desire to open up the field to difference. Melbourne's *Green Room Awards* in the field of dance now includes diversity as a sub-category of evaluation, www.greenroom.org.au/, accessed November 7, 2019.

52 Jon Willis, "Dying in Country: Implications of culture in the delivery of palliative care in Indigenous Australian communities", *Anthropology and Medicine* 6, no. 3 (1999): 429.

53 Ibid., 427.

54 Gunaratnam writes:

> It is the extent to which behaviours by Black and ethnic minority people threaten such standards, which can also determine the extent of accommodation or resistance to particular behaviours. For example, although hospice staff were in an unanimous agreement about the need for multi-cultural food and for multi-faith support, there was a greater reticence towards public mourning rituals within hospice wards. Wider romanticised beliefs about the therapeutic benefits of ritual became suspended or subsumed by the overriding need for control of the physical and emotional environment.
>
>   (Jasmin Gunaratnam, "Culture Is Not Enough: A Critique
>   of Multi-culturalism in Palliative Care", in *Death, Gender
>   and Ethnicity*, ed. David Field, Jenny Hockey and Neil Small
>   [London and New York: Routledge, 1997], 180)

55 Thomas F. DeFrantz, "African American Dance: A Complex History", in *Dancing Many Drums: Excavations in African American Dance*, ed. Thomas DeFrantz (Madison, Wisconsin: University of Wisconsin Press, 2002), 6.

56 Thomas F. DeFrantz, "The Black Beat Made Visible: Hip Hop Dance and Body Power", in *Of the Presence of the Body*, ed. André Lepicki (Middletown, CT: Wesleyan University Press, 2004), 64–81.

57 This issue was discussed recently by a roomful of critics at the *RealTime* magazine retrospective, held during the Sydney Performance Space season, *Liveworks*, October 21, 2018. One critical limit situation was canvassed concerning the ability (authority) of the non-Indigenous critic to engage with Indigenous dance works. A number of views were expressed in the room, ranging from a reluctance to engage (as a non-Aboriginal critic) to a more reflexive critical stance which engages through an acknowledgement of the problematic relation between Indigenous work and white spectatorship.

58 David Morley, "Texts, Readers, Subjects", in *Culture, Media, Language*, ed. Stuart Hall et al. (London: Hutchinson, 1980), 163–173.

59 Foster, "Worlding Dance: An Introduction", 7.

60 Csordas, "Somatic Modes of Attention", 146.

61 Russell Dumas, "Russell Dumas: On Film: An Interview by Deborah Jowitt", *Writings on Dance* 17 (1997): 7.
62 Cited by Elizabeth Dempster, "Ballet and Its Other: Modern Dance in Australia", in *Movement and Performance (MAP) Symposium: 25th and 26th July,* 1998, ed. Erin Brannigan (Melbourne: Ausdance, 1998), 10.
63 Ibid., 16.
64 The question could also be asked of a number of diasporic dance traditions that are currently positioned as multicultural, whether they are able to function as a form of counter-tradition.
65 Stephen Page, "Dance as Great Medicine: Interviewer, Rachel Fensham", in *Bodies of Thought: Twelve Australian Choreographers*, ed. Erin Brannigan and Virginia Baxter (Adelaide: Wakefield Press and RealTime, 2014), 127.
66 Ibid., 127.
67 See Rachel Fenhsam, "Stephen Page: Belonging to Country", in *Bodies of Thought: 12 Australian Choreographers*, ed. Erin Brannigan and Virginia Baxter (Adelaide: Wakefield Press and RealTime, 2014), 216.
68 Andrew Taylor, " 'Ooga-Booga' Dancing Not On: Says Bangarra", www.smh.com. au/entertainment/dance/oogabooga-dancing-not-on-says-bangarra-20110625-1gkwb.html, accessed November 20, 2018. To be clear, Page is not dismissing traditional Aboriginal dance. Bangarra consistently draws on traditional culture in its work, working in remote communities and with master practitioners. What he is rejecting is the colonial desire to reduce his work to an emblematic form of traditional culture contained within an anthropological format.
69 Lena Hammergren notes a similar frustration on the part of Swedish choreographer, Rani Nair: "At times, she expressed dissatisfaction over the manner in which her winning choreography [*Future Memory*] made critics singularly speak about the Indian qualities of her work. She was a contemporary choreographer, and wanted criticism to address aesthetic issues in that same way", Lena Hammergren, "The power of classification", in *Worlding Dance*, edited by Susan Foster (London: Palgrave Macmillan, 2009), 26–27.
70 Fiona Nicoll, "Aboriginal Art: It's a White Thing, Framing Whiteness", in *The Art of Politics: The Politics of Art: The Place of Indigenous Contemporary Art*, ed. Fiona Foley (Southport, Queensland: Keeaira Press, 2006), 1–5.
71 Taylor writes: "The leaders of Bangarra are also frustrated at being called on to perform at international events by governments wanting to show off", " 'Ooga Booga' Dancing Not On, Says Bangarra". The company's Executive Director, Catherine Baldwin, noted that Bangarra is often called upon to represent Australian culture, yet does not receive funding that recognises their role in creating an Australian culture that is able to claim 50,000 years of tradition, Ibid. There to "show off" the wealth and diversity of Australian culture, subject to criticism for not performing what Page calls "ooga-booga dancing", Bangarra finds itself in a double-bind, " 'Ooga-Booga' Dancing Not On, Says Bangarra".
72 Ranajit Guha, "The Authority of Vernacular Pasts", *Meanjin* 51, no. 2 (1992): 299–302.
73 Bangarra's reterritorialization of tradition flies in the face of the primitivism that, according to Chris Healy, locates Indigenous art "outside of history, fixed in another time to modernity and the present", Chris Healy, *Forgetting Aborigines* (Sydney: UNSW Press, 2008), 46. Nicholas Thomas writes of the cultural colonization according to which settler societies "situate Indigenous people firmly

in the past, or in a process of waning, while settlers are identified with what is new and flourishing and promising", Nicholas Thomas, *Possessions: Indigenous Art: Colonial Culture* (London: Thames and Hudson, 1999), 109. Drawing on Thomas' claim that *contemporaneity* can incorporate difference beyond a single temporal axis, *Bangarra* can be seen as both traditional and contemporaneous, vernacular and hybrid, Thomas, *Possessions,* 174.

74 Appadurai, *Modernity at Large*. See esp. Chapter Nine, "The Production of Locality". Appadurai draws on the concept of the neighbourhood to indicate the wider social forces through which locality is realized, ibid., 179.

75 Jane Desmond argues for a reconsideration of dance ethnography in light of recent emphases on culture and representation, which tend to treat the dance in textual terms, "Terra Incognita: Mapping New Territory in Dance and 'Cultural Studies'", *Dance Research Journal* 32, no. 1 (Summer 2000): 44. For Desmond, a combined ethnographic, textual approach would require an understanding and training in fieldwork as well as a nuanced understanding of dance history and critical studies.

76 David Morley, "British Cultural Studies, Active Audiences and the Status of Cultural Theory: An Interview with David Morley", *Theory, Culture, Society* 28, no. 4 (2011): 124–144.

77 Ibid., 131.

78 Ibid., 128.

79 Ibid., 132.

80 Anita Arangham, "Arangham", www.arangham.com/anita/anita.html, accessed December 4, 2018.

81 Ibid.

82 *MA3KA, The Triad Supreme.* Choreographed by Anita Ratnam, 2009.

Bibliography

Abu-Lughod, Lila. *Remaking Women: Feminism and Modernity in the Middle East.* Princeton: Princeton University Press, 1998.

Ahmed, Sara. *Strange Encounters: Embodied Others in Post-coloniality.* Hoboken: Taylor and Francis, 2013.

Appadurai, Arjun. *Modernity at Large: Cultural Dimensions of Globalization.* Minneapolis: University of Minnesota Press, 1996.

Arangham, Anita. "Arangham". www.arangham.com/anita/anita.html, accessed December 4, 2018.

Becker, Anne, E. "Nurturing and Negligence: Working on Others' Bodies in Fiji". In *Embodiment and Experience: The Existential Ground of Culture and Self*, edited by Thomas Csordas, 100–115. Cambridge: Cambridge University Press, 1994.

Bleeker, Maaike. "Movement as Lived Abstraction: The Logic of the Cut". In *Performance and Phenomenology: Traditions and Transformations*, edited by Maaike Bleeker, Jon Foley Sherman, and Erini Nedelkopoulou, 35–53. London and New York: Routledge Books, 2015.

Bourdieu, Pierre. *Distinction: A Social Critique of the Judgement of Taste.* Translated by Richard Nice. Cambridge: Harvard University Press, 1984.

———. "Structures, *Habitus*, Practices", in *Contemporary Sociological Theory*. Translated by Richard Nice, edited by Craig Calhoun, 276–288. Oxford: Blackwell, 2002.

Browning, Barbara. *Samba: Resistance in Motion*. Bloomington: Indiana University Press, 1995.

Coorlawala, Uttara. "Speaking Back". *Dance Research Journal* 33, no. 1 (Summer 2001): 93.

Csordas, Thomas. "Somatic Modes of Attention". *Cultural Anthropology* 8 (1993): 135–156.

———, editor. *Embodiment and Experience: The Existential Ground of Culture and Self*. Cambridge: Cambridge University Press, 1994.

———. *The Sacred Self: A Cultural Phenomenology of Charismatic Healing*. California: University of California Press, 1997.

———. "Embodiment and Cultural Phenomenology". In *Perspectives on Embodiment: The Intersections of Nature and Culture*, edited by Gail Weiss and Honi Fern Haber, 143–162. New York and London: Routledge, 1999.

DeFrantz, Thomas F. "African American Dance: A Complex History". In *Dancing Many Drums: Excavations in African American Dance*, edited by Thomas DeFrantz, 3–35. Madison, Wisconsin: University of Wisconsin Press, 2002.

———. "The Black Beat Made Visible: Hip Hop Dance and Body Power". In *Of the Presence of the Body*, edited by André Lepicki, 64–81. Middletown, CT: Wesleyan University Press, 2004.

Dempster, Elizabeth. "Ballet and Its Other: Modern Dance in Australia". In *Movement and Performance (MAP) Symposium, 25th and 26th July*, 1998, edited by Erin Brannigan, 10–17. Melbourne: Ausdance, 1998.

Desjarlais, Robert. *Body and Emotion: The Aesthetics of Illness and Healing in the Nepal Himalayas*. Philadelphia: University of Pennsylvania Press, 1992.

Desmond, Jane. "Terra Incognita: Mapping New Territory in Dance and 'Cultural Studies'". *Dance Research Journal* 32, no. 1 (Summer 2000): 43–51.

Dumas, Russell. "Russell Dumas: On Film: An Interview by Deborah Jowitt". *Writings on Dance* 17 (1997): 1–14.

Fensham, Rachel. "Belonging to Country". In *Bodies of Thought: 12 Australian Choreographers*, edited by Erin Brannigan and Virginia Baxter, 120–126. Adelaide: Wakefield Press and RealTime, 2014.

Foster, Susan. "Dancing Bodies". In *Incorporations*, edited by Jonathon Crary and Sanford Kwinter, 480–495. New York: Zone Books, 1992.

———. "Worlding Dance: An Introduction". In *Worlding Dance*, edited by Susan Foster, 1–13. Basingstoke and New York: Palgrave Macmillan, 2009.

Foucault, Michel. "Nietzsche, Genealogy, History". In *Language, Counter-Memory, Practice: Selected Essays and Interviews by Michel Foucault*. Translated by Donald F. Bouchard and Sherry Simon, edited by Donald F. Bouchard, 139–164. New York: Cornell University Press, 1977.

Gallagher, Shaun. "Body Schema and Intentionality". In *The Body and the Self*, edited by José Luis Bermudez, Anthony Marcel and Naomi Eilan, 225–244. Cambridge, MA: MIT Press, 1995.

Grau, Andrée. "When the Landscape Becomes Flesh: An Investigation into Body Boundaries with Special Reference to Tiwi Dance and Western Classical Ballet". *Body and Society* 11, no. 4 (2005): 141–163.

Guha, Ranajit. "The Authority of Vernacular Pasts". *Meanjin* 51, no. 2 (1992): 299–302.

Gunaratnam, Jasmin. "Culture Is not Enough: A Critique of Multi-culturalism in Palliative Care". In *Death, Gender and Ethnicity*, edited by David Field, Jenny Hockey and Neil Small, 166–185. London and New York: Routledge, 1997.

Grosz, Elizabeth. *Sexual Subversions: Three French Feminists*. Sydney: Allen and Unwin, 1989.

Hammergren, Lena. "The Power of Classification". In *Worlding Dance*, edited by Susan Foster, 14–31. London: Palgrave Macmillan, 2009.

Haraway, Donna. "Situated Knowledges: The Science Question in Feminism and the Privilege of Partial Perspective". *Feminist Studies* 14, no. 3 (1998): 575–599.

Healy, Chris. *Forgetting Aborigines*. Sydney: UNSW Press, 2008.

Kaeppler, Adrienne, L. "The Mystique of Fieldwork". In *Dance in the Field: Theory, Methods and Issues in Dance Ethnography*, edited by Theresa Buckland 13–25. Basingstoke: Palgrave Macmillan, 1999.

Kirstein, Lincoln. "The Classic Ballet: Historical Development". In *The Classic Ballet: Basic Technique and Terminology*, edited by Lincoln Kirstein, Muriel Stuart and Carlus Dyer, 3–17. London: Adam and Charles Black, 1977.

Lingis, Alphonso. "Imperatives". In *Merleau-Ponty Vivant*, edited by M.C. Dillon, 91–115. Albany, NY: State University of New York Press, 1991.

MA3KA, The Triad Supreme. Choreographed by Anita Ratnam, 2009.

Martin, Randy. "Dance as a Social Movement". *Writings on Dance* 8 (Winter 1992): 9–21.

Morley, David. "Texts, Readers, Subjects". In *Culture, Media, Language*, edited by Stuart Hall et al., 163–173. London: Hutchinson, 1980.

———. "British Cultural Studies: Active Audiences and the Status of Cultural Theory: An Interview with David Morley". *Theory, Culture, Society* 28, no. 4 (2011): 124–144.

Nelson, Lisa. "The Sensation is the Image: It's What Dancing is to Me". *Writings on Dance* 14 (Summer 1995/1996): 4–16.

Ness, Sally Ann. "Being a Body in a Cultural Way: Understanding the Cultural in the Embodiment of Dance". In *Cultural Bodies: Ethnography and Theory*, edited by Helen Thomas and Jamilah Ahmed, 123–144. Oxford: Blackwell, 2004.

Nicoll, Fiona. "Aboriginal Art: It's a White Thing: Framing Whiteness". In *The Art of Politics: The Politics of Art: The Place of Indigenous Contemporary Art*, edited by Fiona Foley, 1–5. Southport, Queensland: Keeaira Press, 2006.

Novak, Cynthia. *Sharing the Dance: Contact Improvisation and American Culture*. Madison: University of Wisconsin Press, 1990.

O'Shea, Janet. *At Home in the World: Bharata Natyam on the Global Stage*. Middletown, CT: Wesleyan University Press, 2007.

Ou Yang, Baya. "Interview #36: Dr Priya Srinivasan". www.liminalmag.com/interviews/priya-srinivasan, accessed November 11, 2019.

Page, Stephen. "Dance as Great Medicine: Interviewer, Rachel Fensham". In *Bodies of Thought: Twelve Australian Choreographers*, edited by Erin Brannigan and Virginia Baxter, 127–131. Adelaide: Wakefield Press and *RealTime*, 2014.

Reason, Matthew and Dee Reynolds. "Kinesthesia, Empathy and Related Pleasures: An Inquiry into Audience Experiences of Watching Dance". *Dance Research Journal* 42, no. 2 (Winter 2010): 49–75.

Sanders, John T. "Affordances". In *Perspectives on Embodiment: The Intersections of Nature and Culture*, edited by Gail Weiss and Honi Fern Haber, 121–141. New York and London: Routledge, 1999.

Saukko, Paula. *Doing Research in Cultural Studies: An Introduction to Classical and New Methodological Approaches*. London: Sage, 2003.

Sklar, Deirdre. "On Dance Ethnography". *Dance Research Journal* 32, no. 1 (Summer, 2000): 70–77.

———. *Dancing with the Virgin: Body and Faith in the Fiesta of Tortugas: New Mexico.* Los Angeles: University of California Press, 2001.

———. "CORD Awards Panel 2014: Celebrating the Scholarship of Dierdre Sklar, Rigor: A Personal Essay", *CORD Proceedings 2015* (Fall 2015): 19–23.

Srinivasan, Priya. "A 'Material'-ist Reading of the Bharata Natyam Dancing Body". In *Worlding Dance*, edited by Susan Foster, 53–75. London: Palgrave Macmillan, 2009.

———. *Sweating Saris: Indian Dance as Transnational Labor*. Philadelphia: Temple University Press, 2012.

Taylor, Andrew. " 'Ooga-Booga' Dancing Not On: Says Bangarra". www.smh.com.au/entertainment/dance/oogabooga-dancing-not-on-says-bangarra-20110625-1gkwb.html, accessed November 20, 2018.

Thomas, Nicholas. *Possessions: Indigenous Art: Colonial Culture.* London: Thames and Hudson, 1999.

Victora, Ceres. "Inside the Mother's Body: Pregnancy and the 'Emic' Organ 'the Body's Mother' ". *Curare* 12 (1997): 169–175.

Visweswaran, Kamela. *Fictions of Feminist Ethnography.* Minneapolis: University of Minnesota Press, 1994.

Willis, Jon. "Dying in Country: Implications of Culture in the Delivery of Palliative Care in Indigenous Australian communities". *Anthropology and Medicine* 6, no. 3 (1999): 423–435.

4 Keeping it Korean

The pluralization of space and time in Korean dance

Introduction

This chapter is a continuation of the thinking of the last, on the imposition of kinaesthetic value, via a case study of sorts. It offers a select example, of the ways in which western modes of perception impact upon the vernacular and hybrid practices of Korean dance. The discussion that follows focuses on the work of two choreographers, Kim Mae-ja and Kim Jae-duk. Kim Mae-ja is a well-recognized artist, who established her own company, ChangMu Dance, in 1976, publishes a monthly dance magazine (*Momm Magazine*), curates an annual dance festival (ChangMu International Arts Festival) and runs a performance space (ChangMu Arts Centre) located in Seoul. Kim Jae-duk, director of dance company, Modern Table, belongs to a younger generation of dance makers. What unites these two artists is their commitment to traditional Korean dance and culture. And yet, their work has also been described as modern and contemporary respectively. How are these descriptors to be deployed and what factors condition Kim Mae-ja and Kim Jae-duk's ability to characterize their work on their own terms?

Lena Hammergren addresses the problem of classification in dance as a question of power relations, which involve "connections between global and local experiences".[1] For Hammergren, the invocation of historical systems of classification can be problematic. This is because the dance landscape is less stable and more complicated than is suggested by a set of fixed categories, also because a system of classification may have emerged in one context, only to be deployed in another. Hammergren forwards the notion of a bodyscape, as a means of portraying the kinaesthetic landscape within which work is received.[2] The bodyscape pertains to "the construction of cultural modernity in corporeal form".[3] Its corporeal focus poses modernity in genealogical terms, in relation to the production of the local within a wider global and transnational context. What factors condition the construction of the bodyscape in Korean dance today, and how do these bear upon the characterization of Kim Mae-ja and Kim Jae-duk's work? How do global and transnational factors impact upon the classification of their dance? The following discussion is informed by a series of visits to Korea, made between 2008 and 2014.[4] Much of its thinking is drawn from personal communication with many Korean artists, commentators and critics, including Kim Mae-ja and Kim Jae-duk, from watching a great many dance performances, as well as the corporeal generosity of a number of master practitioners, many of whom are embodied bearers of Korean culture.[5] I have watched dance performed in black box, proscenium arch theatre spaces, on the courtly stage, the public arena and street, in rice fields, traditional courtyards, on the beach and in the university. I have danced in select master classes, followed the moves of master dancers and joined a mobile milieu of dancers and musicians. It should be noted that I have a very limited and partial grasp of the breadth and depth of Korean dance. That limitation is symptomatic of this chapter's argument regarding the undue influence and authority of western (kin)aesthetics in relation to the bodyscape of non-western dance.

Korean dance embodies a rich and long-standing tradition of local, traditional, shamanistic (*gut*) and courtly practices.[6] It is beyond the scope of this chapter, and the abilities of its author, to do justice to the field.[7] It is worth noting, however, the impact of recent Korean history, including its colonization by Japanese forces, the Second World War (WW2), its partition into North and South Korea, the Korean war, and the soft diplomacy exerted by the US during the Cold War period. These events inform Kim Ch'ae-hyŏn's classification of the two eras in dance immediately following WW2 as the "Chaotic Period" (1945–1961), which for its part led to a number of

Figure 4.1 Hahoe, South Korea, 2010, courtesy of SIDance, director, Lee Jong-Ho.

confusions and distortions in the ensuing "Groping Period" (1962–1972).[8] These dynamic and unstable political and cultural moments set the scene for thinking through the question of modernity and modernization within Korean dance.

Now and then

In 2008, a number of dance critics were invited to participate in a round-table discussion with Korean choreographers, dancers and critics in a session entitled, "Limitations and Possibilities of Korean Dance in the Global Arena", to be held in a well-known arts centre in Seoul.[9] Having seen a mere dozen or so works, foreign critics were invited to evaluate what we'd seen in terms of the export potential of Korean dance.[10] What does global mean in this context? Commentators took it to mean Europe and the US, thought in market terms. The question of 'translation' was thereby given over to the authority of a handful of western critics, who were asked to identify suitable prospects for export to their own countries.[11]

During the course of the discussion, one of my colleagues remarked that the work of ChangMu Dance company (director Kim Mae-Ja) might be seen as 'dated' in the US. Kim Mae-Ja's choreography has an emotional intensity that, it was argued, could be seen as 'harking back' to the aesthetics of Martha Graham. Perhaps my colleague was right, that the company's work might be thought 'out of date'. Yet the director of ChangMu Dance, and one of the seminal figures of recent Korean dance, Kim Mae-Ja, resists attributing her modernization of traditional movement vocabularies to a Graham style of modernism.[12]

In company publicity materials entitled "Modern Take on Traditional Dance", Kim is described as a "veteran traditional choreographer" who "strongly objects to the idea that traditional dance cannot be categorized as modern dance".[13] Elsewhere, these materials claim, "Because Kim's works, though based solidly on Korean tradition, interpret aspects of our modern daily lives and thoughts, critics have characterized her choreography as a role model for the modernization of Korean dance without giving up its Koreanness".[14] The dance critic, Kim T'ae-won supports this view, locating Kim Mae-Ja's work under the category "Korean dance", rather than "Modern dance".[15] Ramsay Burt and Michael Huxley classify a choreography as modern insofar as "it speaks to the experience of modern life".[16] Kim Mae-ja would seem to adhere to this view. If she is right, that her work engages with modern daily life, then her work is modern in this sense. For Kim Mae-Ja and Kim T'ae-Won, ChangMu's modernism is not sourced from the west. The question is complicated somewhat by the fact that Graham technique has historically had an influence throughout Asia, where it was taken up at the Ehwa Women's University where Kim Mae-Ja once taught.[17] It is also present in the modern dance stream taught at the Korean National University of the Arts, Seoul.[18]

Figure 4.2 The Eye of Heaven, choreographed by Kim Mae-Ja, artistic director, ChangMu Dance Company, courtesy of the artist.

How to unravel the modernist origins of a Korean choreographer's *oeuvre*? Does Kim Mae-Ja need to establish an untouched modernism in order to claim Korean credentials for her modernization of Korean dance? R. Radhakrishnan reflects upon a similar problem with regard to the emergence of nationalism, where non-western "nationalisms have to assimilate something alien to their own cultures before they can become modern nations".[19] This is distinct from European nationalisms (French, German, English) which are free to "generate their own models of autonomy from within".[20] There is also the complication of foreign influence. Radhakrishnan writes:

> This process seems difficult to avoid since the immediate history of these nations happens to be Western and there are no easy ways available to reclaim a pure and uncontaminated history.[21]

Kim Mae-Ja is similarly unable to claim a pure and uncontaminated history as the basis for her modernization of traditional dance.[22] Does this disqualify her from claiming a Korean mode of modernization, generated from within rather than sourced from without?

According to Theodore Adorno, modern art can be distinguished from other art traditions in virtue of its relation to the new.[23] For Adorno, the new in modern art realizes a break with tradition.[24] This notion of modern aesthetics is affiliated with the logic of an aesthetic avant-garde, which discerns the movement of modern art in terms of an aesthetic vanguard that inaugurates a shift in aesthetic concerns.[25] How do these notions sit with traditional Korean aesthetics, which has its own manner of valuing innovation? Professor of Korean art at Ehwa Women's University, Choi Joon-Sik, characterizes traditional Korean aesthetics as that which values individual interpretation, creativity and expresses a resistance towards imitation (mimesis).[26] Choi uses a number of descriptors to suggest a degree of aesthetic flexibility in Korean aesthetics, such as improvisation, spontaneity, emotion and situation, also through the idea of "techniqueless technique", "intentionless intention" and "schemeless scheme".[27]

According to Choi, improvisation is a key component of the relation between dancers and musicians in traditional dance. In October 2009, I spent an evening with several master dancers, their pupils and guests at the dance facility of Jeong Young-man, UNESCO Intangible Asset no. 82 of Korea, in Tongyeong province, under the guidance of Jin Ok-seop, director of *Festive Land*, an organization dedicated to the performance of traditional dance repertoires. Throughout the evening, individuals were plucked out of the communal circle by Jin and encouraged to improvise with the musicians. The fine temporality of Korean traditional gestures – felt through the flick of a wrist,

Figure 4.3 The Dynamics of Force, choreographed by Kim Mae-Ja, artistic director, ChangMu Dance Company, courtesy of the artist.

the hunch of a shoulder and the propulsion from one foot to another – lends itself to an in the moment elasticity of rhythm.[28] The dancing is itself a live dialogue between movement and music, able to be attenuated, the audience part of this open-ended sense of temporality. Master Ha Yong-bu, UNESCO Intangible Asset no. 68, spoke in response to my own dance improvisation with the evening's musicians, suggesting that I wait in my heart for inspiration rather than predetermine the flow of movement. Ha's point was that I could have enriched my dancing by playing with the moment of my decision-making, an art well-honed in Korean traditional dance. Over the course of the evening, a number of masters in traditional dance from different genres and schools took their turn to dance, offering a range of exquisite attenuations, comic moments and rhythmic syncopations, in support of Choi's aesthetic propositions. Audience expectations speak to this elasticity of time, where the dancer's choice when to lower the foot to the floor can provoke a vocal appreciation.[29] Erin Manning writes of the moment before weight is committed as "the virtual momentum of a movement's taking form before we actually move".[30] In my limited experience, watching and dancing, Korean traditional dancers and their audience are fully cognizant of what Manning calls "the elasticity of the almost".[31] Audiences hoot and clap in relation to that virtual play between the inevitable step and its momentary enunciation. This was the basis of Ha's advice to me, not to pre-empt the not-yet of movement. There are thus multiple sources of value in relation to the question of innovation from within and without Korean tradition, in which there exists an acknowledged space for allowing new elements to emerge.[32] Who then is authorized to determine the source of the new within Mae-ja's work?

In *Provincializing Europe,* Dipesh Chakrabarty writes of an asymmetry between western and non-western modes of historical knowledge, whereby European historians can produce work in relative ignorance of non-western histories but that non-western historians cannot return the favour for fear of appearing old fashioned or outdated.[33] According to Chakrabarty, the dominance of Europe in relation to historical knowledge is expressed along a single timeline, a "secular, linear calendar", which runs from the traditional past to the present. This temporal linearity underpins "a homogenizing narrative of transition" that moves from an archaic past through to modernity. In the case of dance, we might ask whether a transition narrative likewise situates non-modern dance along a single axis of modernization. And if modern dance has already happened (in the US and Europe), we might also ask whether its non-western articulations are to be calibrated along the same axis, as occurring before, during or after its emergence in the west. A modernism that does not refer (defer) to this western moment may be considered old fashioned, in aesthetic ignorance of that which defines modern dance and has already established itself. It is little wonder then that Kim Mae-Ja's work is liable to be perceived to be both modern *and* outmoded, as out of joint with aesthetic developments centred elsewhere or, in Radhakrishnan's terms, as "hopelessly out of sync with the 'international' present of modernity".[34]

Figure 4.4 The Eye of Heaven, choreographed by Kim Mae-Ja, artistic director, ChangMu Dance Company, courtesy of the artist.

It is as if the single temporal axis of modernity has installed a western aesthetic centre to which all developments must inevitably refer. Such a conception perhaps underlies Kim Ch'ae-hyŏn's conviction that Korean cultural tradition needs to counter western modernization.[35] Kim Mae-Ja rejects the view that modernization is inherently non-Korean (western), stating that she "strongly objects to the idea that traditional dance cannot be categorised as modern dance".[36] And yet, western aesthetic references recur as benchmarks of modernity, in Kim's claim that Korean dance is "best experienced in humble settings, close to the audience. So, Korean dance is more modern than you might expect".[37]

On the one hand, Kim Mae-Ja posits the modern in local, Korean terms, and yet, western modern dance values (such as performative proximity) are invoked as a kinaesthetic 'due north', as signifiers of what counts as the modern within dance – Korean dance is modern because, like in the west, it is performed in proximity to its audience. One could ask, why aren't elements of Korean modern dance used to mark the status of western modern dance values? The phallocentric tendency for western modern dance to function as the implicit measure of all things modern invites non-western practices to make the comparison (and simultaneously invoke a sense of lack). Why should modern dance have one meaning or origin? Is it possible to pluralize the modern within dance?[38] Is tradition incommensurable with the contemporary?

Jin Ok-seop argues the contemporary status of traditional Korean dance over western concert dance on the basis that traditional Korean dance is constantly in flux, adapting itself to new circumstance and performative contexts, while the western choreographic repertoire remains the same over time.[39] The suggestion that there is nothing more contemporary than tradition reflects Anton Cramer's perception of Japanese Noh theatre as "positing itself whole-heartedly in the now".[40] Cramer contests the idea that contemporary artworks should be able to be shown anywhere in the world in relation to some global sense of value.[41] The de-localizing logic of cultural capital underlies the authority invested in those international critics participating at the Roundtable (referred to earlier). And yet, Korean producers and presenters were not wrong in appealing to the sensibilities of their international guests as arbiters of the market. To provincialize Europe, in Chakrabarty's terms, is to bring to the fore the conditions under which Europe managed to 'acquire' the adjective modern for itself.[42] A provincializing focus on the European or western origins of the 'modern' in modern dance might similarly look to the conditions according to which European/American dance came to acquire for itself the horizon of modernity within dance. It might investigate which kinds of kinaesthetic sensibility authorize the application of the term as a way of setting out the bodyscape for the so-called "global arena". It might also examine whether the transition from traditional to modern dance is always governed by a single, temporal logic. Finally, it might also aim to de-authorize the 'international critic' whose lack of literacy can only be rectified through a different articulation of local and international points of view.[43]

Adorno's notion of modern aesthetics is enunciated in part through the notion of innovation in art. Mark Franko has commented on the close conceptual relationship between modernist aesthetics and the reception of modern dance as "so 'blindly' modernist that critical distance from its tenets appears at first unconscionable".[44] The assumption that modern dance is bound up with modernist aesthetics has led to a progressive conception of modern dance, as that which moves from one kinaesthetic sensibility to the next. Franko discerns one such narrative in modern dance, which begins with Duncan, moves through Wigman and Graham, and ends with Cunningham.[45] Franko contests the progressive paradigm, by conjoining canonical with lesser known figures, and through thinking their practices in relation to wider ranging political concerns. He makes an interesting observation, that the changes embedded in these dance forms suggests an interior dynamic he characterizes as "internal critique".[46] For Franko:

> The recourse to innovation sets in motion a new becoming at the same time that it permits the preservation of that which, by its very permanence, continues to particularize and to define culture. The issue of change is no longer uniquely one of progress, but partially one of return.[47]

What kind of return might we see in Kim Mae-ja's modernization of Korean traditional dance? What new becomings emerge in the midst of its preservation of kinaesthetic value? If modernization combines the new with the old, and the new is (in the case of Korean dance) a feature of the old, how are we to conceive the modernizing moment in Kim Mae-ja's choreographic work?

Chakrabarty's project of provincialization contests the singular temporality of historical time that underlies western conceptions of modernity. Radhakrishnan contrasts the European licence to define itself as modern in autonomous terms with the colonial predicament, compelled to appeal to western modernity as arbiter of modernization. The desire to produce an autonomous modernization is, according to Radhakrishnan, already complicated by western influence. Historical contamination rules out the fantasy of "colonial revenge" as Leela Ghandi puts it, which believes it can 'legislate' against western influence.[48] Kim Ch'ae-hyŏn's view that the Korean system of intangible cultural assets functions as a bulwark against "the rough waves of modernisation and westernisation" has in it something of the postcolonial desire for revenge insofar as it imagines itself outside western influence.[49] This is not to denigrate the importance of the intangible asset system, nor to reject postcolonial strategies to counter western ethnocentrism, merely to suggest that the complex history of modernity and colonization, partition and civil war in Korea complicates the kinaesthetic landscape. Chakrabarty

Figure 4.5 The Dynamics of Force, choreographed by Kim Mae-Ja, artistic director, ChangMu Dance Company, courtesy of the artist.

suggests opening up the singular axis of historical time to a conception of temporal plurality, one which does not aim to commensurate difference under the one narrative of then and now.[50] Kim Mae-ja's modern dance is an example of a pluralizing trajectory, which resists reduction to the singular logic of western (kin)aesthetics. Her appeal to western kinaesthetic values (performative intimacy) as a mark of her modernism need not detract from the Koreanness of her modernism, a reworking of traditional culture that remains on the plane of tradition.

Here and there

The pluralization of time may welcome a dynamics of space which allows for a strategic reworking of place. What follows is a discussion of choreographer Kim Jae-duk's work in relation to the regional space of an Asian spectatorship thought apart from the influence of the western gaze. Japanese critic and author, Muto Daisuke, has inaugurated a strategic approach to Asian dance that is neither oriented towards the west nor explicitly turned away from it.[51] As a member of the organizing committee for the *10th Indonesian Dance Festival*, Muto invited the Korean choreographer Kim Jae-Duk to show his work, *Darkness Poomba,* in Jakarta. *Darkness Poomba* invokes and plays with elements of Korean culture, music and dance.[52] The poomba is a poor Korean man, a singer, often depicted in comic terms, celebrated and caricatured in

Figure 4.6 Darkness Poomba, choreographed by Kim Jae-Duk, artistic director, Modern Table. Photographer: Layza Vasconcelos.

festivals.[53] *Darkness Poomba* begins with dancer-poombas dressed accordingly, working the audience, clowning and eating from rice bowls, to Korean pansori music. The work develops towards a jazz-rock hiatus, with a live band onstage, once again moving through the audience, opening out the performance from within through surges of energy and intensity. According to Muto Daisuke:

> Kim Jae-Duk does not just apply the form of traditional culture to his performance but rather grasps the essence of Korean tradition that is grounded in the popular mentality of common people, which can easily be understood by a contemporary audience as well.[54]

It is by no means clear where *Darkness Poomba* would sit in relation to a traditional/contemporary dichotomy. Kim Jae-duk speaks of drawing on the figure of the poomba in order to connect with contemporary audiences.[55]

It is interesting to note Muto's use of the term "contemporary audience" to account for the reception of Korean work in Indonesia for an English language newspaper, *The Jakarta Post*. What kind of contemporary sensibility is at stake here?

Muto writes of *Darkness Poomba's* Indonesian reception:

> I felt like that I was witnessing a process of reception of a foreign culture; a form of Korean aesthetics was accepted, hesitantly at first, but enthusiastically in the end, by Indonesian people. I think my trial of making a fold within the region called Asia revealed itself as certainly successful.[56]

Muto's strategy of making folds within Asian dance is not the pursuit of sameness (Asia is one). Rather, it aims to pursue relationships of difference within the region. It is the attempt to facilitate local encounters, to connect as a matter of neighbourly proximity. These encounters belong to a region, conceived by Muto as a "disidentity":

> what if we, renouncing essentialist way[s] of thinking, regard it [Asia] as an amorphous site just like streets which are crowded with numerous people and cultural differences? This region, always noisy and bustling, has been characterized for its openness for difference of cultures and values and their ceaseless transformations, loosely organized around some axes of great civilizations like China or India since long time ago. There is no identity of Asia but it has infinite diversity. Then "Asia" could be re-imagined as a symbol of the diversity and its dynamic motions.[57]

Thus the encounter between an Indonesian audience and a Korean aesthetic is a genuine relation of difference. The notion of an Asian disidentity able to connect without erasing its internal differences recalls Luce Irigaray's depiction of female plurality against phallocentric sameness.[58] Irigaray forwards a corporeal figuration, formed from two genital lips, in touch, neither one nor two.[59] Muto's conception of Asian culture could be posed in relation to Irigaray's anti-phallocentric gesture, as an appeal to difference and proximity without invoking the cardinal norm of western cultural sensibility. Its resistant assertion of Asian disidentity offers one kind of response to Ananya Chatterjea's rhetorical question: "Why do Asians care to be 'readable' to the West?", by turning away from western spectatorship towards another kind of readability, for another spectatorship.[60] Folding Asian dance could be conceived as a provincializing strategy that works through strengthening while producing its own version of locality, a strategy Irigaray might pose as the movement of "commodities amongst themselves".[61] It is in such a space that Kim Mae-ja and Kim Jae-duk can command a degree of authority in relation to their own work, beyond the classifying tendencies to which they are nonetheless subject. If Kim T'ae-won is right, that western aesthetic categories are an inadequate means of addressing Korean dance,[62] it is also possible that Kim Jae-Duk's work is able to provoke an aesthetics of tradition that allows for innovation, impact and intensity. Kim Jae-duk's citation of tradition within his work need not be seen as harking back, so much as drawing on traditions that are already present in Korean popular culture and everyday life. Like Kim Mae-ja, Kim Jae-duk is also interested in thinking his work in relation to multiple sources of inspiration, including western philosophy and the work of Akram Khan in the UK.[63] These sensibilities enrich Kim's engagement with his 'contemporary audience', inside and outside Korea.

Like modernism, the notion of the contemporary in contemporary dance has its own reductive tendencies. Ananya Chatterjea writes:

> Repeatedly I have bemoaned the erasure of difference under the wonderfully unifying and legitimizing aesthetic categories of "contemporary dance" (really meaning Euro-American modern/contemporary dance) that seems to dominate much of what is seen of "Asian" choreography in these fora that currently represent the global stage.[64]

For Chatterjea, there is a tendency for Asian dance to be assessed according to a single notion of the contemporary, "inevitably drawn from Western modern/ contemporary dance".[65] As a consequence, the contemporary credentials of Chatterjea's own choreography was questioned on the basis that she is "*still* using footwork and hand gestures" (emphasis mine).[66] One could well imagine the same questions being directed towards an avowedly contemporary Korean choreography that 'still' utilizes distinctive shoulder and foot dynamics but maybe not of dancing that embodies high leg extensions and jumps drawn from western classical ballet. There are numerous examples of contemporary Korean choreographers who draw on traditional Korean sensibilities in their work on an overt and subtle basis. Such is the legacy and provenance of Korean dance that traces of these sensibilities remain or, in Franko's words, return. The problem, to use Chatterjea's formulation, concerns their 'read-ability' as contemporary.

Does a traditional gesture 'mean' a work is bound to be classified as trad-itional and not contemporary? Or could we suggest, as Nicholas Thomas argues, that we reject the either/or logic of tradition versus the contemporary in art in favour of a Deleuzean notion of machinic seriality, able to draw upon whatever lies to hand?[67] In once sense it doesn't matter which category Kim and Kim's work falls under, but in another sense it does. Hammergren recounts the views of an Indian–Swedish choreographer who wanted her work to be appreciated in contemporary and not merely traditional terms.[68] There

Figure 4.7 Sinawi, choreographed by Kim Jae-Duk, Kangdong Arts Center. Photographer: Sangyun Park.

is a force at work in Korean dance circles today, pushing choreographers to frame their work as contemporary rather than traditional, to buy into an either/or classification so as to secure a greater share of state funding amidst economic scarcity.[69] Categories matter in the mattering of movement. A corporeal reflection of their own concerns and kinaesthetic sensibility, the work of Kim Mae-ja and Kim Jae-duk can be seen as a relatively autonomous gesture of art making that has its place within the diversity of Korean dance. Thought in terms of pluralization rather than progression, Korean dance can be located within a wider network of Asian performance and spectatorship as a way of promoting kinaesthetic relations of difference beyond the notion of a singular kinaesthetic centre.

Coda

The discussion thus far has focused on whether and how the terms 'contemporary' and 'modern' might be invoked in relation to Korean dance. Questions of authority, authorization, temporality and literacy were raised in an attempt to rethink the nature and place of tradition beyond a single axis that contrasts the past of tradition with the modernizing thrust of aesthetic innovation. According to Adorno's formulation, the modern artwork is that which breaks with a perceived aesthetic past. The avant-garde emerges here as the precursor and signifier of that break. Work that fails to break with its past is, by definition, pre- or unmodern. By implication, insofar as Korean dance purports a contiguous relation with its own past, it is relegated to the backwaters of traditions, which for their part cannot be simultaneously contemporary.

One option is to refuse a notion of time that, according to Bruno Latour, "passes irrevocably and annuls the entire past in its wake".[70] Chakrabarty's *Provincializing Europe* suggests a dual strategy of temporal pluralization and geo-political regionalization.[71] If successful, western universalism would become a regional sphere of influence, perhaps demoted with respect to its hegemonic purchase. What then of its claim to represent and model modernity? In *We Have Never Been Modern*, Latour traces the complicity between modernity and an irreversible sense of time. Latour writes:

> one can go forward, but then one must break with the past; one can choose to go backward, but then one has to break with the modernizing avant-gardes, which have broken radically with their own past. This diktat organized modern thought until the last few years – without, of course, having any effect on the practice of mediation, a practice that has always mixed up epochs, genres, and ideas as heterogeneous as those of the premoderns.[72]

Latour calls into question the western presupposition that 'we' are living in a time that moves determinably forwards, arguing that the purist conception of modern time is only made possible by a (nonmodern) amalgam of practices, temporalities and sensibilities. To be modern for Latour is to *constitute* the modern notion of time and its difference from other, non-modern modalities. This requires work:

> Modernizing progress is thinkable only on condition that all the elements that are contemporary according to the calendar belong to the same time. For this to be the case, these elements have to form a complete and recognizable cohort.[73]

The cohort of the present time is thus made and not given. And for this to happen, "entities *have to be made contemporary*".[74] When deemed contemporary, events and entities are seen to be "moving in step".[75] No wonder it was suggested that Kim Mae-ja's purportedly modern work was liable to be thought out of step with the present day. That it was up to a small cohort of largely western critics to decide which Korean works might make the global cut, only underlines Latour's claim that modernism "was only the provisional result of a selection made by a small number of agents in the name of all".[76] Latour posits another sphere of practice, an unacknowledged side of the modern paradigm, which he theorizes in terms of hybrids and networks.[77] The unilateral flow of time, with its proper assortment of contemporary practices, would not be possible were it not for this other kind of contaminated and contaminating practice. The view that Korean dance can be simultaneously modern, Korean, traditional and contemporary recalls this disavowed side of modern thinking. If Latour is even half-right, it is as modern a way of thinking as the classifying gestures of the authorized western critic.

Notes

1 Lena Hammergren, "The Power of Classification", in *Worlding Dance*, ed. Susan Foster, (London: Palgrave Macmillan, 2009), 18.
2 The term "bodyscape" is Paula Saukko's term, an adaption of the work of Arjun Appadurai on globalization, locality and movement, cited in Hammergren, ibid., 18.
3 Ibid., 20.
4 During this period, I was a guest of the Seoul International Dance Festival (SIDANCE) over several years, serving as a dance critic representing Australia at the *Seoul Performing Arts Critics* forum (SPAC), inaugurated in 2008. Over this period, SIDANCE (dir. Lee Jong-ho) facilitated a number of educational and participatory programs on Korean culture and dance (curated by Lee Dong-min and Kim Seo-ryoung) which included master classes, lectures, regional tours, seminars and meetings, as well as exposure to many dance performances. Due to the hospitality embedded in these events, I have been able to connect, speak, eat, drink and dance with numerous master dancers, choreographers, critics, producers, arts administrators and curators. SIDANCE also arranged for a number of meetings and interviews which form the basis of this discussion.

5 South Korea has, since 1962, availed itself of the UNESCO tangible and intangible cultural asset system of cultural preservation, which includes the identification of national living treasures, who are able to contribute to the ongoing sustainability of art practice.

6 Sang-suk Nam and Hae-suk Gim, *Introduction to Korean Traditional Arts* (Seoul: School of Korean Traditional Performing Arts, 2002).

7 Judy Van Zile's *Perspectives on Korean Dance* offers an excellent introduction to Korean dance based on many years' experience, Judy Van Zile, *Perspectives on Korean Dance* (Middeltown, CT: Wesleyan University Press, 2003). See also Yunesŭk 'o Han'guk, *Korean Dance, Theatre and Cinema* (Seoul: Si-sa-yong-o-sa Publishers, 1983).

8 Ch'ae-hyŏn Kim, "1946–1980: The Will to Form Dance Infrastructures and Dance Style", in Yi Tu-hyŏn et al., *Korean Performing Arts: Drama, Dance and Music Theatre*, (Seoul: Jipmoondang Publishing, 1997), 104.

9 The Roundtable discussion, held on October 14, 2008, at *Sangsang Madang*, Seoul, was the final session of the first *Seoul Performing Arts Critics Forum 2008*, organized by the South Korean Section of the International Dance Council CID-UNESCO and coinciding with the 11th Seoul International Dance Festival (dir. Lee, Jong-Ho), October 2008.

10 The South Korean section of the International Dance Council of CID-UNESCO has been offering a series of annual dance programs entitled "Korean Identity through Dance", since 1996. In 2008, SPAC forum critics had seen one such offering.

11 Although most of the critics came from Europe, others also came from Israel, Australia, China and Japan. There was also a panel of Korean critics although, from memory, they were not asked to comment on the export potential of the Korean dance.

12 Interview with Kim Mae-Ja, October 2009, translated by Chung Eunju.

13 ChangMu Dance, Publicity materials, October 2008.

14 Ibid.

15 Kim T'ae-won, "1981–1987: The Rapid Growth of Creative Activity and the Appearance of New Dance Genres and Generations", 124.

16 Ramsay Burt and Michael Huxley, *Dancing Modernism and Modernity* (Milton: Routledge, 2019), 5.

17 Victoria Geduld looks at the ways in which the US used the tours of Martha Graham during the cold war as a form of soft diplomacy, Victoria Phillips, "Dancing Diplomacy: Martha Graham and the Strange Commodity of Cold-War Cultural Exchange in Asia 1955 and 1974", *Dance Chronicle* 33, no. 1 (2010): 44–81. These kinds of political, cultural gesture inform the presence and persistence of Graham technique in Korea. The Ehwa Women's University was the first institution to teach dance (other than through private schools) beginning in 1963, Kim, "1981–1997: The Rapid Growth of Creative Activity", 149–150. See also Zile, *Perspectives on Korean Dance*, 22–23.

18 I visited the School of Dance at the Korean National University of the Arts in October 2008 (Dean, Chung, Seoung-hee), where students specialize in classical, traditional or modern dance. The modern dance class I watched consisted of Graham floor work, contraction and release.

19 R. Radhakrishnan, "Nationalism, Gender and Narrative", in *Nationalisms and Sexualities*, ed. Andrew Parker (New York and London: Routledge, 1992), 86.

20 Ibid., 86.
21 Ibid.
22 Prior to World War Two, modernization in dance occurred in the context of Japanese colonization. Judy Van Zile and Park Sang Mi both trace dance modernism in Korea through the figure of Ch'oe Sŭng-hŭi, an important figure in twentieth-century modern dance, whose work was influenced by Japanese modern dancer Ishii Baku, Judy Van Zile, "Performing Modernity in Korea: The Dance of Ch'oe Sŭng-hŭi", *Korean Studies* 37 (2013): 124–149; Park Sang Mi, "The Making of a Cultural Icon for the Japanese Empire: Choe Seung-Hui's US Dance Tours and 'New Asian' Culture in the 1930s and 1940s", *Positions* 14, no. 3 (2006): 597–632.
23 Theodor Adorno, *Aesthetic Theory,* trans. Robert Hullot-Kentor (London: Bloomsbury Publishing 2013).
24 Ibid., Chapter 2. See also Peter Bürger, *Theory of the Avant-Garde*, trans. Michael Shaw, 59–63.
25 See Bürger, *Theory of the Avant-Garde.*
26 Choi, Joon-sik, "Exploring the Spirit of Korean Traditional Arts", lecture on Korean aesthetics at Post Theatre, Seoul, October 13, 2009.
27 Ibid.
28 Van Zile writes:

> Another distinguishing feature that pervades many forms of traditional dance is a feeling of suspension. The dancer begins a movement that rises, in some fashion, and then appears to stop abruptly. That dancer briefly remains poised, as if deciding whether to lift even higher or to move on to something else. As the contained energy verges on explosion, the performer quickly rises just a bit higher, almost like a small hiccup, before releasing everything into a gently downward movement. This movement of suspension, a delicate hovering, provides strong, dynamic tension for the viewer and contributes to the visual sigh of relief created by the shoulder dance.
>
> (*Perspectives on Korean Dance*, 13)

29 Van Zile writes:

> Yet another distinctive feature of traditional dance is a particular way of using the floor. Koreans are quick to point out that their dance is characterized by walks in which the dancer steps first on the heel rather than the toe or the ball of the foot. But what is unique in this movement, is the way in which dancers seem to caress the floor with their feet, curling their toes upward before placing the heel on the floor and then gently rolling the entire foot down.
>
> (*Perspectives on Korean Dance*, 13)

30 Erin Manning, *Relationscapes: Movement, Art, Philosophy* (Cambridge, MA: MIT Press, 2012), 6.
31 Ibid., 9.
32 The point of claiming innovation within Korean tradition is not to replace other (read, western) sources of innovation and improvisation but to indicate that these values can be sourced from within Korean aesthetic practices. In a similar vein, Leila Ahmed contrasts two sources of feminist politics in the Middle East, one internal to the Middle East, the other western in origin. According to Ahmed, western ideas of nationhood, civil and political rights were taken up in the nineteenth century and oriented towards an Arabicized and Islamicized notion of political rights. As a consequence, local forms of feminism were able to be criticized as

"a 'Western' and 'un-Islamic' import whose consequences would destroy the fabric of Islamic Society", Leila Ahmed, "Feminism and Cross-Cultural Inquiry: The terms of the Discourse in Islam", in *Coming to Terms: Feminism, Theory, Politics,* ed. Elizabeth Weed (London and New York: Routledge, 1989), 143. It is Ahmed's contention that Islam and Islamic history is equally able to offer the intellectual means to contest injustice against women committed in the name of Islam, ibid., 151. The point is not necessarily to fix one source as a replacement for the other, to invert western dominance, so much as to remain open to the strategic possibilities of multiple sources for an Islamic feminist politics.

33 Dipesh Chakrabarty, *Provincializing Europe: Postcolonial Thought and Historical Difference* (Princeton, NJ: Princeton University Press, 2000).

34 R. Radhakrishnan, "Nationalism, Gender and Narrative", 86.

35 Kim, "1946–1980: The Will to Form Dance Infrastructures and Dance Style", 110.

36 Kim Mae-ja, Press Release, October 2008.

37 Ibid.

38 Sanjay Seth argues against the view that thinking the concept of modernity is necessarily Eurocentric, "Is Thinking with Modernity Eurocentric?", *Cultural Sociology* 10, no. 3 (2016): 385–398. For Seth, the origins of the question, its milieu and local conditions, impact upon the concept, its deployment and effect. To adapt this argument towards the case of Mae-ja, one might suggest that localized (Korean) values of aesthetic innovation render the deployment of the category modern entirely compatible with tradition, giving modernization in Korean dance its own timbre.

39 Personal communication, Seoul, October 2011. Jin Ok-seop is renowned nationally for his published work on traditional Korean dance, as a curator, writer, supporter of the form and Artistic Director of *Festival Land* whose mandate is the promotion of traditional dance.

40 Anton Franz Cramer, "Speaking Africa: A German-Côte d'Ivoire Performing Arts Dialogue", in *Choreography and Corporeality: Relay in Motion,* ed. Thomas F. DeFrantz and Philipa Rothfield (London: Palgrave Macmillan, 2016), 135.

41 Ibid., 136.

42 Chakrabarty, *Provincializing Europe*, 16.

43 For my own part, my understanding and perception of Korean dance was greatly assisted by taking a master class (with master dancer, Kim Tae-Won, ChangMu Arts Centre, Post Theatre, October 2008). This experience made it clear to me that I needed to understand the dance through my own body, which at the same time lacks the literacy to adequately understand the field.

44 Mark Franko, *Dancing Modernism: Performing Politics* (Bloomington: Indiana University Press, 1995), ix.

45 Ibid., ix. Franko argues that the grand narrative of modern dance is indebted to the modernist paradigm, ix.

46 Ibid., xi.

47 Ibid.

48 Cited in Chakrabarty, *Provincializing Europe*, 16.

49 Kim, "1946–1980: The Will to Form Dance Infrastructures and Dance Style", 110.

50 Chakrabarty refers to Appiah, Kosambi and Kenyatta's lived experience, arguing that, "They refer us to the plurality that inheres in the 'now', the lack of totality, the constant fragmentariness, that constitutes one's present", *Provincializing Europe*, 243.

51 Daisuke Muto is a dance critic, choreographer and academic, working in Japan. He is interested in the modern history of dance in Asia and theories of choreography.

52 Darkness Poomba premiered in 2010 and was performed at the 10th Indonesian Dance Festival (2010). It was choreographed by Kim Jae-Duk, director of the dance company, *Modern Table*. Kim has a PhD in dance. In 2016, he won the Dance Culture Performance Award for performance of the year for his work, Darkness Poomba, which has been performed around the world. Kim also received first prize at the 2007, 28th Seoul Dance Festival. Kim's company, *Modern Table*, has been showing work since 2008.

53 For example, the Eumseong Pumba Festival is held annually in Seoul.

54 Muto, Daisuke, "Kim Jae-Duk: Across the Arts". *The Jakarta Post*, June 26, 2010, www.thejakartapost.com/news/2010/06/26/kim-jaeduk-across-arts.html, accessed April 5, 2011.

55 Kim Jae-duk, interview, October 2011.

56 Muto, Daisuke, "Making Folds in Asian Dance Cultures: In Search of Inner Contacts", paper presented to Seoul Performing Arts Critics (SPAC) Forum, Seoul, October 2010.

57 Ibid.

58 Luce Irigaray, *This Sex Which Is Not One*, trans. Catherine Porter (Ithaca, NY: Cornell University Press, 1985).

59 Ibid.

60 Ananya Chatterjea, "On the Value of Mistranslations and Contaminations: The Category of 'Contemporary Choreography' in Asian Dance", *Dance Research Journal* 45, no. 1 (2013): 15.

61 Irigaray, *This Sex Which Is Not One*, 192.

62 Kim T'ae-won, personal communication, 2011.

63 Kim Jae-duk, personal communication, 2014.

64 Chatterjea, "On the Value of Mistranslations and Contaminations", 10.

65 Ibid., 10.

66 Ibid., 10.

67 Thomas writes: "The significance and effects of indigenous art can only be misunderstood if we insist on celebrating *either* the so-called 'traditionalist' expressions *or* the 'contemporary' ones, instead of acknowledging both", *Possessions*, 199.

68 Hammergren writes of Rani Nair's frustration "over the manner in which her winning choreography made critics singularly speak about the Indian qualities of her work. She saw herself as a contemporary choreographer, and wanted criticism to address aesthetic issues in that same way", "The Power of Classification", 26–27.

69 This observation was made to me by a number of commentators, both Korean and French.

70 Bruno Latour, *We Have Never Been Modern,* trans. Catherine Porter (Cambridge, MA: Harvard University Press, 1993), 47.

71 Chakrabarty, *Provincializing Europe.*

72 Ibid., 69.

73 Ibid., 73.

74 My emphasis, ibid., 72.

75 Ibid., 72.

76 Ibid., 76.

77 Ibid., 11.

Bibliography

Adorno, Theodore. *Aesthetic Theory*. Translated by Robert Hullot-Kentor. London: Bloomsbury Publishing, 2013.

Ahmed, Leila. "Feminism and Cross-cultural Inquiry: The Terms of the Discourse in Islam". In *Coming to Terms: Feminism, Theory, Politics*, edited by Elizabeth Weed. London and New York: Routledge, 1989.

Bürger, Peter. *Theory of the Avant-Garde*. Translated by Michael Shaw. Minneapolis: University of Minnesota Press, 1984.

Burt, Ramsay and Huxley, Michael. *Dancing Modernism and Modernity*. Milton: Routledge, 2019.

Chakrabarty, Dipesh. *Provincializing Europe: Postcolonial Thought and Historical Difference*. Princeton, NJ: Princeton University Press, 2000.

Chatterjea, Ananya. "On the Value of Mistranslations and Contaminations: The Category of 'Contemporary Choreography' in Asian Dance". *Dance Research Journal* 45, no. 1 (2013): 7–21.

Choi Joon-sik. "Exploring the Spirit of Korean Traditional Arts". Lecture on Korean aesthetics at Post Theatre, Seoul, October 13, 2009.

Cramer, Franz Anton. "Speaking Africa, *Logobi*: A German-Côte d'Ivoire Performing Arts Dialogue". In *Choreography and Corporeality: Relay in Motion*, edited by Thomas F. DeFrantz and Philipa Rothfield, 135–151. London: Palgrave Macmillan, 2016.

Franko, Mark. *Dancing Modernism: Performing Politics*. Bloomington: Indiana University Press, 1995.

Geduld, Victoria Phillips. "Dancing Diplomacy: Martha Graham and the Strange Commodity of Cold-War Cultural Exchange in Asia 1955 and 1974". *Dance Chronicle* 33, no. 1 (2010): 44–81.

Hammergren, Lena. "The Power of Classification". In *Worlding Dance*, edited by Susan Foster, 14–31. London: Palgrave Macmillan, 2009.

Irigaray, Luce. *This Sex Which Is Not One*. Translated by Catherine Porter. Ithaca, NY: Cornell University Press, 1985.

Kim, Ch'ae-hyŏn. "1946–1980: The Will to Form Dance Infrastructures and Dance Style". In Yi Tu-hyŏn et al., *Korean Performing Art: Drama, Dance and Music Theatre,*103–122. Seoul: Jipmoondang Publishing, 1997.

Kim, T'ae-won, "1981–1997: The Rapid Growth of Creative Activity and the Appearance of New Dance Genres and Generations". In Yi Tu-hyŏn et al., *Korean Performing Arts, Drama, Dance and Music Theatre,*123–154. Seoul: Jipmoondang Publishing, 1997.

Latour, Bruno. *We Have Never Been Modern*. Translated by Catherine Porter. Cambridge, MA: Harvard University Press, 1993.

Manning, Erin. *Relationscapes: Movement, Art, Philosophy*. Cambridge, MA: MIT Press, 2012.

Morley, David. *Media, Modernity and Technology: The Geography of the New*. London: Routledge, 2007.

Muto, Daisuke. "Kim Jae-Duk: Across the Arts". *The Jakarta Post*, June 26, 2010. www.thejakartapost.com/news/2010/06/26/kim-jaeduk-across-arts.html, last accessed April 5, 2011.

———. "Making Folds in Asian Dance Cultures: In Search of Inner Contacts". Paper presented to Seoul Performing Arts Critics (SPAC) Forum, Seoul, October 2010.

Nam, Sang-suk and Gim, Hae-suk. *Introduction to Korean Traditional Arts*. Seoul: School of Korean Traditional Performing Arts, 2002.

Park Sang Mi. "The Making of a Cultural Icon for the Japanese Empire: Choe Seung-Hui's US Dance Tours and 'New Asian' Culture in the 1930s and 1940s". *Positions* 14, no. 3 (2006): 597–632.

Radhakrishnan, R. "Nationalism, Gender and the Narrative of Identity". In *Nationalisms and Sexualities*, edited by Andrew Parker et al., 77–95. New York and London: Routledge, 1992.

Seth, Sanjay. "Is Thinking with Modernity Eurocentric?" *Cultural Sociology* 10, no. 3 (2016): 385–398.

Van Zile, Judy. *Perspectives on Korean Dance*. Middletown, CT: Wesleyan University Press, 2003.

———. "Performing Modernity in Korea: The Dance of Ch'oe Sŭng-hŭi". *Korean Studies* 37 (2013): 124–149.

Wiwŏnhoe, Yunesŭk'o Han'guk. *Korean Dance, Theatre and Cinema*. Seoul: Si-sa-yong-o-sa Publishers, 1983.

Part II

5   Nietzsche and the ontology of force

Introduction

Thus far, we have posed the activity of dancing as the work of the dancer, thought through a phenomenological conception of difference. According to this paradigm, difference pertains to the variable conditions of kinaesthetic agency exercised by the dancer. These include the dancer's cultural and kinaesthetic milieu, specific training, experience, ways of working and performing. Cultural phenomenologist, Thomas Csordas' concept of somatic attention – as an inherently cultural act – gives expression to the corporeal impact of culture upon perception. The cultural dimension of the dancer's perception is felt in terms of her kinaesthetic sensibility – the many factors that come together to produce this person's manner of sensing and moving. The dancer's movement subjectivity brings together notions of agency, perceptual orientation and kinaesthetic specificity as they impact upon the dancer's field of practice. The acknowledgement of the dancer's milieu and provenance is able to take note of the different factors that impinge upon and shape the dancer's agency. To that extent, this is a corporeal reading of subject-production, thought in terms of kinaesthetic variation.

Although its attention to difference resists the universalizing tendencies of phenomenology, this manner of thinking remains inside the domain of the subject, seeking the conditions and specificities of agency, as they are expressed in movement and felt within perception. The merits of such an approach cluster around the nuances of lived experience: How does the dancer feel herself moving? What are the ways in which she pays attention to her own body, the bodies of others (dancers and audience) and her environs? How is her agency shaped and expressed in practice? This phenomenological approach is also able to track the hegemonic imposition of dominant perceptual norms upon the field, at the expense of what Foucault would call subjugated knowledges. The field of dance is articulated on uneven ground, such that its values and modes of evaluation are steeped in political factors that prevail within the field and more broadly. The political economy of dance, its modes of production, manners of exchange, funding and commodification influence what it is and what's possible within the field. Such an approach rises above the humanist tendencies of phenomenology by allowing difference to enter the domain of kinaesthetic sensibility and movement subjectivity. Subjectivity thereby has a history, which both constrains and makes possible the field of action. Although difference performs a kind of decentring action here, towards a heterogeneous conception of subjectivity, this approach adheres to the plane of the subject. The act of dancing is seen to be the work of the dancer, whatever the influences that shape her dancing.

This chapter marks an ontological break with the phenomenological approach to dance, as that which attributes the activity and agency of the dance to the dancer. In so doing, it will offer an alternative conception of dance, one which looks to the workings of force in the production of movement. The shift towards a conception of relational force as that which produces the body aims to rethink what a body is and what a body does. The Nietzschean conception of force destabilizes the singular identity of things, putting in their place a more mutable and dynamic sense of that which happens. Its displacement of subjectivity can be traced to Nietzsche's *On the Genealogy of Morality*, which gives clear expression to the critique of the subject as 'doer', leading to a focus on action as such.[1] Its focus on the difference between action and reaction, in the context of master versus slave methods of valuation, paves the way for Deleuze's fine elaboration of force in *Nietzsche and Philosophy*.[2] Deleuze takes up Nietzsche's conceptual *oeuvre* in order to tease out the different ways in which forces combine. He highlights the difference between forces which combine to produce a body, and those that turn inwards to create a subjective interior. Apart from clarifying Nietzsche's claim that "there is no 'being' behind the deed", Deleuze's close reading of force enables a typology of dancing which looks to the various ways in which agency arises in its midst.[3] According to this mode of thought, agency does not belong to the subject, nor is it predicated of 'the body' as the one who acts. Agency is instead posed as the work of a composite and composing multiplicity. Such are the becomings of force.

The account begins with an ontological reformulation of dance in terms of bodies and forces. According to this approach, the body is a momentary formation, a provisional resolution of relations of force. Such a view will form the basis for a focus on the different ways in which forces combine so as to produce movement. Although no longer thought of as the site and source of agency, there is a place for subjective sensation, thought and imagery within this framework, as grist for the activities of force. Subjectivity is likewise able to be activated within this context, not as a staging ground for some metaphysical comeback, but as a stepping stone towards what Deleuze might call the affirmative arts of "dance, laughter and play".[4] These questions, of the nature and place of subjectivity within an ontology of force, will be addressed in Chapter 6. The following discussion begins by addressing the difference between phenomenology's emphasis upon subjectivity and Nietzsche's sceptical critique of its epistemological and metaphysical underpinnings. Nietzsche's sceptical attitude towards the subjective point of view and all that it entails paves the way for a treatment of action, beyond the domain of the subject.

The Nietzschean break with subjectivity

However derived, produced, situated and constrained, phenomenology thinks of the subject as the centre and source of human action. Our experience reflects this point of view, positing the subject at the centre of its field of action. According to this paradigm, even habitual actions, which transpire without the benefit of consciousness, occur by virtue of the subject. Habits enable the lived body to take up elements of its existential situation, freeing thought to occupy itself with other considerations. Dance functions within this conceptual milieu as the work of the dancer. Practice enters the scene through contextualizing the dancer's movement subjectivity and kinaesthetic sensibility. Although agency is in part produced through practice, the actions of the dancer are still seen as her own.

Nietzsche does not buy into this picture, seeking a quite different account of its derivation. His critical project, developed on multiple fronts, is prompted by the sense that things could be different, that human being could, in a certain sense, be overcome. Nietzsche would not deny that we feel ourselves to be the agents of our own destiny. Indeed, he acknowledges the difficulty of thinking otherwise.[5] Hence his multi-faceted assault on our philosophical good sense as it applies to questions of agency and its experience:

> The primeval delusion still lives on that one knows, and knows quite precisely in every case, how human action is brought about ... Is the "terrible" truth not that no amount of knowledge about an act *ever* suffices to ensure its performance, that the space between knowledge and action has never yet been bridged even in one single instance? Actions are *never* what they appear to be![6]

Nietzsche calls into question the idea that we are the ones who express agency within action. The critique of agency is taken up in *On the Genealogy of Morality*, where Nietzsche famously stated that "there is no 'being' behind the deed, its effect and what becomes of it; 'the doer' is invented as an afterthought – the doing is everything".[7] For Nietzsche, adding the subject to our account of action merely muddies the ontological waters.

The fact that our experience appears to support the phenomenological conception of agency doesn't count for much here. This is because experience for Nietzsche has no purchase upon that which happens and thus lacks probity. Nor does the coherence of experience guarantee its veracity:

> The habits of our senses have woven us into lies and deception of sensation: these again are the basis of all our judgements and "knowledge" – there is absolutely no escape, no backway or bypath into the *real world!*

We sit within our net, we spiders, and whatever we may catch in it, we can catch nothing at all except that which allows itself to be caught in precisely *our* net.[8]

There are thus two elements to Nietzschean scepticism towards the subject: one, that experience is not an accurate reflection of the way things are, and two, that we are nonetheless caught within its web. The failure of experience to live up to its promise merely ratifies Nietzsche's search for an alternative account of action, one which appeals to a multiplicity of underlying factors as their basis and not human agency.

For Nietzsche, all our actions and feelings can be traced to the work of underlying drives or forces. Drives (forces, instincts or impulses) compete with one another, achieving gratification at the expense of their rivals. Nietzsche writes:

Every drive is a kind of lust for domination, each has its perspective, which it would like to impose as a norm on all the other drives.[9]

Our problem is that we have no inkling of their machinations, beyond a series of opaque encounters with their outcome.[10] The 'task' of subjectivity is to make sense of these subterranean goings-on, to interpret their workings from a subjective point of view, a project doomed to fail, partly because of our compulsion to maintain ownership of our actions, and partly because we have no direct access to that which determines them. We are thus compelled to interpret the workings of force as if they were the product of our own intentional actions. These interpretations, which are taken on board by phenomenology, are not, for Nietzsche, an accurate picture of human action. To that extent, Nietzsche likens waking life to dreaming – in each case, an imaginary turn of events is superimposed upon underlying nervous stimuli (corporeal affect).[11] Between the drives and their experience lies an imaginary layer of subjective interpretation, whose content is itself the work of underlying drives.[12] The Nietzschean project of genealogy digs beneath these layers of interpretation and reinterpretation, which have covered over the origins of subjectivity in the workings of force.[13] Such an approach resonates with post-structural readings of subjectivity which appeal to the influence of underlying social and political forces. Nietzsche's genealogy of the subject does not stop at the production of human agency, however, but rather seeks the agency of things between and amongst relations of force, in the ways in which forces work other forces.

Bodies and forces

The body is a key figure in this shift, away from a metaphysics of the subject and towards an ontology of force. Nietzsche often appeals to the body as a source of value. Not only is it his "guiding thread",[14] the body functions as a mode of resistance to the putative identity of the subject.[15] The body paves the way for a conception of life which is based upon multiplicity and diffe-rence, rather than unity and identity. Nietzsche's emphasis on the body reveals "a tremendous multiplicity"[16] beneath its apparent unity:

> what is more astonishing is the *body*: there is no end to one's admiration for how the human *body* has become possible; how such a prodigious alliance of living beings, each dependent and subservient and yet in a cer-tain sense also commanding and acting out of its own will, can live, grow, and for a while prevail, as a whole.[17]

According to this thought, the body is not one centre but consists of a multiplicity of interrelated activities, organs, actions and reactions, which come together according to moments of order, selection, arrangement and connection.[18] The notion of multiplicity opens the body up to difference, both within and without, posing the body as its dynamic and transitory outcome.

Although Nietzsche did not develop a theory of the body as such, a number of his commentators have drawn upon his writings in order to think through the corporeal dimension of his philosophy. Pierre Klossowski was a key figure in the French post-war 'rehabilitation' of Nietzsche, a precursor of Deleuze and Foucault's engagement with Nietzschean thought. Klossowski's novel reading of Nietzsche makes sense of the claim that a tremendous multi-plicity underpins the body's apparent unity.[19] It also offers a way of thinking the body as an inherently mobile formation. Klossowski looks to the body as a site of dynamic transformation which must be thought apart from subject-centred modes of explanation. While we tend to merge the body with subject-ivity, Klossowski draws an ontological and epistemological wedge between the felt identity of the self on the one hand, and the dynamic activities of the body on the other.[20] He begins by positing the body as a series of corporeal states, which come into being then pass.[21] This dynamic and changing con-ception of the body is not organized under the rubric of an overarching iden-tity – a form of sovereign subjectivity – but is instead the outcome of myriad interactions between the body's constitutive impulses. An impulse is a ten-dency, an indeterminate state of affairs, which takes shape through forming relationships with other tendencies. The body is that which temporarily ensues from these evolving relationships. Its apparent unity – as 'a body' – masks its component, underlying, impulsive states. A momentary body forms, for Klossowski, because its constituent, contestatory elements (impulses) resolve their differences in a particular way.[22] Such resolution emerges by way of cor-poreal formation. The body is thus an 'outcome', an assemblage, albeit a pro-visional and transitory one.

Klossowski sees the activity of the impulses as a kind of interpretive pro-cess superimposed upon an underlying chaotic multiplicity (of impulses). The impulses combine to give shape to that which is inherently indeterminate. They access and take up corporeal circumstance, forming a movement towards the production of new corporeal circumstance. Klossowski calls this process a semiotic of impulses. The notion of a semiotic suggests an interpretive facility on the part of the impulses. This is less linguistic than ontological, in that the body represents a kind of momentary organization – which brings something into being – out of that which is inherently disorganized. Eric Blondel addresses the notion of an organizing set of impulses by posing the body as a midpoint of Nietzschean becoming: "an intermediary between the absolute plural of the world's chaos, and the absolute simplification of intellect".[23] The body is a mediating figure here, a provisional mode of organization that emerges from the "chaotic and contradictory diversity of impulses".[24] The body's intermediary status allows Nietzsche to get closer to the myriad impulses that underlie the body's becoming. To that extent, it differs from subjectivity. Nietzsche writes:

> The danger in all direct questioning of the subject about the subject, and all self-contemplation of the mind, is that it could be useful and important for the subject's activity to misinterpret itself. This is why we ask *the body*, and reject the testimony of the sharpened senses: we try, so to speak, to see whether the subordinated themselves can't take up communication with us. (my emphasis)[25]

Klossowski takes up the project, foreshadowed earlier, of finding a way to 'communicate' with those impulses that constitute the flow of corporeal states. His starting point is not that these impulses are the result of 'a doer' but rather that the impulses pursue their own 'semiotic' trajectory. Their coherence (determinacy) ensues from the provisional modes of organization which comprise the successive formation of each corporeal state.

The successive and changing nature of corporeal states is at odds with the everyday experience of the embodied subject embedded in the phenomenological point of view. Klossowski outlines two quite distinct orders in order to explain these two perspectives: that of the body – conceived as a singular succession of corporeal states – and that which belongs to the domain of human understanding. The difference between these two orders suggests that our understanding and interpretation of the body are not a simple matter. The problem for us is that our understanding is constrained by language, a mediating semantic system Klossowski calls the "code of everyday signs".[26] The code of signs is the very technology of thought: we can only think "as a product of the code".[27] The code of signs is an interpretation of Nietzsche's work on the relation between consciousness and language.[28] It reflects Nietzsche's view that language is a generalized means of exchange/understanding. On the one hand then, consciousness is founded on the sociality of language, which is geared towards an intersubjective, shared means of understanding; on the other hand, a body arises in the particular instance, as a singular resolution of contestatory impulses. According to Klossowski, these two registers – social and singular – come from and serve very different interests. The problem for consciousness is that it must understand the serial specificity of corporeal states through the social medium of language.[29] The "deciphering of the messages transmitted by the impulses" on the part of the subject offers a necessarily distorted conception of the body's 'messages', which are distilled via the code of signs.[30] The hermeneutic function of the code of signs is to assimilate the body's activities under the aegis of the subject, thereby to produce a coherent form of subjective experience. Subjectivity is thus founded on a corporeal misrecognition. Bound to the 'herd' perspective embedded in the code of signs, it is destined to miss its own constitutive and dynamic minutiae. The body, on the other hand, offers its own unique perspective, one which shifts with each new arrangement of impulses. What Klossowski makes clear is the sense in which the code of signs is unable to capture the changing face of corporeal life.[31] The body participates in a quite distinct form of corporeal semiosis, following its own semiotic of impulses, towards corporeal differentiation.

Klossowski's work on the difference between the body and its conscious apprehension marks a point of departure for Deleuze's *Nietzsche and Philosophy*. Deleuze incorporates many of Klossowski's insights regarding the breach between subjectivity and corporeality through seeking their explanation in an explication of force (an alternative to the term, impulse). Deleuze introduces the Nietzschean body as a corrective to the philosophical prioritization of consciousness.[32] The body is not the servant of consciousness here, nor its intertwining. Rather, the body is the superior formation, a mode of becoming to be valued apart from the workings of consciousness. According to Deleuze, the body's activity lies in the provisional resolution of its constituent and constituting forces. A body can arise within many registers:

> Every relation of forces constitutes a body – whether it is chemical, biological, social or political.[33]

Deleuze emphasizes the body's mobility through denying its status as any kind of fixed ground or site of struggle.[34] The Nietzschean body is neither an identity nor a substance that undergoes change, rather a series of changes that arrive at the putative identity of the body/self. Nietzsche treats the body as shorthand for a plethora of interrelated elements, "whose interaction the thing we call 'body' is the best simile".[35] This approach offers a mobile, provisional and transitory account of corporeal formation.

The body in Nietzsche thus destabilizes rather than supplements subjectivity. The body is not a stable, well-organized identity to which we can attribute agency – an embodied substitute for disembodied subjectivity – nor is it a stable identity which moves. Rather, its moving gives a body, a coagulation of forces, a temporary and provisional equilibrium. The body signals this momentary gathering of forces. How to think the momentary in this context? Conceptually, this relates to the way the notion of position sometimes functions within dance. Positions are conceptual, heuristic moments, a means of pinning down that which is in motion. They can be useful gathering points for sensation, recognition and stability, offering a temporary holding pattern, a chance to catch up with the moving body. But their identity is itself in flux. The temptation with respect to dance is to reduce movement to a series of positions (fixed identities), devaluing that which happens in between. This attitude can be observed in motion, in situations where dancers can be seen moving between a series of positions, without paying attention to the in-between moments that make such arrival possible. This way of thinking and sensing dancing promotes the position at the expense of the transition, rather than understanding dancing as itself transitional. Brian Massumi criticizes the way in which the position is privileged within cultural theory at the expense of transformation, such that:

> The very notion of movement as qualitative transformation is lacking. There is "displacement," but no transformation; it is as if the body simply leaps from one definition to the next.[36]

Yet there is a sense in which *all* moving is transitional. Such is the nature of movement. Steve Paxton's *Small Dance* draws attention to this state of affairs, opening up the dancer's perception to the micro-adjustments implicit in stillness. Trisha Brown's *Watermotor* likewise foregrounds the transitional quality of its moving, never quite crystallizing into place, allowing initiations to overlap as they play themselves out. And yet, transitoriness extends beyond its fine expression within post-modern choreography. Classical ballet equally requires the management of dynamic instability – subtle shifts of weight, breathing, muscular textures, which change over time – in order to achieve the held, visual clarity of, for example, an arabesque. The position is thus conceptual, perhaps experiential, but it is not achieved at the expense of moving. Rather, it occurs in virtue of it. The momentary is similarly conceived as a stabilizing gesture, a scan, a provisional equilibrium formed in the midst of movement that occurs in "the passing moment".[37] The Nietzschean conception of the body is thus far more dynamic than its phenomenological counterpart. It is a mobile formation, a momentary resolution between the multiple, changing forces of the world, an open-ended site of biological difference and corporeal differentiation.

The plurality of force

Force is one way of conceptualizing the many factors that comprise the body in the course of movement. Force is a dynamic concept, one which assumes multiple roles. Nietzsche writes of force as the force of becoming:

> And do you know what "the world" is to me? Shall I show you it in my mirror? This world: a monster of force, without beginning, without end, a fixed, iron quantity of forces which grows neither larger nor smaller, which doesn't exhaust but only transforms itself, ... as force everywhere,

as a play of forces and force-waves simultaneously one and "many", accumulating here while diminishing there.[38]

In the context of dance, the notion of force stands for the multiplicity of tendencies found in movement. Forces are virtual tendencies, whose emergent character depends upon their eventual articulation with other modes of virtual tendency. Force takes shape in relation to other forces. Because force is not singular but relational, the field of future possibility is not contained in any one force (as a predetermined identity; bent leg, straight leg and so on) but depends upon the way in which forces combine over time. The field is itself in process, arising from those practices which give rise to its constituent elements. Conceptually singular, force exists in the plural, to be found in its concrete elaboration with other forces.[39] Depending on their context, the tendencies of force can also be referred to as drives, impulses or instincts, even thoughts, feelings or affects.[40]

Forces are heterogeneous and polymorphic. They hail from multiple sources. All kinds of force, ecological, biological, physiological, economic, cultural, social, kinaesthetic and habitual, enter into relation in the course of movement, which would not occur but for their complex and interrelated interactions. Dance is a field of selection within this wider field of relations of force – cultural, social, historical, cosmological. The body equally enters into and emerges from this complex mix of relations, conditions, modes of organization and reorganization.

Movement and mastery

A distinctive feature of the Nietzschean approach is the view that the body's constituent forces are not equal, nor do they come together in a cooperative fashion. Nietzsche refers to asymmetrical relations between forces as hierarchical modes of order or rank, which involve relations of command and obedience, play and counter-play.[41] Impulses contradict one another inasmuch as they represent different directions or pathways, movements not yet formed. Forces thus compete for different things, different kinds of resolution. Over time, their mutual tensions find a provisional resolution, and in so doing, transit towards new relations of force, new tensions, new histories. Whatever occurs does so, for Nietzsche, because some forces (or sets of force) *master* others. According to this mode of thought, movement expresses mastery. Movement occurs because force *imposes* itself upon other forces, using them, drawing upon them, mastering them, to generate an action or event; using the floor to push off, drawing on traditional idiom in order to stage a contemporary departure, creating phrase material through deconstruction and reconstruction, resisting habit, to enable new movement possibilities. Contestatory relations of force yield a contingent and passing resolution of evolving potential trends, a resolution between tendencies achieved through the ascendency of one tendency at the expense of the others. A snapshot of that resolution reveals one force commanding others, expressing certain active qualities found through forming a relation with and drawing upon other forces. The activity of force is not the elimination of other, competing possibilities, rather a mode of interaction with them.

The hierarchical conception of force analyses relations of force by distinguishing between the roles played by each participant force. This is to be found in motion, as a quality of their concrete becoming. Deleuze writes:

> In a body the superior or dominant forces are known as *active* and the inferior or dominated forces are known as reactive.[42]

The difference between active and reactive force concerns the way in which forces function in relation to one another. Bodies form because forces resolve their differences in certain ways, thereby to produce a new corporeal formation out of the old. In that sense, the body is a form of movement. An action occurs because one force exerts itself upon other, selected forces which, for their part, react, respond and accommodate. Forces are neither inherently active nor reactive but become so in the context of their joint becoming. The notion of active and reactive allows us to differentiate between the different roles played by forces in the particular instance. Nietzsche characterizes active force in relation to the expression of "aggressive, expansive, re-interpreting, re-directing and formative powers".[43] Active force differs from reactive force because it expresses mastery over that which differs. Deleuze asks:

> What is active? – reaching out for power (VP II 43/WP 657). Appropriating, possessing, subjugating, dominating – these are the characteristics of active force. To appropriate means to impose forms, to create forms by exploiting circumstances.[44]

Reactive forces respond to the initiations of active force, offering the means whereby active force is able to make its mark. Interdependent yet distinct, the two qualities of force (active and reactive) together provoke a change in circumstance. Dancing embodies this state of affairs inasmuch as it requires the ongoing and shifting mastery of multiple factors, whether gravity and weight, muscular textures, relations with other bodies or by drawing upon the quasi-givenness of movement material, such as a form, or score. Circumstance represents these many facilitating and contextualizing factors. Circumstance provides the (reactive) means whereby the activity of force is able to emerge. Mastery engages circumstance, its field of operation. Mastery masters but it is also dependent upon this field of exertion, which for its part, maintains its own interlocutory character – its textures, resilience, constraints and manner of cooperation. The activities of force do not eradicate other forces, rather they make use of their characteristic tendencies, drawing upon their very difference.[45] Active and reactive forces are both necessary factors in the production of movement. It is in this sense that Nietzsche and Deleuze speak of the pathos of distance (reminiscent perhaps of Merleau-Ponty's notion of the chiasm (écart) in *The Visible and the Invisible*).[46]

Force of circumstance

According to this mode of thought, dancing is the expression of mastery upon a field of circumstance. Movement consists of an active component, which works circumstance, and a reactive component, which manifests itself through the ways in which circumstance enters movement. The two aspects are intertwined, for mastery is tied to the circumstances of the body writ large. Martha Graham once remarked that it takes 10 years to make a dancer.[47] Those 10 years and more are to be found in and around the body, in its facility, background and milieu. Provenance comes into play through becoming a circumstance of movement, via the accumulation of training and technique or when an element of the field enters into the body's activities. Mastery selects its circumstance, rendering it available for movement. The greater the mastery, the finer the grasp of its circumstance. The availability of circumstance is a measure (and function) of the mastery found in motion. This requires a degree of sensitivity (and therefore affectivity) between forces. Active force must yield in order to work the resilience of the ground, must soften sufficiently to register and activate the shifting textures of the body, and must draw on the right amount of resident strength in the legs to push out of the floor.[48] The quality of the dancing – for example, its management of gravity and weight – determines the degree to which and how the floor enters the movement. Circumstance is not given then (as though the floor must enter the body in a particular way) so much as made available *through* an activity which both embraces and works circumstance. The distinctive footwork of Korean dance works the floor, the kinaesthetic elements that guide its execution, the temporal field, and where the body is at, to enunciate its mastery of circumstance. That which ensues does so in virtue of force forging certain kinds of relation with other, facilitating (or resistant yet compliant) forces: the foot descends in its own time, working with and against gravity, playing with time; the plié descends towards the floor, giving in to gravity, while maintaining its shape, opening hip and knee joints so as to enable the bending that occurs beneath an erect torso. Different forces come into play in the plié, cooperating, allowing, driving, requiring, enabling. They compete insofar as they represent a disjunctive set of possibilities or tendencies: different qualities of movement engage force differently, whether an overly muscular rendition of a plié, one that gives in to gravity on the way down, holds onto or releases the breath, softens where it can and so on. In each case, active force is expressed in the way in which the action-plié works its various participant elements: muscularity, gravity, technique, momentary qualities and tendencies found in and beyond the body. Habit also clearly comes into play – providing habitual modes of organization that pre-dispose towards a characteristic usage of force. Established habit can be framed as a circumstance of the body, as the

tendency towards certain kinds of movement. Habit also illustrates the potentially resistive force of circumstance. It illustrates the sense in which mastery
does not eliminate that which is different but rather works that very difference.
Such is the force of circumstance.

Kinaesthetic custom (cultural habit) likewise speaks to the ways in
which for example the circumstance of the floor is to be utilized. Custom
privileges certain manners of engagement and makes aesthetic determin-
ations as to its preferred movement intentions/outcomes. The dancing that
occurs within these milieus works in relation to these pre-conceptions, yet
at the same time must engage circumstance to achieve its goals. The performative nature of dancing must perforce embrace and work with the
force of circumstance, which for its part exerts its own reactive riposte to
activity. Klossowski writes of "organized" impulses being "put to use by
a new body" in the context of a "search for new conditions".[49] Movement
represents that search for new conditions, drawing on modes of organization past, manifesting their potential for mastery in that which follows.
What the new signifies here is the difference implied by the passage of
forces from one formation to another. The differentiation of the body from
its former state is itself a form of movement, utilizing the past in the course
of corporeal articulation.

Force of history

Social and political forces also enter the mix. They are brought to bear on the
bodies of dancers, the interests and concerns of choreographers, the sustainability of tradition, the desires of practitioners, audiences, dance communities
and the influence of wider cultural and national interests. Their emergence
and field of operation depend upon the ways in which circumstance is selected
within the dance: Social forces may be resisted, countered, accommodated
and/or transformed (or confirmed, entrenched and perpetuated). They can
also be activated in the making of movement. To return to the case of Korean
modern dance by way of illustration,[50] Judy Van Zile and Sang Mi Park discuss the colonial context within which Ch'oe Sŭng-hŭi made work, performed
and toured.[51] Van Zile points out the multiplicity of factors, kinaesthetic, aesthetic and political that formed the circumstances of early twentieth-century
Korean dance:

> The links between dance and place and time in Korea during the 1920s
> and 1930s clearly reflect the multiplicity and complexity of concurrent
> socio-political and cultural events. Further, as pointed out by Japanese
> and Korean art curator Ken Voss, despite the darkness brought on by
> the Japanese Empire, the colonial era in Korea was a period of "great
> cultural dynamism". It can be argued that dance and Ch'oe Sŭng-hŭi were
> significant players in that dynamism.[52]

How to theorize that dynamism in relation to active and reactive forces? Van Zile lays out a complex set of social and political circumstances which comprised the colonial milieu within which Ch'oe Sŭng-hŭi exerted an aesthetic dynamism. A tension is depicted here between the domination of colonizing forces on the one hand, and their affirmative cultural deployment on the other. In the case of early twentieth-century Korean dance, Japanese colonization was a key factor of social and political life. Ch'oe Sŭng-hŭi functioned within these circumstances, whilst also drawing upon Korean dance culture. She travelled to Japan, where she studied with dancer, Ishii Baku, a key figure of Japanese dance modernism, subsequently performing across Asia, Europe and the US. The interpretive question concerns the identification of active and reactive moments within and in relation to these events. For example, Park traces the sense in which Ch'oe was orientalized for an American audience, identifying the imposition of colonizing modes of spectatorship on Ch'oe's work. Could it be said that this response is fundamentally reactive, an interlocutory resistance and response to Ch'oe's dancing? Or was it rather imposing an active, orientalizing interpretation upon the circumstance of her work? The difference between these interpretations depends upon which elements are taken to prevail, and which are thought to be subordinated. Van Zile offers an active interpretation of Ch'oe's choreographic output, arguing that her dancing expressed an active relation towards its circumstances to articulate a distinctive, Korean modernism. The suggestion here is that Ch'oe's choreography worked its colonial circumstance towards a form of kinaesthetic difference.[53] Then there is the question of Ch'oe's kinaesthetic provenance. The kinaesthetic residue of working with Ishii would have provided an embodied kinaesthetic which included a mediated form of Mary Wigman's German Expressionism which, according to Van Zile, informed much of Ch'oe's work.[54] To think these factors in relation to force is to draw out that which constituted Ch'oe's milieu, and to seek the activation of circumstance within her choreographic and performative practice, its reception and impact. Van Zile highlights the activity inherent Ch'oe's work, drawing on Korean traditional culture, the complex modernity of Korea under Japanese rule, and the provenance of her own dancing, developed between Korea and Japan, to suggest that Ch'oe introduced foreign audiences to "*her* version of what constituted Korean dance, a version that embraced both a sense of modernity and Korean-ness" in the midst of prevailing colonizing and modernizing tendencies.[55] Mark Franko's notion of the 'return' (within dance modernism) could prove fruitful here, as a way of tracing the role of traditional choreographies in Ch'oe's dance in a modernist context.[56] Bruno Latour's notion of hybrid formation could equally be brought to bear on Ch'oe's distinctive conjunction of these disparate practices.[57] Van Zile shows a number of photographs of Ch'oe, which appear to range between European expressionism and traditional Korean dance, suggesting a mélange of origins and styles selected and featured in the form of the solo dance.[58]

It may not always be clear in the given instance whether social and political forces express an active or reactive role. Circumstances are complex, and their manner of engagement can be both ambiguous and indeterminate. For example, theatrical expressions of Australian Indigenous dance can be seen in a number of ways: as expressing the force of cultural tradition in relatively autonomous terms, or as a mode of resistance to the forces of colonization, cultural devaluation and suppression, or as appropriating and reinterpreting western aesthetic values through situating work in relation to proscenium arch modes of spectatorship or as a vehicle of dominant western aesthetic values or a fluctuating mixture of all these possibilities. These questions are often posed in relation to the emergence of Aboriginal fine art.[59] Any purported resolution of these questions raises further issues of cultural authority around issues of interpretation, criticism, critique and analysis. To take up a position on these matters is itself a matter of force working force, on questions of interpretation and representation, evaluation and authority, politics and resistance, cultural identity and aesthetic narration. It matters which corporeal formations take up these questions, which forms of cultural authority are invoked and according to what kinds of perspective.[60]

The issue of western hegemony and the pluralization of historical time raised in Chapter 4 in relation to Korean dance could be framed in terms of relations of force, between competing conceptions of modernity and modernism, through mutations of tradition that are undecidably internal or western, and the competing authorization of critical judgement, whether local or foreign. Expressions of authority, judgement and interpretation form a discursive tissue around dance practice. The Nietzschean approach to force sees their formation as a complex of active and reactive relationships, whose occurrence itself constitutes a mode of corporeal formation (remembering that the Deleuzian body can be political, biological or social).

Social and political factors also impact upon our concept of what a dancing body is able to do, bringing into relief socially normative presumptions that pre-figure the 'proper' dancing body. For example Brenda Dixon Gottschild details the norms of exclusion that call into question the 'proper' status of the black dancing body in the US, by invoking an "unnamed, 'normal' standard – white dance".[61] Gottschild focuses on the ways in which the black dancing body has been produced within the US, to draw out the politics that condition the positioning and provenance of dancers, white and black. These are the circumstances within which Ishmael Houston-Jones curated two seasons of performance in New York, 30 years apart, around the participation of black bodies in postmodern, "non-mainstream" dance, in part to reterritorialize assumptions around whiteness and the postmodern but also, according to Eva Asentewaa, to broaden "the aesthetic possibilities for Black dancers while making room for black perspectives within the white-predominant avant-garde".[62] Houston-Jones' work (both performative and curatorial) could be posed in relation to, but also as a reconfiguration of, the circumstances of the black dancing body. He joins a cohort of artists whose work takes up and reterritorializes the prevailing political force of racialized dance culture. Scholars also draw out the affirmative component of these works. For example Takiyah Nur Amin speaks of centring Back Dance in order to let it "enjoy its ontological status as a foundational mode of creative possibility".[63] From this point of view, Black Dance activates its circumstances towards the production of new forms of life: "Black Dance as an answer to Black life".[64]

The entry of differently abled bodies upon the scene of concert dance has contested and altered the forces of selection and exclusion that presume to limit dance to certain kinds of body, opening up new ways of moving and perceiving dance, expanding the field of possibility for what a dancing body can do.[65] Differently abled bodies do not merely dance 'just like' conventional bodies, mastering force to the same ends, they utilize force differently, select different forces, to achieve new forms of movement, in turn challenging normative conceptions (themselves formed from relations of force) around who can dance. This is well expressed by dancer Melinda Smith, in Dianne Reid's recent work, *Dance Interrogations* (2015).[66] In the course of the dance, Smith manages the intense instability associated with cerebral palsy, finding balance in relation to sudden shifts of weight and muscular tone. At one point, Smith abandons her chair as a stabilizing device, so as to set up a circumstance of extreme, dynamic instability which she negotiates in motion. Smith's virtuosic management of these muscular variations is quite specific to the challenges of her own corporeal situation. In that sense, it could be said that her dancing selects and utilizes the force(s) of circumstance affiliated with her corporeality, actively working those forces that pertain to her bodily situation. Her dancing recalls the fine nuance of the tightrope walker, who must at each and every moment deal with the dynamic instability of the rope. In some circumstances, this has a knock-on effect on other participating bodies, opening up new abilities in those formerly seen as 'already able'. Smith's remarkable dancing not only opens the spectator's understanding of what a body can do, it also provokes new capacities in fellow performer, Reid. *Dance Interrogations* features a duet between Smith and Reid, also featured in the documentary, *Nothing but Bones in the Way.*[67]

As Reid lies on her back with her legs in the air, Smith lowers her body onto Reid. Reid now has to deal with the diversity of muscular impulses and adjustments emanating from Smith's body, finding equilibrium through managing change from moment to moment. By joining forces, Reid has the opportunity to find new ways of managing change, in the process, developing new forms of skill, especially in relation to matters of balance and weight-bearing.

Christel Stalpaert looks at the potential for a work to provoke something new in its audience, here, around age-based conceptions of the 'proper' dancing body. Stalpaert discusses Katarzyna Kozrya's *Rite of Spring*, as a work that contests the idealization of youth embedded in earlier canonical versions, most notably in the work of choreographer Maurice Béjart. Stalpaert argues that Kozrya's installation reterritorializes the dancing body, beyond its "pre-programmed representations, form and functions" so as to "force the

Figure 5.1 Melinda Smith and Dianne Reid, *Nothing but Bones in the Way* (documentary), courtesy of director Dianne Reid.

spectator to think the yet unthought".[68] For Stalpaert, the *Rite of Spring* takes up prevailing (western) norms around age-based dancing as its circumstance, producing different iterations of the dancing body. She writes:

> In Kozyra's *Rite of Spring*, the spectator must again and again devise new procedures to free affect from personal feeling, perception from common perception, thinking from common sense.[69]

These shifts, regarding age and ability, race and culture, represent new configurations of force, new understandings of what dancing can be when opened up to a greater diversity of bodies within the scene of dance.

Force and the will to power

Thus far, force has been conceived in the following terms: forces are found in relation to one another. Their relations enable the formation of things, the coagulation of forces, which arise through their modes of alignment with other forces. Relations of force express a mode of mastery, of force selecting and working force. In the context of dance, this is found through the ways in which active force works the circumstances of dance, including that of the body. The notion of force speaks to the activity of dancing, to the ways in which the dance draws upon a wide range of factors, orienting them, while making use of them in the course of movement. A foot which pushes off the ground utilizes the texture of the floor, the musculature and sinews of the foot, the weight of the body falling through the foot, its connection into the hip joint, the subtle counter-balances continually playing themselves out in movement. Softening the body enables the muscles to find release; inhibition of habit works habit, engaging and redirecting its tendencies; kinaesthetic traditions and narrative heritages are mined to produce new performative arrangements. A broader, more fulsome picture would also incorporate the many relations and networks of social, political and cultural forces that situate and make possible these activities and their articulation within a larger ecology of circumstance. Such are the fluctuations and variations of relations of force. Michel Haar speaks of forces "forever in conflict, alternately imposing themselves and subordinating themselves".[70] The ontological conception of force is open to far-reaching analyses of that which enters into the activity of dance, and the role of the body within it. To a certain extent, it explains the variety of approaches that can be taken towards dance – their various emphases on subjectivity, representation, language, politics and discourse, as well as physiology, technique, training and tradition. For these differing emphases represent distinct kinds of focus on the variety and fields of force which undergird and make possible particular modes of practice. The body traces the contours of these shifting relationships. It is not the agent behind their movement, rather the momentary, passing (and enduring) modes of organization which they engender. Becoming traces the movement from and between one set of forces towards another, between one multiplicity and another. While this movement is not ascribed to an agent, it nonetheless exhibits a kind of (embedded) agency or internal dynamic, which Nietzsche calls the will to power.[71] In a famous passage, Nietzsche speaks of the will to power as a necessary supplement to the notion of force.[72] Although force and the will to power are conceptually distinct, the will to power is internal to relations of force, an element of their relationship. It is embedded within them, an aspect of force but not reducible to it. The will to power enhances the essentially active picture formed out of the activity of force upon force. It complements the differential nature of force, tracing their dynamic reconfiguration, their intensification towards new forms of difference. The will to power represents all that is active in life, its proliferation and diversification. It underlies the body's capacity for recalibration, its incorporation "of the most diverse life".[73] The will to power discerns the active interplay of organizations, structures, habits and new formations that make up the body in movement.

Will to power as a principle of synthesis

The bipartisan nature of relational force situates this sense of impulsive agency in their differences, in the way forces relate and resolve. To that end, Deleuze describes the will to power as "synthetic".[74] The will to power is a polymorphous principle of synthesis or "bipolarity" because it is nested within relations of force, in the many ways in which active force works its modes of reaction, and in reaction's response to such activity.[75] This is its distinction from force; that it is a principle of difference, to be found amongst the plurality of forces. To that extent, it embraces a duality of perspective, the point of view of active force and that of its reaction.[76] The will to power encompasses the differing perspectives of force, their characteristic thrust as exerted upon one another, a "moving diversity of perspectives", continually producing new diversities.[77] The will to power is the working of difference towards new forms of difference. Alphonso Lingis writes of the will to power as an "original difference",[78] as the "differential element of force".[79] It is tempting to think force apart from the will to power, as a series of singular entities which are severally articulated prior to their conjunction. But force only emerges in relation: "To Nietzsche, what is unformed is not matter, but force, is not passive, but chaotic".[80] The chaotic indeterminacy of forces (their unformed potential) takes shape according to their selection, relation and passage from one arrangement to another. Their shape is itself a matter of folding and unfolding along a series of divergent and diverging states. We on the other hand tend to assimilate differences, working becoming into being, difference into identity. Lingis writes:

> Thus Being, *physis*, incessant unfolding of a show of ever new, ever divergent appearances – continual differentiation – is also continual *logos*, continual assembling, assimilation of all that appears ... To comprehend is to see the identical ... in the different.[81]

Nietzschean thought sometimes avails itself of the notion of a 'mask'.[82] The mask is the veneer of constancy, of sameness, a bridge which covers over the movement implicit in becoming. It enables the different to be perceived as the one.[83]

Will to power as a principle of transformation

The concept of the will to power reveals being as itself a mode of transience, as that which has and will become.[84] The will to power is thus a protean principle of change. It is the genetic impulse found in movement. As the generative element of becoming, the will to power moves between one arrangement of force to another. The will to power expresses the specific, internal, immanent qualities of dynamic transformation inherent in all that which becomes. There are myriad wills to power; emergent, relational, generative modes of self-differentiation. Their singularity calls for individual interpretation and analysis of each particular dynamic. Nietzsche's work is quite occupied with the variety of ways in which the will to power produces change. Genealogical analysis traces the shift in relations of force that underlie the givenness (being) of phenomena. Although there is an element of growth, overcoming and self-differentiation in the dynamic shifts afforded through the will to power, the will to power is also able to achieve pathological modes of inversion, which express power through its renunciation. These pathologies belong specifically to the sphere of human being, in the form of morality, *ressentiment*, nihilism and asceticism.[85] To that end, Deleuze discerns two qualities of the will to power in Nietzsche, affirmative and negative. These qualities resonate with the two types of force, active and reactive, but that the will to power is a transformative power: it traces the *movement* from one arrangement of active and reactive force to another. The qualities of the will to power are thus qualities of becoming:

> Affirmation is not action but the power of becoming active, *becoming active* personified. Negation is not simple reaction but a *becoming reactive*. It is as if affirmation and negation were both immanent and transcendent in relation to action and reaction; out of the web of forces they make up the chain of becoming.[86]

Genealogical analysis traces these movements of force, their joint interpretation of the chaotic forces of the world.

Plasticity in the will to power

Deleuze writes of the will to power as "an essentially *plastic* principle that is no wider than what it conditions, that changes itself with the conditioned and determines itself in each case along with what it determines".[87] The suggestion is that the will to power draws force from the world, that its becoming ensues from the qualities of its constituent forces. The will to power is indebted to its component forces, each iteration a question of the differential and relational impact of force upon force. The plasticity of the will to power marks a point of difference from law-like notions of causality, in that its generative function is quite specific and singular. Hence its plasticity, the capacity to address the qualities of force inherent in this particular passing moment. Plasticity implies a kind of sensitivity towards an event's constituent forces, towards their coming together as they do. That forces forge a relationship, however hierarchized, signals an ability to affect one another, to exert or respond. Nietzsche wrote of the "feeling of power".[88] Feeling in this context is not an experience to be had by a subject but an indicator of the dynamic interchange between forces, of their capacity to affect and influence one another. Relations of force require proximity (the capacity to enter into relationship), but also difference, the "pathos of distance", reminiscent of Merleau-Ponty's work on the chiasmic nature of the flesh, but without recourse to a subject who feels.[89] Feeling (in the will to power) is expressed dynamically, in the fact of forces coming together and in their subsequent moving. In that sense, agency and affect collaborate: the agency which generates; the affectivity which underlies generativity. Terms usually reserved for the plane of the subject (affect, sensibility, sensation) are here imported into an alternative register of becoming.[90]

In a Spinozan gesture, Deleuze conjoins capacity with its expression: the capacity of forces to affect one another, felt within the will to power, is expressed in the sensible becomings of force. We encounter capacity through the concrete encounters of force; how certain forces engage and work others, how the multiplicity of forces are able to generate movement, what works, what feels, what's felt, what kinds of response enable this kind of move. For Deleuze then, the will to power:

> manifests itself as the sensibility of force; the differential element of forces manifests itself as their differential sensibility.[91]

Taken together, the intertwining of force and will to power offers an alternative conception of agency and affect. Agency arises in the formation of a relation of forces, through the mastery inherent in active force and the interlocutory character of its reactions.

Virtuosity in the will to power

Deleuze connects Nietzschean philosophy with Spinoza on two counts. Firstly, that the capacity for being affected is felt through its expression: affectivity is to be seen in the relation of force to force and not prior to it.[92] And secondly, the greater the affectivity of a body, the greater the power. A body which emerges out of the fine workings of force, which expresses a delicate and dedicated mastery of its circumstance expresses great power in this Spinozan sense. Such an approach which deems affectivity to be the active expression of force reframes the field of sensibility, away from the field of subjective apprehension and towards that of active engagement. Deleuze writes:

> Similarly for Nietzsche, the capacity for being affected is not necessarily a passivity but an *affectivity*, a sensibility, a sensation. It is in this sense that Nietzsche, even before elaborating the concept of the will to power and giving it its full significance, was already speaking of a *feeling of power*.[93]

The notion of the will to power's sense and expression of affective feeling (and capacity) lends itself to a particular notion of virtuosity in dance. Haar writes of strength in relation to the will to power:

> When affirmative and strong, the Will to Power takes upon itself variety, difference and plurality.[94]

Skilful dancing can be construed along these lines, as the informed manipulation of divergent forces. Virtuosic dancing takes up a great diversity of forces, orienting them towards the finest movement, the "grand simplification that perfect mastery can produce".[95] This is dancing that takes up all that a body has to offer, as it draws force from the universe. Such dancing avails itself of that which each particular style selects – the audience, timing, breath, surrender, relation to self, relation to others, release, muscular control, focus, energy, spiritual connection, serendipity, and draws upon these forces to produce movement. While virtuosity ensues from the particular kinaesthetic selections of the field, and therefore has many faces, in general terms, it takes up the plurality of forces and orients them in movement: to suggest the pure line of the arabesque, to stretch time, to open up to the unexpected, to bring the multiplicity of the corporeal along, incorporating and appropriating, executing, deploying and orienting.

Although virtuosity is kinaesthetically and culturally specific, the notion of strength in the will to power, of embracing the plurality of the moment to produce movement, raises the stakes in any field of practice. What is it that makes for great dancing? It could be what Haar calls grand simplification, evoking the forms and lines of classical ballet's movement landscape. Or it could be a question of engagement in the dancing itself, of keeping the field of possibility alive through bringing forces into proximity, into the affective reach of movement's will to power. Many improvisers speak of being in the moment, of finding ways to open the body up to the multiplicity of possibilities that lie in the path of movement. Russell Dumas evokes a sense of variety, difference and plurality through resisting the tendency to foreclose movement possibility in the execution of set choreography. Dumas posits the great dancer as the one who is able to summon an expanded field of virtual possibility, a horizon which clusters around that which actually emerges. Dumas' account of performative virtuosity resonates with Chapter 4's description of elastic temporality in traditional Korean dance. Although theorized in different terms, Dumas' perspective and the Korean example could be posed in relation to Massumi's notion of the inseparable "charge of indeterminacy carried by a body".[96] For Massumi, the body's openness to difference arises through an incorporeal dynamic, an abstract element that is itself transformed in movement. Thought in these terms, we might suggest that virtuosity engages this duality, of material emergence and its attendant incorporeal dynamic.[97] To evoke or keep open a horizon of movement possibility, without foreclosing that which follows, is to work with the "abstract" potential of a body, that shifting field of possibility associated with but not reducible to actual movement.[98] Virtuosity in this way of thinking plays the indeterminacy of the body through a transformative resolution of its embodied forces, thereby evoking and engaging the incorporeal dimensions of dancing though the dynamics of corporeal formation.

Dumas used to recount the example of the mature Margot Fonteyn who was able to evoke an aura and suggestion of greater possibility and extension with respect to her poses and held positions. To be able to evoke a horizon, a virtual field of different trajectories, while nonetheless following a path, brings a certain aliveness to dancing with the suggestion that more could happen. Not to anticipate (by pre-empting), and yet to orient force, to produce a field of availability *out* of a field of availability. Korean traditional dance follows an analogous path, of keeping the relation between the dancer and the music alive in the exquisite hover of a foot above the floor, a delight

Figure 5.2 Russell Dumas, artistic director, Dance Exchange, courtesy of the artist.

shared with the audience who themselves represent a breadth of available forces. From a performative point of view, one can also think about opening up to the multiplicity of forces in the present moment, to resist the tendency to be overly teleological by staying alive to what's happening right now. The notion of presence in dance signifies an openness to the plurality of forces which gather around the momentary body. Linda Sastradipraja encourages dancers to maximize the greatest range of incipient sensations as they arise in movement rather than mechanistically foreclose around a normative conception of what ought to happen or what ought to be felt. Such a practice works towards an increase of affective capacity, felt in the dancing as it emerges. This could be thought of as an ongoing project of maximizing variety, of enjoying difference whilst simultaneously giving way to a series of expressions of the will to power, that is, whilst following the path of making movement. Another aspect of embracing variety, difference and plurality is not second guessing movement by trying to 'control' it but rather opening up to its eventfulness, activity and aliveness. The body thereby becomes through performing rather than functioning as 'the one' who directs performance. Mastery belongs to the moment rather than to some implied puppet master.

The Nietzschean account offers a distinctive take on virtuosity, as that which expresses an affirmative and strong will to power, through managing plurality, variety and difference. Virtuosity turns multiplicity into fine dancing. There are as many forms of virtuosity as there are kinaesthetic fields and their exponents. Their common element is breadth, selection and the orientation of force taken to the max. In this context, this means something like the maximization of difference, the expansion of affective capacity and the wide engagement of plurality. What is great about great dancing is its ability to keep multiplicity in play, to draw upon and deploy the width and breadth of force. If virtuosic dancing embraces difference, it also turns difference to its own ends. The will to power *orients* force. It does so according to the selections and values of the particular kinaesthetic field within which it finds expression. In this sense, virtuosity is a cultural concern, the product of a kinaesthetic context that is itself articulated within a wider social and cultural milieu.[99]

Towards an active interpretation of dance

Deleuze's adaptation of Nietzsche's distinction between action and reaction, affirmation and negation offers a fine qualification of the becomings of force – in principle. In practice, the discernment of these qualities in action is complex, in part due to the bipolar nature of relational force but also because corporeal formation represents a shifting terrain of myriad constitutive forces. The qualitative character of force, will to power and their joint becoming make sense of Nietzsche's claim that "there are no facts, only interpretations".[100] This is not because interpretation is a mere subjectivism or relativism but because interpretation is the wrenching of perspective out of the impulsive morass. If perspective ensues from the workings of force, generating new perspectives and new modes of resolution, then interpretation must be situated (and implicated) within these workings, as itself the production of perspective. Nietzsche sees interpretation as an expression of the will to power, an ontological rather than hermeneutic production: "One mustn't ask: 'So *who* interprets?' –instead, the interpreting, as a form of the will to power, itself has existence (but not as a 'being'; rather as a process, as a *becoming* ...".[101] Lingis writes:

> What interprets is not a contemplative spirit both impotent to act on the things and omnipotent to charge them with its meanings; what interprets is power, Will to Power, and there can be no such thing as absolute power, solitary power. And if it takes power to interpret, to give sense to, to

orient, it is because the thing being interpreted is itself a force, affirming itself, generating divergent perspectives.[102]

Deleuze's own reading of Nietzsche can be seen as the imposition of perspective on the force of Nietzschean thought, one which highlights the role of force within becoming.[103] Its resultant focus on force and the will to power charges all becomings with a sense of their differences, transformations and emergent qualities. Turning these emphases towards dance is equally an interpretive gesture, a reconfiguration of thought towards the moving body.

The notion of force and the will to power offer a picture of dance thought as a series of interrelated activities and transformations. A further elaboration would need to discern the ways in which forces function in the particular instance, paying attention to their character and quality, provenance and function. There are two ways in which this might occur within the Nietzschean landscape: first, as a form of attention towards their concrete elaboration, a specific reading which might identify an action's active and reactive forces, including the ways in which active force selects and works its particular circumstance. A second mode of Nietzschean engagement assumes a form of distance, to gain perspective upon the differentiation of forces, with a view to discern their patterns of engagement and consequent types of becoming. The latter represents the search for an understanding of the different types of relationship of force, and their subsequent modes of becoming, called typology. Typology critically identifies and evaluates forms of existence by seeking their manner of becoming. According to Deleuze, Nietzsche created "a whole typology to distinguish active, acted and reactive forces and to analyse their varying combinations".[104] Typology is a way of approaching phenomena with a view to drawing out their manner of resolution. Deleuze lauds Nietzsche's rejection of what he calls "personalist" modes of interpretation in favour of a focus on the event.[105] The event is a mode of becoming. It consists of a signature relation of forces, a movement. Insofar as these relations achieve a certain pattern and relation of active and reactive forces, they form a type, a type of becoming, which is in turn intimately connected to the will to power.

As we will see in the following chapter, typological analysis not only draws upon the distinction between active and reactive forces, it also seeks their manner of combination and therefore becoming. In the process, a difference in kind is discerned between forces that together produce action (and therefore corporeal formation) and those which combine to create the interior landscape of subjectivity. Such a difference in kind reflects Nietzsche's distinction between master and slave morality, which for its part distinguishes between unconscious activity and conscious apprehension. What follows is an extension of Nietzschean typology into the field of dance, an elaboration of its types, ultimately to rethink the character of subjectivity and its role within the activity of dance.

Notes

1 Friedrich Nietzsche, *On the Genealogy of Morality*, trans. Carol Diethe, ed. Keith Ansell-Pearson (Cambridge: Cambridge University Press, 1994).
2 Gilles Deleuze, *Nietzsche and Philosophy*, trans. Hugh Tomlinson (New York: Columbia University Press, 1983).
3 Nietzsche, *On the Genealogy of Morality*, 28.
4 Deleuze, *Nietzsche and Philosophy*, 194.
5 "I notice something and look for a reason for it – that originally means I look for an *intention* in it, and above all for someone who has intentions, for a subject, a doer .... What gives us the extraordinary strength of our belief in causality is *not* the great habit of the succession of occurrences but our *incapacity* to *interpret* what happens other than as happening out of our intentions", Friedrich Nietzsche, *Writings from the Late Notebooks*, trans. Kate Sturge (Cambridge, Cambridge University Press, 2003), 74.
6 Friedrich Nietzsche, *Daybreak: Thoughts on the Prejudices of Morality*, trans. R.J. Hollingdale (Cambridge, Cambridge University Press, 1997), 72.
7 Nietzsche, *On the Genealogy of Morality,* 28.
8 Nietzsche, *Daybreak*, 117.
9 Nietzsche, *Writings from the Late Notebooks*, 139.
10 "But at the moment when we finally do act, our action is often enough determined by a different species of motives than the species here under discussion, those involved in our "picture of the consequence" ... for though I certainly learn what I finally *do*, I do not learn which motive has therewith actually proved victorious", Nietzsche, *Daybreak*, 129–130.
11 Having noted that dreaming involves the free interpretation of nervous stimuli, Nietzsche writes, "... do I have to add that when we are awake our drives likewise do nothing but interpret nervous stimuli and, according to their requirements, posit their 'causes'? that there is no *essential* difference between waking and dreaming?", ibid., 119.
12 "What is clearly the case is that in this entire procedure our intellect is only the blind instrument of *another drive* which is a *rival* of the drive whose vehemence is torturing us .... While "we" believe we are complaining about the vehemence of a drive, at bottom it is one drive *which is complaining about another*," ibid., 110.
13 Foucault writes:

> Genealogy, as an analysis of descent, is thus situated within the articulation of the body and history. Its task is to expose a body totally imprinted by history and the process of history's destruction of the body ... Genealogy, however, seeks to re-establish the various systems of subjection: not the anticipatory power of meaning, but the hazardous play of dominations. Emergence is always produced through a particular stage of forces ... Emergence is thus the entry of forces; it is their eruption, the leap from the wings to center stage.
>> (Michel Foucault, "Nietzsche, Genealogy, History", in *Language, Counter-Memory, Practice*: *Selected Essays and Interviews by Michel Foucault*, ed. Donald F. Bouchard [New York: Cornell University Press, 1977], 148–150)

14 Nietzsche, *Writings from the Late Notebooks*, 27, 30.

15 "The assumption of the *single subject* is perhaps unnecessary; perhaps it is just as permissible to assume a multiplicity of subjects on whose interplay and struggle our thinking and our consciousness in general is based?", ibid., 46.

16 Ibid., 77. Nietzsche writes: "All unity is only unity as organisation and connected activity", ibid., 76.

17 Ibid., 29.

18 Ibid., 29–30, 77.

19 Pierre Klossowski, *Nietzsche and the Vicious Circle*, trans. Daniel W. Smith (London and New York: Continuum books, 1997).

20 To be clear, Klossowski's discussion of mind and body is not a form of Cartesian dualism. Klossowski does not settle on the mind as the seat of philosophical knowledge, nor is the body that which is animated by the mind. For Klossowski, the Nietzschean body is the source and basis of action. Doing is a corporeal act, not the result of any animating intentionality. Klossowski's body makes sense of Nietzsche's claim that there is no doer behind the deed, merely the act itself. As the following discussion will show, the body's formation is due to the activity of underlying forces – impulses – it is a mobile and changeable formation, not the material identity of Cartesian thinking. For Klossowski, the identity of the body is an interpretation produced by the mind. Consciousness functions in concert with language within Klossowski's work. Its role is not to animate inanimate matter, rather to make sense of the body's relatively autonomous activities. In that sense, Klossowski writes of Nietzsche taking the side of the body, "against" consciousness, ibid., 19.

21 Ibid., 21–22.

22 Ibid., 22.

23 Eric Blondel, *Nietzsche, The Body and Culture: Philosophy as Philological Genealogy*, trans. Sean Hand (London: Athlone, 1991), 207.

24 Michel Haar, "Nietzsche and Metaphysical Language", in *The New Nietzsche*, ed. David B Allison (Cambridge, MA: MIT Press, 1985), 11.

25 Nietzsche, *Writings from the Late Notebooks*, 44.

26 Klossowski, *Nietzsche and the Vicious Circle*, 29.

27 Ibid., 29. First published in 1969, *Nietzsche and the Vicious Circle* was written at the same time as structuralism was establishing itself in French intellectual circles. Structuralism's focus on the linguistic sign is reflected in Klossowski's notion of the code of signs. Structuralism posed the linguistic system as that which made possible the individual exercise of language (parole). In doing so, it privileged the social aspect of signification as that which individuals must utilize. The emphasis on the underlying social system of signification and the role of the individual sets the scene for the development of non-humanist notions of subjectivity, reflected in concepts such as anti-humanism, de-centred subjectivity and the death of the author. Klossowski's claim that the subject thinks as a product of the code reflects these linguistic approaches towards de-centered subjectivity. What structuralism lacks, however, is a focus on the corporeal, a point of difference made explicit in the work of Foucault.

28 In *The Gay Science*, Nietzsche claims that consciousness developed as a means of communication amongst the social group, that language functions in the interests of the herd rather than the individual:

> My idea is clearly that consciousness actually belongs not to man's exist-ence as an individual but rather to the community and herd-aspects of his

nature; that accordingly it is finely developed only in relation to its useful-
ness to community or herd; and that consequently each of us, even with the
best will in the world to *understand* ourselves as individually as possible, "to
know ourselves", will always bring to consciousness precisely that in ourselves which is "non-individual", that which is "average" ... our thoughts
themselves are continually as it were *outvoted* and translated back into the
herd perspective.

> (Friedrich Nietzsche, *The Gay Science: With a Prelude in German
> Rhymes and an Appendix of Songs*, trans. Josefine Nauckhoff
> [Cambridge, Cambridge University Press, 2001], 213)

29 "The body wants to make itself understood through the intermediary of a language of signs that is fallaciously deciphered by consciousness. Consciousness
itself *constitutes this code of signs* that inverts, falsifies and filters what is expressed
through the body", Klossowski, *Nietzsche and the Vicious Circle*, 20.

30 Ibid., 21.

31 This is made clear by his distinction between that which is singular as opposed
to gregarious, ibid., 59. Corporeal states are singular, individual modes of
becoming, whereas gregariousness "presupposes exchange, the communicable,
language: being equivalent to something else ...", ibid., 60. Inter-subjectivity
functions via an economy of sense making, the circulation of signs. Corporeal
specificity has no equivalent. This leads Klossowski to ask; "What, in lived experience, refers to the singular?", ultimately to conclude that the gregarious and the
singular are opposed to one another, and that the body carries a charge of unintel-
ligibility, ibid., 60.

32 Deleuze, *Nietzsche and Philosophy*, 39.

33 Ibid., 40.

34 Ibid., 39.

35 Nietzsche, *Writings from the Late Notebooks*, 30.

36 Brian Massumi, *Parables of the Virtual: Movement, Affect, Sensation* (Durham:
Duke University Press, 2002), 3.

37 Deleuze treats the passing moment as that which forces us to think of
becoming: "That the present moment is not a moment of being or of present 'in
the strict sense', that it is the passing moment, *forces* us to think of becoming,
but to think of it precisely as what could not have started, and cannot finish,
becoming", Deleuze, *Nietzsche and Philosophy*, 48.

38 Nietzsche, *Writings from the Late Notebooks*, 38.

39 "Every *thought*, every feeling, every will is *not* born of one particular drive but is
a *total state*, a whole surface of the whole consciousness, and results from how
the power of *all* the drives that constitute us is fixed at that moment—thus the
power of the drive that dominates just now as well as of the drives obeying and
resisting it." (Ibid., 60)

40 See Haar, "Nietzsche and Metaphysical Language", 10; also Klossowski, *Nietzsche
and the Vicious Circle,* Nietzsche, *Daybreak*; also Nietzsche, *Writings from the Late
Notebooks*, 60 (on thoughts, feelings, and affects). When drawing on *Daybreak,*
this chapter will use the notion of drive but otherwise will rely on the notion of
force, the term utilized in Nietzsche, in *On the Genealogy of Morality* and Deleuze,
in *Nietzsche and Philosophy*.

41 Nietzsche, *Writings from the Late Notebooks*, 8, 30, 46.

42 Deleuze, *Nietzsche and Philosophy*, 40.
43 Nietzsche, *On the Genealogy of Morality*, 56.
44 Deleuze, *Nietzsche and Philosophy*, 42.
45 Nietzsche, *Writings from the Late Notebooks*, 25.
46 Merleau-Ponty, *The Visible and the Invisible*.
47 Martha Graham, *Blood Memory* (New York: Washington Square Press, 1991), 4.
48 The idea that a body must draw force in order to act is reflected in somatic prac-
    titioner, Bobbie Bainbridge Cohen's notion of yield. For Cohen, a body must
    yield in order to draw force from its environment, Body Mind Centering work-
    shop, Bonnie Bainbridge Cohn, "Embodying the Basic Neurocellular Patterns",
    Melbourne, March 27, 2017. Yield involves both sensitivity and activity. It differs
    from collapse in that the work of yielding implies an active encounter which allows
    something to come forth, rather than mere submission (to gravity for example).
    See Bonnie Bainbridge Cohen, "Yield versus Collapse", www.bodymindcentering.
    com/yield-verse-collapse/, February 25, 2019.
49 Klossowski, *Nietzsche and the Vicious Circle,* 26.
50 See my Chapter 4.
51 Park Sang Mi. "The Making of a Cultural Icon for the Japanese Empire: Choe
    Seung-Hui's US Dance Tours and 'New Asian' Culture in the 1930s and 1940s",
    Positions 14, no. 3 (2006): 597–632, and Judy Van Zile, "Performing Modernity in
    Korea: The Dance of Ch'oe Sŭng-hŭi", *Korean Studies* 37 (2013): 124–149.
52 Van Zile, "Performing Modernity in Korea", 128–129.
53 Ibid.
54 Ibid., 132.
55 Ibid., 128.
56 Mark Franko, *Dancing Modernism: Performing Politics* (Bloomington: Indiana
    University Press, 1995), xi, see my Chapter 4.
57 Bruno Latour, *We Have Never Been Modern,* trans. Catherine Porter (Cambridge,
    MA: Harvard University Press, 1993), see my Chapter 4.
58 Van Zile, "Performing Modernity in Korea".
59 Chris Healy traces the narration of modern Aboriginal art at Papunya, offering
    a counter-narrative to its conventional rendering, which sees it as the product of
    western mentorship and influence, *Forgetting Aborigines* (Sydney: UNSW Press,
    2008). Healy writes:

> Those who were involved as painters or advisers, and those with a serious
> stake in Aboriginal art as critics, historians, anthropologists or curators, also
> know that 'Papunya' as a metonym is a selective condensation of varied stories
> and actual historical experiences, a figure that stands in for the contingent and
> particular reality of historical processes.
>
> (Ibid., 71)

60 For further discussion of Australian Indigenous dance, see Chapter 7, on the per-
    formance of Indigenous sovereignty.
61 Brenda Gottschild, *The Black Dancing Body* (New York: Palgrave Macmillan,
    2003), 18.
62 Eva Yaa Asentewaa, "Platform 2012, Parallels", *Dance Magazine* (April 4, 2012),
    www.dancemagazine.com/platform-2012-parallels-2306891500.html,   accessed
    February 26, 2019. See also Ishmael Houston-Jones, "Excerpt: Ishmael-Houston

Jones' Curatorial Statement from Parallels Catalogue", www.danspaceproject.org/2012/01/27/excerpt-ishmael-houston-jones-curatorial-statement-from-parallels-catalogue/, accessed February 27, 2019.

63 Thomas F. DeFrantz and Takiyah Nur Amin, "Talking Black Dance", in *Talking Black Dance, Inside out, Outside In*, ed. Thomas F. DeFrantz and Takiyah Nur Amin, *Society of Dance History Scholars* XXXVI (2016): 12.

64 Ibid., 13.

65 See, for example, Anne Cooper Albright, *Choreographing Difference: The Body and Identity in Contemporary Dance* (Middleton, CT: Wesleyan University Press, 1997); Petra Kuppers, *Disability and Contemporary Performance Bodies on Edge* (London and New York: 2004); Carrie Sandahl and Phillip Auslander, eds., *Bodies in Commotion: Disability and Performance* (Ann Arbor: University of Michigan Press, 2005); and Anna Hickey-Moody, *Unimaginable Bodies: Intellectual Disability, Performance and Becomings* (Rotterdam, NL: Sense Publishers, 2009).

66 *Dance Interrogations: A Dyptich*, Melbourne Fringe Festival, September 23–October 3, 2015, Ceres and Abbotsford Convent, Melbourne. Concept and Video by Dianne Reid. Performed by Dianne Reid and Melinda Smith.

67 *Nothing but Bones in the Way*. Directed by Dianne Reid, 2017.

68 Christel Stalpaert, "Dancing and Thinking Politics with Deleuze and Rancière: Performing Hesitant Gestures of the Unknown in Katarzyna Kozrya's *Rite of Spring*", in *Choreography and Corporeality, Relay in Motion*, ed. Thomas F. DeFrantz and Philipa Rothfield (London: Palgrave Macmillan, 2016), 181.

69 Ibid., 186.

70 Haar, "Nietzsche and Metaphysical Language", 10.

71 For example, in *The Gay Science*, he writes: "… the great and small struggle revolves everywhere around preponderance, around growth and expansion, around power and in accordance with the will to power, which is simply the will to life", Nietzsche, *The Gay Science*, 208, also *Daybreak*, 130–131.

72 "The triumphant concept of "force", with which our physicists have created God and the world, needs supplementing: it must be ascribed an inner world which I call "will to power", i.e., an insatiable craving to manifest power; or to employ, exercise power as a creative drive etc. The physicists cannot eliminate "action at a distance" from their principles, nor a force of repulsion (or attraction). There is no help for it: one must understand all motion, all "appearances", all "laws" as mere symptoms of inner events, and use the human analogy consistently to the end. In the case of an animal, all its drives can be traced back to the will to power: likewise all the functions of organic life to this one source", Nietzsche, *Writings from the Late Notebooks*, 26–27.

73 Ibid., 29.

74 Deleuze, *Nietzsche and Philosophy*, 52.

75 Haar, "Nietzsche and Metaphysical Language", 12.

76 These two perspectives, active and reactive, represent the different ways in which an event might be interpreted. Deleuze bemoans our tendency to see things from the reactive point of view, from the perspective of reaction and accommodation rather than activity and imposition. This is symptomatic of the 'human all too human' failure to recognize the active dimension inherent in all becoming, all movement.

77 Haar, "Nietzsche and Metaphysical Language", 10. We will later return to this matter as a question of interpretation: If all events and all becomings embody a polarity of perspective, from what point of view, from which perspective is a particular mode or instance of change to be interpreted? For Nietzsche:

> Every willing unites a multiplicity of feelings: the feeling of the state to be *left*, the feeling of the state to be *reached*, the feeling of this 'leaving and reaching' itself, the feeling of the duration of the process, then lastly an accompanying feeling of the muscles which begins its play through a kind of habit.
>
> (*Writings from the Late Notebooks*, 36)

These questions are finely elaborated in *Daybreak*, where Nietzsche looks at the genealogy of moral values, revealing their non-moral origins, their transmission and accumulation of moral force and ultimate appearance to those who are born into a moral universe. See also Nietzsche, *On the Genealogy of Morality*, in relation to our interpretations of good and evil, and the characterization of our perspective in reactive terms.

78 Alphonso Lingis, "The Will to Power", in *The New Nietzsche*, ed. David B. Allison (Cambridge, MA: MIT Press, 1985), 40.

79 Ibid., 41.

80 Ibid.

81 Ibid., 39.

82 Ibid., 40. Lingis writes: "The identical, the ideal being ... functions as the condition for the possibility of things", ibid., 34. The mask is the thing, the identity constructed out of divergences, the perception of similarity within the different.

83 Lingis writes: "A thing, metaphysically understood, is a unity that recurs across time, that reiterates itself across time and space and, in doing so, generates a sequence of differing appearances of itself", ibid., 40.

84 "A being, a sequence of appearances, is not founded on the reiteration of unity, of identity; difference is original – unity, identity, is something *become*", ibid., 42.

85 These three expressions of human being are diagnosed and teased apart in Nietzsche's *On the Genealogy of Morality*. *Nietzsche and Philosophy* traces their formation as a matter of pathology as well as potential reconfiguration beyond the realm of the human.

86 Deleuze, *Nietzsche and Philosophy*, 54.

87 Ibid., 50.

88 Nietzsche, *Writings from the Late Notebooks*, 72.

89 Ibid., 166.

90 These concepts represent an account of affect embedded in the becomings of force. Forces relate. They do so because of their capacity to affect one another. This is reflected in the following remarks of Deleuze, Nietzsche and Lingis, respectively: "All sensibility is only a becoming of forces"; Deleuze, *Nietzsche and Philosophy*, 63; Nietzsche writes that the will to power is "the primitive form of affect, *Writings from the Late Notebooks*, 256; Lingis writes of the will to power as "essentially affective", as incorporating a notion of feeling, feeling other forces, relating to them so as to work them, Lingis "Will to Power", 51.

91 Deleuze, *Nietzsche and Philosophy*, 63.

92 Ibid., 62.

93 Ibid.

94 Haar, "Nietzsche and Metaphysical Language", 12.

95 Ibid., 12.

96 Massumi, *Parables of the Virtual*, 5.

97 Massumi writes of these two interrelated elements as a "Fellow-travelling dimension of the same reality", ibid., 5. The conceptual tension between materiality and incorporeality is for Massumi played out in terms of movement; "potential and process", "becoming" and "event", ibid., 5.

98 Ibid., 5.

99 Virtuosity will be considered somewhat differently in the following chapter, through the notion of subject-formation as the work of culture, and the Sovereign Individual in Nietzschean thought.

100 Deleuze, *Nietzsche and Philosophy*, 58. Nietzsche writes: "Against the positivism which halts at phenomena – 'There are only facts' – I would say: no, facts are just what there aren't, there are only interpretations", *Writings from the Late Notebooks*, 139.

101 Nietzsche, *Writings from the Late Notebooks*, 91. Nietzsche writes:

> the development of an organ is an interpretation; the will to power sets limits, determines degrees and differences of power. Power differences alone wouldn't be able to feel themselves as such: there has to be something that wants to grow in terms of its value. *In this* like – – In truth, *interpretation is itself a means of becoming master of something. (The organic process presupposes constant interpreting).*
>
> (Ibid., 90)

102 Lingis "Will to Power", 44.

103 "This book attempts to define and analyse the different forces", Deleuze, *Nietzsche and Philosophy*, x. Such analysis consists in approaching phenomena, things, organisms, societies, consciousness in terms of their constituent forces, Deleuze, *Nietzsche and Philosophy*, x.

104 Deleuze, *Nietzsche and Philosophy*, x.

105 Ibid., xi.

Bibliography

Asentewaa, Eva Yaa. "Platform 2012, Parallels". *Dance Magazine* (April 4, 2012). www.dancemagazine.com/platform-2012-parallels-2306891500.html, accessed February 26, 2019.

Blondel, Eric. *Nietzsche, The Body and Culture: Philosophy as Philological Genealogy*, translated by Sean Hand. London: Athlone, 1991.

Cohen, Bonnie Bainbridge. "Embodying the Basic Neurocellular Patterns". Body Mind Centering workshop, Melbourne, March 27, 2017.

———. "Yield versus Collapse". www.bodymindcentering.com/yield-verse-collapse/, accessed February 26, 2019.

Cooper Albright, Ann. *Choreographing Difference: The Body and Identity in Contemporary Dance*. Middleton, CT: Wesleyan University Press, 1997.

Dance Interrogations: A Dyptich, Melbourne Fringe Festival, September 23–October 3, 2015, Ceres and Abbotsford Convent, Melbourne. Concept and Video by Dianne Reid. Performed by Dianne Reid and Melinda Smith.

DeFrantz, Thomas, F. and Takiyah Nur Amin. "Talking Black Dance". In *Talking Black Dance: Inside out, Outside In*, edited by Thomas F. DeFrantz and Takiyah Nur Amin. *Society of Dance History Scholars* XXXVI (2016): 10–13.

Deleuze, Gilles. *Nietzsche and Philosophy*. Translated by Hugh Tomlinson. New York: Columbia University Press, 1983.

Foucault, Michel. "Nietzsche, Genealogy, History". In *Language, Counter-Memory, Practice: Selected Essays and Interviews by Michel Foucault*, edited by Donald F. Bouchard, 139–164. New York: Cornell University Press, 1977.

Franko, Mark. *Dancing Modernism: Performing Politics*. Bloomington: Indiana University Press, 1995.

Gottschild, Brenda. *The Black Dancing Body*. New York: Palgrave Macmillan, 2003.

Graham, Martha. *Blood Memory*. New York: Washington Square Press, 1991.

Haar, Michel. "Nietzsche and Metaphysical Language". In *The New Nietzsche*, edited by David B Allison, 5–36. Cambridge, MA: MIT Press, 1985.

Healy, Chris. *Forgetting Aborigines*. Sydney: UNSW Press, 2008.

Hickey-Moody, Anna. *Unimaginable Bodies: Intellectual Disability, Performance and Becomings*. Rotterdam, NL: Sense Publishers, 2009.

Houston-Jones, Ishmael. "Excerpt: Ishmael-Houston Jones' Curatorial Statement from Parallels Catalogue". www.danspaceproject.org/2012/01/27/excerpt-ishmael-houston-jones-curatorial-statement-from-parallels-catalogue/, accessed February 27, 2019.

Klossowski, Pierre. *Nietzsche and the Vicious Circle*. Translated by Daniel W. Smith. London and New York: Continuum books, 1997.

Kuppers, Petra. *Disability and Contemporary Performance: Bodies on Edge*. London and New York: 2004.

Latour, Bruno. *We Have Never Been Modern*. Translated by Catherine Porter. Cambridge, MA: Harvard University Press, 1993.

Lingis, Alphonso. "The Will to Power". In *The New Nietzsche*, edited by David B. Allison, 37–63. Cambridge, MA: MIT Press, 1985.

Massumi, Brian. *Parables of the Virtual: Movement, Affect, Sensation*. Durham: Duke University Press, 2002.

Nietzsche, Friedrich. *On the Genealogy of Morality*. Translated by Carol Diethe, edited by Keith Ansell-Pearson. Cambridge: Cambridge University Press, 1994.

———. *Daybreak: Thoughts on the Prejudices of Morality*. Translated by R.J. Hollingdale, Cambridge, Cambridge University Press, 1997.

———. *The Gay Science: With a Prelude in German Rhymes and an Appendix of Songs*. Translated by Josefine Nauckhoff. Cambridge, Cambridge University Press, 2001.

———. *Writings from the Late Notebooks*. Translated by Kate Sturge. Cambridge, Cambridge University Press, 2003.

Nothing but Bones in the Way. Directed by Dianne Reid, 2017.

Park Sang Mi. "The Making of a Cultural Icon for the Japanese Empire: Choe Seung-Hui's US Dance Tours and 'New Asian' Culture in the 1930s and 1940s". *Positions* 14, no. 3 (2006): 597–632.

Sandahl, Carrie and Phillip Auslander, editors. *Bodies in Commotion: Disability and Performance*. Ann Arbor: University of Michigan Press, 2005.

Stalpaert, Christel. "Dancing and Thinking Politics with Deleuze and Rancière: Performing Hesitant Gestures of the Unknown in Katarzyna Kozrya's *Rite of Spring*". In *Choreography and Corporeality, Relay in Motion*, edited by Thomas F. DeFrantz and Philipa Rothfield, 173–191. London: Palgrave Macmillan, 2016.

Van Zile, Judy. "Performing Modernity in Korea: The Dance of Ch'oe Sŭng-hŭi". *Korean Studies* 37 (2013): 124–149.

6 Subjectivity three ways
In Nietzsche and Deleuze

Introduction

This chapter looks to the fate of the subject within an ontology of force. It will outline three accounts of subjectivity, each somewhat different. The first offers a way of thinking action and therefore dancing outside the agency of the dancer. It does so through depicting experience as a mode of interiority that inhibits action. Gilles Deleuze's portrayal of subjectivity in Nietzsche shows how forces fold inwards, to create an interior, felt as conscious experience (thoughts, feelings and sensations). Force functions to produce consciousness here, via the momentary suspension of action. This depiction of the subjective field signals the triumph of reactive over active force. It recalls the sense in which the Nietzschean slave defeats the master through reaction and *ressentiment* (negation). This picture is at odds with the phenomenological paradigm which ascribes agency – the capacity to act – to an agent, who is deemed to be the subject of experience. Instead of attributing agency to the dancer as subject, in this chapter, action and its experience are treated as distinct formations of force. The dancer's agency is thereby recast, beyond the notion of a singular agency and toward a dynamic plurality of relations of force. The formation of subjectivity through force turning inwards is markedly different from the notion of action (as successive corporeal formation) depicted in Chapter 5. Deleuze shows how the formation of subjectivity functions at the expense of corporeal formation. It's a case of one or the other: either forces produce a transitory corporeal becoming or they conspire to turn inwards. The Deleuzian distinction between subjectivity and corporeal becoming, founded on Nietzschean thought, is adapted to an action-based account of dance thought in terms of corporeal and subject-formation.

The second account of subjectivity looks to the formation of the subject within culture, through the cultural deployment of force to produce the trained individual. This section brings together Michel Foucault and Gilles Deleuze in order to show the ways in which culture works through subject-formation and the cultivation of corporeal disposition in the subject. Foucault's work on disciplinary power argues the correlative emergence of facility on the one hand (*qua* the trained individual), and subjection (to culture) on the other. The discussion of culture follows Deleuze's tri-partite treatment of the cultural in pre-historic, historic and post-historic terms. Cultural analysis shows how forces come to be gathered in the trained individual in such a way that they become "suitable for being acted", that is, poised for deployment.[1] Culture produces the dispositional tendency for force to express itself in customary ways. This is felt in the body and expressed in action. The work of culture is thereby framed as that which makes force available to be acted in line with customary and cultural norms. This approach to subjectivity adopts a dual perspective: the point of view of culture, oriented towards subject-production and the creation of dispositional tendencies, and the point of view of the individual, trained and technically proficient. In the field of dance, the trained individual is a pre-condition for the emergence of the Sovereign Individual, culture's "ripest fruit".[2] A Nietzschean concept, the Sovereign Individual is a product of culture, yet is able to redeploy culture, to its own ends. The Sovereign Individual utilizes all that culture has to offer, its inscriptions and norms, facility and techniques, towards a recalibration of culture. The figure of the Sovereign Individual lends itself to a reconceptualization of virtuosity, beyond conventional displays of excellence, and towards the formation of new modes of value and valuation.

The third treatment of subjectivity pursued here examines the relation between subjectivity and its overcoming. The undoing of subjectivity raises the possibility that reactive formations can be displaced so as to make room for other kinds of (non-human) becoming. Deleuze conceptualizes this in terms of active destruction. Active destruction is a mode of transformation that moves beyond the reactive sphere, bringing about a radical transformation of type on the part of, or rather, beyond the subject. This chapter will review the suggestion that the subject can will its own downfall, *in action*. In so doing, it aims to open up a range of perspectives on the strategic possibilities available to the dancer, framed from the point of view of force. The discussion in this section draws on the notion of overcoming in the field of dance to suggest that there is a manner of dancing which could be seen in terms of desubjectification, that is, as a movement beyond the self. The suggestion is that certain practices, such as those found for example in postmodern dance and potentially further afield, can be framed as the strategic deployment of subjectivity in the manner of its (own) overcoming. This is illustrated by reference to a number of choreographic strategies which create in the dancer the formation of that which I call the Workerly Type. The Workerly Type is an attitude towards the dancing self, found in action and oriented towards its own displacement. This last section represents a speculative (re)interpretation of Deleuze's writing on overcoming and active destruction, as the work of the one who wants to be overcome.

Section 1: Genealogy of the reactive type

Deleuze's account of subjectivity within Nietzsche is founded upon a typological distinction between two key types, active and reactive. Typology is a Nietzschean concept, a mode of discrimination, which distinguishes between types or patterns of becoming.[3] Typology seeks to differentiate the ways in which force is found in particular "modes of existence".[4] It applies itself to specific ontologies of becoming, seeking their existential character through an analysis of force. Deleuze writes:

> Nietzsche was responsible for creating a whole typology to distinguish active, acted and reactive forces and to analyse their various combinations. In particular, the delineation of *a genuinely reactive type* of forces constitutes one of the most original points of Nietzschean thought.[5] (my emphasis)

Deleuze assumes a typological approach towards the production of this genuinely reactive type, that is to say, human subjectivity. An art of distinction, typology contrasts the active type, best understood in relation to the Nietzschean master, with the reactive consolidation of consciousness, the mark of the slave. The active and reactive types draw upon a distinction between the body on the one hand, and consciousness on the other. While corporeal formation makes possible the formation of the active type, consciousness obstructs it.

The typological focus on "active, acted and reactive forces" leads to the claim that forces combine in one of two ways.[6] The first way is found in corporeal formation. Chapter 5 posited corporeal formation as the imposition of active force upon a differing tendency, reactive force, which offers its own interlocutory response. The body is conceived here as a mobile formation, a provisional resolution of contestatory impulses which become active and reactive in relation to one another. Their difference is found in active forces expressing mastery over a selected field of circumstance, which for its part reacts and responds. These qualities of active and reactive force are specific to the relation: force becomes active in relation to another force, which emerges through reacting to active force. Such a conception of bodily becoming reveals a great multiplicity of arrangements of force, modes of organization, actions and reactions within but also beyond the human body. The body is a focus of activity, active force defined through its expression of mastery upon a field of reaction or circumstance. The activity of dancing can be posed in these terms, as an engagement of circumstance towards the production of movement. The notion of circumstance is widely construed, a question of provenance in the dancer, kinaesthetic value and heritage as well as social, political and cultural context. Active force represents the selection and utilization of these contextualizing factors, reactive force that which is both taken up and orients itself towards active force. The relationship between these two kinds of force is that which produces the body as its transitory and provisional outcome. When reactive force is selected and worked by active force, it is said "to be acted".[7] To be acted is to enter into corporeal formation in relation to the myriad exertions of active force.

The second kind of formation differs from the domain of the corporeal. It includes the entire field of subjective experience, all that which belongs to the plane of the subject.[8] It represents "the triumph of reaction", over the active type to form what Deleuze calls the reactive type. The reactive type represents a combination of forces in which reactive force is no longer acted – and when this happens, action no longer ensues. The reactive type is closely related to the slave in Nietzsche's treatment of the master–slave relationship. This is because the slave functions by way of reaction, to the master. The story begins with the master who assumes a positive stance towards her actions, thereby creating value in an affirmative manner. Affirmation is nested in action here, in its "strong, free [and] happy" character.[9] The master's actions are said to express a form of morality. According to master morality, an action creates its own sense of value, according to which it is judged good. It does not appeal to that which is outside itself to deserve the title, good. Slave morality by contrast follows a different pathway. The slave does not affirm the value of action through doing but rather takes a negative attitude towards the actions of the other:

> in order to come about, slave morality has to have an opposing external world ... its action is basically a reaction.[10]

The slave 'reacts' to the master by way of moral critique, condemning the master for lacking a moral compass. By comparing itself to the master, the slave's inaction (restraint from wrongdoing) is deemed good. Slave morality is thus parasitic and negative, master morality, affirmative and autonomous. Nietzsche criticizes slave morality. He sees it as filled with hatred (*ressentiment*) toward the master, without sharing in the master's positive and creative means of expression. While the master acts (through corporeal formation), the slave merely reacts (through forming negative judgements).

The figure of the slave offers a model for the formation of subjectivity (*aka*, the reactive type). While the master functions through the deployment of "necessarily unconscious" forces, the slave operates in the domain of consciousness.[11] Deleuze's treatment of Nietzschean thought seeks to show how consciousness requires the inhibition of action. Just as the slave detracts from the master through a negative "revaluation", consciousness withdraws from action to form the inside of subjectivity.[12] Subjectivity thus represents a second type or pattern, quite unlike corporeal formation. Key to this account is the view that consciousness represents a redirection of active force away from action (corporeal formation), and towards the construction of an interior arrangement of force. Deleuze names this particular arrangement "the reactive apparatus". The reactive apparatus is the seat of subjectivity, the means whereby experience is produced, thinking occurs and feelings are felt. It is the means whereby consciousness occurs, perchance to persist in the form of *ressentiment*, a problematic range of attitudes and actions at odds with that which is called "the active type".[13]

The fluid paradigm

Deleuze explains the reactive apparatus by way of a contrast, between a fluid conception of consciousness able to entertain the new, and one liable to get stuck. He cites Freud's conception of consciousness as a skin, formed at the border between the internal and external world, able to receive excitations but, equally importantly, able to refresh itself so as to make room for the new.[14] According to the fluid paradigm, consciousness is that which receives input of one sort or another, forming reactions in response. A feature of this mode of consciousness is its ability to entertain *new* reactions, to open itself to the influx of new content. In order to do this, consciousness must be able to organize a "constantly renewed skin surrounding an ever fresh receptivity".[15] Deleuze credits the faculty of forgetting with making the renewal of consciousness possible. He draws on the Nietzschean insight that forgetting is neither a lapse nor a form of deterioration, but is "rather an active ability to suppress, positive in the strongest sense of the word".[16] For Nietzsche, forgetting enables consciousness "to make room for something new".[17] It is through forgetting that consciousness is able to open up to new experience. When consciousness actively forgets, one content is able to give way to another. Deleuze sees active force as doing the work of conscious renewal, through 'forgetting' reaction. In such a case, active force 'acts' those reactions that form in the reactive apparatus towards forgetting and therefore renewal. This treatment of reaction enables consciousness to remain free of the mnemonic trace (memory). Through resisting the formation of conscious reaction, consciousness maintains a "freshness" and "fluidity", ready for new experiences, new modes of reaction,[18] recalling Nietzsche's claim that "what we simply live through, experience, take in, no more enters our consciousness during digestion (one could call it spiritual ingestion) than does the thousand-fold process which takes place within our physical consumption of food, our so-called ingestion".[19] We could think of this regenerative process as that which resists the formation of conscious experience in the reactive apparatus, for as soon as reactions arise, active force acts them away from conscious registration.

Malfunction in the reactive apparatus

The fluid conception of consciousness is made possible by the faculty of forgetting. Forgetting supports the plasticity of consciousness and forestalls the formation of *ressentiment* in the reactive apparatus. Consciousness functions as a mobile staging ground here, a place of momentary entertainment. The fluid conception of consciousness represents an exceptional state of affairs, at odds with the business as usual of human subjectivity, which is marked by the tendency to retain and respond to conscious experience. The purpose of Deleuze's treatment of the reactive apparatus is to show how it functions to support the reactive type, "the man of *ressentiment*" who experiences the world as an encroachment to be answered.[20] A wholly fluid consciousness cannot found the reactive point of view, "which blames the object in order for its own inability to escape from the traces of the corresponding excitation".[21] Hence the following depiction of another kind of formation, one which enables the production of such conscious tenacity:

> Suppose there is a lapse in the faculty of forgetting: it is as if the wax of consciousness were hardened, excitation tends to get confused with its trace in the unconscious and conversely, reaction to traces rises into consciousness and overruns it.[22]

The "ascent of memory into consciousness" that occurs through this lapse in the faculty of forgetting enables reactions to become the stuff of experience.[23] It enables reactions in the reactive apparatus to rise to consciousness and thereby extend their psychical tenure. The reactive apparatus has now become the framework for the constant flow and generation of reactive content. When forgetting fails, the reactive apparatus is subject to the rich and varied life of consciousness. This is the field of subjectivity, that which we experience, think and feel.

What is distinctive about this account is that it sees the emergence of consciousness as a failure on the part of the reactive apparatus. Such failure has immense consequences, both within the reactive apparatus and further afield. This is because "at the same time as reaction to traces becomes perceptible, reaction ceases to be acted".[24] In other words, the sedimentation of reaction within consciousness simultaneously insulates it from deployment by active force:

> We can thus finally see in what way reactive forces prevail over active forces: when the trace takes the place of the excitation in the reactive apparatus, reaction itself takes the place of action, reaction prevails over action.[25]

When reaction prevails within the reactive apparatus, it can no longer become forgotten in the active sense. Such is the means whereby the subject is able to form a reactive interpretation on all that happens. The failure of active force to maintain the plasticity of consciousness underlies the formation and triumph of a new type. Deleuze writes:

> We rediscover the definition of ressentiment: *ressentiment* is a reaction which simultaneously becomes perceptible and ceases to be acted: a formula which defines sickness in general.[26]

What is 'sick' about *ressentiment* is its inability to let go of its reactions, and the tendency to see the world as an intrusion, to be answered by way of further reaction. *Ressentiment*, the mark of the reactive type, differs from the active type through the way in which the world and its experience are regarded. For the reactive type, the world is experienced through its effects upon the subject. For the active type, the world is a field of circumstance, to be deployed. Consciousness supports the reactive paradigm insofar as it enables *ressentiment* to take hold.

There are thus two models, two modes of functioning within the reactive apparatus: one whereby consciousness renews itself, the other a breakdown through which it acquires memory. Such an account is able to delineate two sorts of formation, conscious and corporeal. Deleuze's discussion reveals the way in which consciousness arises at the point at which reactive force 'escapes' the actions of active force: for when consciousness forms, reactive forces are no longer able to be acted. This is key to understanding the difference between consciousness and action, each of which represents a different pattern of relationship between active and reactive forces. In contrast to the phenomenological approach, conscious subjectivity is not the seat of agency here. Indeed, consciousness in all its enduring forms requires a diversion of force away from action and into the reactive apparatus, which for its part momentarily obstructs action. This explains why all actions involve the participation of "necessarily unconscious forces" – for to be acted is to avoid becoming conscious.[27]

The dual character of Deleuze's analysis not only reflects Nietzsche's claim that there is no doer only the deed, it also poses consciousness as a formation endemic to the reactive type. Apart from its critique of *ressentiment* as the tenacious and degenerative power of consciousness, its critical calibration of relations of force calls for an approach towards the event that differentiates its elements according to a basic distinction between action and its experience. The typological approach decentres subjectivity and destabilizes corporeal identity as a way of opening up to the becomings of force. It takes a mercurial approach towards corporeality, one which posits a wide and changing field of component forces. It also displaces human agency for the agency of forces found in corporeal formation. The subject – or at least subjective experience – is a formation of force which is diverted away from action and folded inwards. This isn't merely a dispute about agency, however, it also explains why forces can either function towards corporeal formation or become perceptible. It poses these two types in contestatory terms.

In terms of force, the typology of the subject works with three key terms: corporeal formation, the active and reactive types. The active type is found in affirmative actions that create and affirm their own forms of value. While belonging to the field of action (corporeal formation), not all actions belong to the active type. Whether they do so in the particular instance depends upon a characterization of their creative footprint. The notion of the active type is open to a variety of interpretations. It need not be thought that the active type depends upon the creation of aesthetic values (in the manner of an aesthetic avant-garde). An act could be attributed to the active type in virtue of its practice-based nuances: a well-executed pirouette perhaps, or an inspired improvisational contribution or a movement that reveals a quality, a moment, a depth of feeling.

Dance and the activities of force

Deleuze's treatment of the master and slave, force and the body, consciousness and *ressentiment* makes sense of the claim that there is no doer behind the deed. Its displacement of human agency for the workings of force opens itself to a very different notion of dancing from the phenomenological conception. Deleuze makes the point that:

> for Nietzsche, what counts is not the quantity of force considered abstractly but a determinate relation in the subject itself between the different forces of which it is made up this is what he means by a type.[28]

The suggestion is that there are within the subject a multiplicity of actions and reactions, forces and formations, and that this is a matter to be discerned in the particular instance. The typological perspective draws attention to that which in the subject turns inwards, becomes forgotten, rises to consciousness or becomes deployed in corporeal formation. Any one movement will undoubtedly call upon myriad simultaneous and overlapping combinations of force. While typology institutes a divide between action and its experience, it is worth remembering that the human body is a multiplicity, comprising myriad relations, operations and organizations, deploying multiple fields and levels of circumstance, all of which coalesce in motion. The dancing body inevitably encompasses and expresses many different relations of force. Compatible and competing modes of organization reside in the body: at any one moment, there will be a range of indeterminate possibilities which are nevertheless informed by the plural circumstances of dance. Thoughts circulate, movements emerge, qualities arise and forces regroup. Multiple activities occur in the one flow of movement.

Corporeal formation is a dynamic state of affairs. Its boundaries swell and contract, depending upon the activities of force and their selected fields. Movement draws force from many quarters, beyond the boundaries of the human body narrowly conceived. The relational conception of corporeal formation doesn't stop at the boundaries of the human body. A relation between bodies or with elements of the environment can be seen as the formation of a new (if momentary) body. Drawing upon culture, history or others are all ways of forming new bodies, kinaesthetic, social or political. Erin Manning's conception of the "becoming body" is a timely reminder that the boundaries of the body arise from the becomings of force found in the event.[29] A hermeneutics of kinaesthetic force negotiates the tension between the identity of the dancer (thought in relation to the reactive apparatus) and that which

Figure 6.1 Russell Dumas, artistic director, Dance Exchange, courtesy of the artist.

the dancing draws upon and produces by way of corporeal formation – the movement. The key issue is to identify that which acts and that which reacts in the momentary and provisional organization of force. Remembering that a body can be chemical, biological, social or political, force enjoys a diversity of origins and a heterogeneity of qualities.[30] The dynamic and transitory nature of corporeal becoming allows for the identification of many kinds of momentary formation. From the body politic of activist choreography,[31] the joint corporeality of the participatory event,[32] to the momentary elaboration and reconfiguration of corporeal identity,[33] the activities of force can conform, resist, reconstitute and/or produce new formations of force that challenge hegemonic forms of value, whether in the field of dance, culture or society. The kinaesthetic and cultural character of corporeal formation is to be found in the circumstances of dance, in its selections, history, customs and habits. These factors qualify the ways in which active and reactive force perform their respective roles. Corporeal circumstance is allied to customs, habits, practices and traditions that value certain kinds and qualities of movement over and above others. Insofar as typology is an existential concern, it can be oriented towards particular domains and fields of practice, articulating their context, preferences, customs and habits. It can also be enlisted to show the forces at work within hegemonic modes of perception, kinaesthetic sensibilities and aesthetic predispositions.

Putting the subjective to work – movement's riposte

Although Deleuze's Nietzsche refuses a metaphysics of human agency in favour of an ontology of force, there is a place for subjective reaction within the activity of dance. There are many modes of movement that put elements of the subjective to work. Deleuze describes an oscillation between reaction and action, between the tendency for reactive force to hinder or delay, and active force's tendency to deploy and work reactive force. The type of the master (the active type) is the one who never gets bogged down in forming reactions to that which happens but readily redeploys reactions in "a burst of creativity", described by Deleuze as a form of "riposte".[34] Such is the active type, whose reactions are, according to Nietzsche, "consumed and exhausted in an immediate reaction".[35] Dancing represents its own riposte to the formation of experience in the reactive apparatus. The riposte includes all manner of movement which selects and acts experience. Such a model accounts for the many ways in which consciousness, perception, feeling and imagination can feature within movement. This riposte represents the sense in which action is able to engage and work with reaction, towards the production of movement. Movement's riposte consists of two stages: the formation of reaction (*qua* experience) and its subsequent activation (according to corporeal formation). The figure of the riposte is an important aspect of all those momentary formations that enact sensation, feeling and thought. It makes room for the entry and incorporation of experience, without resorting to a metaphysics of the subject, for here, it is the activity – the moving – that incorporates and acts experience. The riposte is able to incorporate a wide range of reactions, depending upon the customary preferences of the field, whether for sensation, thought, imagery or other kinds of reaction.

For example, dancers often focus upon and utilize *sensations* felt in the body. Their content and quality are able to inform the dancing that follows: these include feelings of weight, tension, touch, tone or rhythm. Dancing can be enriched by the incorporation of felt sensation in movement, which lend the dancing a certain quality of attention, and offers the dancer a retrospective yet experiential perspective on (the elsewhere of) action. *Thoughts* are also taken up and acted in movement. This is quite evident in the field of improvisation – a momentary perception, impulse or observation is promptly converted, generating those felicitous moments of surprise, rupture or creative elaboration. Skilled performers allow themselves to become the vehicle of the riposte, to get out of the way by letting go of conscious reaction and allowing the movement to take over.

Other kinds of somatic practice focus upon the use of *imagery* for movement. In the case of ideokinesis, for example, movers lie in constructive rest and entertain a great range of images: some abstract, some anatomical and others metaphorical. These images are for the most part dynamic metonyms that stand in for actions or qualities to be found in the body: the swelling and contraction of the diaphragm (as the opening and closing of an umbrella), the downwards flow of scapulae (shoulders attached to the front sternum as a flowing cape), movement from one side of the pelvis to the other (through the pelvis as a bridge between the legs) and the body relaxing and releasing (through a collapsing suit of clothes).[36] Images are not folded into movement in any simple way. They are entertained while lying down in the constructive rest position, away from the action-based norm of verticality. Participants are exhorted not to 'do' the image as this would be to revert to habitual movement pathways. In that sense, the image is destined to replace the subject's usual motor intentionality. There are a few ways to account for the ideokinetic image in action: it could be that the image works the body, as an active force that appropriates and displaces the subject's usual habitus. Or, the image might mingle with the body to produce a fecund circumstance, which is in turn acted by the ensuing movement. In either case, entertainment of the image within the reactive apparatus and in relation to the body has become deployed in action. Many somatic practices draw upon image-based methodologies to disrupt the movement subjectivity that has become enmeshed in the body, with a view to investing the image with a dynamic sense of agency. For example, Skinner Releasing Technique™ also relies upon imagery as a way of provoking particular qualities of movement.[37] Joan Skinner works with the notion of a "partner graphic", as a means of dynamic provocation.[38] These tactile strategies, expressed through the touch of another, produce feelings which may become (re)deployed in action. If the image is felt and then followed by movement, then this constitutes an instance of movement's riposte. Releasing technique aims to disable the muscular anacrusis of action, in which the dancer prepares for movement through a muscular form of anticipation. Releasing into movement sidesteps muscular corporeal thinking in favour of other qualities and actions. Bonnie Bainbridge Cohen's Body Mind Centering constructs its own imaginary field, formed through drawing upon a distinctive mix of anatomy, physiology and, more recently, embryology, as a methodological means of movement provocation.[39]

Thought typologically, these examples show a range of approaches that deploy subjective reactions in action. They are by no means exhaustive. There is no single formula for the shift between reaction-formation and its entry into movement. The specific character of perceptible reaction is a cultural, kinaesthetic state of affairs. Reactions draw force from culture. They are contextual and contingent. Their (re)deployment in action is informed by the practices, social, cultural and kinaesthetic, within which they occur. The heterogeneity of images, thoughts, feelings, strategies, perceptions, anticipations and apprehensions are all potential reactions which may be felt then acted. Whatever these reactions are, and from whatever tradition or practice, their redeployment in action offers them the pragmatic destiny of felt reactions that enter the sphere of corporeal formation.

The discussion thus far has centred upon the difference between that which forms a body and that which results in consciousness. It represents the Nietzschean view that we are not the authors of our actions. It shows how consciousness is formed from force turned inwards, as distinct from that which results in corporeal formation. And finally, although a decentred account of action and agency, it is able to accommodate the many ways in which the subjective is able to be deployed in the course of movement.

Section 2: The subject of culture

The open-ended nature of the riposte serves as a reminder that dancing is an intensely cultural and kinaesthetic state of affairs. Kinaesthetic culture informs what kinds of reaction are produced and selected within movement's riposte, also their manner of deployment. It's not that any and all reactions are suitable for redeployment. Each field, style, tradition and context maps out its own domain according to which the riposte makes sense, *as dancing*. Dance practices mark out their own form of territory. This can be thought in terms of culture. Culture territorializes through practice, producing the subject as its intermediary formation. For Nietzsche, culture works through the individual. Culture is a force for conformity, the individual its means of reproduction. And yet, the individual is no ultimate guarantor of conformity. Although critical of the individual's alliance to the herd, Nietzsche also praises the individual as the one who is able to overcome culture. Culture is therefore ambivalent, a force for reproduction but equally a basis for renewal. As we will see, the Sovereign Individual expresses this ambivalence, embodying culture on the one hand, yet able to overcome it on the other.

Culture and the pre-historic

Nietzsche is very clear that subjectivity is a placeholder for culture, the subject its mode and means of transmission. He developed a term, the morality of custom (*der sittlichkeit der sitte*), to signify the bond between society and the individual.[40] The morality of custom poses the subject as a vehicle for the transmission of cultural value. It suggests that individuals feel themselves (morally) bound to conform to the tenets of their culture. Through compliance with its values, they become its conduit. Deleuze writes:

> Every historical law is arbitrary, but what is not arbitrary, what is prehistoric and generic, is the law of obeying laws.[41]

The notion of the prehistoric construes subjectivity in functional terms – subjectivity's function being to reflect and reproduce the particular cultural milieu. The task of culture is to produce subjects who embody the values and dispositions of the field. This is culture's "generic" moment.[42] Deleuze looks at culture as a selective process, one which identifies and 'schools' reactive forces so that they become available for deployment:

> The activity of culture is, in principle, exercised on reactive forces, it gives them habits and imposes models on them in order to make them suitable for being acted.[43]

There are two claims here: one that culture selects and treats reactive forces so that they are ready to enter action in culturally pre-determined ways; the other, that this all occurs in the field of subjectivity. In principle, exercised on reactive force; in practice, managed through the subject, culture's means of transmission. Subjectivity is posed here as an intermediary formation which enables the selection and deployment of force. If culture selects those reactions pertinent to its signature practices, training is that which equips them for action. Training involves the inculcation of reaction in the form of a subjective disposition or readiness to act:

> It is always a matter of giving man habits, of making him obey laws, of training him. Training man means forming him in such a way that he can act his reactive forces.[44]

The trained dancer is the one in whom reactions are concentrated and rendered suitable for deployment according to the practices of the field. Dance training is in large part concentrated upon producing the dancer who is able to act according to custom. Custom can be seen as a characteristic selection and deployment of reaction, whether this concerns the kinds of perceptions that mark out the field, movement qualities, modes of attention and focus, or the ways in which thought and movement combine. Each tradition, style or form of dance will have its own way of mapping out its signature kinaesthetic territory and means of subject-production. Many will involve the acquisition of habit. Habit-formation is another way of thinking the cultivation of law-like behaviour in the individual. Habit is the disposition to act, an acquired tendency.[45] Habits can be a useful means of capacity-building. Habit gathers and disperses reactions in the individual, forging in the subject the means to render them suitable for action. In this context, habit reflects the needs of culture by taking up culture's particular selections and cultivating them in the body in the form of skill.

Habit is training's way of adhering to the body, not just in the past, but oriented towards the future. It is training's legacy. The point of habituation is to ensure that skill remains available in the body. In dance, habits are often maintained through repetition. For example, the ballet *barre* is an important element of the ballet dancer's daily regimen. The *barre* enables and reinforces ballet's particular territorialization of movement, felt through its characteristic demeanour, pull up, turn out, muscular qualities and emblematic lexicon. The trained dancer is the one disposed and able to act her reactive forces according to the dictates of the field. For training to succeed in the Deleuzian sense, reactions must remain accessible and deployable. Practice supplements training and reinforces habit, to ensure the ongoing availability of reaction. The more complex the movement form, the greater the need to keep it alive in the body, however this is to be achieved. The daily *barre* is one way of thinking the maintenance of training. Repetition, rehearsal, performance, practice, class, workshop and investigation represent other ways and means.

Rather than thinking human agency as a given, this account looks toward cultural production and kinaesthetic practice as working, gathering and shaping force around the body and through the reactive apparatus. The subject is an assemblage of forces, concentrated around a mutable body, itself selected by culture, established and maintained through practice. From an individual point of view, training and practice produce the dancer's skill. From culture's point of view, the dancer is the one in whom reactions are rendered suitable for being acted. Both points of view represent a form of utility, either for the individual, or for culture itself.[46] Another illustration can be found in the practice of Deborah Hay's choreography.[47] Hay has created and conducted a series of works entitled, *The Solo Performance Commissioning Project*.[48] The project is a durational event, held in a number of locations, over several years. It is to be undertaken by numerous individual dancers, who, amongst other things, make a commitment to regularly practise its specific choreography over many months, leading to a performance outcome. Although the work requires daily practice of the choreography, unlike ballet, its daily reiteration is liable to produce significant forms of difference. Hay has over many years developed a unique choreographic approach. She does not create movement material which dancers are supposed to emulate but rather constructs challenging suppositions for the dancer to work with. These suppositions may reframe what it is to be a body, or require perceptual shifts on the part of the dancer or ask for highly unusual actions.

Hay's work functions at the interface of intention and movement, and often undoes or challenges the dancer's knowing subjectivity.[49] Susan Foster describes her work in this project as wanting "to create a kind of dance that never becomes fixed, repeatable or knowable".[50] Dancers undertake her work not knowing how they are going to perform her choreographic instructions each and every time they work through them. As a result, the performance of her choreography is liable to differ with each reiteration. The dancer cannot depend upon established movement patterns nor settle upon a given solution. And yet, the project calls for great fealty to the work, to its processes and choreographic demands, requiring a dedication which opens up the body by way of habit to the emergence of new and surprising reactions, which nonetheless qualify as performance of the work. The singularity of each iteration is matched by the habitual dedication needed to make this possible. Although Hay's work does not depend upon making recognizable shapes nor repeating found material, it can be seen as a mode of training, an ongoing process of subject-formation that is nested within the work. It takes skill to let go of prior training, to open up to the different demands of Hay's work, to not know what will come next and to stick to instructions that are liable to leave the dancer in the dark.[51] The point of the example is to distinguish between the subjectivity formed in the context of Hay's work from that which is produced by a tradition such as ballet that involves an established lexicon. While both examples create a milieu within which the dancer's subjectivity is shaped, and both depend upon daily practice, the similarity stops there. Ballet works in the zone of the familiar, in a known kinaesthetic

Figure 6.2 The Match, choreographed by Deborah Hay, 2004. Photographer: Rino Pizzi.

context, whereas Hay's work defamiliarizes as it is enacted. While Susan Foster sees this as problematizing "the very process of subject-formation",[52] Lena Hammergren discerns the exhibition of a certain kind of mastery in the performance outcome component of the project.[53] For Hammergren, the regular practice embedded in the project produces a discernible competence. Perhaps there are two contrary tendencies within Hay's work, both towards and against subject-formation.[54] The habituation of engaging in the practice engenders a kind of subject-formation felt in terms of mastery of the work, while the choreographic mien embedded in its practice deconstructs that very formation.[55]

The body and history – the historical

If culture selects its reactions and their manner of deployment, practice secures it in the body through historical means. For Foucault, the (Nietzschean) body is the primary site of cultural production.[56] Foucault, like Deleuze, sees the body in provisional and transitory terms, as "a volume in perpetual disintegration".[57] The body is not substance. And yet, the body *has* a history, of myriad practices and events which are inscribed upon its surfaces. It is not that the body pre-exists inscription then. Rather, it emerges in virtue of these inscriptive encounters, which leave their mark by means of corporeal formation.[58] In *Discipline and Punish*, Foucault traces the formation of the military body to show how discipline can be viewed in productive terms by way of corporeal formation and subject-production.[59] For Foucault, the body is articulated through the imposition of daily rhythms, regimes and regimens, which work "slowly through each part of the body, mastering it, making it pliable, ready at all times, turning silently into the automatism of habit".[60] Their cumulative effect is to engrave memory in the form of habits and *habitus*,[61] along with a corresponding turning inwards of force.[62] Deleuze credits Foucault with showing how, in historical terms, subjectivity is produced through folding the body's forces to form an inside of thought.[63] Subjectivation is the name given to the process which "bends" force to become the interior landscape of subjectivity.[64] Interiority is not a metaphysical given here, rather it is produced through practice, via inscription. Deleuze writes that it is:

> as if the relations of the outside [were] folded back to create a doubling, allow[ing] a relation to oneself to emerge and constitute an inside which is hollowed out and develops its own unique dimension ... self-mastery.[65]

In the context of training and practice, self-mastery is expressed through the dancer's skills, kinaesthetic background and movement subjectivity.

Foucault's work draws attention to the discursive and inscriptive means by which history and the body coalesce. It unpacks the territorialization of culture in relation to the body, which functions as "the inscribed surface of events".[66] Once inscribed, the body evokes an associated depth or 'correlate', understood by Deleuze as force folded inwards.[67] Depth is the means whereby the body is able to become intelligible to itself. Subjectivity in the dancer speaks to this notion of depth. It is in particular concerned with the body's own intelligibility or self-interpretation, which in turn informs the interpretation of other bodies. Klossowski most clearly recognized the sense in which culture produces its own means of corporeal understanding. For Klossowski, corporeal intelligibility mediates experience. There is no independent experience of the body. Corporeal intelligibility is linked to practice, to its habituated sensibilities. Nietzsche writes:

> The habits of our senses have woven us into lies and deception of sensation: these again are the basis of all our judgements and "knowledge" – there is absolutely no escape, no backway or bypath into the *real world*.[68]

Practice produces its own signature habits, perceptual foci and preferred sensations. The dancer's kinaesthetic thinking is formed within and according to this milieu. Foucault writes that although we believe "that the body obeys the exclusive laws of physiology and that it escapes the influence of history", the body is in fact imprinted by "a great many distinct regimes".[69] The regime produces its own distinctive corporeal intelligibility, an intelligibility which may itself claim unmediated access to the body. It is perhaps a mark of such a depth that its thinker is seamlessly transported into the body. The question that history poses is *which* body.

Thought broadly, dance is a mode of history in the body, a regime and a regimen. As such, it produces the characteristic abilities and subjectivities belonging to the field, including their allied attitudes, interpretations and modes of intelligibility. Dance training generates habits, dispositions, signature reactions and their preferred manner of deployment. Kinaesthetic culture works reaction and its deployment through the reins of the subject-position, an intermediary formation embedded in the intertwining of history and the body.

The Sovereign Individual – the post-historic

In principle, training leads to conformity.[70] Training, for Deleuze, is a kind of domestication, one which works our animal nature into a form of 'docility'.[71] To be docile is not to be inert in the face of outside pressures. Rather it is to function within certain limits, to occupy the field in a positive sense. The Foucauldian docile body is an emergent formation, the product of disciplinary practice.[72] The docile body is produced through education, reinforcement, habituation and repetition, which Deleuze calls training and selection. From one point of view, discipline is a creative process, facilitating the emergence of skill in the body. And yet, once skill becomes embedded in a body (and therefore available), the body cleaves to that particular way of organizing force. It follows the designated pathways established through corporeal formation. Foucault sees disciplinary modes of production as manifesting this double tendency:

> Discipline increases the forces of the body (in economic terms of utility) and diminishes these same forces (in political terms of obedience). In short, it dissociates power from the body; on the one hand, it turns it into an "aptitude" and "capacity", which it seeks to increase; on the other hand, it reverses the course of energy, the power that might result from it, and turns it into a relation of strict subjection.[73]

Subjection in this sense is a type of corporeal subjectification – a formative process that subjects insofar as it produces a certain kind of corporeal tendency.

Although discipline, training and selection equip the body for cultural reproduction, skill can be deployed against the cultural grain. Resistance is the underside of conformity, drawing on the same forces but acting them towards other ends. Foucault writes of the "meticulous work of power" to invest in a body which, for its part, may act "against power".[74] Nietzsche conceived the reworking of cultural force 'against power', as a particular form of mastery – over culture. The expression of mastery over culture is the expression of a particular type, called by Nietzsche, the Sovereign Individual. Nietzsche sees the Sovereign Individual as culture's "ripest fruit", ripe because she is cultivated through culture yet active in relation to it, able to create rather than to merely reproduce.[75] The Sovereign Individual claims "the right to say 'yes' to itself", an affirmative gesture reminiscent of the master.[76] But the Sovereign Individual emerges through culture. The Sovereign Individual, graduate of kinaesthetic culture, has all the facility that training can produce: the right reactions and the capacity to deploy them well. What differentiates the Sovereign Individual from the merely trained is that the Sovereign Individual has "power over himself", whereas the merely trained has become wholly domesticated.[77] Culture thus works in two inimical directions:

(1) Towards conformity through the herd's affiliation to hegemonic forms of value, and
(2) Towards culture's potential overcoming in the form of the Sovereign Individual.

For Deleuze, history secures the triumph of reaction – felt in the gathering of reaction within subjectivity, through subjectivation and corporal formation. History is realized in the emergence of the herd, which functions as "a means of preserving, organising and propagating the reactive life".[78] The Sovereign Individual, by contrast, is pure activity, affirming (and therefore creating) value in the midst of culture. Deleuze locates the Sovereign Individual in the post-historic, after (the work of) culture. While the pre-historic depicts the structural nature of subjectivity (its capacity for the acquisition and reproduction of the socio-cultural habitus) and the historic conjoins the body with history (through discursive practices, technologies of power and the institutional customs within which subjectivity emerges), the post-historic belongs to another kind of activity, one which is not simply acted by culture but is "like only to itself ... an autonomous, supra-ethical individual".[79]

Virtuosity and the untimely

The Sovereign Individual is a less form of subjectivity, than an activity: the redeployment of culture. Sovereignty is expressed in action here, through 'acting' culture. The Sovereign Individual turns culture itself into a reaction, to be reinterpreted, reinvigorated, reframed or reimagined. The sovereign type is the one who acts culture rather than is acted by it. The body is its means, the very reactions and abilities cultivated by culture but now expressed through turning culture on its head.[80]

Virtuosic dancing is one way of looking at sovereign expressivity. If culture forms the background of virtuosity, the virtuosic acts that very terrain as its circumstance. The virtuosic dancer is thoroughly trained, the ultimate exponent of her field. While Nietzsche and Deleuze use terms such as freedom and autonomy, it is important to realize the *corporeal basis* of that freedom. If the virtuosic dancer is the one who acts culture, her means of expression begins with the body produced by culture. Virtuosity doesn't transcend the body, it must find a way to work with and through it. Given the dancer's strong attachment to her skills (as that which makes her a dancer), this is no easy task. It is not that unusual to observe classically trained dancers working in a contemporary context pull out an *attitude*, a leg extension or a *jeté*, almost as if they are expressing their "dancerness" as they know it in their own bodies.[81] This is in part a matter of habit, the habit of enunciating one's identity as a dancer. Attachment to one's habits can be a strong force within dance, since their expression gives a sense of pleasure, alongside feelings of mastery within the kinaesthetic terrain. Displacing that terrain through non-conformist behaviour risks foregoing the recognition embedded in known forms of value.[82] The difficulty with kinaesthetic innovation according to an emergent standard of value is that others/the herd do not adhere to these values. To create value is to move onto new kinaesthetic territory, to reterritorialize the given. What sovereignty does is destabilize historical and corporeal forces, through taking them as their circumstance. Dance combines stability and instability. Its iterative, performative character opens it up to corporeal variation: repetition being the generation of difference. And yet, the corporeal basis of dance grounds its iteration in the trained body, in the one for whom the norms of culture are given. These two tendencies (towards conformity and variation) underlie and inform the virtuosic.

Sovereign virtuosity can be seen to function on two fronts, individual and collective. In an individual sense, virtuosic dancing draws on culture's selections, but gives them its own inflexion through the ways in which they are deployed. What is it that makes for great dancing? To be sure, each field will have its own criteria but the virtuosic is able to address those criteria, to take up a perspective on them, in action. Such is its relative autonomy. To what extent this remains within or lies beyond the terms of the particular cultural milieu is a matter for judgement and debate, in part a question of the identity and limits of the dance form. While some dance forms have clear boundaries (e.g. a fixed lexicon or form), there will always be a degree of equivocation when culture is itself reworked. Is a work still traditional when it draws on new kinds of force? How open is technique to variation? There are so many contextual factors at play in any given performance; it is difficult to (pre)determine what constitutes historical repetition as distinct from an untimely variation that subverts the form. Butoh and traditional Korean dance each incorporate an element of improvisation within their kinaesthetic palette. Where does improvisation end and virtuosic reconfiguration begin? If virtuosity is difficult to achieve on the part of the dancer, there is no guarantee it will be recognized as such in that kinaesthetic perception carries its own presumptions and perspective. Kinaesthetic qualities and values have a history, are transmitted from body to body and engender their own forms of literacy which come into play when determining the virtuosic qualities of the dance. It is in this sense that Nietzsche uses terms such as irresponsibility and immorality to signal a departure from the morality of custom and the inauguration of new forms of value. At the very least, virtuosity acts its kinaesthetic, cultural base. This may be contained within the particular field, as excellent dancing in conformity with cultural norms, or it may move the form itself into new territory. The creation of value defies easy recognition based on the old values, requiring a perception of difference founded on new territory.

The collective expression of sovereignty may not seem to fit the Nietzschean paradigm insofar as it is not the work of an individual. Perhaps the collective is just another version of the herd? And yet, if sovereignty actively refashions culture, there is a sense in which political collectivities determine their own standard of value. The collectivity forms a new body in Deleuzian terms, a community of bodies which, together, act culture.[83] Grosz poses the possibility of "strategic counter-reinscription" as a way of thinking culture against the grain.[84] Feminist activism constitutes one means of redeploying patriarchal givens. Artistic creation offers another. In kinaesthetic terms, the suggestion is that the body (or bodies) can be redeployed, towards a different cultural vision. Matthew Bourne's inversion of gender codes in *Swan Lake* could be seen as a sovereign destabilization of ballet culture. Christel Stalpaert offers another example of cultural destabilization, through Katarzyna Kozrya's restaging of *Rite of Spring* in a dance installation featuring older bodies.[85] Stalpaert claims that Kozyra's *Rite of Spring* goes against clichéd thinking about the proper body of dance, issuing a challenge to the spectator's normative thinking around what a (dancing) body should be like.[86] For Stalpaert, the work provokes the composite body of the visitor-spectator to encounter corporeal otherness with wonder rather than recognition, leading to a new capacity in the cultural body, to "see age differently".[87]

The ability to open up to difference can be an integral aspect of culture, particularly within minority or resistant (sub)cultures. Thomas DeFrantz writes of the ways in which kinaesthetic variation is valued within black social dance.[88] Not only are "gestures of innovation" recognized by the group, the form itself embraces the new in order to move forwards.[89] According to this way of thinking, black social dance invites virtuosic variation, posed by DeFrantz as a mode of queer resistance. In this context, virtuosity can be collective or individual, performed by a same-sex athletics team, by couples or by an individual for the group. The 'right' to virtuosic expression is conferred upon all members of the group, who together dance their cultural form. DeFrantz writes "*Queer* in this articulation refers to the non-normative flashes of gender performance that contribute to unexpected renderings of social identity".[90] The non-normative flash recalls Deleuze's capture of the active type's "burst of creativity".[91] The Sovereign Individual of black social dance queers the form towards new "explorations of [the] dance form". In so doing, an untimely black futurity is made possible. DeFrantz identifies the two aspects of cultural force that underlie virtuosity: the cultural basis that feeds the virtuosic, alongside the potential for variation. On the one hand, Afrofuturism "needs history to stabilise its ambitions"[92], and on the other, black futures are "already in creative play".[93] Such is the tension within sovereignty, between historicity and the untimely.

Section 3: Desubjectification

We have seen how culture can be transformed through the virtuosic, on an individual and collective level. What we haven't yet considered is whether and why subjectivity might itself be overcome. Nietzsche's multifaceted critique of subjectivity is motivated by the sense that we could be so much more. For Nietzsche, the very things that define our humanity – a sense of responsibility, morality and virtue – stand in the way of our fully embracing life. It's not that all good deeds are 'wrong', rather, the moral imperatives within which good and evil arise are limiting. Nietzsche often frames this state of affairs as a form of sickness endemic to human being. He poses the overman as an antidote to the pathological tendencies of the human, seeing in the figure of the overman a movement towards better health.[94] The overman is an ideal, a type which overcomes the human in us. Like Nietzsche, Deleuze is keen to posit a difference in kind between the human and the overman.[95] An implication of this difference is the view that subjectivity cannot be overcome by some new version of subjectivity. It must give way to another type altogether:

> We should not think of Nietzsche's overman as simply a raising of the stakes: he differs in nature from man, from the ego. The overman is

defined by *a new way of feeling*: he is a different subject from man, some-thing other than the human type.[96]

If the human is our starting point, how does the overman come about? Deleuze refers to Nietzsche's *Thus Spake Zarathustra* as offering a range of (mostly inadequate) types and tendencies.[97] Their collective problem is that, although they strive for betterment, they are firmly situated within the human domain. To that end, Deleuze outlines a mode of becoming on the part of the subject, which inaugurates its own demise. He calls it active destruction:

> Zarathustra praised the man of active destruction: he wants to be over-come, he goes beyond the human, already on the path of the overman.[98]

Active destruction is found in the one who wants to be overcome, who "wills his own downfall".[99] It is not a form of submission – to some greater force – but the work of the one who actively destroys himself. The subject of active destruction is a liminal figure, poised to leave the realm of reaction to become that which affirms all becoming. For Deleuze, active destruction is the decisive moment, an instant which values creativity over and above that which is already known.[100] Active destruction signifies the 'transmutation' of the human realm into the affirmative arts of dance, laughter and play. To create in such a way is "to set free what lives", to generate new values while inventing new forms of life.[101]

What follows is a line of interpretation which aims to take up the gesture of active destruction if not its ultimate destiny. Its goal is to seek out the circumstances in which subjectivity can be played strategically, towards its own overcoming – for kinaesthetic gain. Although the dancer is unlikely to will her own downfall as such, there is in dance a sense in which the dancer may take a critical stance towards her own (movement) subjectivity. Such an impetus is founded on the recognition that subjectivity narrows the corporeal field. Often predicated upon a critique of habit, these strategic moves share the sense that, under the right circumstances, the body can be encouraged to pursue its own course, beyond any conscious direction that the dancer can supply.

Active destruction in the dancer represents a movement away from subject-ivity and towards a greater plurality of corporeal becoming. It resonates with Klossowski's corporeal reading of overcoming, which pits the body against the self. Klossowski writes of Nietzsche's distinction between the body's rela-tion to the self (as a property of the self, as something we own and con-trol) and the body's own activities which follow their own impetus.[102] In the first case, the body is subjected to the subjective sphere, understood in con-formity with the experience and ongoing identity of the self. In the latter case, the body is seen on its own terms, as the dynamic product of contestatory forces (impulses) which find serial resolution in corporeal terms. While the body cleaves to the workings of force that comprise its formation, the self is committed to a very different hermeneutic, one whose interests are social in nature. For Klossowski (and Nietzsche), the sociality of human understanding depends upon a communicative principle of exchange and equivalence, at odds with the singular unfolding of corporeal states.[103] The body and the self thus represent antithetical interests. Taking the side of the body rather than that of the self, Klossowski asks how the body might "subtract" the self.[104] The aim of subtraction is to destabilize and liberate the corporeal from the confines of subjectivity.

Like Deleuze, Klossowski interprets overcoming as a form of desubjectification which involves an "expropriation of the agent, of the self".[105] For Klossowski, however, overcoming the self has a *corporeal* aim, namely, to restore "corporealizing forces (impulses) to thought".[106] Klossowski claims that expropriating the self makes space for another kind of intellect, "infinitely more vast than the one that merges with our consciousness".[107] The body's myriad corporeal states found the emergence of this wider perspective, which follows its own semiotic of impulses. The body's 'semiotic' is a line of corporeal interpretation, a dynamic hermeneutics of force, which situates thought in the body rather than in the reactive apparatus. Subtracting the self, for Klossowski, makes possible this new kind of corporeal perspective, conceived apart from consciousness. Klossowski thereby gestures towards a corporeal trajectory, able to differ on its own terms, freed from the distorting intelligibility of the subject. He writes:

> Once the body is recognized as the product of the impulses (subjected, organized, hierarchized), its cohesion with the self becomes fortuitous. The impulses *can be put to use by a new body*, and are presupposed in the search for new conditions.[108]

Subtracting the self from the body enables the body to remain on the plane of the corporeal, rather than finding itself subject to human understanding. In Deleuzian terms, it resists the diversion of force into the reactive apparatus, thereby to support the body's affirmative status. In short, subtraction widens the field of corporeal becoming.

Overcoming through dance

Overcoming in Nietzsche opens itself up to a number of interpretations and rationales. Deleuze treats active destruction as a thought, a moment that completes nihilism and ushers in a fully affirmative domain. Klossowski looks at subtraction as a journey away from the subject's lucidity and towards greater corporeal activity. From a kinaesthetic point of view, overcoming is an action, to be performed in the midst of movement. It puts forward the idea that dancers might want to deconstruct elements of their own subjectivity in order to promote another notion of corporeal possibility. Fleshing out such a possibility depends upon the ways in which dancerly subjectivity is conceived and problematized – in practice. Postmodern dance is offered as one example of such an approach. Certain somatic approaches such as the Alexander Technique explicitly critique habit. Other instances are embedded in the work of individual artists who conspire to resist the formation of subjectivity in their dancing. These examples, each in their own way, embrace overcoming as a means to enhance corporeal formation. Although they qualify as expressions of desubjectification, their field of concern is practical, the measure of their success an aesthetic, functional or empirical matter. The kinaesthetic context within which these examples arise suggests a cultural reading of Klossowski's corporeal semiotic. To that end, the body's semiosis is not situated outside of culture but rather amalgamates body and culture. Active destruction is thus given a cultural inflexion, as that which finds expression through corporeal formation in its broadest sense.

The discussion begins with the work and impact of Yvonne Rainer on the status of the performative self. While Rainer's signature manifesto, " 'No' to Spectacle", challenged the value of spectacle within dance, it was the dancing of *Trio A* (1978) which established another kind of performativity, linked to Merce Cunningham's critique of expressivity within modern dance.[109] Rainer writes:

> what Merce was trying to express was the idea that anything the human body does is expressive, and that the self is at best irrelevant and, at worst, a distraction from the real business of dancing.[110]

Rainer builds upon Cunningham's critique of the self to elaborate the sense in which *Trio A* purports:

> a provisional or ambiguous self that is at once produced, erased, and confounded. It can be said that the performing self of *Trio A* takes care of its self *and* its expression by a mode of expression that recuses the self.[111]

The suggestion is that something of the dancer's subjectivity is given up by the dancer in *Trio A*. If not an explicit attempt to undo subjectivity, *Trio A* nonetheless requires a "selfless, cool absorption in the *work* of dancing".[112] Active destruction is one way of framing this performative modality, characterized by pragmatic absorption in the work of dancing. I call this particular version of active destruction the expression of a Workerly Type.

The Workerly Type subsumes her performative self, not merely to subvert the dancer's sense of self-expression, but to allow another kind of dancing to emerge, one which is led by the body rather than the self. Sara Rudner speaks of dancing *Trio A*:

> When it came right down to it, and you were there to do the dance, the best thing that happened was the body took over and the dance happened.[113]

The Workerly Type characterizes an absorption in the work of dancing, one which 'brackets' the self so as to promote the corporealization of force. While many forms of dance are absorbing, each in their own way, the Workerly Type speaks to those activities that actively *problematize* the performative self. It belongs to the range of postmodern strategies and treatments of movement material that undermine the subject (dancer) presumed to know through kinaesthetic defamiliarization. These are best known through techniques of cut and paste and retrograde variation. Movement material that may have arisen because it felt good or familiar or reflects habitual, characteristic ways of moving is here subjected to somewhat arbitrary breaks and (re)assemblages. Rather than selecting movement because it *feels* right, slicing and suturing movement requires an adaptation on the part of the body towards a new corporeal logic. It destabilizes and displaces the dancer's familiar kinaesthetic sensibility in favour of unknown flows of force. In a similar vein, working out the retrograde version of phrase material follows none of the intuitive pathways that may have inspired its original formulation. The process (of adaptation) on the part of the dancer is itself at the centre of this way of working, not the development of 'mastery'. There is an ethos within these practices, away from finding a fixed 'solution' (way of dancing phrase material), and towards a more active, interrogatory approach. Linda Sastradipradja writes:

> Dancing is problem solving. The problem is never solved, if you are dancing.
> If you are showing a solution to a previously solved problem then you are not dancing. You are assuming a position, or you are presenting a position or stance.
> Embodied dancing is active solving of a problem in real time. An "accomplished" dancer is not necessarily one who has previously accomplished a solution and then repeats it as a "feat".[114]

Rather than the dancer as 'the subject presumed to know', these approaches sideline knowing subjectivity in favour of an expanded corporeal field.

Allied to this process-oriented approach is the tendency to take a critical perspective towards one's movement habits. Elizabeth Dempster writes of the postmodern body's engagement in "processes of deconstruction and bricolage", where habitual tendencies and patterns are called into question.[115] Melanie Bales similarly speaks of paring back habitual, muscular patterns. For Bales, undoing these patterns requires the dancer "to get out of the way", thereby to practise a kind of Zen non-doing.[116] According to Dempster, the resultant instability engendered by these kinds of activity enables the postmodern body to become "available" to a greater range of active forces.[117] In Dempster's view then, deconstruction and bricolage are a means to widen the field of available force.

This is no easy task. The problem, for Russell Dumas, is that the dancer is invested in her (movement) habits and therefore resistant to their over-coming.[118] Dumas used to say that he couldn't leave his dancers to rehearse on their own because they would only practise their 'bad habits'. The challenge of active destruction is that it calls for the abdication of that which quali-fies the dancer *as* a dancer.[119] The achievement of greater 'availability' on the part of the body thus depends upon relinquishing feelings of mastery. Dumas has over the years developed a number of strategies aimed towards kinaes-thetic desubjectification: displacing dancers from their familiar contexts and relocating to other cultural and kinaesthetic milieus, working late so as to undermine the 'night watchman', drinking (small amounts of) alcohol and an activity he calls "slow rendering".[120] Dumas writes:

> "slow rendering" involves distracting the conscious mind with detailed complex physical activities. In the best scenario, the mind abdicates con-trol over how these tasks are achieved within the body and the body unconsciously utilizes the deeply efficient pattern of running. As trust and confidence in this body wisdom increases, development occurs "behind your back".[121]

Slow rendering is a counter-strategy, aimed to retard the subject-formation implicit in the act of 'mastering' movement.

To what extent these activities constitute a form of active destruction on the part of the dancer depends in part on the concrete ways in which the dancer conducts herself, in motion. Certain choreographies may also be seen as supporting or even requiring a kind of desubjectification. For example, postmodern choreographer and dancer, Trish Brown, spoke of the impossi-bility of tracking her movement and speech in *Accumulation with Talking Plus Watermotor.*[122] The task of keeping these two activities in play may benefit from a certain kind of subjective decentring. In like fashion, Dumas would sometimes insert what he calls 'smart dancing' into his choreography. For example, one side of the body begins a series of movements and the other side follows in canon. Managing the simultaneous complexity of these tasks in real time requires relinquishing any sense of conscious control. However achieved, there is a sense in which the body is entrusted to enact that which sovereign subjectivity cannot. Deborah Hay's work functions on another plane again, at the level of movement selection on the part of the dancer. Yet her multi-faceted instructions and (counter-factual) suppositions can be construed as deconstructive techniques that destabilize and decentre the dancer's subject-ivity, thereby to retard the process of subject-formation.[123] For example, the choreographic instruction, "here and gone", "here and gone", to be repeat-edly deployed in action, palpably subverts (or subtracts) the formation of the memorial self in the midst of movement.[124] Like slow-rendering, "here and gone" distracts the conscious mind away from its usual observations and judgements in order to enable the emergence of another kind of corporeal thinking, felt in action. Hay's recent project, *Being a Pig* (2019), is predicated on a number of instructions that equally retard subject-formation, including for example the following directives:

> No obvious sequence of movement
> No cause and effect composition
> No prolonged narrative movement
> No hanging out in the body[125]

Taken together, these directives tend towards the deformation of the dancer as dancer. Hay writes:

> My work relies on the persistent presence of the questions, rendering useless a reliance on memory and anticipation.[126]

Although the Workerly Type nested in certain strands of postmodern dance resonates with the notion of active destruction, and may further involve strategies that displace the dancer's knowing subjectivity, active destruction need not be confined to a single kinaesthetic context. Japanese performer, Takao Tawaguchi, speaks of his performative approach towards *About Kazuo Ohno* (2013) in a way which suggests a kind of slow rendering of his performative self.[127] Although *About Kazuo Ohno* was constructed from detailed examination of film and video archives of the Butoh master, and input from Ohno's son, Yoshito Ohno, Tawaguchi resisted settling on a fixed version of Ohno's dancing, even though he performed a number of Ohno's celebrated dances in costume. When asked whether he felt that he, Takao, was performing his understanding of Ohno, Tawaguchi responded that he resisted the sense that he understands or knows Ohno's work.[128] He similarly denied that, through performing the work, he came to 'know' Ohno.[129] Rather than assuming a kind of knowing subjectivity, Tawaguchi would return time and again to the video materials and his extensive sketches of Ohno. Neither vesting authority in the absent master/authorial source (as object), nor assuming authorship himself (as subject), but keeping a certain indeterminacy alive, *About Kazuo Ohno* destabilizes these two terms, drawing upon new corporeal circumstances according to each performance. Working from the outside-in, to evoke the work of a performer who worked from "the heart" to create "form", the work undermines the presumption of mimesis and authenticity in a work that on the surface seeks an accurate reproduction of a corporeal past.[130]

Somatic practices, such as Skinner Releasing Technique™, Body Mind Centering, Feldenkrais and Alexander Technique, can also be seen in light of overcoming, particularly in relation to habit. Western dancers regularly supplement their dancing technique by engaging in one or more forms of somatic practice.[131] These approaches often involve critical examination of the subject's movement habits, as a way of seeking greater facility, range or efficiency. Some somatic practices, such as Alexander Technique, are explicitly critical of the role habit plays within everyday life. Others, such as Feldenkrais technique, are less directive but equally aim to open the body up to a greater diversity of movement possibilities. Each approach maps out its own morphological commitments, including a hermeneutic corporeal intelligibility through which they approach movement.[132] Alexander Technique is of the view that our everyday tendency to contract the body in action gets in the way of our living with greater ease and efficiency.[133] Alexander Technique offers a strategic response to this state of affairs, one which aims to inhibit habit so as to facilitate the possibility of moving otherwise. Rebecca Nettl-Fiol writes:

> The word inhibition, as used in the context of Alexander technique, means to stop when you notice yourself responding to a stimulus in your habitual way. This moment of stopping opens the door to new possibilities.[134]

Inhibition is an attempt to overcome unreflective habits. Rather than absorption, inhibition aims to arrest the habitual every day so as to create "the space for something different to occur".[135] Its space of possibility is less a place of enhanced agency than a domain of *non-doing*. Non-doing extends inhibition into the realm of movement. Nettl-Fiol describes it as "getting out of one's own way".[136] Non-doing deconstructs (subjective) agency by forwarding a sense of movement that incorporates the Alexander directions.[137] The Alexander directions are an antidote to the endemic tendency to contract into action. Their aim is to open up the body (and the self) to another "means whereby" life can be lived, and movement can be enacted.[138] The Alexander Technique gives pause to action. It subtracts the self, both through inhibition and non-doing, while supporting a different kind of action.

Ideokinesis and image-based work likewise embrace the notion of non-doing (here, through entertaining but not 'doing' the image) but deals with habitual repatterning in another way. Anne Thompson sees ideokinesis as working beneath conscious intentionality:

> The process demands engagement in imagining not a willing of change. Willing change to occur prevents the body finding the change, necessary and particular, for its own freedom of operation. It is important to allow the images to find their own resolution, to allow oneself to be, potentially, retrospectively surprised by the effects of the imagined movement.[139]

The ideokinetic subject lies in constructive rest when entertaining the image.[140] Disrupting the vertical every day (through assuming the constructive rest position) arguably displaces the vertical organization of subjective sovereignty over the body, paving the way for the entry of new kinds of corporeal force.[141] Entertaining but not doing the image and lying in constructive rest can be seen as an attempt to desubjectify experience so that other sensations and movement qualities are able to emerge. Moving from the image into action is not a prescribed process, rather the opportunity to allow new neuro-muscular qualities and sensations to transpire, in motion. Non-doing remains a key component of allowing the image to act the body, such that the image becomes present without effort.[142] Jane Refshauge traces four moments in the life of an image (as told to Mabel Todd): "Seeing the image, thinking it, and finally, forgetting it, so that it can happen".[143] In this way, the image enters a horizontal zone of experiential displacement, ultimately to act a new body into motion. Forgetting enables experience to enter into movement's riposte, acted by the image into motion. Manny Emslie discusses Joan Skinner's similar sense that the dedicated use of imagery in her work is able to produce a sense of 'transparency' in the body, of the "image moving the dancer who then becomes the dance rather than dancing it".[144] Whether these practices 'qualify' as successful versions of active destruction or merely *gesture* towards overcoming is difficult to say. What somatic practices do is offer a strategic means for dancers to quieten their habitual agency in favour of an expanded corporeal field.

Thought through Klossowski's corporeal reading of overcoming, active destruction in dance decentres the dancer's movement subjectivity. This can occur in numerous ways, through the absorption embedded in the Workerly Type, via slow rendering, memorial deconstruction, inhibition or non-doing. Each of those practices within which active destruction is embedded incorporates the view that subjectivity cannot furnish the entire gamut of movement possibility and that, strategically, subjectivity can be deployed in such a way that the self can be subtracted. They are founded on the recognition that subjectivity inhibits the corporeal field. Whether overcoming can ever be *achieved* is entirely moot. After all, active destruction in Deleuze is a speculative moment in a conceptual journey towards the affirmation of difference. In Klossowski, subtraction is achieved at the cost of the subject's lucidity. In dance then, active destruction is an asymptote, a movement towards rather than an arrival. Never fully realized, it nonetheless signifies an ethos, the inauguration of a new mode of valuing, one which distinguishes between the self and the body and which acknowledges the relative autonomy of corporeal life.

Conclusion

There are a number of ways in which subjectivity can be reconfigured within Nietzschean philosophy. The first approach taken in this chapter offers an action-based account of dancing founded upon relations of force. Using typology to distinguish between the active and reactive types, it depicts subjectivity as a failure on the part of the reactive apparatus to ensure the fluidity of consciousness. Experience is depicted here as that which cannot let go. While the reactive type represents the many ways in which experience and thought persist, movement's riposte highlights the sense in which dancing is ever poised to re-enter the field of action. To that extent, subjectivity's 'retreat' from action is once again returned to the fold of corporeal formation. Overall, this approach represents a reading of Nietzsche's claim that there is no doer behind the deed. Its focus on the dynamic plurality of forces paves the way for a wide conception of that which enters the dance, depending upon the activity and identification of force in the particular instance, whether psychic, social, cultural, spiritual, political, kinaesthetic, environmental and so on.

Culture can also be seen as a means of shaping and producing subjectivity, generating the subject as its intermediary formation. Culture functions through the individual, to ensure the reproduction and transmission of its embedded values. Training and selection, habituation and practice enter the picture as the means whereby subjectivity can become culture's reaction *writ large*. The cultural perspective not only concentrates upon the means whereby subjectivity is produced (the pre-historic role of culture), it also acknowledges the articulated specificity of cultural practices (culture's historical dimension). If culture is that which acts subjectivity, then virtuosity for its part acts culture. This is the post-historic moment of cultural production. Virtuosic dancing turns culture on its head, operating via singular reinterpretation or collective reconfiguration.

The third treatment of subjectivity set out in this chapter concerns its strategic redeployment, in action. Drawing on the Nietzschean concept of overcoming and active destruction, it looks to the ways in which dance might be said to enunciate a relation to the dancing self – one which seeks its own displacement. Such an approach is elucidated through an interpretation of certain postmodern and somatic practices, the discernment of a Workerly Type, and the claim that there is a sense in which movement need not seek a sovereign subjectivity.

In the Preface to *Nietzsche and Philosophy*, Deleuze writes of Nietzsche's image of thought as an arrow shot into the air and picked up "by another thinker".[145] Thought moves in myriad directions in the field of dance. Some of it is inherited, in the form of training and technique, but also through cultural and kinaesthetic precedent. Culture fosters the gathering of those forces in the body that come to be deployed in action. Culture is the concentration of force, to become a mode of practice or technique. It is also found in the distinctive subjectivity of the dancer, the customs and character of the dance, its history, milieu and kinaesthetic context. In practice, culture is the historical means by which a body acquires its habits. What a body does leaves its mark on the body. These factors determine what counts as thought in the field of movement. Thought is transmitted through culture and is expressed in the many rituals and performative habits embedded in dance practice. Thought can also shift between types, from movement to its experience and back to movement. It may be expressed through faithful reiteration or virtuosic play. The many thoughts that form the dancer may also be strategically deployed towards a mode of overcoming, so as to promote a corporeal line of flight, into new territory. The circumstances of dance may as a result be reconfigured, to produce new modes of thought beyond the dictates of custom.

The Nietzschean ontology of force and its allied concepts offers a different take upon the dancer and the dancing than that proposed by the phenomenological perspective. While undermining the metaphysical givenness of the dancer as agent, it casts a wider net to capture the vicissitudes of corporeal formation. Its emphasis on the dynamic play of force opens itself to a broad conception of the circumstances of dance, which are acted into motion. These circumstances are local and variable, also determining and historical. History is a key circumstance of dance, that impacts upon subject-formation, corporeal disposition, kinaesthetic literacy, intelligibility and perception. It draws political force as both circumstance and its activation. The political circumscribes the body of dance, to be recruited in a variety of forms and on a number of levels. The fact that a body can be social, political or individual, biological or virtual suggests the many ways in which this might be understood. The nuances of these activities and their associated events is a matter of interpretation – of perception and critique, literacy and openness. One of Nietzsche's key insights is the view that interpretation is not an innocent process but itself draws force from specific quarters and interests. The following chapter illustrates the dynamic character of interpretation, felt in political terms. Located in Indigenous/non-Indigenous relations, within an Australian context, it aims to deploy the Nietzschean approach to corporeal formation in the political theatre of race relations Australian style.

Notes

1 Gilles Deleuze, *Nietzsche and Philosophy*, trans. Hugh Tomlinson (New York: Columbia University Press, 1983), 134.
2 Friedrich Nietzsche, *On the Genealogy of Morality*, trans. Carol Diethe, ed. Keith Ansell-Pearson (Cambridge: Cambridge University Press, 1994), 40.
3 Nietzsche writes, "I distinguish between a type of ascending life and another type of decay, disintegration, weakness. Is it credible that the question of the relative rank of these two types still needs to be posed?", Friedrich Nietzsche, *Will To Power*, trans. Walter Kaufmann and R.J. Hollingdale (New York: Random House, 1968), 457. Also, Nietzsche, *Will To Power*, 472, 476, 477, and 479. Nietzsche uses the term 'rank' to distinguish between different kinds of formation or type, for example, the slave, the master, the noble and the herd. *Thus Spake Zarathustra* also depicts and evaluates a number of types, Friedrich Nietzsche, *Thus Spake Zarathustra*, trans. R.J. Hollingdale (London: Penguin Books, 2003).
4 Deleuze, *Nietzsche and Philosophy*, x.
5 Ibid., x.
6 Ibid.
7 Ibid., 111. This is an odd turn of phrase which, according to the translator of *Nietzsche and Philosophy*, Hugh Tomlinson, is also odd in the original French, ibid., 211. Nonetheless, it does indicate the sense in which reactive force orients itself towards active force. It suggests a level of compliance, if also response, to the workings of active force.

8 The plane of the subject is a form of words, a shorthand for philosophical approaches that suppose the importance of the subject for metaphysics. Although pervasive, not all philosophers adhere to a metaphysics of the subject, most notably, Deleuze and Guattari, who argue that "Subject and object give a poor approximation of thought. Thinking is neither a line drawn between subject and object not a revolving of one around the other. Rather, thinking takes place in the relationship of territory and the earth", Gilles Deleuze and Félix Guattari, *What Is Philosophy?*, trans. Hugh Tomlinson and Graham Burchell (New York: Columbia University Press), 95.

9 Nietzsche, *On the Genealogy of Morality*, 18.

10 Ibid., 21.

11 Deleuze, *Nietzsche and Philosophy*, 41.

12 Nietzsche, *On the Genealogy of Morality*, 19–20.

13 Deleuze, *Nietzsche and Philosophy*, 117.

14 Ibid., 112.

15 Ibid., 113.

16 Nietzsche, *On the Genealogy of Morality*, 38.

17 Ibid., 38.

18 Deleuze, *Nietzsche and Philosophy*, 113.

19 Nietzsche, *On the Genealogy of Morality*, 38.

20 Deleuze, *Nietzsche and Philosophy*, 116.

21 Ibid., 116.

22 Ibid., 114.

23 Ibid.

24 Ibid.

25 Ibid.

26 Ibid.

27 Ibid., 41.

28 Ibid., 115.

29 Erin Manning's *Relationscapes* is predicated on the concept of the becoming body, which is thought in conjunction with a number of other movement- and process-based conceptions. The becoming body is posed as "a sensing body in movement, a body that resists predefinition in terms of subjectivity or identity, a body that is involved in a reciprocal reaching-toward that in-gathers the world even as it worlds", Erin Manning, *Relationscapes: Movement, Art, Philosophy* (Cambridge, MA: MIT Press, 2012), 6. Manning draws on the work of Whitehead to elaborate the relation between thought and movement. The becoming body enters into this relation as a formation in motion. Manning writes:

> The becoming body has no fixed form – it is an exfoliating body. It creates space through both intensive and extensive movement, appearing as such only momentarily in its passage from incipiency to the elasticity of the almost. The body in Riefenstahl's work is not given but produced – produced not in its entirety but in passing, in movement.
>
> (Ibid., 124)

30 Deleuze, *Nietzsche and Philosophy*, 40.

31 See Susan Foster, "Choreographies of Protest", *Theater Journal*, 55, no. 3 (October 2003): 395–412; Anusha Kedhar, "Hands up Don't Shoot: Gesture, Choreography and Protest in Ferguson", *Dancehouse Diary* 10, (2018): 14–15; and Thomas

DeFrantz, "Bone Breaking: Black Social Dance and Queer Corporeal Orature", *The Black Scholar* 46, no. 1 (Spring 2016): 66–74.

32 Co-creation is one way of thinking this. Venke Sortland writes of the sense in which Ingri Fiksdal's work, *Urskog*, and the work of Diego Gil, Irina Müller, and Trajal Harrell, involves its audience as "co-creators", Venke Sortland, "When Experience is the Artwork: The End of Performance?", in *Writing Movement: Expeditions in Dance Writing 2012–2014*, ed. Ine Therese Berg and Inta Balode (Norway: Dance Information Norway, 2014), 146. See also Shaun McLeod, *The Movement Between: Dance Improvisation, Witnessing and Participatory Performance*, unpublished PhD thesis (Melbourne: Deakin University, 2016), for an articulation of an emergent joint corporeal formation between the audience and dancers in a performative version of authentic movement.

33 Manning's account of relational movement in tango dancing, for example, suggests a mutable sense of corporeal boundary, *Relationscapes*, 14–15.

34 Deleuze, *Nietzsche and Philosophy*, 111.

35 Nietzsche, *On the Genealogy of Morality*, 23.

36 The notion of the sternum as a flowing cape was introduced to me by Pam Matt, a former student of Barbara Clark, the pelvis as a bridge by Shona Innes, drawing on the work of John Rolland, and the body as a collapsing suit of clothes originated in the work of Lulu Sweigard, *Human Movement Potential* (Lanham, MD: Harper & Row, 1974). See Chapters 2 and 3 for further discussion of imagery and ideokinesis.

37 Manny Emslie writes: "As with many other dance practices, the use of guided imagery and metaphor is core to the work of SRT. For example in class two, students are presented with imagining their 'breath transforming into a white mist'", "Skinner Releasing Technique: Dancing from Within", *Journal of Dance and Somatic Practices* 1, no. 2 (2009): 172.

38 See Elizabeth Dempster, "Releasing Aesthetic with Joan Skinner", *Writings on Dance* 14 (1995/1996): 17–26.

39 Bainbridge Cohen calls the process of movement incorporation (of images), embodiment. Embodiment is the corporeal realization of the image. This can be thought in individual or collective terms or in relation to the spatiality of the room created by those engaged in the process of corporeal realization, Bonnie Bainbridge Cohen, *Sensing, Feeling and Action: The Experiential Anatomy of Body-Mind Centering* (Northhampton, MA: Contact Editions, 1993).

40 Friedrich Nietzsche, *Daybreak: Thoughts on the Prejudices of Morality*, trans. R.J. Hollingdale (Cambridge: Cambridge University Press, 1997), 8–9.

41 Deleuze, *Nietzsche and Philosophy*, 133.

42 Ibid., 133.

43 Ibid., 134.

44 Ibid., 133.

45 For further discussion of habit and its acquisition, see Félix Ravaisson, *On Habit*, trans. Clare Carlisle and Mark Sinclair (London and New York: Continuum, 2008); Philipa Rothfield, "Beyond Habit: The Cultivation of Corporeal Difference", *Parrhesia* 19 (2013): 100–112; and Elizabeth Grosz, "Habit Today: Ravaisson, Bergson, Deleuze and Us", *Body and Society* 19, nos. 2–3 (2013): 217–239.

46 For Foucault, bodily discipline engenders utility:

> The historical moment of the disciplines was the moment when an art of the human body was born, which was directed not only at the growth of its skills,

nor at the intensification of its subjection, but at the formation of a relation that in the mechanism itself makes it more obedient as it becomes more useful, and conversely.

(Michel Foucault, *Discipline and Punish: The Birth of the Prison*, trans. Alan Sheridan [Harmondsworth: Penguin Books, 1977], 137–138)

47 Hay has enjoyed an extensive career as a renowned choreographer and dancer. A member of the Judson Dance Theatre in the early days of postmodern dance, she has developed a unique choreographic practice, which she has taught in large-scale performance workshop form for many years. Hay also has a long-standing practice of performing solo works.

48 Deborah Hay, "Turn Your F∧*cking Head" screening and Q & A, with Philipa Rothfield, Dancehouse, Melbourne, Australia, March 8, 2014.

49 The Dancehouse, Melbourne website states that

For 43 years Deborah Hay's research has been based on the observation and realisation that all of us are, both consciously and unconsciously, choreographed by culture, gender, politics, job, history, art, etc. Her interest as a choreographer is not to maintain or refine a choreography, but rather to destabilize learned movement that keeps us on a treadmill of replication.

(www.dancehouse.com.au/development/training/trainingdetails. php?id=136, accessed June 8, 2018)

50 Lena Hammergren and Susan Foster, "Dancing the Political", in *Choreography and Corporeality: Relay in Motion*, ed. Thomas F. DeFrantz and Philipa Rothfield (London: Palgrave Macmillan, 2016), 297.

51 The lack of foreknowledge on the part of the dancer was made very clear me (as spectator) in a series of solo performances, *In the Dark*, which arose from a solo project, taught by Hay and Ros Warby in Australia, 2008, *In the Dark*, choreographed by Deborah Hay (2008). Whatever the choreographic instruction, dancers revealed themselves without anticipation in relation to that which was yet to come. See Philipa Rothfield, "Present Sense: Deborah Hay: In the Dark", *RealTime Magazine* 98 (August–September 2010): 22, www.realtime.org.au/present-sense/, accessed February 27, 2019.

52 Hammergren and Foster, "Dancing the Political", 298.

53 Ibid., 299.

54 Hay is herself reluctant to abandon the concept of the dancer's subjectivity on the basis that her work calls for enormous effort on the part of the dancer, Hay, "Turn your F∧*king Head", and personal communication, January 2019. Whether such effort reinforces or undermines subject-formation is open to debate. The question is whether that effort includes a resistance to subjectification or even paradoxically, calls for a subjective commitment towards desubjectification (see next section).

55 See Conclusion for further discussion of this tension.

56 Michel Foucault, "Nietzsche, Genealogy, History", in *Language, Counter-Memory, Practice: Selected Essays and Interviews by Michel Foucault*, ed. Donald F. Bouchard, trans. Donald F. Bouchard and Sherry Simon (New York: Cornell University Press, 1977), 139–164.

57 Ibid., 148.

58 For further discussion of the inscriptive paradigm, see Philipa Rothfield, "Bodies and Subjects", in *Troubled Bodies: Critical Perspectives on Postmodernism, Medical Ethics and the Body*, ed. Paul K. Komesaroff (Durham: Duke University Press,

1995), esp. 182–197, also Elizabeth Grosz, "Inscriptions and Body Maps", in *Feminine, Masculine and Representation*, ed. Terry Threadgold and Anne Cranny-Francis (Sydney: Allen and Unwin, 1990), 62–74.

59 Foucault, *Discipline and Punish*, esp. Part 3.

60 Ibid., 135.

61 Pierre Bourdieu, "Structures, *Habitus*, Practices", in *Contemporary Sociological Theory*, ed. Craig Calhoun, trans. Richard Nice (Oxford: Blackwell, 2002), 276–288.

62 "If the surplus power possessed by the king gives rise to the duplication of his body, has not the surplus power exercised on the subjected body of the condemned man given rise to another type of duplication? That of a "non-corporal", a "soul" as Mably called it. This history of this "micro-physics" of the punitive power would then be a genealogy or an element in a genealogy of the modern "soul" … it exists, it has a reality, it is produced permanently around, on, within the body", Foucault, *Discipline and Punish*, 29.

63 Gilles Deleuze, *Foucault*, trans. Séan Hand (Minneapolis: University of Minnesota Press, 1986). See esp. "Foldings or the Inside of Thought (Subjectivation)", 94–123. See also Foucault, *Discipline and Punish*, 29.

64 Deleuze, *Foucault*, 106.

65 Ibid., 100.

66 Foucault, "Nietzsche, Genealogy, History", 148.

67 In *Discipline and Punish*, Foucault writes of the soul as the correlative effect of corporeal technologies of power. For Foucault, subjectivity is "the element in which are articulated the effects of a certain type of power", 29.

68 Nietzsche, *Daybreak, 73.*

69 Foucault, "Nietzsche, Genealogy, History", 153.

70 "What is tradition? A higher authority which one obeys, not because it commands what is *useful* to us, but because it *commands*", Nietzsche, *Daybreak*, 9.

71 Deleuze bemoans the reactive turn enabled through training which operates "in order to turn man into a gregarious, docile and domesticated animal", Deleuze, *Nietzsche and Philosophy*, 139.

72 See Foucault, *Discipline and Punish*, Part Three, Chapter 1, "Docile Bodies".

73 Foucault, *Discipline and Punish*, 138.

74 Michel Foucault, *Power/Knowledge: Selected Interviews and Other Writings 1972–1977*, ed. Colin Gordon (Brighton: Harvester Press, 1980), 56.

75 Nietzsche, *On the Genealogy of Morality*, 40.

76 Ibid., 41.

77 Deleuze, *Nietzsche and Philosophy*, 137.

78 Ibid., 139.

79 Nietzsche, *On the Genealogy of Morality*, 40.

80 Keith Ansell-Pearson writes:

> The paradox is this: the process by which man becomes moralized is one which, in its beginnings, operates by coercion and violence; but once the human animal has become disciplined it is, at least potentially, capable of living beyond morality (*Sittlichkeit*) and autonomously.
>
> (Keith Ansell-Pearson, "Editor's Introduction: Nietzsche's 'Overcoming'", in Friedrich Nietzsche, *On the Genealogy of Morality*, trans. Carol Diethe, ed. Keith Ansell-Pearson [Cambridge: Cambridge University Press, 1994], xvi)

81 The notion of dancerness comes from Rebecca Hilton, who uses the term to capture the dancer's perspective on her own dancing, Rebecca Hilton, "Dancerness", *Performance Paradigm* 13 (2017): 196–200. Dancerness is an expression of the dancer's movement subjectivity, in action. It qualifies that which counts as dancing, from the dancer's point of view.

82 Martha Graham writes of her early days of making work:

> To many people, I was a heretic … I felt at the time that I was a heretic. I was outside of the realm of women. I did not dance the way that people danced. I had what I called a contraction and release. I used the flexed foot. I showed effort. My foot was bare. In many ways I showed onstage what most people came to the theatre to avoid.
>
> (Martha Graham, *Blood Memory* [New York: Washington Square Press, 1991], 114)

And yet, Graham acknowledges the corporeal basis of her work:

> As with a child, as with a little animal that has to be trained, there has to be discipline and it has to be consistent. You rebel against it, but you enjoy the boundaries. And there's a will to do things of which we're completely unconscious–it is the force of life using us as a channel, and we have to submit to that. We are an instrument.
>
> (Ibid., 124)

83 Faye Driscoll's *Thank You for Coming: Attendance* could be seen as an attempt to create a performative community of bodies, *Thank You for Coming: Attendance*, choreographed by Faye Driscoll, 2016. See Rothfield, "Utopia Unsettled", in which I argue *Thank You for Coming* seeks a mode of becoming-community:

> This active form of participation brings joy to the group – it is reflected in their bodies and faces, as they become absorbed by the group. *Thank you for coming* is an ontological piece – it aims to create a mode of social being through performance. Its intention to enact its vision shows a commitment to making a kind of political reality, one which is able to leave a trace in the bodies of the audience beyond participation through mere spectatorship.
>
> (Philipa Rothfield, "Utopia Unsettled", *RealTime Magazine* 135 [October–November, 2016]: www.realtime.org.au/utopia-unsettled/, accessed March 2, 2019)

84 Grosz, "Inscriptions and Body-Maps".

85 *Rite of Spring*, a video installation by Katarzyna Kozyra, shown at *TransFormes*, Paris, Centre de La Danse, January 14–17, 2005.

86 Christel Stalpaert, "Dancing and Thinking Politics with Deleuze and Rancière: Performing Hesitant Gestures of the Unknown in Katarzyna Kozrya's *Rite of Spring*", in *Choreography and Corporeality: Relay in Motion*, ed. Thomas F. DeFrantz and Philipa Rothfield (London: Palgrave Macmillan, 2016), 173–191.

87 Ibid., 186.

88 DeFrantz, "Bone Breaking", 68.

89 Ibid., 66.

90 Ibid., 69.

91 Deleuze, *Nietzsche and Philosophy*, 111.

92 DeFrantz, "Afrofuturist Remains: A Speculative Rendering of Social Dance Futures v2.0", in *Choreography and Corporeality: Relay in Motion*, ed. Thomas F. DeFrantz and Philipa Rothfield (London: Palgrave Macmillan, 2016), 218.

93 Marc Deary, cited in DeFrantz, "Afrofuturist Remains", 220.

94 "The need to show that as the consumption of man and man-interests becomes more and more economical and the 'machinery' of interests and services is integrated ever more intricately, a counter-movement is inevitable. I designate this as the secretion of a luxury surplus of mankind: it aims to bring to light a stronger species, a higher type that preserves itself under different conditions from those of the average man. My concept, my metaphor for this type is, as one knows, the word 'overman'", Nietzsche, *Will to Power*, 463.

95 "Not "mankind" but *overman* is the goal", ibid., 519.

96 Deleuze, *Nietzsche and Philosophy*, 163.

97 Ibid., 164–166. Nietzsche, *Thus Spake Zarathustra*.

98 Deleuze, *Nietzsche and Philosophy*, 174.

99 Ibid.

100 "Active destruction means: the point, the moment of transmutation in the will to nothingness", ibid., 174.

101 Ibid., 185.

102 Pierre Klossowski, *Nietzsche and the Vicious Circle*, trans. Daniel W. Smith (London and New York: Continuum books, 1997), 24.

103 See Chapter 5.

104 Klossowski, *Nietzsche and the Vicious Circle*, 24.

105 Ibid., 25.

106 Ibid.

107 Ibid., 26.

108 Ibid.

109 Yvonne Rainer is a choreographer, dancer and filmmaker. She was a founding member of the Judson Dance Theatre. Her work, *Trio* A, is often cited as a marker of American postmodern dance but she also made many avant-garde and experimental works in dance and in film. Yvonne Rainer, "'No' to Spectacle", *Tulane Drama Review* 10, no. 2 (1965): 178.

110 Yvonne Rainer, "Where's the Passion? Where's the Politics? *Or, How I Became Interested in Impersonating, Approximating, and End Running around My Selves and Others', and Where Do I Look When You're Looking at Me?*", *Theater* 40, no. 1 (2010): 47–48.

111 Ibid., 49.

112 Ibid., 51.

113 Sara Rudner, in *Post-modern Dance Judson Theater and the Grand Union*, dir. Richard Sheridan (New York: ARC on Videodance).

114 Linda Sastradipradja, *Agency, Authorship and Embodied Aesthetics: The Dancer as Auteur*, unpublished PhD (Melbourne: Victoria University, 2019), 15.

115 Elizabeth Dempster, "Women Writing the Body: Let's Watch a Little How she Dances", in *The Routledge Dance Studies Reader, Second Edition*, ed. Alexandra Carter and Janet O'Shea (London and New York: Routledge, 2010), 229.

116 Bales, "A Dancing Dialectic", in *The Body Eclectic: Evolving Practices in Dance Training*, ed. Melanie Bales and Rebecca Nettl-Fiol (Urbana and Chicago: University of Illinois Press, 2008), 15.

117 Dempster, "Women Writing the Body", 229.

118 Russell Dumas, "Necessary Incursions: Rethinking the Unstable Body in Dance", unpublished PhD (Melbourne: Victoria University, 2014).

119 Nietzsche writes of such a quandary as a question of mutiny versus authority:

> There is a wicked dilemma to which not everyone's courage and character are equal: as a passenger on a ship to discover that the captain and steersman are making dangerous mistakes and that one is their superior in nautical knowledge – and then to ask oneself: how if you should incite a mutiny against them and have them both seized? Does your superiority not give you the right to do so? And would they not also be in the right if they locked you up for undermining discipline?
>
> (*Daybreak*, 186)

120 Dumas, "Dance for the Time Being", *Dancehouse Diary* 1 (2012): 10, also www.dancehousediary.com.au/wp-content/uploads/2014/09/Issue-01-Mobile-Minds.pdf, accessed March 1, 2019.

121 Ibid., 10.

122 *Accumulation with Talking Plus Watermotor*, choreographed by Trisha Brown (1979). Trisha Brown is a key figure in American postmodern dance. She was a choreographer and dancer, who established a venerable body of work over several decades, under the auspices of Trisha Brown Dance Company.

123 Discussed earlier in relation to Hammergren and Foster, "Dancing the Political".

124 Deborah Hay, *Learning Curve Workshop* (Melbourne: Dancehouse, 2014).

125 Email communication, via Jane Refsahuge, June 23, 2018.

126 Ibid.

127 *About Kazuo Ohno*, choreographed by Takao Tawaguchi, Asiatopa Festival (Melbourne: Dancehouse: February 25–27, 2017).

128 Personal communication, February 2017.

129 Ibid.

130 Ibid.

131 Rebecca Nettl-Fiol, "Somatics: An interview with Martha Myers", in *The Body Eclectic, Evolving Practices in Dance Training*, ed. Melanie Bales and Rebecca Nettl-Fiol (Urbana and Chicago: University of Illinois Press, 2008), 89–110; Bales, "A Dancing Dialectic", 1–2.

132 As noted earlier, the notion of morphology used here adheres to an Irigarayan concept of the body thought through and not outside culture. See Chapter 3.

133 Alexander began his work with the observation that he tended to pull his head back and down when speaking. Alexander worked with this insight, ultimately to develop a set of directions aimed to counteract this tendency in others, See F. Matthias Alexander, *The Essential Writings of F. Matthias Alexander: The Alexander Technique,* selected and introduced by Edward Maisel (New York: Carol Communications 1989).

134 Rebecca Nettl-Fiol, "First it was Dancing: Reflections on Teaching and Alexander Technique", in *The Body Eclectic: Evolving Practices in Dance Training*, ed. Melanie Bales and Rebecca Nettl-Fiol (Urbana and Chicago: University of Illinois Press, 2008), 112.

135 Ibid., 105.

136 Ibid., 122.

137 "Let the neck be free, to allow the head to go forward and up, and the back to lengthen and widen", ibid., 122.

138 Alexander, *The Essential Writings of F. Matthias Alexander*, 13–15.

139 Anne Thompson, "A Position at a Point in Time", *Writings on Dance* 1 (1985): 6.

140 Elizabeth Dempster writes:

> The constructive rest position – lying on the back, knees bent, flat feet on the floor – is a rest position which requires minimal muscular effort to maintain. The effect of gravity and a relative positioning of body parts, which encourages mechanical balance throughout the skeleton, act together to assist release of excessive muscle tension. Interference from habitual patterns of inefficient alignment and movement is thus reduced, enhancing the ability of the body to receive new information.
>
> (Elizabeth Dempster, "Image-Based Movement Education", *Writings on Dance* 1 [1985]: 14–15)

141 Klossowski writes: "Since everything leads to the 'head' (the upright position), the message is deciphered in a way that will maintain this 'vertical' position; *there would be no message as such* if this position were not habitual and specific", *Nietzsche and the Vicious Circle*, 38.

142 Jane Refshauge, *Winter Intensive Workshop*, Dancehouse, June 25, 2012.

143 Ibid. Forgetting conforms to the model of movement's riposte, where experience is folded into action.

144 Emslie, "Skinner Releasing Technique", 173.

145 Deleuze, *Nietzsche and Philosophy*, x.

Bibliography

About Kazuo Ohno. Choreographed by Takao Tawaguchi, Asiatopa Festival. Melbourne: Dancehouse: February 25–26, 2017.

Accumulation with Talking Plus Watermotor. Choreographed by Trisha Brown (1979).

Alexander, F. Matthias. *The Essential Writings of F. Matthias Alexander: The Alexander Technique*, selected and introduced by Edward Maisel. New York: Carol Communications 1989.

Ansell-Pearson, Keith. "Editor's Introduction: Nietzsche's 'Overcoming'", Friedrich Nietzsche, *On the Genealogy of Morality*, translated by Carol Diethe, edited by Keith Ansell-Pearson, ix–xxiii. Cambridge: Cambridge University Press, 1994.

Bainbridge Cohen, Bonnie. *Sensing, Feeling and Action: The Experiential Anatomy of Body-Mind Centering*. Northhampton, MA: Contact Editions, 1993.

Bales, Melanie. "A Dancing Dialectic". In *The Body Eclectic: Evolving Practices in Dance Training*, edited by Melanie Bales and Rebecca Nettl-Fiol, 10–21. Urbana and Chicago: University of Illinois Press, 2008.

Bourdieu, Pierre. "Structures, *Habitus*, Practices". In *Contemporary Sociological Theory*. Translated by Richard Nice, edited by Craig Calhoun, 276–288. Oxford: Blackwell, 2002.

DeFrantz, Thomas, F. "Afrofuturist Remains: A Speculative Rendering of Social Dance Futures v2.0". In *Choreography and Corporeality: Relay in Motion*, edited by Thomas F. DeFrantz and Philipa Rothfield, 209–222. London: Palgrave Macmillan, 2016.

———. "Bone Breaking: Black Social Dance and Queer Corporeal Orature". *The Black Scholar* 46, no. 1 (Spring 2016): 66–74.

Deleuze, Gilles. *Nietzsche and Philosophy*. Translated by Hugh Tomlinson. New York: Columbia University Press, 1983.

Deleuze, Gilles and Félix Guattari. *What Is Philosophy?* Translated by Hugh Tomlinson and Graham Burchell. New York: Columbia University Press, 1994.

Dempster, Elizabeth. "Image-Based Movement Education". *Writings on Dance* 1 (1985): 13–17.

———. "Releasing Technique with Joan Skinner". *Writings on Dance* 14 (1995/ 1996): 17–26.

———. "Women Writing the Body: Let's Watch a Little How She Dances". In *The Routledge Dance Studies Reader, Second Edition*, edited by Alexandra Carter and Janet O'Shea, 229–235. London and New York: Routledge, 2010.

Dumas, Russell. "Dance for the Time Being". *Dancehouse Diary* 1 (2012): 10. www. dancehousediary.com.au/wp-content/uploads/2014/09/Issue-01-Mobile-Minds. pdf, accessed March 1, 2019.

———. "Necessary Incursions: Rethinking the Unstable Body in Dance". Unpublished PhD, Melbourne: Victoria University, 2014.

Emslie, Manny. "Skinner Releasing Technique: Dancing from Within". *Journal of Dance and Somatic Practices* 1, no. 2 (2009): 169–175.

Foster, Susan. "Choreographies of Protest". *Theater Journal* 55, no. 3 (October 2003): 395–412.

Foucault, Michel. *Discipline and Punish: The Birth of the Prison*. Translated by Alan Sheridan. Harmondsworth: Penguin Books, 1977.

———. "Nietzsche, Genealogy, History". In *Language, Counter-Memory, Practice: Selected Essays and Interviews by Michel Foucault*. Translated by Donald F. Bouchard and Sherry Simon, edited by Donald F. Bouchard, 139–164. New York: Cornell University Press, 1977.

——. *Power/Knowledge: Selected Interviews and Other Writings 1972–1977*, edited by Colin Gordon. Brighton: Harvester Press, 1980.

Graham, Martha. *Blood Memory*. New York: Washington Square Press, 1991.

Grosz, Elizabeth. "Inscriptions and Body Maps". In *Feminine, Masculine and Representation*, edited by Terry Threadgold and Anne Cranny-Francis, 62–74. Sydney: Allen and Unwin, 1990.

———. "Habit Today: Ravaisson, Bergson, Deleuze and Us". *Body and Society* 19, nos. 2–3, (2013): 217–239.

Hammergren, Lena and Foster, Susan, L. "Dancing the Political". In *Choreography and Corporeality: Relay in Motion*, edited by Thomas F. DeFrantz and Philipa Rothfield, 291–305. London: Palgrave Macmillan, 2016.

Hay, Deborah. *Learning Curve Workshop* (Melbourne: Dancehouse, 2014).

———. "Turn Your F^*cking Head". *Screening and Q & A, with Philipa Rothfield*, Dancehouse, Melbourne, Australia, March 8, 2014.

Hilton, Rebecca. "Dancerness". *Performance Paradigm* 13 (2017): 196–200.

In the Dark, choreographed by Deborah Hay (2008).

Kedhar, Anusha. " 'Hands Up! Don't Shoot!' Gesture, Choreography and Protest in Ferguson". *Dancehouse Diary* 10 (2018): 14–15, originally published in *The Feminist Wire*, October 6, 2014.

Klossowski, Pierre. *Nietzsche and the Vicious Circle*. Translated by Daniel W. Smith. London and New York: Continuum books, 1997.

Manning, Erin. *Relationscapes: Movement, Art, Philosophy*. Cambridge, MA: MIT Press, 2012.

McLeod, Shaun. *The Movement Between: Dance Improvisation, Witnessing and Participatory Performance*, unpublished PhD thesis. Melbourne: Deakin University, 2016.

Nettl-Fiol, Rebecca. "First it was Dancing: Reflections on Teaching and Alexander Technique". In *The Body Eclectic: Evolving Practices in Dance Training*, edited by Melanie Bales and Rebecca Nettl-Fiol, 101–125. Urbana and Chicago: University of Illinois Press, 2008.

———. "Somatics: An Interview with Martha Myers". In *The Body Eclectic: Evolving Practices in Dance Training*, edited by Melanie Bales and Rebecca Nettl-Fiol, 89–100. Urbana and Chicago: University of Illinois Press, 2008.

Nietzsche, Friedrich. *The Will to Power*. Translated by Walter Kaufmann and R.J. Hollingdale. New York: Random House, 1968.

———. *On the Genealogy of Morality*. Translated by Carol Diethe, edited by Keith Ansell-Pearson. Cambridge: Cambridge University Press, 1994.

———. *Daybreak: Thoughts on the Prejudices of Morality*. Translated by R.J. Hollingdale. Cambridge: Cambridge University Press, 1997.

———. *Thus Spake Zarathustra*. Translated by R.J. Hollingdale. London: Penguin Books, 2003.

Post-modern Dance: Judson Theater and the Grand Union. Directed by Richard Sheridan (Series: Eye on Dance). New York: ARC on Videodance.

Rainer, Yvonne. " 'No' to Spectacle". *Tulane Drama Review* 10, no. 2 (1965): 178.

———. "Where's the Passion? Where's the Politics? *Or, How I Became Interested in Impersonating, Approximating, and End Running around My Selves and Others, and Where Do I Look When You're Looking at Me?*". *Theater* 40, no. 1 (2010): 47–55.

Ravaisson, Félix. *Of Habit*. Translated by Clare Carlisle and Mark Sinclair. London and New York: Continuum, 2008.

Refshauge, Jane. *Winter Intensive Workshop*. Melbourne: Dancehouse, June 25, 2012.

Rite of Spring. A video installation by Katarzyna Kozyra, shown at *TransFormes*, Paris, Centre de La Danse, January 14–17, 2005.

Rothfield, Philipa. "Bodies and Subjects". In *Troubled Bodies: Critical Perspectives on Postmodernism, Medical Ethics and the Body*, edited by Paul K. Komesaroff, 168–201. Durham: Duke University Press, 1995.

———. "Present Sense: Deborah Hay: In the Dark". *RealTime Magazine* 98 (August–September 2010): 22. www.realtime.org.au/present-sense/, accessed February 27, 2019.

———. "Beyond Habit: The Cultivation of Corporeal Difference". *Parrhesia* 19 (2013): 100–112.

———. "Utopia Unsettled: Faye Driscoll: *Thank you for Coming*, Attendance". *RealTime Magazine* 135 (October–November, 2016), www.realtime.org.au/utopia-unsettled/, accessed March 2, 2019.

Sastradipradja, Linda. *Agency, Authorship and Embodied Aesthetics: The Dancer as Auteur*, Unpublished PhD. Melbourne: Victoria University, 2019.

Sortland, Venke Marie. "When Experience is the Artwork: The End of Performance?" In *Writing Movement: Expeditions in Dance Writing 2012–2014*, edited by Ine Therese Berg and Inta Balode, 144–150. Norway: Dance Information Norway, 2014.

Stalpaert, Christel. "Dancing and Thinking Politics with Deleuze and Rancière: Performing Hesitant Gestures of the Unknown in Katarzyna Kozrya's *Rite of Spring*". In *Choreography and Corporeality: Relay in Motion*, edited by Thomas F. DeFrantz and Philipa Rothfield, 173–191. London: Palgrave Macmillan, 2016.

Sweigard, Lulu. *Human Movement Potential*. Lanham, MD: Harper & Row, 1974.

Thank You for Coming: Attendance. Choreographed by Faye Driscoll, 2016.

Thompson, Anne. "A Position at a Point in Time". *Writings on Dance* 1 (1985): 4–12.

7 Staging sovereignty

To set foot on Australian soil is to set foot on Aboriginal land. The continent of Australia belongs to the Aboriginal peoples who have lived here for over 50,000 years. They have never ceded their sovereignty, which is held by the many First Nations that make up the land mass of Australia. Although a conceptual work, this book is also grounded in practice, practices which have a place. It is custom now, at public events, to acknowledge the Traditional Owners of this land, to pay respects to elders past, present and emerging. This chapter aims to acknowledge those owners by focusing on matters of Indigenous sovereignty in relation to dance and sport, two divergent fields, united by their performative, embodied character. Its focus is upon the relation between embodied Indigenous sovereignty and white spectatorship, in particular, upon the ways in which such spectatorship can be destabilized, so as to set free the repressed colonial underpinnings of white nationhood and its allied forms of subjectivity.

Sovereignty can be understood in many ways: according to international law and political philosophy as that which belongs to the properly constituted nation.[1] It can also be defined by those to whom it belongs.[2] Aileen Moreton-Robinson writes that Aboriginal sovereignty exists in corporeal, ontological and epistemological terms, and is grounded in complex relations between "ancestral beings, humans and land".[3] Indigenous sovereignty is embodied – "carried by the body" – finding expression in myriad ways: through resistance, in everyday life and according to the many cultural, familial and extended bodies politic.[4] Irene Watson sees Aboriginal sovereignty in heterogeneous terms, as embracing a diversity of sovereign bodies, peoples and practices.[5]

The British colonization of Australia in 1788 inaugurated the dispossession of Aboriginal peoples from their land, law and culture, through massacre, murder, forced removal and relocation under the lock and key of Christian missions. The British asserted ownership of Australian territory via the doctrine of *terra nullius*, the claim that Australia was uninhabited, a patent misrepresentation. Larissa Behrendt writes:

> The British claimed Australia on the basis that it was *terra nullius* – vacant and/or without a sovereign. This claim ignored the international

standards of the time, failing to recognize the sovereignty of Indigenous Australians and Aboriginal customary laws, including property laws. Instead of admitting the land was invaded, the British used the doctrine of *terra nullius* to create a myth that the land was "settled". This myth was institutionalized in the legal system.[6]

Gary Foley notes that the international standards at the time of the British occupation offered three ways in which a colonizing power could legally acquire sovereignty over new lands: one, via conquest over their inhabitants – in which case the colonizing nation needed to compensate a country's Indigenous peoples; two, through Indigenous people's ceding their sovereignty, in which case compensation and reparation needed to be negotiated; or three, by claiming a land was uninhabited via the notion of *terra nullius*.[7]

The British asserted their sovereignty by availing themselves of the third option. This didn't stop them from massacring nor dispossessing the people who were supposedly not there, nor from developing case law which denied Aboriginal property ownership as defined by British legal precedent.[8] Whatever the justificatory claims made out by the state and its judiciary, Foley, amongst many others, makes clear that Indigenous people never acknowledged the legitimacy of colonial rule nor ceded their sovereignty.[9] Having traced the long history of political actions staged by Aboriginal activists from the eighteenth century until today, Foley points out that:

> From the very beginning, Indigenous peoples resisted and opposed the invasion and occupation of their lands. Since the 1860s as the Aboriginal peoples in regional areas of southeastern Australia experienced the spread of white invasion and forcible occupation of their homelands, there can be said to have been significant resistance, both passive and active ... Land and the implicit question of sovereignty continued to be at the heart of Aboriginal concerns and protests over many decades, and numerous disputes were conducted at a local level.[10]

The 1970s saw the establishment of the Aboriginal Tent Embassy on the lawns of the Australian Federal parliament.[11] This political action was in part provoked by Prime Minister McMahon's 1972 Australia Day speech in which he rejected Aboriginal land rights, offering instead pastoral leases to those Indigenous citizens who proved themselves 'worthy'.[12] Activists involved in the embassy action saw themselves represented as aliens in their own land, condemned to rent land off the state.[13] The notion of an embassy as a vehicle of communication between Aboriginal peoples and the Australian government asserts the existence of two distinct bodies, the Commonwealth of Australia and the Indigenous body politic.[14] It refutes the claim that Australia's Indigenous peoples are mere members of the greater citizen state.

It is in this context of sovereign assertion that Torres Strait Islander, Eddie Mabo, declared his ownership in a landmark case that went all the way to the High Court.[15] The *Mabo* case is notable for the majority judgement of the High Court that *terra nullius* was never valid. The decision is significant for raising by implication the question of the legitimacy of British occupation, recognition of Aboriginal sovereignty and for putting the matter of compensation on the table. Unfortunately, the majority *Mabo* judgment side-stepped these issues by finding that the newly acknowledged native title is extinguishable by the subsequent creation of leasehold and freehold title (private property). The vast settlement of Australia was therefore insulated from Indigenous claims. Foley writes:

> This aspect of the Mabo decision represents the greatest single act of dis-possession in Australian history since 1788.[16]

Having abandoned the legal myth of *terra nullius*, the Crown ought to have addressed the question of compensation, while entering into bilateral talks with the land's Traditional Owners (under one of the two remaining means of territorial acquisition). Instead, *Mabo* confined native title to Crown land. Despite this radical narrowing of the field, *Mabo* nonetheless prompted political anxieties which were fuelled by politicians who wanted to quarantine, if not reverse, the *Mabo* decision.[17] The ensuing debate led to the introduction of native title legislation, which effectively contained the revolutionary potential of *Mabo*.[18]

The invalidation of *terra nullius* should by rights have destabilized the entire basis of Australian sovereignty, requiring negotiation with the land's original and continuing owners. The notion of a treaty between the white nation and an Aboriginal polity has been proposed over the years by a range of constituted bodies.[19] The stumbling block for moving forwards on the matter of a national treaty is a lack of willingness on the part of the Federal Government to enter into any bilateral form of relationship.[20] The momentous 2017 "Uluru Statement from the Heart", which called for a First Nations voice in parliament, was summarily dismissed by the government of the day.[21] Prime Minister Malcolm Turnbull and Attorney-General George Brandeis rejected the call for constitutional reform, arguing that creating "a constitutionally enshrined representative assembly for which only Indigenous Australians could vote" would undermine the universal character of democracy which "is built on the foundation of all its citizens".[22] The question of Indigenous recognition was thereby nullified by assimilating indigeneity into an undifferentiated whole. The totalizing claim that Australian democracy already represents all its citizens ignores the historical and continuing challenge posed by Aboriginal sovereignty. The rhetoric of democracy is thereby used to trump sovereignty.

The rejection of an offer to form a bilateral relationship between Aboriginal peoples and the white Australian nation rests on the assumption that the nation *already* represents and incorporates all 'its' peoples. And yet, the ongoing refusal to acknowledge Aboriginal sovereignty *reduces* the nation to an expression of what Moreton-Robinson calls "white possessive" interests.[23] Aboriginal difference is thus effaced by the universal logic of white patriarchal sovereignty, which can only understand difference on its own totalizing terms. The phallocentric nature of a universal logic which masks its specificity extends to discursive representations of Aboriginality, which are structured around colonizing interests.[24] Michael Dodson critiques non-Indigenous representations of Aboriginality as a mere reflection of colonial interests.[25] He writes:

> Our constructed identities have served a broader purpose of reflecting back to the colonizing culture what it wanted or needed to see in itself ... In the construction of "Aboriginality", we have been objects to be manipulated and used to further the aspirations of other peoples.[26]

In other words, non-Indigenous representations of Aboriginality are a "mirror" for colonial interests.[27] Dodson thereby distinguishes between a "genuine relationship" that holds between two parties and the phallocentric tendency to reduce otherness to "more of the same".[28]

Indigenous scholar, Marcia Langton, observes a similar cultural phenomenon in non-Indigenous representations of Aboriginal subject-matter.[29] She writes:

> Australians do not know and relate to Aboriginal people. They relate to stories told by former colonists.[30]

These one-sided narratives are made possible by the ongoing sense of *terra nullius* embedded in the Australian cultural imaginary. Cultural *terra nullius* enables the assumption of relationality in the absence of genuine dialogue. And yet:

> "Aboriginality" only has meaning when understood in terms of intersubjectivity, when both the Aboriginal and the non-Aboriginal are subjects, not objects.[31]

Langton's formulation contests the long-standing practice of constructing Aboriginal subjects as objects of white knowledge, in anthropological discourse but also within governmental instrumentalities. Media representations of Indigenous social problems typically combine moral panic with 'tragedy porn', extending objectification into discursive abjection. Langton draws attention to the ways in which Indigenous lives thereby became a "public spectacle, played out in a vast 'reality show' through the media, parliaments, public service and the Aboriginal world".[32]

Indigenous sovereignty and the being of the occupier

It is in this context that Toula Nicolacopoulos and George Vassilacopoulos invert the colonizing gaze, so as to focus on the being of the colonizer.[33] Nicolacopoulos and Vassilacopoulos deal with the intercultural nature of Aboriginality through addressing the obstacles to forming a genuine relationship between Indigenous and non-Indigenous people. For Nicolacopoulos and Vassilacopoulos, the problem is ontological, a question of unresolved being on the part of non-Indigenous Australia. Their analysis begins with a distinction between three types of being: sovereign being, foreigner being and occupier being.[34] Much depends upon the kinds of relation that arise between these modes of being. For example, sovereign being is in a position to offer hospitality to the foreigner. Without the extension of such hospitality, however, foreigner being becomes that of an occupier, "unjustly dwelling" on the land of another.[35] Nicolacopoulos and Vassilacopoulos apply this framework to relations between Indigenous and non-Indigenous Australia. Having neither negotiated settlement nor recognized Indigenous sovereignty, non-Indigenous Australia exists today as a form of occupier being.[36] Those who inhabit occupier being (non-Indigenous Australians) may very well deny their status as occupiers, purporting legitimacy as settled identities on a land essentially without owners. The allied view, that Australia's colonial history has no moral purchase on the present, frees up the non-Indigenous citizen from any sense of responsibility or complicity.[37]

And yet, the persistence of sovereign being on the part of Australia's First Nations peoples constitutes a form of address that names occupier being as such. Nicolacopoulos and Vassilacopoulos argue that sovereign being "perpetually commands white Australians to name our selves as the bearers of the being of an occupier of foreign land".[38] They claim that the command calls for a truthful account of our existential status and origins. The command functions as a call for truth, if not (yet) reconciliation.[39] The command is intersubjective and intercultural. It presupposes the existence of the two modes of being – sovereign and occupier. Once addressed by virtue of the command, the addressee becomes responsible for the whole world of the occupier.[40] The command thus calls for a response on the part of the non-Indigenous subject, one which acknowledges and takes responsibility for our political state of affairs. It is a form of address that issues from Indigenous sovereign being to call out the complicity of the colonizing other.

There is no guarantee the command will produce an adequate response on the part of occupier being. Nicolacopoulos and Vassilacopoulos trace the ways in which white Australia has historically repudiated its position as occupier, through concealment, denial, amnesia, historical quarantine and white supremacist politics. The practical effect of these gestures is to subvert the command, perchance to bolster the imagined status of the colonizer. One way in which this occurs is to create a mode of hierarchical difference between white Australian and 'less-than' Australian subjectivity. Nicolacopoulos and Vassilacopoulos look at the ways in which white Australia has historically constructed certain modes of 'foreigner being' in order to establish the rightful status of the established Australian. They argue that occupier self-legitimation is staged through identifying a class of "perpetual-foreigners-within", migrants in relation to whom 'old' Australians can assert their imagined difference.[41] Identification of the unassimilated other affirms, through negation, the claims of white Australia. It adopts the Nietzschean slave's *modus operandi*, of creating value through negation:

> You don't come from here
> I am not like you
> Therefore, I belong.[42]

Zenophobia towards the unassimilated other is also expressed in Australia's asylum seeker policy of 'border protection' and offshore detention. In other words, the foreigner can be posed as an internal or external threat, as long as the other affirms the putative legitimacy of the white Australian subject. The identity of the perpetual-foreigner-within has historically shifted over the years: from Chinese, to Jewish, to southern European, to Asian, Southeast Asian, to Muslim and, more recently, to Sudanese migrants. The perpetual-foreigner-within is a place holder, which functions so as to deflect attention away from Indigenous sovereignty and to confer legitimacy upon white Australian subjectivity.[43] Although Australia historically embraced a pluralistic multiculturalism in the 1970s:

> in practice a profound inequality continued to define state-citizen relations since the dominant British-Australian group had assigned itself the historical mission of managing the state's supposed neutrality ... Once the idea of the neutral state had been successfully tested in the public-political domain, the dominant Anglophone group progressively expanded its role from that of managing the state's neutrality to serving as the guarantor of the culturally diverse nation's unity.[44]

The perpetual-foreigner-within is a mere cipher then, the functional means by which Anglophone subjects legitimate their tenure. And yet, the gesture is doomed to fail. Occupier being is inherently liable to destabilization, unable to ward off the threat exerted by expressions of Indigenous sovereignty. The following discussion seeks to unpack two such threats, drawn from two very different fields of endeavour – sport and dance. What these examples share is an ability to exert a destabilizing force, to expose the undercurrent of denial, concealment and anxiety that attends occupier being. They do so through staging an embodied, sovereign subjectivity which interpellates its white spectatorship. By being named as such, the stabilized identity of the non-Indigenous spectator is disrupted, subject to the return of that which is repressed within the Australian political imaginary.

Chris Healy writes of a certain kind of amnesia that besets the Australian white experience of Indigenous peoples.[45] Amnesia functions at the level of the everyday *habitus*, according to which non-Indigenous people fail to notice Indigenous presence.[46] Although legally obsolete, Nicolacopoulos and Vassilacopoulos argue that the idea of *terra nullius* still operates within the Australian social and political imaginaries, enabling the white nation to feel itself as one.[47] Larissa Behrendt identifies the ability of the nation to adopt what she calls "psychological *terra nullius*".[48] The capacity to act *as if* Australia were still *terra nullius* is expressed in the ability to experience life essentially unaffected by Indigenous presence. Such forgetting (of Indigenous presence and its implications) informs the habitual every day of white Australia. The survival of Indigenous peoples is however at odds with the forgetting that characterizes white Australian being.[49] Indigenous presence reminds white Australia that *terra nullius* is a political fiction. It functions as a provocation, not merely to remember, but to account for one's presence. It is in such a context that Indigenous artist, SJ Norman, and footballer, Adam Goodes, invoke the dual character of white-Aboriginal relations, commanding the white spectator to acknowledge their investment in the white nation.

SJ Norman

SJ Norman is a trans-identified, cross-disciplinary artist and writer. An Indigenous artist of Wiradjuri, Wonnarua and European heritage, their work includes performance, installation, sculpture, text, video and sound.[50] Norman's performance work highlights the body, drawing from a wide range of corporeal forces, including but not limited to their own flesh. Many of their works invoke Australia's colonial history. On the one hand, the body in Norman's work is a morphological body, inscribed by history and culture; on the other hand, it has an agency of its own, able to reconfigure those very same historical and cultural forces.[51] For example, *Corpus Nullius/Blood Country* (2011) involved Norman inscribing their own body, piercing the word *nullius* across their chest, with white pearled pins, while embroidering the word *terra*, on a lambskin.[52] The reference to *terra nullius* acknowledges the legacy of colonization upon their own body and those of their ancestors, and yet the act of piercing re-works the colonizing gesture towards an active (re)inscription, in which Norman's actions declare "their own body as *belonging to no-one*".[53]

Norman's work is also object-focused, often selecting objects which begin as colonial tropes but which become vibrant surfaces for artistic reconfiguration. Norman's corporeal imaginary takes up these material forces of history as a circumstance of their work, reorienting them towards an untimely future. For example, *Bone Library* (2011) was an installation-event, staged over three days in which Norman meticulously engraved a lexicon of so-called extinct Indigenous words onto cattle bones, a metonym for the colonial pastoralism whose destruction of Indigenous culture led to the disappearance of numerous Indigenous languages.[54] Framed by plastic curtains such as might be found in an abattoir or forensic laboratory, Norman's painstaking and methodical process of inscription, cataloguing, display and distribution evokes the curatorial epistemology of a museum culture that appropriated and exhibited Aboriginal remains for scientific and voyeuristic purposes.[55] At the end of the three-day event, individual audience members were given engraved bones for custodial safekeeping, invoking an ethics of care and responsibility on the part of the spectator towards the inscribed cultural artefact.[56] History thereby passes through the present into an indeterminate future, dependent upon the actions of the spectator.

There is a ritual feel to Norman's work, a virtuosic recalibration of culture, connected to the ritual of performance, rituals of body modification and those of historical retelling. Norman writes:

> The principal character of ritual is repetition; it is through repetition that meaning is inscribed and, over time, shifts. Ritual gestures are interesting to me insofar as they are ancestrally haunted, and as such, may provide a visceral pathway to rethinking our histories. It's through ritual that we substantiate and situate ideas within the flesh, and through calling up and repositioning these gestures, we might seek to *agitate* the closed circuits of the encultured body (emphasis mine).[57]

Norman's work accrues a visceral and virtuosic power through its agitation of historical forces so as to trouble the sedentary being of the spectator. By inhabiting an intercultural space of Aboriginality, the white spectator can no longer sustain the fiction of psychological *terra nullius.* The collective title of eight of Norman's pieces in a Sydney performance season, *Unsettling Suite*, plays on the trope of the settler within colonial discourse.[58] The following discussion looks at the ways in which white spectatorship is unsettled in three of Norman's works, presented together as part of Dancehouse's Dance Territories program, held in Melbourne in October 2016.

The River's Children was a performative installation that was staged in a long rectangular space.[59] Seated beside a pile of clothing, Norman silently washes item after item in a large bathtub of water. Finished items are hung out to dry on one of the clothes' lines that criss-cross the space. Spectators are installed along two sides of the room, so as to watch Norman perform the rituals associated with domestic labour. Aboriginal women and girls have historically played a key role in colonial households, providing an enforced and unpaid servitude over many generations.[60] Prior to the performance, audience members had been invited to bring along white items of clothing. From time to time, individuals would get up and offer their items to Norman who would add them to the Sisyphusian pile of washing. The audience becomes complicit in this colonial logic of master and slave. Through our actions, and the history in which they are embedded, we are interpellated, named and implicated.

Norman's embodied presence, the domesticity of her costume and the water in the bathtub sourced from the Murray River attest to the Indigenous sovereignty that commands spectators to acknowledge their occupier being. So too, the slide projections that detail every recorded massacre of Aboriginal peoples.

The command is relational. It recalls the relational space of Aboriginality, theorized by Dodson and Langton. The command institutes an intersubjective meeting place, which cannot be assimilated into a totalizing logic of sameness, but confronts the colonial difference of occupier being in the face of Aboriginal presence. Dodson claims that recognition of Indigenous otherness poses a threat to the "boundaries of identity, knowledge and absolute truth which give the subject a sense of power and control".[61] *Heirloom* and *Take This for It Is My Body* pose such a threat insofar as they problematize the boundaries between Indigenous being and colonizing subjectivity.[62] *Heirloom* consists of a set of ceramic plates, painted with the artist's own blood, in Willow pattern. These plates are displayed in a typical country kitchen cupboard in a small room furnished with a white kitchen table and chairs. Audience members enter the space, overseen by a young Aboriginal woman in domestic attire. A syringe sits beside a bowl of fresh blood, next to a text about the artist's grandmother who literally worked her fingers to the bone, drawing blood which was subsequently baked into the bread that was consumed by her employer's stockmen.[63] We are told that the artist's blood has been incorporated into the scones which form part of a formal tea service laid out on the kitchen table. Seated for afternoon tea, we must decide whether and what to eat and drink, what to say to each other and to the Indigenous woman who silently pours our tea. For Irene Watson, Australia's appropriation and displacement of Aboriginal sovereignty amounts to a kind of cannibalism, the consumption of Indigenous being and culture.[64] Norman's blood and by implication the blood of her ancestors is there to be consumed, has already been consumed. Like *Corpus Nullius, Take This for It Is My Body* troubles the boundaries of the body-subject. Norman's blood is a floating signifier, a material force which is able to traverse the putative corporeal difference between Norman and their audience. The historically repressed suffering of Indigenous domestic workers threatens to return by entering the body of the spectator, who is no longer able to maintain the fiction of *terra nullius*. Indigenous presence enters a process of incorporation, a phase of corporeal becoming in which the abjected other is assimilated. Norman refers to the ritual as a visceral means of accessing that which is "ancestrally haunted".[65] Spectators, white and Indigenous, are relocated in this historically displaced moment of consumption, poised to consume history in a time which is out of joint with its colonial origins.

The destabilization of the proper boundary between Norman and their audience opens up a corporeal uncanny, one which brings the historicity of a colonial past into an untimely present. In "One Manifesto Less", Gilles Deleuze describes a theatrical operation which interrupts hegemonic systems of power whether, theatrical, state or familial.[66] Deleuze calls this interruption, subtraction. The impact of subtraction is to create an instability, which sets in motion a positive process of creation. Deleuze refers to:

> the subtraction of stable components of power, which releases a new potentiality of theatre, a non-representational force always in disequilibrium.[67]

Subtraction differs from political theatres, such as Brecht's, which are based on critique and its revolutionary solution.[68] This is because subtraction destabilizes. It takes away something of the stability that authorizes established political force. Deleuze therefore conceives of subtraction as a mode of activity, one which acts the political towards a state of disequilibrium. It could be said that *Take This for It Is My Body* is subtractive in this sense, in that it sabotages the power relations that enable non-Indigenous subjects to forget their relationship to Indigenous others. Its dismemberment of colonial 'remembering' produces a tension between thought and affect. *Take This for It Is My Body* undermines the ability to assume psychological *terra nullius* by creating an historical fissure, an untimely displacement in which the spectator is given a seat at the table of white colonial privilege. Anne Marsh writes that Norman's work creates an "Other returned to puncture the collective unconscious and make the trauma real".[69] The trauma of colonization has not been properly acknowledged. Hence the call for a process of truth-telling.[70] The trauma of colonization is made real in *Take This for It Is My Body* through the performative drama of blood-letting, its incorporation into food and the prospect of cannibalism. The destabilization of the boundary between colonizer and Indigenous being allows trauma to trouble the 'good conscience' of the participant-spectator.

Yet, at the same time, the reality of trauma has become something else, an otherwise. By engaging colonial force, *Take This for It Is My Body* opens up an indeterminate space of possibility, to become an "event-in-the-making" in which the body of history enters a liminal time and space.[71] History thereby gives way to an untimely variation.[72] It is not that history has no force here – rather, its force is amplified into a plurality of indeterminate futures. Dipesh Chakrabarty writes of a plural history which is not one as an antidote to hegemonic, linear conceptions of history.[73] *Take This for It Is My Body* disturbs Australia's colonial history by questioning its hegemonic status. It joins a growing body of historical research which contests the colonial meta-narrative.[74] But it does so in an untimely fashion. It is not an historical re-enactment, and yet, it cites historical time.[75] Norman's audience must take up its uncanny rendering of the past – written in blood – and take part in a colonial *tableau vivant* formed in the midst of the work. The lack of a script, and the necessity for action, creates an aura of responsibility, an uncanny burden on the part of the spectator. Deleuze writes of subtraction's working the middle, to create a mode of becoming in the midst of things which is subject to "continual variation". Subtraction does not add something then, it disturbs in such a way that "everything remains but under a new light".[76] There is no clear point at which *Take This for It Is My Body* ends and everyday life begins. *Take This for It Is My Body* opens up that which cannot be decisively closed over, namely the vulnerability of occupier being to the command. Its transgression of Norman's own bodily boundaries, to supply the blood for *Take This for It Is My Body* and *Heirloom*, is liable to get under the skin of white, colonial subjects such as myself – in Nietzschean terms, to forge a new body, infiltrated by a colonial past no longer dormant. In *Powers of Horror*, Julia Kristeva poses the abject as that which "disturbs identity, system, order".[77] The spectre of Norman's blood, expelled and incorporated, disturbs the purported separation between Indigenous suffering and colonial complacency, inaugurating a "narcissistic crisis" on the part of the white spectator.[78]

Norman is very careful to leave open the question of interpretation in relation to their work. The above discussion takes up the question of spectatorship in two different registers: one discerns a logic of command and interpellation that challenges the white spectator to take responsibility for the political reality of the Australian nation. It reminds the spectator of that which psychological *terra nullius* would repress. The second approach moves beyond the framework of recognition and its repudiation towards an open-ended sense of positive disequilibrium, one which is subject to "continual variation".[79] History remains but becomes untimely as new possibilities are "lived rather than represented".[80] The result is what Deleuze calls a "living theatre" and Marsh the "real-time" of ritual performance.[81] These treatments are not mutually exclusive. The spectre of interpellation haunts the positive disequilibrium that occurs within Norman's real-time ritual. It informs the spectator's sense of possibility and responsibility.

Norman's corporeal uncanny destabilizes the complacency and collusion of Australian colonial history in which we are immersed to stage a living history which is no longer one. To be inside Norman's installations is to enter a space of decomposition and recomposition, of discombobulation and porous boundaries. There is no one lived experience of Norman's work, nor a single position for the audience to occupy. People bring their own histories, embodied origins and contexts to the table. Indigenous spectators will not be interpellated in the same way as Norman's non-Indigenous audience. Although audience members hail from a multiplicity of origins then, and will feel the impact of these situations each in their own way, everyone must nevertheless take a seat on the disappearing ground of Norman's work.

Adam Goodes

The Sydney Cricket Ground is a sacred space in the Australian sporting imaginary. Sport functions as a unifying factor, a source of national pride within a never-ending drama. Australia celebrates its sporting stars. Adam Goodes is one of them, an Australian Football League (AFL) legend.

Figure 7.1 Adam Goodes. Photographer: Dean Lewis, AAP.

Being a long-time member of the AFL's Sydney Swans, Goodes won the esteemed best and fairest Brownlow Medal twice and played with the Swans to win two Grand Finals. Goodes was named Australian of the Year in 2014. Each year, the AFL hosts an Indigenous round of football to celebrate the game's Indigenous players. May 29, 2015 marked that year's Indigenous round. The Sydney Swans were playing the Carlton Blues. Early on in the game, Goodes kicked a goal in the forward front pocket in front of the Carlton fans. He performed a beautiful, graceful war dance towards the crowd.[82] Goodes later reflected: "Instinctively I knew I was going to dance, the situation couldn't have been more perfect".[83] Goodes advanced sideways towards the crowd, finishing with a boomerang throwing gesture, a war dance he had recently learnt from the AFL's under 16 Indigenous squad, The Flying Boomerangs.[84] The Boomerang's dance was created by young team members on a visit to New Guinea that year, a ritual created to express pride and competitive readiness.[85] The Boomerangs took inspiration from the New Zealand Haka war dance which is performed and recognized around the world. According to the Boomerangs' mentor, Mark Yettica-Paulson, the Boomerang's dance was accompanied by traditional language which said, "We are the Flying Boomerangs and we're coming after you with strong, fast hunting".[86] Yettica-Paulson describes Goodes' performance as "a call to contest" in the sporting arena.[87] For Goodes, performing the Boomerang's war dance was a way of embracing his heritage in the Indigenous round. Interviewed on the ground immediately afterwards, Goodes said that he was inspired by the war dance of the Flying Boomerangs, and that his performance wasn't a reaction to anything untoward but occurred because it was the "Indigenous round, proud to be Aboriginal and represent them".[88]

The reason Goodes was asked whether his dance was a reaction to some untoward incident is because Goodes had been subjected to persistent booing on the ground for almost two years. The booing began in 2013, when Goodes called out a young woman who, during that year's Indigenous round, called Goodes an ape.[89] For Goodes, that incident was a snapshot from the past when people regarded Indigenous people as less than human.[90] The ejection of the young woman from the ground marked the beginning of persistent booing that followed Goodes from game to game. In 2014, he was booed every week. Numerous commentators refused to distinguish between the booing directed towards Goodes and the raucous booing which is part of the game.[91] To their ears, the booing was no more than the usual brinkmanship expressed by the crowd. Poppy de Souza contests the claim that the booing directed towards Goodes had no racial overtones. She argues that sound has a history, and that the boos directed towards Goodes drew on "a settler-colonial form of violence that works through the deployment of sound".[92] De Souza distinguishes between different kinds of listening, as embodied in two very different political formations. The "white ears" that hear no racism in the booing are, for de Souza, invested in maintaining white colonial privilege.[93] For those whose hearing is colour-blind, the sound of booing remains free of political implication. By contrast, for "expert listeners",[94] such as Indigenous journalist, Stan Grant, and media commentator, Waleed Aly, racist bigotry was clearly evident in the sound of the booing.[95] Aly commented that:

> Anyone listening to those boos who is familiar with the dynamics of racism can *hear it in the boos*. There's a certain quality to them. There's something about it that sounds markedly different from the other boos that players get.[96]

These two modes of hearing represent two kinds of somatic attention: one seamlessly bound to a certain vision of the nation and therefore sport, the other felt in the lived body of the racialized other.[97] Larissa Behrendt contrasts the belief that "sport is the great equaliser" with the reality that it nonetheless "remains a litmus test of societal views and prejudices".[98]

At the start of 2015, the booing began again. Sydney Swans management wanted to go to the media to ask for the booing to stop but Goodes suggested waiting a week or so. And so it was, before the game against Carlton, during the Indigenous round of 2015, that Goodes and Indigenous teammate Lewis Jetta agreed that whoever scored first would do a war dance. Goodes kicked the first goal, right in front of the Carlton fans. Commentators were split over Goodes' dance, just as they had been split over whether the persistent booing was racially motivated.[99] Racism against Indigenous players is not new. For Yorta Yorta community and sports leader, Paul Briggs, racism in sport is "linked to the inability of Australia to reach an agreement or a treaty or relationship with Indigenous peoples from the moment that the invasion of Aboriginal lands took place in 1788".[100] Briggs sees racism in sport as a reflection of Australia's unfinished business. Nicolacopoulos and Vassilacopoulos see it as symptomatic of the ongoing denial of our occupier being.

Goodes was not the first Aboriginal player to call out racism. On April 17, 1993, St Kilda star, Nicky Winmar famously responded to racist abuse by lifting his jumper and pointing to his chest saying, "I'm black and I'm proud to be black".[101] The moment was captured and published on the front page of *The Sunday Age* newspaper.[102] The image of Winmar's upright and defiant gesture has become iconic, for taking a stand against racism on and off the field.[103]

Winmar's action became an important moment in the game's tolerance of express racism, as was Michael Long's subsequent complaint against Damian Monkhorst for on-field racial vilification.[104] According to Klugman and Osmond:

> Winmar's gesture helped transform both the way Australian rules football was played on the field and the behaviour of footy fans in the crowd. Indeed, Colin Tatz has argued that it was the most important act in the history of Australian rules football.[105]

At the time of Winmar's action, the club president of the opposing team, Allan McAlister, claimed that his club had no problem with Indigenous players:

> As long as they conduct themselves like white people, well, off the field, everyone will admire and respect ... As long as they conduct themselves like human beings, they will be all right. That's the key.[106]

Goodes' dance was not an attempt to conduct himself "like white people". It was a demonstration of his Indigenous, embodied sovereignty, commanding "white people" to take stock of their own position. In football parlance, it was time for the white nation to take a long hard look at itself.

Not everyone saw it that way. The most notorious criticism of Goodes was expressed by Sam Newman on the commercial television program, *The Footy Show*.[107] According to Newman, as Australian of the Year, Goodes ought not to have drawn attention to his being Indigenous. Or, having "provoked" his audience by doing so, ought not to complain about being vilified for it. Newman began his tirade by addressing Goodes: "from one Australian to another Australian". In so doing, Newman refused to recognize Goodes' indigeneity. Newman continued, "it is on you, as Australian of the Year, to unite and placate people, not to divide and be a provocateur". Nicolacopoulos and Vassilacopoulos contend that the command can

Figure 7.2 Nicky Winmar, "Winmar, I'm Black and Proud of it", *The Age* newspaper, April 18, 1993. Photographer: Wayne Ludbey.

be repudiated by annihilating the question (implicit in the command) or by discrediting the questioner (as entitled to issue such a challenge).[108] Newman did both. He attempted to undermine Goodes' assertion of Indigenous sovereignty by addressing him as an Australian rather than an Indigenous person. If Goodes is merely Australian, he has no right to make Indigenous claims on the field. By charging Goodes with the obligation to "unite and placate people", Goodes is held responsible for dividing a nation which is otherwise one.[109] By embodying his indigeneity and declaring it to the crowd, Goodes' dance commanded the white Australian public to acknowledge its occupier being. Newman's response consists in denying Goodes the right to issue such a command, to embody his sovereignty. Newman's condemnation of Goodes' dancing denied his sovereign right to stage his Indigenous being. His criticism was cloaked in the rhetoric of political holism – implying that Goodes fell short of his civic duties as an Australian (of the Year) by exhibiting 'divisive' behaviours. In other words, the question embedded in the command is declared unethical for its dividing the nation.

Australia's First Nations peoples are supposed to compete on behalf of the nation but not their culture. And yet, football has an Indigenous history, of Aboriginal teams that were established in the late 1980s and continue to today.[110] Playing together enabled Indigenous sportspeople to make links across the country.[111] It is in light of that history that Paul Briggs suggests that footballers such as "Michael Long and Adam Goodes, and others, would be playing for their ancestors and their culture and their people as much as for the fans of their respective clubs".[112] Like Goodes, Olympic gold medallist, Cathy Freeman, declared her Aboriginality as a badge of honour on the sports field. When Freeman ran a victory lap of honour at the 1994 Commonwealth Games flying the Aboriginal flag, she sparked public debate over whether she was 'entitled' to do so.[113] By commanding the crowd on the Indigenous round with a newly minted war dance, Goodes broke with the "Great Australian Silence" on Indigenous sovereignty.[114] Commentators such as Newman sought to admonish Goodes by arguing that he 'got what he asked for'. Grant and Aly both remark that Goodes acted "beyond his station".[115] If they are right, then Goodes' 'provocation' is to have turned the negation embedded in racist booing into an affirmative gesture of sovereign being. The real problem with Goodes' war dance then is that it affirms his Indigenous sovereignty (and by implication those of all Indigenous Australians), implying an ontological difference at odds with the psychological *terra nullius* that characterizes the public sphere. Goodes' action formed a new body, a political formation of thought, composed of contestatory impulses – colonial investments, Indigenous counter-narratives and embodied innovations – which were selected and taken up in the ensuing debate. Using the circumstance of his own Indigenous heritage, and the force of Indigenous participation in football, Goodes affirmed his sovereign being, in the words of Stan Grant, "talking to a country that didn't like what it heard".[116] This in turn led to two sorts of reaction: acknowledgement of nation's Indigenous peoples and their sovereign rights or denial of Indigenous sovereignty in the hate speech of *ressentiment*. It is testimony to the destabilizing power of Goodes' actions that the whole nation from the Prime Minister down felt compelled to respond, whether in acknowledgement or denial of its status as occupier. The year 2019 has seen the release of two major documentaries on the matter, *The Final Quarter* and *The Australian Dream*.[117] While the Australian Football League and its 18 clubs issued a public apology for not standing by Goodes, Waleed Aly argues that the entire situation cannot be confined to football because it is made possible by a culture war "as big as the nation".[118]

As a whole, the Australian nation has not shown itself willing to acknowledge Indigenous sovereign being, condemning itself to the compulsive repetition of colonizing rhetoric. For Nicolacopoulos and Vassilacopoulos, the being of Australian sovereignty is empty, lacking in substance. That lack explains why the racism embedded in the booing of Indigenous players is an expression of *ressentiment,* towards the affirmative character of Indigenous sovereignty. Founded on the originary negation of *terra nullius* – an historic reaction par excellence – the Australian body politic cannot become otherwise unless it opens itself to Indigenous being. Marcia Langton writes:

> Aboriginal people have invented a theatre of politics in which self-representation has become a sophisticated device, creating their own theories or modes of intercultural discourse such as land rights, self-determination, "white Australia has a black history" and so on.[119]

Sarah Jane Norman and Adam Goodes staged their own rituals of embodied sovereignty in the real-time theatre of intercultural Aboriginality. Their reterritorialization of colonial history, in bodily, cultural and aesthetic terms, pulled a thread from the fabric of Australia's ongoing *terra nullius*. It is testimony to the power of their dance that, for a time, an atmosphere of disequilibrium prevailed, making possible the emergence of something other than mere repetition of our colonial past.

Notes

1 Hagen Schultz-Forberg writes that the notion of sovereignty emerged in early modern Europe as "the core concept of legitimate statehood", "Sovereignty", in *Encyclopedia of Global Studies*, ed. Helmut Enheier and Mark Juergensmeyer (Los Angeles: Sage Publications, 2012), 1588. For Schultz-Forberg:

> Sovereignty still constitutes a core concept of political authority. It has been of central importance since the early modern period when it began to be applied to describe a mode of rule within a certain territory that rested in the hands of the state.
>
> (Ibid., 1588)

Schultz-Forberg acknowledges that legal (*de jure*) claims to sovereignty may well not match the actual (*de facto*) sovereignty exercised over a particular territory.

2 Padraig Kirwan acknowledges the existential and therefore conceptual distinction between Native sovereignty and its Western counterparts, "Mind the Gap: Journeys in Indigenous Sovereignty and Nationhood", *Comparative American Studies: An International Journal* 13, nos. 1–2 (June 2015): 51. He supports the view that "it is necessary to excavate the widest possible meaning(s) of Indigenous self-determination with regard to sovereignty" so that a better understanding of its *in situ* differences can emerge, ibid., 51.

3 Moreton-Robinson, "Sovereign Subjects", In *Sovereign Subjects: Indigenous Sovereignty Matters*, ed. Aileen Moreton-Robinson (New South Wales: Allen & Unwin, 2007), 21. Aileen-Moreton Robinson is a Geonpul scholar, Director of the National Indigenous Research and Knowledges Network (NIRAKN), and Distinguished Professor of Indigenous Research at Queensland University of Technology.

4 Ibid., 21.

5 Irene Watson, "Settled and Unsettled Spaces: Are We Free to Roam?", in *Sovereign Subjects: Indigenous Sovereignty Matters*, ed. Aileen Moreton-Robinson (Sydney: Allen and Unwin, 2007), 38. Irene Watson belongs to the Tanganekald, Meintangkt Boandik First Nations peoples, of the Coorong and the south east of South Australia. She is a professor of law and pro vice-chancellor of Aboriginal Leadership and Strategy at the University of South Australia.

6 Larissa Behrendt, "White Picket Fences: Recognizing Aboriginal Property Rights in Australia's Psychological *Terra Nullius*", *Constitutional Forum* 10, no. 2 (1999): 51. Larissa Behrendt is a Eualeyai/Kamillaroi scholar, professor of law and director of research at Jumbunna Indigenous House of Learning, at University of Technology, Sydney.

7 Gary Foley, "The Australian Labor Party and the Native Title Act", in *Sovereign Subjects: Indigenous Sovereignty Matters*, edited by Aileen Moreton-Robinson (Sydney: Allen and Unwin, 2007), 134–154. Professor Gary Foley (Victoria University) is a Gumbainggir scholar, activist and historian. He was co-founder of the Redfern Aboriginal Legal Services (1971) and the Aboriginal Tent Embassy (1972) and was involved in the establishment of the National Black Theatre.

8 *Coooper v. Stuart* (1889) 14 AC 285.

9 See also Moreton-Robinson, "Sovereign Subjects", 21.

10 Foley, "The Australian Labor Party and the Native Title Act", 136.

11 See Gary Foley, Andrew Schaap, and Edwina Howell, eds., *The Aboriginal Tent Embassy: Sovereignty, Black Power, Land Rights and the State* (New York: Routledge, 2014).

12 Gary Foley, Andrew Schaap and Edwina Howell, "Introduction", *The Aboriginal Tent Embassy*, xxv.

13 Ibid.

14 Moreton-Robinson, *Sovereign Subjects*, 138.

15 *Mabo and Ors v Queensland* (No. 2) (1992) 175 CLR 1.

16 Foley, "The Australian Labor Party and the Native Title Act", 147.

17 Ibid., 149; and Behrendt, "White Picket Fences", 54–55.

18 The *Native Title Act 1993* acknowledges that Aboriginal and Torres Strait Islanders were the original inhabitants of Australia, and that they have suffered dispossession of their lands. It also acknowledges the *Mabo* decision that native title is extinguished by the creation of freehold and leasehold interests. According to the act, once dispossessed of particular lands, native title cannot be claimed for that land. The aim of the act is to determine the processes and mechanisms for recognising native title in those areas that were not turned into freehold or lease-hold estates. Native title is thereby limited to "unallocated Crown land, original reserved land, land reserved for use not inconsistent with native title", Foley, "The Australian Labor Party and the Native Title Act", 153. In effect, a group wishing to establish native title needed to show its continuing traditional connection to the

land in question. Interruption via dispossession extinguishes the possibility of any claim. Foley writes:

> Thus the vast majority of Aboriginal people in Australia are now formally deemed to have been dispossessed without the possibility of compensation. All of this has been achieved by the judiciary and government, conveniently without having to address the primary underlying issue of Indigenous sovereignty

(Ibid., 154)

Bunjalong author, Fabienne Bayet-Charlton writes that native title has in practice been watered down so that "claiming native title these days is a bit like me saying to you, 'in your *second* language, prove to me reality'", "Overturning the doctrine: Indigenous Peoples and Wilderness: Being Aboriginal in the Environmental Movement", in *Blacklines: Contemporary Critical Writing by Indigenous Australians*, ed. Michele Grossman (Melbourne: Melbourne University Press, 2003), 180.

19 The Council for Aboriginal Reconciliation (CAR) was created by Federal legislation with a view to producing a strategy for reconciliation ready for the centenary of Australian federation. In 2000, the Council for Aboriginal Reconciliation presented to the nation the National Reconciliation documents *Corroboree 2000: Towards Reconciliation* and a *Roadmap for Reconciliation*. Reconciliation Australia was then created to continue the process inaugurated by CAR.

20 The State Government of Victoria is currently working towards forming a Treaty with the Indigenous people of Victoria, having recently enacted *Advancing the Treaty Process with Aboriginal Victorians Act 2018*. The process is in its early days, the first of its kind in Australia.

21 Referendum Council. "Uluru Statement from the Heart", www.referendumcouncil. org.au/sites/default/files/2017-05/Uluru_Statement_From_The_Heart_0.PDF, accessed November 25, 2019. It begins:

> Our Aboriginal and Torres Strait Islander tribes were the first sovereign Nations of the Australian continent and its adjacent islands, and possessed it under our own laws and customs. This our ancestors did, according to the reckoning of our culture, from the Creation, according to the common law from "time immemorial", and according to science more than 60,000 years ago. This sovereignty is a spiritual notion: the ancestral tie between the land, or "mother nature", and the Aboriginal and Torres Strait Islander peoples who were born therefrom, remain attached thereto, and must one day return thither to be united with our ancestors. This link is the basis of the ownership of the soil, or better, of sovereignty. It has never been ceded or extinguished, and co-exists with the sovereignty of the Crown.

(Ibid.)

22 Calla Wahlquist, "Indigenous Voice Proposal Not Desirable Says Turnbull", *The Guardian*, October 26, 2017, www.theguardian.com/australia-news/2017/oct/26/indigenous-voice-proposal-not-desirable-says-turnbull, accessed November 25, 2019.

23 Moreton-Robinson writes:

> Whiteness in its dominant contemporary form in Australian society is Anglicized, institutionalized, and culturally based. Australian culture is less white than it used

to be, but Anglicized whiteness forms the center where white men established institutions encouraging a possessive investment in whiteness.

> (Aileen Moreton-Robinson, *The White Possessive: Property, Power, and Indigenous Sovereignty* [Minneapolis: University of Minnesota Press, 2015], 65–66)

Patriarchal whiteness is manifest in law, through legalistic definitions of whiteness but it also has a wider remit. Moreton-Robinson writes:

> Patriarchal whiteness can be deployed simultaneously or separately as status, identity, and property. As a form of property, patriarchal whiteness is a valuable possession warranting protection. Patriarchal whiteness invests in property rights and is possessive and protective about asset accumulation and ownership
>
> (Ibid., 67)

It is also a rubric of power and power relations. By refusing Indigenous recognition and constitutional participation, the Australian government of the day retained the function of the Australian state as protector and perpetuator of patriarchal whiteness.

24 Phallocentric modes of representation conceive of otherness on the basis of their own hegemonic self-identity. The critique of phallocentric notions of sexual difference is articulated in the work of Luce Irigaray. "This Sex Which Is Not One" opens with the statement that "Female sexuality has always been conceptualized on the basis of masculine parameters", Luce Irigaray, *This Sex Which Is Not One*, trans. Catherine Porter (Ithaca, NY: Cornell University Press, 1985), 23. Irigaray's point is that sexual difference is oriented around masculine sameness, that there are not two sexes so much as one sex and its other: "Woman, in this sexual imaginary, is only a more or less obliging prop for the enactment of man's fantasies", ibid., 25. Phallocentrism can be extended to modes of representation which are structured around an economy of sameness, and not genuine difference. Elizabeth Grosz writes: "Phallocentrism is not simply, as Ernest Jones defined it, the primacy of the phallus ... but can be identified with a more general process of cultural and representational *assimilation*", Elizabeth Grosz, *Sexual Subversions: Three French Feminists* (Sydney: Allen and Unwin, 1989), 105. It arises from a model of human subjectivity that sees all "variations of subjectivity" in relation to a univocal male ("Western, capitalist, white, Eurocentric") model, ibid., 105.

25 2009 Australian of the Year, Michael Dodson is a member of the Yawuru people of the Broome region of Western Australia. He directed the Northern Land Council from 1988 to 1990 and served as counsel to the *Royal Commission into Aboriginal Deaths in Custody* (1987–1991).

26 Michael Dodson, "The End in the Beginning: Re(De)Finding Aboriginality", in *Blacklines: Contemporary Critical Writing by Indigenous Australians*, ed. Michele Grossman (Melbourne: Melbourne University Press, 2003), 36.

27 Ibid., 38.

28 Ibid., 37.

29 Indigenous scholar Marcia Langton is an anthropologist and geographer and holds the Foundation Chair of Australian Indigenous studies at the University of Melbourne. She gave the 2012 Boyer lectures entitled, "The Quiet Revolution: Indigenous People and the Resources Boom", and is author of *Marcia Langton's Welcome to Country,*

A Travel Guide to Indigenous Australia. She is associate provost at the University of Melbourne.

30 Marcia Langton, "Aboriginal Art and Film: The Politics of Representation", in *Blacklines: Contemporary Critical Writing by Indigenous Australians*, ed. Michele Grossman (Melbourne: Melbourne University Press, 2003), 119.

31 Ibid., 118.

32 Marcia Langton, "Trapped in the Aboriginal Reality Show", *Griffith Review* 19 (Autumn 2008): 143–159.

33 Toula Nicolacopoulos and George Vassilacopoulos, *Indigenous Sovereignty and the Being of the Occupier: Manifesto for a White Australian Philosophy of Origins* (Melbourne: re.press, 2014).

34 Ibid., 10.

35 Ibid.

36 Ibid., 22.

37 See Janna Thompson, "Collective Responsibility for Historic Injustices", *Midwest Studies in Philosophy* 30 (2006): 154–167, for a discussion of shared responsibility in the face of historical wrongs.

38 Nicolacopoulos and Vassilacopoulos, *Indigenous Sovereignty and the Being of the Occupier*, 11.

39 Like the truth commission of the South African TRC, Indigenous bodies have called for truth-telling to be part of reconciliation or negotiated settlement. The theme of the 2018 Yolngu Garma festival was truth-telling: Yolngu elder, Djawa Yunupingu, stated that:

> That is what *Garma* is – a ceremony – and here this year we have promised to tell the Truth – *Yuwalk Lakamara.* And to get to my point, the Truth is that we are not United in this country – we are not Comfortable – and we remain uncertain and troubled by this Truth. Because we live side by side – Two People – Two Laws – One Country.
> (Djawa Yunupingu, "Djawa Yunupingu: Speech August 4, 2018", Yothu Yindi Foundation, www.yyf.com.au/news/detail.aspx?SubjectID=1& ArticleID=155, accessed November 25, 2019)

40 Nicolacopoulos and Vassilacopoulos, *Indigenous Sovereignty and the Being of the Occupier,* 12.

41 Ibid., 14.

42 Ibid.

43 Whiteness is not always literally understood in this context insofar as a number of communities are counted as white in relation to Indigenous identity, yet will be seen as non-white, or in Nicolacopoulos and Vassilacopoulos's terms, "white-non-white" and "white-but-not-white-enough" if not simply black or non-white when used to affirm Australian possessive whiteness, ibid., 91.

44 Ibid., 27. When, for example, conservative columnist, Andrew Bolt, ostensibly bemoans the 'divisive' ghettoised behaviours of unassimilated migrants, his own ethnicity is lauded for its assimilation into the undifferentiated whole of Australian society, Andrew Bolt, "There is no 'us', As Migrants Form Colonies", *Herald Sun*, August 2, 2018, www.heraldsun.com.au/blogs/andrew-bolt/there-is-no-us-as-migrants-form-colonies/news-story/919f583813314a3a9ec8c4c74bc8c091, accessed November 25, 2019. Bolt writes: "Once we might have assumed that such migrants – just like my own parents – would assimilate into the wider

'us'", ibid. The article not only presumes a unified form of Australian-ness, it blames recent migrants for breaking up the party. The good migrant (with origins such as his own) cannot express any distinction, but must assimilate (annihilate) its differences in the name of the unified whole. The unassimilated migrant thereby affirms Bolt's status, as Australian, legitimate representative and safe-keeper of national unity.

45 Chris Healy, *Forgetting Aborigines* (Sydney: UNSW Press, 2008).

46 Ibid., 29–35.

47 The unity of the nation has become a troubled question in the public arena, a debate that has come to be played out in relation to Australia Day. On the one hand, Australia Day is a vehicle for patriotic ideologies of belonging and national virtue, and on the other hand, it is an opportunity to express doubts about the genealogy of the nation. While official events are held across the nation on Australia day, many cities host marches against Australia Day on the basis that it is a celebration of invasion and Indigenous dispossession. Tradition demands that citizenship ceremonies are held on Australia Day. In 2017, a number of local councils voted to hold their citizenship ceremonies on another day, to support finding another day to celebrate the nation (rather than the date of its invasion) and to educate the community on Aboriginal perspectives on Australia Day. As a result, the Prime Minister, amongst others, accused them of dividing the nation, Elias Clure, "City of Yarra Council's 'Attack on Australia Day' Angers Malcolm Turnbull", *ABC News Online*, August 16, 2017. www.abc.net.au/news/2017-08-15/melbourne-council-votes-to-ban-references-to-australia-day/8810286, accessed November 25, 2019.

48 Behrendt, "White Picket Fences", 51. Psychological *terra nullius* is manifest in the notion that recognition of native title is a gain for Aboriginal people, rather than recognition of property rights that existed long before European colonization. When native title is posed as a threat to the givenness of farming and mining interests, it would appear that native title is a recent construction, one which threatens to superimpose itself upon legitimately established interests.

49 Technically, White Australia is not entirely white, nor ever has been. Chinese migration has been a feature of Australian colonial society from the outset. White Australia is a political construction and critique, an imaginary yet real mode of citizenship which applies to non-Indigenous Australians. As Dipesh Chakrabarty once remarked, it is a mark of the success of the Indigenous political movement that Australians such as himself are deemed white, Chakrabarty, personal communication, 1993. On the other hand, the recent influx of African migrants on top of a sizeable Asian and Indian population could be forwarded as a reason to rethink the term "white Australian identity" while critiquing its political force and function. For Moreton-Robinson, the empirical mix of migrant ethnicity does not take away from the dominance of patriarchal whiteness in the Australian state, a topical subject of debate in the Australian media, Julia Baird and Sam Bold, "Conservative Parties around the World Have a Problem – and Women Are Losing Patience", *ABC News Online*, February 8, 2019, www.abc.net.au/news/2019-02-07/women-in-parliament-labor-liberal/10783234, accessed November 25, 2019.

50 SJ Norman, "SJ Norman: About", www.sarahjanenorman.com/about, accessed November 25, 2019.

51 Derived from the work of Luce Irigaray, morphology is a way of thinking the body in material, social and historical terms. Corporeal formation is an emergent process of social, material and historical forces.

52 *Corpus Nullius/Blood Country,* created and performed by SJ Norman as part of *Unsettling Suite*, Sydney: Carriageworks, February 23–March 10, 2013. See also SJ Norman, "SJ Norman: Corpus Nullius: Blood Country", www.sarahjanenorman. com/corpus-nulliusblood-country, accessed November 25, 2019.

53 SJ Norman, "SJ Norman: Corpus Nullius", www.sarahjanenorman.com/corpus-nulliusblood-country, accessed November 29, 2019.

54 *Bone Library*, a performance installation, created and performed by SJ Norman, Melbourne: Melbourne City Library, *Next Wave Festival*, May 23–27, 2012. See also SJ Norman, "SJ Norman: Bone Library", www.sarahjanenorman. com/bone-library, accessed November 26, 2019. On the impact of colonization on the life of Indigenous languages, see for example, Colin Yallop and Michael Walsh, eds. *Language and Culture in Aboriginal Australia* (Canberra: Aboriginal Studies Press, 1993), and Jeanie Bell, "Australia's Indigenous Languages", in *Blacklines: Contemporary Critical Writing by Indigenous Australians*, ed. Michele Grossman (Melbourne: Melbourne University Press, 2003), 159–180.

55 Gemmia Burden, "The Violent Collectors who Gathered Indigenous Artefacts for the Queensland Museum", *The Conversation*, May 28, 2018, https:// theconversation.com/the-violent-collectors-who-gathered-indigenous-artefacts-for-the-queensland-museum-96119, accessed November 25, 2019.

56 The ostensible loan of the artefact, subject to an apocryphal recall, supplants the sorry history of Aboriginal remains taken to Britain and now subject to recall for proper burial. See, for example, Reuters, "Bones to Return Home", *Sydney Morning Herald*, May 11, 2007, www.smh.com.au/national/bones-to-return-home-20070511-gdq46a.html, accessed November 25, 2019.

57 SJ Norman, "On Rituals", *Dancehouse Diary* 13, no. 7 (2014): 13, www. dancehousediary.com.au/?p=2509, accessed November 26, 2019.

58 *Unsettling Suite* was staged at Sydney's Performance Space in 2013. Eight works were presented in a large immersive installation, styled as a farmhouse, as well as a catalogue of essays, SJ Norman, *Unsettling Suite: Sarah Jane Norman*, ed. Jeff Kahn (Sydney: Performance Space, 2013). See also SJ Norman, "SJ Norman: Unsettling Suite", www.sarahjanenorman.com/unsettling-suite, accessed November 9, 2018.

59 *The River's Children*, a performance installation, created and performed by SJ Norman, Melbourne: *Dance Territories*, Melbourne Festival, Dancehouse, October 14–16, 2016. See also SJ Norman, "SJ Norman: The River's Children", www.sarahjanenorman.com/the-rivers-children, accessed November 25, 2019.

60 See *Servant or Slave*, dir. Steven McGregor, 2016.

61 Dodson, "The End in the Beginning", 37.

62 *Heirloom*, an installation created by SJ Norman. Melbourne: *Dance Territories*, Melbourne Festival, Dancehouse, October 14–16, 2016. See also SJ Norman, "SJ Norman: Heirloom", www.sarahjanenorman.com/heirloom, accessed November 26, 2019. *Take This for It Is My Body*, a performance installation, created by SJ Norman, performed by Carly Shepherd. Melbourne: *Dance Territories*, Melbourne Festival, Dancehouse, October 14–16, 2016. See also SJ Norman, "SJ Norman: Take This for It Is My Body", www.sarahjanenorman.com/take-this-for-it-is-my-body, accessed November 26, 2019.

63 Stan Grant's mother, a Kamilaroi woman, also engaged in work "that would leave her hands red raw, cracked and bleeding", *Talking to My Country* (Sydney: Harper Collins, 2016), 52.

64 Irene Watson writes of the colonial appropriation of Indigenous being:

> In the process of absorption, we are to be consumed by the state and its citizens and, in their consumption of us, they are to become us. They anticipate coming into their own state of lawfulness through the consuming of our sovereign Aboriginality.
>
> ("Settled and Unsettled Spaces", 35)

Watson raises a number of possible scenarios according to which white Australia might become otherwise, ibid., 36. She offers a model of Aboriginal sovereignty that differs from state sovereignty. To that end, Aboriginal sovereignty purports a change in sovereign power, towards diversity and inclusivity rather than appropriation and dominance, ibid., 38.

65 Norman, "On Rituals", 13.

66 Gilles Deleuze, "One Manifesto Less", in *The Deleuze Reader*, ed. Constantin V. Boundas (New York: Columbia University Press, 1993), 204–222.

67 Ibid., 207.

68 Ibid., 218.

69 Anne Marsh, *Performance, Ritual, Document* (Melbourne: Macmillan, 2014), 177.

70 Referendum Council, "Uluru Statement from the Heart".

71 The term "event-in-the-making" comes from the innovative work of the Sense Lab under the direction and input of Erin Manning and Brian Massumi, to bring together thought and art, concept and creation through an ethos of experimental hospitality, https://senselab.ca/wp2/about/, accessed November 29, 2019. The event-in-the-making is emergent, underdetermined, open to that which enters into its elaboration. Richard Schechner is known for his work on ritual and performance, for drawing out the ritual qualities of performance. In "The Future of Ritual", Schechner draws on the work of Victor Turner to suggest that ritual opens up a "liminal-liminoid time and space", Richard Schechner, "The Future of Ritual", *Journal of Ritual Studies* 1, no. 1 Winter (1987): 15. Even though rituals embody prescribed behaviours, there is also a sense in which they depend upon the "not-yetness" of the unfolding event, ibid., 23. In that sense, rituals are events-in-the-making, all the more so where history is shifted onto indeterminate ground.

72 Deleuze writes, "It is in the middle where one finds the becoming, the movement, the velocity, the vortex … It is neither the historical nor the eternal, but the untimely", Deleuze, "One Manifesto Less", 208.

73 Dipesh Chakrabarty, *Provincializing Europe: Postcolonial Thought and Historical Difference* (Princeton, NJ: Princeton University Press, 2000), 250. See Chapter 4, for further discussion of temporal pluralization.

74 There are a great many works on Aboriginal history that take up the colonial rendition of Indigenous dispossession, for example, Reynolds, *Frontier: Aborigines, Settlers and Land* (Sydney: Allen and Unwin, 1996), Bruce Pascoe, *Dark Emu: Black Seeds: Agriculture or Accident* (Broome, WA: Magabala Books, 2014), Bain Attwood, *Telling the Truth about Aboriginal History* (Sydney: Allen and Unwin, 2005).

75 Stan Grant writes of his country as "eternal and still. Time folds into itself and history isn't history at all. It is not something past – it is present", *Talking to My Country*, 77.

76 Deleuze, "One Manifesto Less", 209.

77 Julia Kristeva, *Powers of Horror: An Essay in Abjection*, trans. Leon S. Roudiez (New York: Columbia University Press, 1982), 4.

78 Ibid., 14.

79 Deleuze, "One Manifesto Less", 214.

80 Ibid., 219.

81 Deleuze, "One Manifesto Less", 219, Marsh, *Performance, Ritual, Document*, 181.

82 Adam Goodes, www.youtube.com/watch?v=kBljMnLw9-4, accessed October 5, 2018.

83 *Ahn's Brush with Fame*, Adam Goodes, ABC Television, Series 3, Episode 3, aired August 1, 2018.

84 Ibid.

85 NITV News, "Adam Goodes's War Dance Was Created for the Under 15s Development Squad on Tour in Papua New Guinea", SBS Television, aired August 3, 2015.

86 Ibid.

87 Ibid.

88 Adam Curley, "Proud Goodes Stands by War Cry Celebration", May 30, 2015, www.afl.com.au/news/2015-05-30/proud-goodes-stands-by-war-cry-celebration, accessed November 29, 2019. Also, www.youtube.com/watch?v=6Ii7OMETavU, accessed October 5, 2018.

89 Adrian Crawford, "Adam Goodes Gutted by Racial Slur but wants AFL Fan Educated", www.abc.net.au/news/2013-05-25/goodes-gutted-but-places-no-blame/4712772, accessed November 25, 2019.

90 *Ahn's Brush with Fame*, Adam Goodes.

91 For example, Paul Sheehan, "The Adam Goodes Fire Was Lit by His Conduct: Not His Race", *Sydney Morning Herald*, July 29, 2015, www.smh.com.au/opinion/the-adam-goodes-fire-was-lit-by-his-conduct-not-his-race-20150729-gimxzy.html; also Allison Jackson, "Australians Keep Booing This Football Star, and Swear It's Not Racist", *Global Post Online*, August 7, 2015, www.pri.org/stories/2015-08-07/australians-keep-booing-football-star-and-swear-it-s-not-racist, accessed November 26, 2019. On the other hand, many articles diagnosed the booing of Goodes as clearly racist, for example, Lauren Wood, "AFL Sorry It Didn't Act Quicker People Booing Adam Goodes During His Final Season", *Herald Sun*, March 18, 2016, www.heraldsun.com.au/sport/afl/more-news/afl-sorry-it-didnt-act-quicker-people-booing-adam-goodes-during-his-final-season/news-story/6ebb ec1712615777173c5ce59b70449e, accessed November 25, 2019; Jeremy Stanford, "Booing Adam Goodes: Are We Even Aware We're Racists?", *The Drum, ABC News Online*, 28 July, 2015, www.abc.net.au/news/2015-07-28/standford-booing-adam-goodes:-are-we-even-aware-were-racists/6653108, accessed November 25, 2019; Safi, Michael. "AFL Great Adam Goodes is Being Booed across Australia. How Did It Come to This?", *The Guardian*, 29 July 2015, www.theguardian.com/sport/blog/2015/jul/29/afl-great-adam-goodes-is-being-booed-across-australia-how-did-it-come-to-this, accessed November 25, 2019.

92 De Souza, "What Does Racial (In)Justice Sound Like? On Listening: Acoustic Violence and the Booing of Adam Goodes", *Continuum* 32, no. 4 (2018): 463.

93 Ibid., 460.

94 Ibid., 464.

95 Stan Grant writes: "To Adam's ears, the ears of so many Indigenous people, these boos are a howl of humiliation", *Talking to My Country,* 219.

96 Aly, cited in de Souza, "What Does Racial (In)Justice Sound Like?", 464. See also Pedestrian.tv, "Watch Waleed Aly Absolutely Nail the Adam Goodes Debate", www.pedestrian.tv/sport/watch-waleed-aly-absolutely-nail-the-adam-goodes-debate/, accessed November 25, 2019.

97 Grant writes: "Australians can consign history to a bygone era. Indigenous people are now told to do the same. We are told to let it go. But our history is a living thing. It is physical. It is noses and mouths and faces. It is written on our bodies", *Talking to My Country*, 69.

98 Behrendt, "The Backlash Against Adam Goodes Is the Reason His War Dance Is Important", *The Guardian*, June 1, 2015, www.theguardian.com/commentisfree/2015/jun/01/the-backlash-against-adam-goodes-is-the-reason-his-war-dance-is-important, accessed November 25, 2019.

99 See www.youtube.com/watch?v=6Ii7OMETavU, for an excellent review of commentators' remarks as they watched Goodes dance.

100 Paul Briggs, "The Long Walk: Philipa Rothfield in Conversation with Paul Briggs", *Dancehouse Diary* 10 (2018): 37, www.dancehousediary.com.au/?p=3467, accessed November 25, 2019.

101 Winmar reflected on the racism directed towards him: "we got spat on, people would throw beers and stuff. I hated it. I was very emotionally upset", Adam Manovic, "'I'm Black and I'm Proud to Be Black': Nicky Winmar's Gesture 25 Years On", *NITV News*, www.sbs.com.au/nitv/article/2018/04/11/im-black-and-im-proud-be-black-nicky-winmars-gesture-25-years, accessed November 25, 2019.

102 *The Sunday Age*, April 18, 1993.

103 Ibid.

104 The event led to mediation between the players and ultimately, the adoption of racial anti-vilification policy on the part of the AFL, AAP. "Michael Long and Damian Monkhorst Look Back on AFL Racism Incident 20 Years On", *ABC News Online*, April 29, 2015, www.abc.net.au/news/2015-04-29/michael-long-damian-monkhorst-remember-afl-racism/6432104, accessed November 25, 2019.

105 Matthew Klugman and Gary Osmond, "That Picture: Nicky Winmar and the History of an Image", *Australian Aboriginal Studies* 2 (2009): 79.

106 Cited in Klugman and Osmond, "AFL: The Ugly Game of Enlightened Racism", *Sydney Morning Herald*, April 17, 2013, www.smh.com.au/opinion/afl-the-ugly-game-of-enlightened-racism-20130416-2hy9b.html, accessed March 5, 2019.

107 Sam Newman, *The Footy Show*, Channel 9, June 4, 2015, www.youtube.com/watch?v=J2g1ow2j_E0, accessed November 25, 2019.

108 Nicolacopoulos and Vassilacopoulos, *Indigenous Sovereignty and the Being of the Occupier*, 17.

109 Grant writes:

> we are often told we should all just be Australians. It is a noble sentiment, and perhaps one day we can find a common identity that encompasses us all, but for much of this country's history we have been told we were anything but Australian.
>
> (*Talking About My Country*, 176)

110 See Briggs, "The Long Walk", 37–38.

111 Briggs recounts

> People like Pat Dodson and Mick Dodson played alongside me in those foot-
> ball teams in the 70s, and we got introduced to people like Michael Mansell
> … We got to talk to Aboriginal people from Western Australia, and South
> Australia, and Queensland, through football. We built really strong social
> networks consisting of very organic conversations. It didn't have a political
> agenda, but it drove people's sense of improving the lives of our mob right
> around the country.
>
> ("The Long Walk", 37)

112 Ibid., 37.

113 Freeman won two races, the 400-m and 200-m sprints. Having won the 400-m
sprint, she ran a victory lap with the Aboriginal flag. Upon winning the 200
m, she displayed the Australian and Aboriginal flags. See Jock Given, "Red,
Black, Gold to Australia: Cathy Freeman and the Flags", *Media Information
Australia* 75 (February 1995): 51, also Scott Gullan, "Commonwealth Games
Flashback: Cathy Freeman's Aboriginal Pride Sparked Arthur Tunstall's Flag
Ban", *Herald Sun*, March 30, 2018.

114 The term belongs to W.E.H. Stanner who gave a lecture in 1968, entitled
"The Great Australian Silence", on the "cult of forgetfulness practised on a
national scale" regarding Indigenous and non-Indigenous history in Australia,
W.E.H. Stanner, "The Boyer Lectures 1968: After the Dreaming" (Sydney,
NSW: Australian Broadcasting Commission, 1969). See Andrew Gunstone,
"Reconciliation and 'the Great Australian Silence'", www.auspsa.org.au/sites/
default/files/reconciliation_and_the_great_australian_silence_andrew_gunstone.
pdf, accessed November 25, 2019.

115 Grant, *Talking to My Country*, 204, Pedestrian.tv, "Watch Waleed Aly Absolutely
Nail the Adam Goodes Debate".

116 Grant, *Talking to My Country*, 204.

117 *The Final Quarter*, dir. Ian Darling (Australia: 2019), and *The Australian Dream*,
dir. Daniel Gordon (Australia: 2019).

118 Sarah Black, "AFL, Clubs Unreservedly Apologise to Goodes for not 'Standing
with him'", www.afl.com.au/news/2019-06-07/afl-clubs-unreservedly-apologise-
to-goodes-for-not-standing-with-him, accessed November 25, 2019; news.com.
au, "Waleed Aly Raises Concerns After Adam Goodes Documentary Airs",
www.news.com.au/sport/afl/waleed-aly-raises-concerns-after-adam-goodes-
documentary-airs/news-story/04961c951beeff64b1db65a67901cab9, accessed
November 26, 2019.

119 Marcia Langton, "Aboriginal Art and Film", 124.

Bibliography

AAP. "Michael Long and Damian Monkhorst Look Back on AFL Racism Incident
20 Years On". *ABC News Online*, April 29, 2015. www.abc.net.au/news/2015-
04-29/michael-long-damian-monkhorst-remember-afl-racism/6432104, accessed
November 25, 2019.

———. "Sydney Swans' Adam Goodes Celebrates Goal with Indigenous War
Dance: Ruffles Feathers". *The Age Newspaper*, May 29, 2015. www.theage.com.au/
sport/afl/sydney-swans-adam-goodes-celebrates-goal-with-indigenous-war-dance-
ruffles-feathers-20150529-ghczbr.html, accessed November 25, 2019.

Ahn's Brush with Fame, "Adam Goodes". ABC Television, Series 3, Episode 3, aired August 1, 2018.

Attwood, Bain. *Telling the Truth about Aboriginal History*. Sydney: Allen and Unwin, 2005.

The Australian Dream. Directed by Daniel Gordon (Australia: 2019).

Baird, Julia and Sam Bold. "Conservative Parties around the World Have a Problem – and Women Are Losing Patience". *ABC News Online*, February 8, 2019. www.abc.net.au/news/2019-02-07/women-in-parliament-labor-liberal/10783234, accessed November 25, 2019.

Bayet-Charlton, Fabienne. "Overturning the Doctrine: Indigenous Peoples and Wilderness: Being Aboriginal in the Environmental Movement". In *Blacklines: Contemporary Critical Writing by Indigenous Australians*, edited by Michele Grossman, 171–80. Melbourne: Melbourne University Press, 2003.

Behrendt, Larissa. "White Picket Fences: Recognizing Aboriginal Property Rights in Australia's Psychological *Terra Nullius*". *Constitutional Forum* 10, no. 2 (1999): 50–58.

———. "The Backlash against Adam Goodes is the Reason his War Dance is Important". *The Guardian*, June 1, 2015. www.theguardian.com/commentisfree/2015/jun/01/the-backlash-against-adam-goodes-is-the-reason-his-war-dance-is-important, accessed November 25, 2019.

Bell, Jeanie. "Australia's Indigenous Languages". In *Blacklines: Contemporary Critical Writing by Indigenous Australians*, edited by Michele Grossman, 159–180. Melbourne: Melbourne University Press, 2003.

Black, Sarah. "AFL, Clubs Unreservedly Apologise to Goodes for not 'Standing with him'". www.afl.com.au/news/2019-06-07/afl-clubs-unreservedly-apologise-to-goodes-for-not-standing-with-him, accessed November 26, 2019.

Bolt, Andrew. "There Is No 'Us': As Migrants Form Colonies". *Herald Sun*, August 2, 2018. www.heraldsun.com.au/blogs/andrew-bolt/there-is-no-us-as-migrants-form-colonies/news-story/919f583813314a3a9ec8c4c74bc8c091, accessed November 25, 2019.

Bone Library, a performance installation, created and performed by SJ Norman. Melbourne: Melbourne City Library, *Next Wave Festival*, May 23–27, 2012.

Briggs, Paul. "The Long Walk: Philipa Rothfield in Conversation with Paul Briggs". *Dancehouse Diary* 10 (2018): 37–38, www.dancehousediary.com.au/?p=3467, accessed November 25, 2019.

Burden, Gemmia. "The Violent Collectors Who Gathered Indigenous Artefacts for the Queensland Museum". *The Conversation*, May 28, 2018. https://theconversation.com/the-violent-collectors-who-gathered-indigenous-artefacts-for-the-queensland-museum-96119, accessed March 5, 2019.

Chakrabarty, Dipesh. *Provincializing Europe: Postcolonial Thought and Historical Difference*. Princeton, NJ: Princeton University Press, 2000.

Clure, Elias. "City of Yarra Council's Attack on Australia Day Angers Malcolm Turnbull". *ABC News Online*, August 16, 2017. www.abc.net.au/news/2017-08-15/melbourne-council-votes-to-ban-references-to-australia-day/8810286, accessed November 25, 2019.

Cooper v Stuart 14 AC 285 (1889).

Corpus Nullius/Blood Country, created and performed by SJ Norman. In *Unsettling Suite*, Sydney: Carriageworks, February 23–March 10, 2013.

Crawford, Adrian. "Adam Goodes 'Gutted' by Racial Slur but Wants AFL Fan Educated". *ABC News Online*, May 27, 2013. www.abc.net.au/news/2013-05-25/goodes-gutted-but-places-no-blame/4712772, accessed November 25, 2019.

Curley, Adam. "Proud Goodes Stands by War Cry Celebration", AFL News, May 30, 2015, www.afl.com.au/news/2015-05-30/proud-goodes-stands-by-war-cry-celebration, accessed November 29, 2019.

Deleuze, Gilles. "One Manifesto Less". In *The Deleuze Reader*, edited by Constantin V. Boundas, 204–22. New York: Columbia University Press, 1993.

De Souza, Poppy. "What Does Racial (in)Justice Sound Like? On Listening: Acoustic Violence and the Booing of Adam Goodes". *Continuum* 32, no. 4 (2018): 459–473.

Dodson, Michael. "The End in the Beginning: Re(De)Finding Aboriginality". In *Blacklines: Contemporary Critical Writing by Indigenous Australians*, edited by Michele Grossman, 25–42. Melbourne: Melbourne University Press, 2003.

The Final Quarter. Directed by Ian Darling (Australia: 2019).

Foley, Gary. "The Australian Labor Party and the Native Title Act". In *Sovereign Subjects: Indigenous Sovereignty Matters*, edited by Aileen Moreton-Robinson, 134–154. Sydney: Allen and Unwin, 2007.

Foley, Gary, Andrew Schaap and Edwina Howell, eds. *The Aboriginal Tent Embassy: Sovereignty, Black Power, Land Rights and the State*. New York: Routledge, 2014.

———. "Introduction", in *The Aboriginal Tent Embassy: Sovereignty, Black Power, Land Rights and the State*, edited by Gary Foley, Andrew Schaap and Edwina Howell, xxv–xxxi. New York: Routledge, 2014.

Fox News. "AFL 360 Discuss Adam Goodes' Dance Indigenous Round 9 2015". YouTube, www.youtube.com/watch?v=6Ii7OMETavU, accessed November 25, 2019.

Given, Jock. "Red, Black, Gold to Australia: Cathy Freeman and the Flags". *Media Information Australia* 75 (February 1995): 46–56.

Goodes, Adam. www.youtube.com/watch?v=kBljMnLw9-4, accessed October 5, 2018.

Grant, Stan. *Talking to My Country*. Sydney: Harper Collins, 2016.

Grosz, Elizabeth. *Sexual Subversions: Three French Feminists*. Sydney: Allen and Unwin, 1989.

Gullan, Scott. "Commonwealth Games Flashback: Cathy Freeman's Aboriginal Pride Sparked Arthur Tunstall's Flag Ban". *Herald Sun*, March 30, 2018.

Gunstone, Andrew. "Reconciliation and 'the Great Australian Silence'". www.auspsa.org.au/sites/default/files/reconciliation_and_the_great_australian_silence_andrew_gunstone.pdf, accessed November 25, 2019.

Healy, Chris. *Forgetting Aborigines*. Sydney: UNSW Press, 2008.

Heirloom, An installation created by SJ Norman. Melbourne: *Dance Territories*, Melbourne Festival, Dancehouse, October 14–16, 2016.

Irigaray, Luce. *This Sex Which Is Not One*, translated by Catherine Porter. Ithaca, NY: Cornell University Press, 1985.

Jackson, Allison. "Australians Keep Booing this Football Star, and Swear It's Not Racist". *Global Post Online*, August 7, 2015, www.pri.org/stories/2015-08-07/australians-keep-booing-football-star-and-swear-it-s-not-racist, accessed December 3, 2019.

Kirwan, Padraig. "'Mind the Gap': Journeys in Indigenous Sovereignty and Nationhood". *Comparative American Studies: An International Journal* 13, nos. 1–2 (June 2015): 42–57.

Klugman, Matthew and Gary Osmond. "That Picture: Nicky Winmar and the History of an Image". *Australian Aboriginal Studies* 2 (2009): 78–89.

———. "AFL: The Ugly Game of Enlightened Racism". *Sydney Morning Herald*, April 17, 2013. www.smh.com.au/opinion/afl-the-ugly-game-of-enlightened-racism-20130416-2hy9b.html, accessed March 5, 2019.

Kristeva, Julia. *Powers of Horror: An Essay in Abjection*. Translated by Leon S. Roudiez. New York: Columbia University Press, 1982.

Langton, Marcia. "Aboriginal Art and Film: the Politics of Representation". In *Blacklines: Contemporary Critical Writing by Indigenous Australians*, edited by Michele Grossman, 109–124. Melbourne: Melbourne University Press, 2003.

———. "Trapped in the Aboriginal Reality Show". *Griffith Review* 19 (Autumn 2008): 143–159.

Mabo and Ors v Queensland (No. 2) 175 CLR 1 (1992).

Manning, Erin and Brian Massumi. "The Sense Lab, About". https://senselab.ca/wp2/, accessed November 25, 2019.

Manovic, Adam. "'I'm Black and I'm Proud to Be Black': Nicky Winmar's Gesture 25 Years On". *NITV News*. www.sbs.com.au/nitv/article/2018/04/11/im-black-and-im-proud-be-black-nicky-winmars-gesture-25-years, accessed November 25, 2019.

Marsh, Anne. *Performance, Ritual, Document*. Melbourne: Macmillan, 2014.

McAlister in Klugman and Osmond, Alan. "That Picture – Nicky Winmar and the History of an Image". *Australian Aboriginal Studies* 2 (2009): 78–89.

Moreton-Robinson, Aileen. "Sovereign Subjects". In *Sovereign Subjects: Indigenous Sovereignty Matters*, edited by Aileen Moreton-Robinson, 21–31. New South Wales: Allen & Unwin, 2007.

———. *The White Possessive: Property, Power, and Indigenous Sovereignty*. Minneapolis: University of Minnesota Press, 2015.

Native Title Act 1993, no. 110. Parliament of Australia, 1993.

Newman, Sam. *The Footy Show.*, Channel 9, June 4, 2015. www.youtube.com/watch?v=J2g1ow2j_E0, accessed November 25, 2019.

news.com.au. "Waleed Aly Raises Concerns after Adam Goodes Documentary Airs". www.news.com.au/sport/afl/waleed-aly-raises-concerns-after-adam-goodes-documentary-airs/news-story/04961c951beeff64b1db65a67901cab9, accessed November 26, 2019.

Nicolacopoulos, Toula and George Vassilacopoulos. *Indigenous Sovereignty and the Being of the Occupier: Manifesto for a White Australian Philosophy of Origins*. Melbourne: re-press, 2014.

NITV News. "Adam Goodes's War Dance Was Created for the Under 15s Development Squad on Tour in Papua New Guinea". SBS Television, aired August 3, 2015.

Norman, Sarah Jane. *Unsettling Suite: Sarah Jane Norman*, edited by Jeff Khan. Sydney: Performance Space, 2013.

———. "On Rituals". *Dancehouse Diary* 13, no. 7 (2014): 13.

———. "SJ Norman: About". www.sarahjanenorman.com/about, accessed November 25, 2019.

———. "SJ Norman: Corpus Nullius: Blood Country". www.sarahjanenorman.com/corpus-nulliusblood-country, accessed November 25, 2019.

Pascoe, Bruce. *Dark Emu: Black Seeds: Agriculture or Accident*. Broome, WA: Magabala Books, 2014.

Pedestrian.tv. "Watch Waleed Aly Absolutely Nail the Adam Goodes Debate". pedestrian.tv, www.pedestrian.tv/sport/watch-waleed-aly-absolutely-nail-the-adam-goodes-debate/, accessed November 25, 2019.

Referendum Council. "Uluru Statement from the Heart". www.referendumcouncil. org.au/sites/default/files/2017-05/Uluru_Statement_From_The_Heart_0.PDF, accessed November 25, 2019.

Reuters. "Bones to Return Home". *Sydney Morning Herald*, May 11, 2007. www. smh.com.au/national/bones-to-return-home-20070511-gdq46a.html, accessed November 25, 2019.

Reynolds, Henry. *Frontier: Aborigines, Settlers and Land*. Sydney: Allen and Unwin, 1996.

The River's Children, a performance installation, created and performed by SJ Norman. Melbourne: *Dance Territories*, Melbourne Festival, Dancehouse, October 14–16, 2016.

Safi, Michael. "AFL Great Adam Goodes Is Being Booed across Australia. How Did It Come to this?" *The Guardian*, July 29, 2015. www.theguardian.com/sport/blog/ 2015/jul/29/afl-great-adam-goodes-is-being-booed-across-australia-how-did-it-come-to-this, accessed November 25, 2019.

Schechner, Richard. "The Future of Ritual". *Journal of Ritual Studies* 1, no. 1 Winter (1987): 5–33.

Schultz-Forberg, Hagen. "Sovereignty". In *Encyclopedia of Global Studies*, edited by Helmut Enheier and Mark Juergensmeyer, 1587–1592. Los Angeles: Sage Publications, 2012.

Servant or Slave. Directed by Steven McGregor, 2016.

Seven Sport. "Adam Goodes War Cry Celebration". YouTube, www.youtube.com/ watch?v=kBljMnLw9-4, accessed November 25, 2019.

Sheehan, Paul. "The Adam Goodes Fire Was Lit by His Conduct: Not His Race". *Sydney Morning Herald*, July 29, 2015. www.smh.com.au/opinion/the-adam-goodes-fire-was-lit-by-his-conduct-not-his-race-20150729-gimxzy.html, accessed November 25, 2019.

Special Broadcasting Service (SBS). "That Adam Goodes War Cry Used a Boomerang Not a Spear: Says Choreographer". *NITV News*, August 3, 2015. www.sbs.com.au/ondemand/video/497197123958, accessed November 25, 2019. SBS Broadcasting.

Stanford, Jeremy. "Booing Adam Goodes: Are We Even Aware We're Racists?" *The Drum, ABC News Online*, 28 July, 2015. www.abc.net.au/news/2015-07-28/standford-booing-adam-goodes:-are-we-even-aware-were-racists/6653108, accessed November 25, 2019. Australian Broadcasting Corporation, 2015.

Stanner, W.E.H. "The Boyer Lectures 1968. After the Dreaming". Sydney, NSW: Australian Broadcasting Commission, 1969.

The Sunday Age, April 18, 1993.

Take This for It Is My Body, a performance installation, created by SJ Norman, performed by Carly Shepherd. Melbourne: *Dance Territories*, Melbourne Festival, Dancehouse, October 14–16, 2016.

Thompson, Janna. "Collective Responsibility for Historic Injustices". *Midwest Studies in Philosophy* 30 (2006): 154–167.

Wahlquist, Calla. "Indigenous Voice Proposal Not Desirable Says Turnbull". *The Guardian*, October 26, 2017. www.theguardian.com/australia-news/2017/oct/ 26/indigenous-voice-proposal-not-desirable-says-turnbull, accessed November 25, 2019.

Watson, Irene. "Settled and Unsettled Spaces: Are We Free to Roam?" In *Sovereign Subjects: Indigenous Sovereignty Matters*, edited by Aileen Moreton-Robinson, 33–50. Sydney: Allen and Unwin, 2007.

Wood, Lauren. "AFL Sorry It Didn't Act Quicker People Booing Adam Goodes During His Final Season". *Herald Sun*, March 18, 2016. www.heraldsun.com.au/sport/afl/more-news/afl-sorry-it-didnt-act-quicker-people-booing-adam-goodes-during-his-final-season/news-story/6ebbec1712615777173c5ce59b70449e, accessed November 25, 2019.

Yallop, Colin and Michael Walsh, eds. *Language and Culture in Aboriginal Australia*. Canberra: Aboriginal Studies Press, 1993.

Yunupingu, Djawa. "Djawa Yunupingu: Speech August 4, 2018". Yothu Yindi Foundation, www.yyf.com.au/news/detail.aspx?SubjectID=1&ArticleID=155, accessed November 25, 2019.

Conclusion

Between the dancer and the dance

> In a book, there is nothing to understand, but much to make use of. Nothing to interpret or signify, but much to experiment with. The book must form a machine with something; is must be a small tool operating on an exterior. The combinations, permutations, utilizations are never internal to the book, but depend on connections with a particular outside.
>
> (Deleuze and Guattari)[1]

Dance and the Corporeal Uncanny follows two tributaries of thought. One is centred upon the subject, *qua* dancer or spectator, the other displaces the subject in order to focus on the activities of force. The body is thought in very different terms, depending upon whether it is integrated with subjectivity or regarded as a formation of force. For Merleau-Ponty, the body is part and parcel of subjectivity. Experience is bodily, perception is bodily and action is the expression of an embodied agency. According to this way of thinking, the dancer is the agent, the one whose actions produce movement. Experience is central to this conception of dance. It offers a way into the workings of the bodily subject, signifying the (motor) intentionality that underlies action. It is the argument of this book that if we are to think experience in relation to the body, then we need to acknowledge the organization of experience through (social) practice. This is felt in individual terms, at the level of the dancer's perceptions, dispositions and preferences (movement subjectivity), also in relation to each field of practice, through its values, commitments and characteristic modes of kinaesthetic sensibility. Practice is widely conceived here, to include physical, social, political, historical and environmental factors. Although focused on the dancer's perceptual and movement experience, the phenomenological body need not be confined to the purview of consciousness. The dancer's actions are not always found within the frame of conscious perception. The body schema is one indication of this, habit formation another. These latter concepts acknowledge the sense in which a greater part of the dancer's organization lies ready to hand, able to emerge without the need for conscious deliberation. Such is the legacy of training and its means of cultivation, practice. Practice conditions the dancer's movement subjectivity. It is the means whereby social, political and kinaesthetic factors come to be embodied. That said, the development of movement subjectivity cannot be reduced to its conditions of production. Dancers bring their own concerns, interests and projects to their dancing. Movement subjectivity thus arises somewhere between the body and its cultural, kinaesthetic milieu.

The phenomenological paradigm is predicated upon a certain conception of embodied subjectivity, agency and action. Taking this as its cue, *Dance and the Corporeal Uncanny* sought to articulate the impact and influence of kinaesthetic, social, cultural and political factors. In so doing, the dancer's subjectivity was recast, so as to acknowledge the sense in which these forces enter into the dancer's movement subjectivity and kinaesthetic sensibility. Practice is key to understanding how such agency emerges, is expressed and is perceived. It poses subjectivity as an emergent formation, rather than as a given that precedes the social. Phenomenology offers an open-ended means of enquiry into the dancer's embodied subjectivity. It is alert to the social and political as it manifests in thought and action. Difference is found in multiple registers, in the field of practice, in the individual dancer, in the intersubjective domain and in the reception and perception of dance. It is finely calibrated through the dancer's movement signature but is also the subject of widespread hegemonic tendencies, which normalize certain kinds of perception at the expense of others. This is found in contexts which authorize particular sensibilities over and above other practices which espouse their own forms of value. It is also found in the institutionalization of norms and conventions that speak to the 'proper' body of dance. The phenomenological approach is a mode of listening to and therefore valuing experience.

Nietzschean thought proceeds altogether differently. It treats subjectivity as a veneer, with its own interpretive needs and interests. The phenomena of subjectivity – experience, thought and perception – are taken to be symptomatic rather than indicative of the relation between thought and action. The symptomatic reading of subjectivity paves the way for a different conception of the body than is discerned through phenomenology. The body in Nietzschean thought is not organized under the aegis of the subject. Deleuze, Klossowski and Foucault develop a reading of the Nietzschean body at odds with experience, giving effect to Nietzsche's claim that it is the body and not consciousness that offers "a guiding thread" for philosophical thought.[2]

For Klossowski, the body figures as a succession of corporeal states, each state a provisional resolution of contestatory impulses. Klossowski distinguishes between two perspectives: that of the body, which follows its own serial pathway of impulse resolution, and that of the subject, whose thinking reflects the social imperative to make sense in terms alien to the trajectory of corporeal articulation. Subjectivity incurs a hermeneutic problematic for Klossowski insofar as it attempts to understand the serial development of corporeal activity. This is because consciousness functions as a vehicle of the group. Individuals think in terms that reflect the group imperative towards communication, signification and the exchange of meaning – that which

Klossowski calls the code of signs.[3] The intersubjective orientation of "the herd" is at odds with the impulsive nature of corporeal becoming.[4] There are thus two modes of signification, the code of signs allied to consciousness and the semiotic of impulses formed through the body.[5] This is quite different to the evidential probity accorded to experience within phenomenological thought. Where phenomenology appeals to experience in order to understand embodiment, Klossowski drives a wedge between conscious thought and corporeal formation. This is not to say that thought can never encounter the body but it may be to suggest that thought cannot really know the body that thinks.

Klossowski's work on thought and the body could be complicated through a more discursive (historicized) understanding of signification and its relation to the body. Foucauldian inscription looks at the relation between language and the body in genealogical terms.[6] For Foucault, like Klossowski, there is no independent access to a body thought outside of, or prior to, culture. But where Klossowski is interested in the body's semiotic (of impulses), Foucault focuses on the corporealization of thought through discursive practices that enable the folding inwards of thought. Movement practices could be seen in these terms, as forming a genealogy of the body, which institutes its own mode of corporeal intelligibility (code of signs) and distinctive manner of corporeal becoming (semiotic of impulses). Qigong, for example, posits and cultivates the movement of Qi, which is in turn informed by the ways in which the body features in Chinese thought and practice. These conceptions, connections, meridians, pathways and locations inform the thinking embedded in the practice and include the cultivation of its corporeal impulses. The corporeal thinking found in Qigong promotes a distinctive range of experiences which are linked to its specific manner of corporeal becoming. Other practices embed their own forms of imagery, imaginary networks, perceptual foci or corporeal order. Their specificity is born from the relation between signification (filtered through each code of signs) and the movement (belonging to each field's semiotic of impulses). These differing links between a movement-based mode of signification and its affiliated semiotic of impulses are forged in practice, a question of history in the body. While Klossowski offers a generic conception of the code of signs (corporeal intelligibility) and the semiotic of impulses (bodily becoming), a more practice-based approach would seek the ways in which field gives shape to these two registers. Eric Blondel conceives the body in Nietzsche midway between the intellect and the chaotic multiplicity of impulses.[7] Following Blondel, we might suggest that practices such as these construct the body in this sense, midway between the intellect and the body's impulsive activity, to create a mode of thought in the body formed and felt in movement.

Like Klossowski, Deleuze distinguishes between subjective experience and corporeal formation. He does so by appealing to an ontology of force which accounts for the body and consciousness in different terms. Also like Klossowski, he treats these two formations as different in kind. The difference between consciousness and the body can be seen through an analysis of their constituent forces. The body in Deleuze belongs to the field of action, which expresses the mastery of force over force, towards corporeal formation. The formation of consciousness breaks with this active norm, towards a momentary mode of inaction. The folding inwards of force to create thought and experience represents the triumph of reaction, however momentary, over movement. Either force resolves into action or it folds inwards.

Dance and the Corporeal Uncanny builds upon Deleuze's Nietzsche to flesh out an account of dance which does not appeal to the dancer as the source of the dance. Its decentred approach towards subjectivity makes sense of Nietzsche's claim that there is no doer behind the deed. The Nietzschean paradigm offers a number of conceptual distinctions which allow for a concrete focus on dancing as an activity that draws upon a multiplicity of factors and forces. According to this mode of thought, force underlies the production of subjectivity and corporeal formation. Movement is the work of forces which variously fold inwards, orient outwards, crystallize, sediment, deploy and respond. Movement draws force from many quarters, towards the formation of myriad bodies, biological, social, political, chemical or cultural. The social and political, cultural and kinaesthetic is that which becomes corporeal in motion. The body's becoming is found in its dynamic and provisional resolution of force. Its boundaries swell and contract. The human body is a changing multiplicity of relational factors that traverse the conventional boundaries between 'the body' and its environment. The relational character of this approach need not delineate between persons and their environment nor between the human and the animal. It could be treated as an invitation to form new relationships –creative formations – that work together to reconfigure what it means to move in ethical ways.

Difference enters this domain at each and every moment of corporeal formation, calling attention to the plurality of underlying forces that make up the field of action. The identification of these forces and their modes of activity is a hermeneutic affair. Nietzschean philosophy sees interpretation (the interpretation of force) as itself the expression of force. In other words, interpretation is never disinterested. Alphonso Lingis writes:

> Interpretation then is not merely projecting over the inert stupor of matter the immaterial glow of meaning visible only to the mind that projects it; to assign meaning to a being is not to exercise absolute sovereignty over it. To give sense to it is to orient it; it is to positively struggle with it, it is to concretely overcome the form it has by force.[8]

Jean Granier similarly poses interpretation as "the creative imposition of form upon matter".[9] The body is a mediating force in this interpretive project, one whose history informs its manner of thoughts, feelings and actions. To interpret dance through the lens of the dancer is to bring into play the force of subjectivity. To see the body apart from the dancer is to draw force from beyond the plane of the subject. Then it is a question of that which is being interpreted, which practice, which aspect of practice, from what point of view. Thomas DeFrantz speaks of the ways in which dance becomes legible and for whom.[10] These factors enter into the perspectival understanding of interpretation as an expression of force on the workings of force.

The notion of force also yields a particular account of subject-formation and its relation to the body. Foucault's genealogical reading of Nietzsche proposes a history of the body through the figure of inscription. Conjoined with Deleuze, Foucauldian genealogy is able to offer a theory of cultural production as it pertains to the dancer. Foucault's work on disciplinary practice demonstrates the sense in which culture inscribes the body to produce a constellation of corporeal dispositions along with a corresponding turning inwards of force (*aka* subjectification). The Deleuzian treatment of culture shows how forces become primed for action through the figure of the subject, ready to act the reactions of the field in conformity with its normative presuppositions. Culture is a key component of dance practice. It functions through training and technique, habit formation, value formation and the ongoing reproduction of the field through practice. The workings of force offer an alternative way of conceiving the social production of movement subjectivity which posits the body schema and its complementary array of body images, theorizing the activity of culture as that which produces in the individual the disposition to act those forces (reactions, circumstances) that define the domain. Foucault's disciplinary analysis shows the dual action of cultural production: the organization of power in the body as aptitude or capacity and its correlative movement towards subjection (subjectification). This is not to say that conformity is guaranteed. There is space in this account for a shift in cultural relations, towards the reconfiguration of force and therefore of social and political power. In dance, this can be seen in the workings of force towards a change of circumstance, through contestation and innovation. It is also embodied in the figure of the Sovereign Individual who draws force from culture in order to act it. *Dance and the Corporeal Uncanny* looks to the concept of virtuosity as the reterritorialization of the kinaesthetic norm towards what Erin Manning might call "the minor gesture".[11] Virtuosity thus conceived is less a marker of (individual) excellence than the reconfiguration of culture, through "counterstrategic reinscription".[12]

Dance and the Corporeal Uncanny has sought to read Deleuze's Nietzsche through the lens of dance: by thinking dance as the activation of circumstance, by discerning the redeployment of experience in action, through analysing cultural production as the corporeal inscription of force – turned inwards and outwards – and via speculating on the virtuosic reconfiguration of culture. Although Deleuze depicts consciousness as the triumph of reactive force, movement's riposte represents the redeployment of reaction towards corporeal formation. Movement's riposte represents the utilization of experience in action without resorting to a metaphysics of the subject. Like all relations of force, felt and formed according to type, it represents a momentary resolution of contestatory impulses, a moment in the flow of becoming otherwise.

The question of subjectivity has a place within this constellation of concepts, open to another interpretation, one which nudges the phenomenological paradigm towards a process of desubjectification. Subjectivity is here strategically played, in the manner of its own overcoming. This is a kind of labour, the labour of a certain kind of dancing, felt through forming the Workerly Type. The strategic deployment of subjectivity represents a line of flight navigated through the Nietzschean concept of overcoming. Although illustrated here in relation to a postmodern sensibility, overcoming could be taken up in a range of ways, in other contexts, for other purposes. It could, for example, be posed as an oppositional force, against the grain of hyper-individualism, diagnosed by Bojana Cvejic.[13] How that might be realized is as yet unclear, but the concept (a concept of overcoming) signals the possibility of another kind of performative practice of the self, away from the commodified individualization embedded in neo-liberalism. It draws force from Foucault's *The Use of Pleasure,* which recognizes the merits of a strategic curiosity, that "enables one to get free of oneself".[14] Foucault writes:

> There are times in life when the question of knowing if one can think differently than one thinks, and perceive differently than one sees, is absolutely necessary if one is to go on looking and reflecting at all.[15]

In philosophical terms, *Dance and the Corporeal Uncanny* is divided into two camps. One, the phenomenological, is focused on the experience, perceptions and agency of the dancer. It sees dancing as the work of the dancer. The other, a combination of Deleuze and Nietzsche, is grounded on an ontology of force, corporeal formation and subjective reaction. It teases out the dance apart from the dancer. Each approach depends upon a distinct view of the body, whether integrated with subjectivity or thought as a multiplicity formed through serial relations of force. And yet there are cross-overs. It is nigh impossible to abandon the plane of the subject. As Deleuze concedes, its "quiverings" fascinate us.[16] Even Louis Althusser admitted his own adhesion to a subject-centred point of view.[17] In terms of the dance, the perspective of the dancer returns again and again in the flow of movement. How could it be otherwise? The point of this book is not to negate the importance or feelings of the dancer and those around her. It is rather to acknowledge the force of subjectivity, while seeking another way in, to thinking movement.

Most of this book was written against a backdrop of practice, of practising and encountering dance. More time was spent writing than in the studio. This concluding chapter will reverse that ratio. It is written in the midst and at the temporal edges of practice, tipping the scales towards dancing rather than writing. It looks to a very specific field of work in order to stage an encounter between philosophy and practice. The emphasis on dancing rather than writing recalls the moment of the relay, mentioned in the Introduction, where theory encounters the brick wall of practice so as to move on. Deleuze

Figure 8.1 No Time to Fly, choreographed by Deborah Hay. Photographer: Rino Pizzi.

writes of artistic practice offering an 'outside' perspective, a form of difference from which to evaluate the conceptual work of the philosopher.[18] The body represents a third term in this relay between art and philosophy, a means of interpretation and conceptual inflexion.

What follows is a conceptual discussion of a two-week workshop conducted by Deborah Hay, entitled, *Being a Pig, Or a Questionable Formula for the Practice of Dance*, and held in Melbourne in January 2019.[19] The aim of this account is to show the ways in which the concepts of this book can be deployed in relation to an event in which "the body commits to practice".[20] *To be a pig* is to take advantage of the environment in which one dances, to snuffle up all that it can offer by putting into play a number of strategic techniques designed to support the link between the body and its milieu. Over two weeks, 28 dancers are encouraged to "practise the practice" in the spirit of experimentation.[21] The practice is strictly impossible to achieve for any length of time. Its suppositions are not bound to the actual, though the work of the dancer is real.[22] Time and again, dancers are encouraged to activate aspects of the practice, severally and together. We are enlisted to perceive each other as likewise engaged in the endeavour. The central tenet of this practice is articulated thus:

> *What if my whole body dancing could be served by how I see the environment in which I dance?*

The question devolves into four thematic moments:

I The non-linearization of experience

Seeing the environment is a key element of this work, which is less concerned with what I see than how I see. Seeing in this context is a momentary state of affairs, a quick grab of the visual field.[23] The idea of the practice is to foster the momentary, not to dwell on any one experience, simply to register it and let it go. This is how we are to see. Hay speaks of "disattaching" from experience, of noticing its affiliated flow of thoughts or perceptual "editing" and letting that go so as to open up to further experience.[24] The aim, from an experiential point of view, is to experience a flow of "non-linear" (non-directed, unreflective) experiences – to see moments of the room, other bodies and the space in between, in smaller and smaller increments.[25] This is an impossible task in that one inevitably starts thinking, reflecting or managing one's perceptions. The *modus operandi* of the practice then is to notice one's attachment to an experience and to disattach from it. The facilitation of the momentary (how I see) depends upon the serial recognition of attachment and the subsequent demand to let go of thought. Hay offers the formulation, "here and gone, here and gone" to encourage momentary engagement without giving in to its inevitable cognitive encroachment.[26] She suggests we open ourselves to environmental perceptions which are near, mid-range and far, all at once; that we think of space as not empty, able to furnish a rich multiplicity of momentary perceptions in smaller and smaller doses.[27] These strategies invite the successive capture of environmental moments, nuggets of space and time. Day after day, I challenge myself to let go of the inevitable train of thought that attaches to my visual experience, returning repeatedly to myriad moments of perceptual apprehension. I look around me, watch others move, moving between the familiar and the uncanny. Our dancing brings us in touch with other bodies. There is a difference between seeing the other as a recognizable person – as Deborah or Niharika – and encountering aspects of a body in movement. Hay's conception of experience requires a degree of recognition, otherwise we would be skimming or surfing the visual field. Clearly there is a fine line between registering an experience and dwelling upon it. Hay suggests that we "have the experience and let it go", that "there is no time to dive in; the depth of the work is on the surface".[28]

II Cellular reconfiguration

Hay has over the years developed a distinctive approach towards the body, which she formulates as the cellular body.[29] She forwards a cellular conception of the body, which consists of trillions of cells, set in motion.[30] The identity of the body (or the dancing self) is reconfigured towards a sense of dynamic multiplicity. Hay writes:

All I can be at any moment is all of myself. If myself is more than fifty trillion cells in radical transformation every moment, I am off the hook of being any one entity. I am flux in a corporeal body. Responsibility to a singular identity is a misconception. Engaging the work of the imagination to translate "I am" into fifty trillion and more cells at once dispossesses fixed ideas from cultivated patterns that continue to determine what dance or dancer should be.[31]

The cellular body reconfigures the unity of the self towards an unfolding multiplicity: "There is no one self. There are a multiplicity of selves".[32] The cellular body undermines what Hay calls the "choreographed body", its habits, body schematic dispositions and tendencies.[33] The "whole body at once" sums up the event-laden dynamism of the cellular body. The "whole body at once" is invoked within the practice to break up the choreographed, habitual body, so as to make it "more than, other than".[34] Appealing to the cellular body opens the body up to difference, beyond its kinaesthetic provenance. Hay remains "in attendance to the feedback" afforded by cellular reconfiguration.[35] This is an imaginary practice, whose adoption may nonetheless take effect. Hay writes: "Dance is the field trip I conduct in order to interface with this experience".[36] Hay claims she can feel the difference between her movement being served by how she sees and movement that conforms to established patterns.[37] Perhaps the non-linearization of experience supports cellular reconfiguration. Perhaps this is what is meant by the whole body dancing being served by how I see.

III Noticing

The third term in this field of practice is the role accorded to noticing. Hay curls her fist above her head to signal that part of the self that watches the work unfold over time: "I am here overseeing the experiment; the body is the field of experimentation; the work is overseeing how the experiment unfolds. You are not the experiment".[38] The dancer oversees the practice, working to enlarge the dance, while simultaneously confining the seriality of experience to smaller and smaller increments. Noticing fixity, the folding inwards of force, requires active destruction. Hay uses the term, "Turn your fucking head" (originally applied to herself) to wake up the self to the practice, also the title of a film about her work.[39] Hay coaches more or less throughout, to remind us of the elements of the practice, its levels, complexities and demands, making strategic suggestions and suppositions:

Think of the dance as a space of practice rather than material ... Whole body at once the teacher ... Step up to the smaller increments of time as a means of not investing ... Defuse the power of the gaze ... I'm juggling with these questions, these parallel dances, the parallel dance of me noticing, overseeing the practice, time passing ... There is a multiplicity of experiences we're juggling simultaneously … My job is to oversee the experiment.[40]

IV Why not?

Hay's workshop can be interpreted along three intersecting axes: one, subject-centred; the second, body-centred; and the third, involving desubjectification. The subject-centred perspective of the practice is simultaneously (or serially) body-centred and engaged in its own undoing. The practice of cellular reconfiguration is a kind of desubjectification, as is the non-linearization of experience. And yet, the work is a form of work on the part of the subject, an enunciation of a Workerly Type.[41] This is work, the work of opening the self to a non-linear flow of experiences (machinic seriality) and to overcome, to actively deconstruct the person as dancer in favour of a greater sense of corporeal possibility. The aim is to move beyond the subject's kinaesthetic sensibility, movement subjectivity, characteristic body schemata and habitual, corporeal self-perceptions. The subject has a role within this practice, to notice momentary attachment, and also to intervene, suppose and reorient: "Front is everywhere, here and here and here".[42] The work of resisting or letting go of attachment to the flow of experience is significant. Time and again, one veers off into thought, reflection, analysis and, time and again, the work demands a return to the machinic seriality of experience. This is a mode of active destruction, of willing to be overcome, of shifting experience towards a lived conception of the cellular body (trillions of cells changing all at once), of fostering a non-linear flow of experience without attachment (sans the *ressentiment* that sustains subjective experience).

To be a pig requires the strategic deployment of subjectivity on the part of the dancer, to deconstruct the dancer in favour of the cellular body. This is both subject-dependent (requiring work on the part of the dancer) and desubjectifying (requiring disattachment) so as to support the reconfiguration of movement subjectivity towards a cellular dynamism (an unfettered semiotic of impulses). *To be a pig* requires an ongoing oscillation between experience and movement's riposte. Movement's riposte is an action-based reply to the formation of experience. Chapter 6 illustrated the riposte in relation to the redeployment of sensation in movement, where droplets of sensory experience (reactions) are returned to motion. And yet, Hay does not highlight corporeal sensation in her work. Her concept of dancing does not depend upon the strategic deployment of sensation in order to compose movement. The kind of riposte envisaged in her work turns thought into action via disattachment or supposition rather than redeployment. It is just as measured, but orients itself towards non-intentional diversification rather than sensory redeployment. Movement for Hay occurs in the space between the non-linearization of experience, its noticing by the subject, and a body freed of the imperative to conform to its genealogical origins.

Being a Pig can also be read in relation to Klossowski's distinction between a technology of thought (the code of signs) and the body's semiotic of impulses.[43] Klossowski writes:

> Once the body is recognized as the product of the impulses (subjected, organized, hierarchized), its cohesion with the self becomes fortuitous. The impulses *can be put to use by a new body*, and are presupposed in the search for new conditions.[44]
>
> To restore these "corporealizing" forces (impulses) to thought amounts to an expropriation of the agent, the self.[45]

Hay verbalizes the non-linear in nonsensical terms as if the practice retreats from imposing a code of signs. She writes:

> I feel like a tower of babble. Millions of voices speak from my body at once – no one voice more dominant – a deliberate exercise to outwit the need to encapsulate. Tower is the continuity of my performance. Babble is the energy.[46]

One of the great pleasures of this workshop was to observe the diversity of movements generated by some of its participants – almost irrational, outlandish moments not easily reconciled with the identity of the body as dancer. To resist the coherence of interpretation in favour of corporeal activity is to affirm the body's 'semiotic of impulses', a flow of movement that takes hold of its own conditions and opens itself to a greater range of impulses than is designated by the body schema (movement habits, capacities and aptitudes) and its cultivated body images (modes of somatic attention). To that extent, the practice aims to support corporeal differentiation with the assistance of non-linear experience (perceptual impulses) and a loosening of subjective grip.

Being a pig oscillates between a designated range of subject-positions (noticer, overseer, disattacher, supposer, reconfigurer) and corporeal lines of flight. It affirms the body, enlisting the self to deconstruct the linear flow of perceptual life. Hay is reluctant to see her work in anti-humanist terms because the practising subject is hard at work.[47] There is a lot of work for the self to do, such as:

1 To notice the formation of attachment to experience and give it up;
2 To notice the passage of time;
3 To resist editing, not to savour experience (i.e., dwell in *ressentiment*);
4 To open up to bodily actions that draw on an enlarged field of circumstance beyond the givens of habit, organization, training and technique; and
5 To commit to the experiment, again and again and again.

Equally, there is a lot for the body to do, to move beyond its constitutive dispositions and habits.

I think that Hay is right to see the work as a form of practice, as practising, rather than achievement. Watching others dance, I notice that some workshop participants tend to remain within their own movement palette, that people dance in recognizably characteristic ways, staying within their version of the practice in the midst of its invitation to expand. That said, it is also possible to see the experiment in motion, to see a contagion of movement between bodies, to notice what a body can do when confronted by its own provenance, sometimes yielding an uncanny glimmer in the serial semiotic of corporeal impulse. Hay encourages dancers to ask *what if* their dancing were served by how they see, by supposing a semiotic of impulses not held in check by the code of signs. Two perspectives are thus in play: one phenomenological, subjective and strategic, and the other deconstructive, geared towards a body without the dancer as agent. According to Deleuze, subtraction allows minor force to become active, by destabilizing that which is dominant, in this case, the coherence of experience and the agency of the dancer as dancer.[48] Deleuze sees subtraction as the destabilization of political force.[49] Displacing the field of movement subjectivity makes sense of Hay's claim that her practice is a form of political activism, not on the global stage, but in terms of its deterritorialization of the dancer and reterritorialization of the kinaesthetic field. These reflections represent an oscillation between the thinking of this book and the specificity of Hay's practice, captured in a particular space and time. They are an example of the Nietzschean view that interpretation is not a disinterested affair, that to make sense is to impose, orient and struggle with that which has its own trajectory of sense-making. The discussion is less a basis for generalization than an interpretive encounter, able to furnish the deployment of the two conceptual paradigms of this book. There are no doubt other practices which call for different emphases, different interpretations and different modes of analysis. *Dance and the Corporeal Uncanny* aims to open up thought to practice in the field of dance. It outlines a philosophy of action with and without a subject. It is the hope of this book that others will pick up its thoughts and take them onto other terrains, by way of other encounters in the field of practice, remembering that the concept is itself a multiplicity in motion, the body its means of interpretation.

Notes

1 Gilles Deleuze and Félix Guattari, cited in Alan Schrift, *Nietzsche's French Legacy* (London and New York: Routledge, 1995), 64.

2 Friedrich Nietzsche, *Writings from the Late Notebooks*, trans. Kate Sturge (Cambridge, Cambridge University Press, 2003), 27. Nietzsche claims that:

> We find it ill-considered that precisely human consciousness has for so long been regarded as the highest stage of organic development and as the most astonishing of all earthly things; indeed as their blossoming and goal. In fact, what is more astonishing is the *body*.
>
> (Nietzsche, *Writings from the Late Notebooks*, 29)

3 A view which can be traced to Nietzsche's remarks in *The Gay Science*:

> My idea is clearly that consciousness actually belongs not to man's existence as an individual but rather to the community – and herd-aspects of his nature; that accordingly, it is finely developed only in relation to its usefulness to community or herd; and that consequently each of us, even with the best will in the world to *understand* ourselves as individually as possible, "to know ourselves", will always bring to consciousness precisely that in ourselves which is "non-individual", that which is "average".
>
> (Friedrich Nietzsche, *The Gay Science: With a Prelude in German Rhymes and an Appendix of Songs*, trans. Josefine Nauckhoff [Cambridge: Cambridge University Press, 2001], 213)

4 Ibid., 213.

5 Just to be clear, Klossowski's position is not a form of Cartesian dualism. Neither Klossowski nor Deleuze think the mind and body in Cartesian terms. Klossowski does not invest agency in consciousness, nor does he pose the body in mechanistic terms. For Klossowski (and Deleuze), the body is the basis of action, the mind an epiphenomenal point of view. Consciousness is not the seat of agency, which is found within and between relations of force/impulses.

6 See Michel Foucault, "Nietzsche, Genealogy, History", in *Language, Counter-Memory, Practice: Selected Essays and Interviews by Michel Foucault*, ed. Donald F. Bouchard, trans. Donald F. Bouchard and Sherry Simon (New York: Cornell University Press, 1977), 139–164.

7 Eric Blondel writes that "The body is therefore an intermediary between the absolute plural of the world's chaos, and the absolute simplification of intellect", Eric Blondel, *Nietzsche, The Body and Culture: Philosophy as Philological Genealogy*, trans. Sean Hand (London: Athlone Press, 1991), 207.

8 Alphonso Lingis, "The Will to Power", in *The New Nietzsche*, ed. David B. Allison (Cambridge, MA: MIT Press, 1985), 44.

9 Jean Granier, "Nietzsche's Conception of Chaos", in *The New Nietzsche*, ed. David B. Allison (Cambridge, MA: MIT Press, 1985), 140.

10 Personal communication, February 4, 2019.

11 Erin Manning, *The Minor Gesture* (Durham: Duke University Press, 2016).

12 Elizabeth Grosz, "Inscriptions and Body Maps", in *Feminine, Masculine and Representation,* ed. Terry Threadgold and Anne Cranny-Francis (Sydney: Allen and Unwin, 1990), 64.

13 Bojana Cvejic's recent research, "The Performing of the Self", focuses on the performative imperative nested in "the experience economy", Bojana Cvejic, "The Performing of the Self: Aesthetic Individualism", public lecture held in conjunction with Dancehouse, Fitzroy Town Hall, Melbourne, Australia, March 2, 2018. Cvejic suggests that capitalism's experience economy compels individuals to perform their identity in aesthetic terms (everyone is an artist). This represents a mode of subjectivation, a form of aesthetic individualism that says to be a subject is to perform one's subjectivity according to the logic of capitalism. Desubjectivation suggests the possibility of resistance, an untimely gesture that runs counter to the political force of hyper-individualism, thought through as a mode of subtraction (active destruction). See also Gilles Deleuze, "One Manifesto Less", in *The Deleuze Reader*, ed. Constantin V. Boundas (New York: Columbia University Press, 1993), 204–222, Stefano Harney and Fred Moten, *The Undercommons: Fugitive*

Planning and Black Study (Wivenhoe, New York: Minor Compositions, 2013), and Manning, *The Minor Gesture.*

14 Michel Foucault, *The Use of Pleasure*: *The History of Sexuality: Volume Two*, trans. Robert Hurley (New York: Vintage Books, 1986), 8.

15 Ibid., 8.

16 Gilles Deleuze, *Nietzsche and Deleuze*, trans. Hugh Tomlinson (New York: Columbia University Press, 1983), 41.

17 I only wish to point out that you and I are *always already* subjects, and as such constantly practice the rituals of ideological recognition … The writing I am currently executing and the reading you are currently performing are also in this respect rituals of ideological recognition.

> (Louis Althusser, "Ideology and Ideological State Apparatuses (Notes Towards an Investigation)", *Essays on Ideology* [London: Verso Editions, 1984], 46–47)

18 Jon Roffe paints the encounter between philosophy and art as an encounter between distinct modes of practice, Jon Roffe, "Practising Philosophy", Jon Roffe, "Practising Philosophy", in *Practising with Deleuze*: *Design, Dance, Art, Writing, Philosophy*, Suzie Attiwill, Terri Bird, Andrea Eckersley, Antonia Pont, Jon Roffe and Philipa Rothfield (Edinburgh: Edinburgh University Press, 2017), 190. This runs counter to that which positions philosophy apart from practice. For Deleuze, philosophy is itself a mode of practice, to be "judged in light of the other practices with which it *interferes*", cited in Roffe, "Practising Philosophy", 190.

19 *Being a Pig* workshop, Abbotsford Convent, Melbourne, Australia, January 14–25, 2019. It was organized by Jane Refshauge with Dancehouse and Deborah Hay. 2019 also marks the focus of Berlin's *Tanz im August* focus on Hay, entitled, *Re-Perspective Deborah Hay: Works from 1968 to the Present*, which included the staging of a number of Hay's choreographic works, alongside a series of seminars, panel discussions and a video installation on the perception of Hay's work.

20 Deborah Hay, *My Body: The Buddhist* (Hanover and London: Wesleyan University Press, 2000), 20.

21 Hay, *Being a Pig* workshop.

22 I am reminded of Priya Srinivasan's *Sweating Saris* and Mark Franko's *The Work of Dance*, both of which draw attention to the labour of dancing, Priya Srinivasan, *Sweating Saris: Indian Dance as Transnational Labor* (Philadelphia: Temple University Press, 2012), Mark Franko, *The Work of Dance: Labor, Movement and Identity in the 30s* (Middletown, CT: Wesleyan University Press, 2002). Conducted in the midst of a heatwave amongst 20-plus sweating bodies, the labour required to engage in Hay's experiment was palpable.

23 In *My Body: The Buddhist*, Hay writes: "I let go of the way vision configures objects and perspective, trying to make things what I want or need them to be", ibid., 2.

24 Hay, *Being a Pig* workshop. Hay cites Chogyam Trungpa Rinpoche on experience:

> once you have that experience of the presence of life, don't hang onto it. Just touch and go. Touch that presence of life being lived, then go. You do not have to ignore it. "Go" does not mean that we have to turn our back on the experience and shut ourselves off from it; it means just being in it without further analysis and without further reinforcement.
>
> (*My Body: The Buddhist*, xxiv)

25 Hay, *Being a Pig* workshop.
26 Ibid.
27 Ibid.
28 Ibid.
29 Susan Foster writes: "One of the dominant and sustaining metaphors in Hay's cultivation of physicality is her postulation of the body as the ever-changing cumulative performance of seventy-five trillion semi-independent cells", "Forward", Deborah Hay, *My Body: The Buddhist* (Hanover and London: Wesleyan University Press, 2000), xii.
30 "I reconfigure the three-dimensional body into an immeasurable fifty-three trillion cells perceived perceiving, all of them, at once", Hay, *My Body: The Buddhist*, xxiv.
31 Deborah Hay, *Lamb at the Altar: The Story of a Dance* (Durham: Duke University Press, 1994), 36.
32 Hay, *Being a Pig* workshop.
33 Ibid.
34 Ibid.
35 Hay, *My Body, My Buddhist*, xxiv.
36 Ibid., xxv.
37 Hay, *Being a Pig* workshop.
38 Ibid.
39 *Turn your F∧*king Head*, dir. Becky Edmunds, 2012.
40 Hay, *Being a Pig* workshop.
41 Although very different, there are a number of points of contact between Hay's choreographic approach and other postmodern practices which appeal to the Workerly Type: firstly, through asking questions within the practice, where the question is danced, and secondly, through absorption of the dancer in the work of dancing. Taken together, these factors offer a point of reference for Hay's shared origins in the Judson Church Theater of the 1960s and 1970s.
42 Hay, *Being a Pig* workshop.
43 Susan Foster writes of Hay enlisting students to pay "rigorous attention to the body's impulses", "Forward", *My Body, My Buddhist*, xiv.
44 Pierre Klossowski, *Nietzsche and the Vicious Circle*, trans. Daniel W. Smith (London and New York: Continuum books, 1997), 26.
45 Ibid., 25.
46 Hay, *My Body, My Buddhist*, 20.
47 Deborah Hay, "Turn your F∧*king Head", showing and discussion, Dancehouse, March 8, 2014, and personal communication, January 2019.
48 Deleuze, "One Manifesto Less".
49 Ibid.

Bibliography

Althusser, Louis. "Ideology and Ideological State Apparatuses (Notes Towards an Investigation)". In Louis Althusser, *Essays on Ideology*, 1–60. London: Verso Editions, 1984.

Blondel, Eric. *Nietzsche, The Body and Culture: Philosophy as Philological Genealogy*. Translated by Sean Hand. London: Athlone Press, 1991.

Deleuze, Gilles. *Nietzsche and Philosophy*. Translated by Hugh Tomlinson. New York: Columbia University Press, 1983.

———. "One Manifesto Less". In *The Deleuze Reader*, edited by Constantin V. Boundas, 204–222. New York: Columbia University Press, 1993.

Foster, Susan. "Forward". In Deborah Hay, *My Body: The Buddhist*, ix–xviii. Hanover and London: Wesleyan University Press, 2000.

Foucault, Michel. "Nietzsche, Genealogy, History". In *Language, Counter-Memory, Practice: Selected Essays and Interviews by Michel Foucault*. Translated by Donald F. Bouchard and Sherry Simon, edited by Donald F. Bouchard, 139–164. New York: Cornell University Press, 1977.

———. *The Use of Pleasure: The History of Sexuality: Volume Two*. Translated by Robert Hurley. New York: Vintage Books, 1986.

Franko, Mark. *The Work of Dance: Labor, Movement and Identity in the 30s*. Middletown, CT: Wesleyan University Press, 2002.

Granier, Jean. "Nietzsche's Conception of Chaos". In *The New Nietzsche*, edited by David B. Allison, 135–141. Cambridge, MA: MIT Press, 1985.

Grosz, Elizabeth. "Inscriptions and Body Maps". In *Feminine, Masculine and Representation,* edited by Terry Threadgold and Anne Cranny-Francis, 62–74. Sydney: Allen and Unwin, 1990.

Harney, Stefano and Fred Moten. *The Undercommons: Fugitive Planning and Black Study*. Wivenhoe, New York: Minor Compositions, 2013.

Hay, Deborah. *Lamb at the Altar: The Story of a Dance*. Durham: Duke University Press, 1994.

———. *My Body: The Buddhist*. Hanover and London: Wesleyan University Press, 2000.

———. "Turn your F∧*king Head", film showing and discussion, Dancehouse, March 8, 2014

———. *Being a Pig* workshop. Abbotsford Convent, Melbourne, Australia, January 14–25, 2019, organized by Jane Refshauge, with Dancehouse and Deborah Hay.

Klossowski, Pierre. *Nietzsche and the Vicious Circle*. Translated by Daniel W. Smith. London and New York: Continuum, 1997.

Lingis, Alphonso. "The Will to Power". In *The New Nietzsche*, edited by David B. Allison, 37–63. Cambridge, MA: MIT Press, 1985.

Manning, Erin. *The Minor Gesture*. Durham: Duke University Press, 2016.

Nietzsche, Friedrich. *The Gay Science: With a Prelude in German Rhymes and an Appendix of Songs*. Translated by Josefine Nauckhoff. Cambridge: Cambridge University Press, 2001.

———. *Writings from the Late Notebooks*. Translated by Kate Sturge. Cambridge, Cambridge University Press, 2003.

Roffe, Jon. "Practising Philosophy". In Attiwill, Suzie, Terri Bird, Andrea Eckersley, Antonia Pont, Jon Roffe and Philipa Rothfield. *Practising with Deleuze: Design, Dance, Art, Writing, Philosophy*. Edinburgh: Edinburgh University Press, 2017.

Schrift, Alan. *Nietzsche's French Legacy,* London and New York: Routledge, 1995.

Srinivasan, Priya. *Sweating Saris: Indian Dance as Transnational Labor*. Philadelphia: Temple University Press, 2012.

*Turn your F∧*king Head*. Directed by Becky Edmunds, 2012.

Index